Evaluation and Accountability in Clinical Training

Evaluation and Accountability in Clinical Training

Edited by

BARRY A. EDELSTEIN
West Virginia University
Morgantown, West Virginia

and

ELLEN S. BERLER
Florida State University
Tallahasse, Florida

Plenum Press • New York and London

ISBN-13: 978-1-4684-5283-9 e-ISBN-13: 978-1-4684-5281-5
DOI: 10.1007/978-1-4684-5281-5

Softcover reprint of the hardcover 1st edition 1987
A Division of Plenum Publishing Corporation
233 Spring Street, New York, N.Y. 10013

B A E

To Carole, Caren, and Allyson

E S B

To Lil and Hy

Contributors

Patricia J. Aletky, American Psychological Association, Washington, DC

Norman L. Berven, Department of Rehabilitation Psychology and Special Education, University of Wisconsin–Madison, Madison, Wisconsin

Alvin G. Burstein, Department of Psychology, University of Tennessee, Knoxville, Tennessee

Daniel M. Chatel, Department of Psychology, University of Arizona, Tucson, Arizona

Mary Beth Crowe, Office of the President, The Pennsylvania State University, University Park, Pennsylvania

Judy E. Hall, New York State Education Department, Cultural Education Center, Albany, New York

Richard H. Hirschenberger, Brainerd Regional Human Services Center, Brainerd, Minnesota

Ann Howard, Human Resources Research, American Telephone and Telegraph Company (AT & T), 550 Madison Avenue, New York, New York

Joseph A. Istvan, Department of Medical Psychology, School of Medicine, Oregon Health Sciences University, Portland, Oregon

Durand F. Jacobs, Psychology Service, Jerry L. Pettis Memorial Veterans' Hospital, Loma Linda, California

Nadine M. Lambert, School of Education, University of California, Berkeley, Berkeley, California

Carl A. Lindsay, Professional Planning Consultants, State College, Pennsylvania

Joseph D. Matarazzo, Department of Medical Psychology, School of Medicine, Oregon Health Sciences University, Portland, Oregon

Peter Nelson Mayfield, Private Practice of Clinical Psychology, Suite 1211, Lenox Towers, 3400 Peachtree Road, NE, Atlanta, Georgia

Patricia S. McGuire, Brainerd Regional Human Services Center, Brainerd, Minnesota

Paul D. Nelson, American Psychological Association, Washington, DC

John C. Norcross, Department of Psychology, University of Scranton, Scranton, Pennsylvania

Samuel H. Osipow, Department of Psychology, Ohio State University, Columbus, Ohio

Robin A. Reed, Department of Psychology, Ohio State University, Columbus, Ohio

Jonathan Sandoval, Department of Education, University of California, Davis, Davis, California

Lee Sechrest, Department of Psychology, University of Arizona, Tucson, Arizona

John F. Stevenson, Department of Psychology, University of Rhode Island, Kingston, Rhode Island

Don R. Thomas, Brainerd Regional Human Services Center, Brainerd, Minnesota

Xenia Tonesk, President, Xenia Tonesk, Inc., Suite 1006, 3101 New Mexico Avenue, NW, Washington, DC

Preface

Accountability in clinical training implies a strong relationship between the training outcomes touted by a training program and the performance of its graduates. The training program and its faculty must be able to ensure that students have the competencies necessary for entering the profession and can offer competent services. In addition, responsibility for the quality and value of training must be assumed by the profession. Pressure for accountability is becoming increasingly apparent as the public learns about fraud, waste, and abuse in publicly funded programs (Fishman & Neigher, 1982). Federally supported clinical training programs have had to defend their training practices against threats of funding loss without the hard data needed to support their practices. Funding seems to have been forthcoming mostly because of our ability to demonstrate the need for clinical, counseling, and school psychologists. Graduates seeking professional careers in such applied fields

> demand considerable trust from their clientele and the public-at-large when they establish themselves, offer and advertise their services, make claims on public monies, and profess to do good and no harm. Neither their clientele nor the public are in the position to evaluate the services of the profession or the claims made for these. (American Psychological Association [APA], 1982, p. 1)

The most alarming finding of the APA Task Force on the Evaluation of Education, Training, and Service in Psychology (1982) was that "there is no evidence that any specific educational or training program or experience is related to professional competence" (p. 2). The report goes on to state that it is "important, perhaps imperative, that psychology begin to assemble a body of persuasive evidence bearing on the value of specific educational and training requirements" (p. 2). It is toward this end that this volume is dedicated.

The objective of our efforts on this volume was to bring together the work of authors who have examined our current training and evaluation practices in professional psychology as well as the work of individuals who have developed innovative methods for evaluating practitioner training. The outline for the volume was originally the outline for a conference we had hoped to hold at West Virginia University. The mercurial funding picture at the time precluded our development of the conference. We decided that the next best thing was to invite the same individuals whom we would have invited to a working conference to contribute to a book that would hopefully serve as an impetus for further research and development in clinical training evaluation. We have brought together experts who can tell us where we currently stand with respect to the evaluation of clinical training in several applied areas in psychology and where we might go given proper information, skills, resources, and commitments.

In Chapter 1 Sechrest and Chatel provide an overview of evaluation and accountability in training for professional psychology and draw heavily upon the report of the APA Task Force on Evaluation of Education, Training, and Service in Psychology (1982). The authors begin with definitions of accountability and show how it is intimately tied to evaluation. They discuss general considerations of how program evaluation could proceed in psychology, followed by comments on the issues and limitations of evaluation and training in other professions. The authors argue for a comprehensive, long-range evaluation plan that is likely to result in improved education and training.

In Chapter 2 Burstein discusses the meaning of quality and how it can be evaluated. One important definition of quality emphasized by Burstein concerns the specification of the essential character or nature of a training program. The author describes the functions of external evaluation as currently performed through the accreditation and reaccreditation processes. Evaluation of quality is considered with an emphasis on the objects of knowledge (i.e., that which is to be learned) at four levels: facts, theories, skills, and attitude. The evaluation of process is considered as an alternative or complement to outcome evaluation. Burstein concludes with comments about quality in the evaluation activity.

Howard's chapter focuses on measurement methods for competency evaluation. She notes that many disciplines have similar needs to evaluate skills and offers work samples and simulations as worthy alternatives to paper and pencil tests. Advantages and disadvantages of using work samples and simulations for comptency assessment are discussed. She provides evidence and examples from competency evaluation in several professions, including the personnel selection work of industrial/organizational psychologists.

Stevenson and Norcross (Chapter 4) survey the status of evaluation and training in clinical psychology. They examine evaluation models, designs, and measures for professional training in clinical psychology. The results of national surveys of clinical psychology training clinics, graduate programs, and predoctoral internships are discussed. Approaches to assessing training processes are addressed followed by a consideration of directions for the future of training evaluation in clinical psychology.

Osipow and Reed focus on training and evaluation in counseling psychology. They first examine the importance of training evaluation and the reasons for its occurrence. They review relevant literature within counseling psychology and also draw upon the counselor education and clinical psychology literatures. The authors then describe the results of a survey they conducted with counseling psychology program directors in an effort to find out the current state of the art of training evaluation. Osipow and Reed end with a discussion of future directions for the evaluation of counseling psychology training.

In Chapter 6 Istvan and Matarazzo discuss the training of health psychologists. They begin with a brief description of the history of the growth of training models in psychology in general. This is followed by a discussion of curricula for health psychology training arising from the recommendations of the 1983 Arden House Conference on Health Psychology Training. The chapter ends with a consideration of licensure for health psychologists.

The status of evaluation of school psychology training is addressec by Sandoval and Lambert. They present a brief history of school psychology and several models for the delivery of school psychological services commonly found in the literature. They proceed to describe a three-dimensional paradigm that can guide data collection during the evaluation process within any service delivery model. Part of their paradigm involves specifying developmental hierarchies of skills through which trainees pass as they achieve competence in a given area. Sandoval and Lambert give specific examples of developmental stages within several skill areas, providing useful groundwork for further development of this innovative evaluation approach.

In Chapter 8 Tonesk describes the current status of medical student evaluation. As editors, we sought a critical examination of medical education because we felt that psychology could learn from the strengths and weaknesses of evaluation practices in other disciplines. Tonesk characterizes education and training along a continuum beginning with clinical courses and ending in the residency (graduate training). The Association of American Medical Colleges report of the general professional education of physicians is discussed. Problems arising from the constraints of the narrow perspective of current evaluation methods (e.g., multiple-choice examinations) are examined. The chapter concludes with an argument for a systems approach for evaluation.

Berven concentrates on evaluation methodology and considers how simulations can contribute to the assessment of counselor competence, as well as counselor training, credentialing, and research. The chapter begins with an examination of competency-based models in counselor training and assessment and proceeds through traditional methods of assessing professional competencies in counseling. He describes the development of simulation methods in medicine, discusses types of standardized simulations in counseling and indicates applications of simulation in assessing counselor competence. The author ends with a discussion of philosophical issues, research needs, and practical considerations.

In Chapter 10 Nelson and Aletky discuss accreditation of professional psychology training programs as a link between training and practice. They begin with a discussion of the values, objectives, and methods of accreditation. Standards for training in professional psychology are examined from a historical perspective. The authors present the evolution of standards for the practice of psychology, with a consideration of the problems and issues of standards implementation. Nelson and Aletky also consider the current status of accreditation of psychological service delivery settings and steps that can be taken to promote psychological accreditation in these settings.

Hall examines licensure and certification of psychologists. She begins by defining competence and relating it to the licensure process. Minimal competence criteria for licensure established by the States and Canadian jurisdictions are provided in detail. Hall also examines the development, validation, and proper use of the Examination for Professional Practice in Psychology (EPPP). The supplementation of the EPPP with oral examinations is considered, as well as the perils of using such examinations. The exciting prospect of using written analyses of problem simulations is explored. Finally, the implications of the licensure evaluation process and competency criteria are considered with respect to clinical training.

In the next chapter, Mayfield describes certification of psychologists by the American Board of Professional Psychology (ABPP). The chapter focuses on the maintenance of standards within the profession as regulated by the ABPP. The history of the ABPP is presented with a discussion of the need to set standards for the profession of psychology. The structure and function of the ABPP are described, including requirements for certification. The examination process is discussed in detail with a consideration of the dimensions of competency covered by the examination. Future trends in credentialing are explored including alternative examination procedures and new areas for certification. Finally, implications of ABPP certification procedures and criteria for training in professional psychology are explored.

In Chapter 13 Hirschenberger, McGuire, and Thomas provide an elaborate example of criterion-referenced, competency-based training in behavior modification. This chapter provides an example of how one can take a knowledge base and sophisticated skills, break them into operationalized components, teach the knowledge and the skills, and evaluate them against very specific criteria. The authors begin with a discussion of the need for competency-based training. They then present critical competencies needed by individuals using intrusive behavior-modification procedures and the methods used by the authors to identify these competencies. This is followed by a discussion of the development and evaluation of specific assessment instruments and training packages based on the targeted competencies. The authors end with an exploration of issues in competency-based instruction and future directions.

For Chapter 14, Lindsay, Crowe and Jacobs were asked to contribute a description of their innovative continuing professional education development project funded by the W. K. Kellog Foundation. Their work provides an illustration of what can be done at the postgraduate level, with significant implications for predoctoral training as well. Their chapter focuses on the role of continuing education as a facet of professional quality assurance. They describe the development, implementation, and evaluation of a practice oriented model of continuing professional education for clinical psychology. Their clinical skills workshop, which included live client simulations, written client vignettes, videotaped therapy vignettes, and various evaluation procedures, is described. The authors then discuss knowledge-based versus practice-oriented approaches to continuing education and their comparative costs. The chapter ends with an exploration of the prospects for practice-oriented continuing professional education.

Although our focus is on the field of psychology, it is our hope that this volume will be read by educators of professional counselors, social workers, and psychiatrists, as well as psychologists who are involved in graduate and postgraduate training. The issues, methodologies, and competencies involved in accountability and evaluation in these disciplines have many commonalities. The chapters in the book can be read in isolation, as they were not intended to be formally integrated. The chapters are relevant to each other, and yet they can each stand alone. We feel that the authors have much to offer those who care about accountability to the profession, their students, and the clients of their graduates.

This volume would not have been possible without the assistance of many individuals. We are particularly grateful for the help of James Scheirer who was Educational Affairs Officer for the American Psychological Association at the time this volume was being planned. Thanks also to Eliot Werner, senior editor at Plenum, who was supportive of our efforts from the inception of this project. Claire Noel ("Mom") deserves our gratitude for her clerical efforts and emotional support. Finally, we are appreciative of the efforts of William Imbornoni who skillfully bugged us at the appropriate times and handled the production of this volume.

BARRY A. EDELSTEIN
ELLEN S. BERLER

REFERENCES

American Psychological Association. (1982). *Report of the Task Force on the Evaluation of Education, Training, and Service in Psychology*. Washington, DC: Author.

Fishman, D. B., & Neigher, W. D. (1982). American psychology in the eighties: Who will buy? *American Psychologist, 37*, 533–546.

Contents

Chapter 7

Jonathan Sandoval and Nadine M. Lambert

Chapter 8

Chapter 9

1

Evaluation and Accountability in Training for Professional Psychology

An Overview

LEE SECHREST and DANIEL M. CHATEL

Psychology has reached a point in its development at which it is desirable, possible, and even necessary to evaluate its education and training activities and requirements. Especially in the health service areas of psychology, professional psychologists are demanding considerable trust from their clientele and the public when they offer and advertise their services, make claims on public and private insurance monies, and profess to do good and no harm. All professions, including psychology, should realize that it is irresponsible to forgo careful evaluation of the hypothesis that the education and training prescribed result in competent and ethical practitioners. Part of the definition of a strong

This chapter draws heavily on the report of the American Psychological Association (APA) Task Force on Evaluation of Education, Training, and Service in Psychology whose members were Lee Sechrest (Chair), Marilyn B. Brewer, Sol Garfield, James Jackson, Ronald Kurz, Samuel Messick, Neal Miller, Donald R. Peterson, and Janet T. Spence. Nonetheless, the views expressed here are those of the authors and should not be attributed individually or collectively to members of the task force.

LEE SECHREST and DANIEL M. CHATEL • Department of Psychology, University of Arizona, Tucson, AZ 85721.

profession is that it requires tangible, technical skills that produce demonstrable results and can be taught and that it can demonstrate specific ways that its education and training are related to the competent delivery of its "product." This is the present, and formidable, task of professional psychology. In a sense, the term *psychologist* is like a trademark of a specific brand of products and services (assessment, psychotherapy, etc.) whose association with the quality of services must be demonstrated if the trademark is to have any value.

We will also contend in this chapter that psychology has reached a point in its development at which processes must be developed to evaluate and certify the capabilities of its individual practitioners. Accountability for a profession entails the ability to vouch for the competencies and other desirable characteristics of members of the profession. It does not suffice simply to assert that "as professionals, we are generally competent and good." We will later refer to a persuasive article by Fallows (1985) that proposes airline pilot certification as a model for the certification of other professions. Few of us would be happy with the notion that when one flies on a commercial plane, one can be assured that *most* pilots are competent and possessed of personal and mental integrity. A recent report on physicians (Inspector General of Health and Human Services [HHS], 1986) expresses dismay at the estimated 5% to 15% of physicians who are not fully competent to practice; that 85% to 95% presumably are competent is not sufficiently reassuring.

Although the definition of terms is now in order, what we mean by evaluation and accountability is just about what most professionals mean when they use them. *Evaluation* refers to the process by which assessments of worth are attached to processes and products. We are evaluating psychological assessment when we say that it is useful, ineffective, valuable, or a waste of time, money, and effort. We are evaluating an educational requirement when we conclude that it results in more effective professional services; and we are evaluating an individual professional when we conclude that the practitioner is only minimally competent, is an effective therapist, or is an expert on child-custody issues. Evaluation may be done in many ways, however, and may itself need to be evaluated. That is, there are good evaluations, not-so-good evaluations, and worthless evaluations. We should not confuse the fact or outcome of evaluation with the adequacy of the process by which it came about. For example, many psychologists get identified as being an "expert" and that identification may be widely accepted without any attention to how the designation was arrived at. The *APA*

Monitor, simply to provide one instance, sometimes describes individual psychologists as experts without any justification of the label at all. Evaluations may be done casually or carefully, objectively or impressionistically. The differences are important.

Accountability refers to the obligations that exist for one person or group to justify its actions to another. In this case, accountability refers to the obligation of professional psychology to justify its actions to its various clienteles. The clienteles are diverse and include individual clients, social agencies, those who foot the bill for services, and those who enact and enforce legislation or regulation favoring psychologists over other groups. Accountability may be assumed voluntarily by a group or an individual or may be imposed by the clientele involved. We believe that voluntary assumption of the obligations of accountability is the mark of a mature profession (see also Sechrest & Hoffman, 1982), but those demands may be inescapable in any case (see also Dumke, 1986). Demands for the accountability of certain professions, particularly those with fiduciary responsibilities, have a long history, but the insistence seems to be broadening rapidly in recent years. Moreover, insistence on accountability of individual members of professions appears also to be increasing. Psychology may be able to put off the time at which accountability will be insisted upon at both the professional and individual levels, but the demand seems bound to descend upon it. For not much longer will we be able to say simply, "Trust us!"

Evaluation is the method by which demands for accountability may be met. Our clienteles want to know that what we are doing is effective and worth paying for; evaluation is a method of demonstrating such effectiveness and worth.

VALIDATING INDIVIDUAL PRACTITIONERS

In the long run, we do not believe that holding members of a profession accountable and evaluating professional activities in general are sufficient to meet the responsibilities of the profession, the eventual demands of the clienteles, and to satisfy the broader public interest. The profession must be responsible and effective, but it is the individual members who will carry out its activities and deliver its services. Regrettably, despite our best efforts, many practicing psychologists, even those trained in good programs, are not competent or otherwise dependable. Although not buttressed by actual evidence, a recent statement attributed to Logan Wright, currently president-elect of the American Psychological Association (APA) and an eminent clinician, is telling: "We are producing a glut and an oversupply of poorly trained and marginally ethical graduates" (Turkington, 1986, p. 14). Professional accountability may require individual accountability and, thus, evaluation at that level. Current evidence indicates that evaluation efforts are unsystematic (Norcross & Stevenson, 1984) and probably inadequate.

Fallows (1985), in a provocative article in *The Atlantic*, provided strong arguments against credentialism, that is, accountability met by requiring certain types of formal training. Although Fallows addressed his article particularly to the business community and the ubiquitous master of business administration (MBA), his arguments are equally applicable to psychology and other professions. Fallows noted the fallibility of the processes that lead to award of credentials and the presumption of once-and-for-all competence that underlies their acceptance. He suggested, for example, that the licensed physician, however competent at the time of licensing, does not necessarily remain competent (see Inspector General of HHS, 1986). Skills erode, and the knowledge base changes. Fallows presented as an alternative model for professional certification the case of commercial airline pilot training and certification. The Federal Aviation Administration (FAA) does not assume that pilots, once trained, remain skillful for the remainder of their careers. In order to maintain their licenses, they must undergo regular competency checks. When they are to undertake a new assignment such as piloting a new aircraft or landing at an airfield they have not used before, they must go through a set of specified procedures to check out their skills.

The comparison of pilot certification to that of professional psychologists is interesting and not in our favor. How many psychologists are out there diagnosing Alzheimer's disease without having had any specific training for that task, let alone without having been "checked out" on their ability to do so? How many psychologists will agree to provide therapy for an anorgasmic female client, although they have never had any specific training in sex therapy of that sort? How many psychologists regularly have their work checked out by a senior peer to make sure they are on track?

Sechrest once observed that there are two characteristics in which almost all adult Americans, at least males, believe they are above average: a sense of humor and the ability to drive an automobile. One suspects that professional psychologists may suffer from a similar peculiar sense of their skills. At least we have met almost no professional psychologists who seem to believe that they are below average as therapists, diagnosticians, or consultants. Can that be so? Obviously not, but most professional psychologists have no good ways of checking on their skills at all—certainly not in a way that would permit them to compare themselves to others. The APA has a self-assessment program that permits psychiatrists at least to check on their knowledge of the basic literature and such other testable skills as diagnostic criteria at intervals as they choose, and such self-assessment programs exist in many other medical specialties. The program has been regarded as quite successful and useful (Quick, Robinowitz, & Wilson, 1981).

A self-assessment program would not be an unreasonable venture for psychology, but a recommendation to that effect from an APA Task Force on Self-Assessment (Sechrest was a member) led nowhere. With effort, psychology might be able to produce useful data bases that would permit individual clinicians to judge their own efforts against those of others. For example, data could be brought together to provide norms for length of treatment of different types of cases, for dropout rates in therapy, for particular outcomes for limited problems, and so on. We are not so naive as to think such norms would have a great impact on the field, but assembling them would be a relatively low-cost effort so that any favorable impact would be worthwhile.

A major problem for professional psychology is, of course, that we do not really know how to specify what psychologists ought to be able to do, ought in fact to do, and we know even less about how well they ought to be able to do anything. The problem is made worse by the insistence of many psychologists that practice is an art and that it cannot be prescribed or assessed.

EVALUATION OF EDUCATION AND TRAINING

Psychology, along with a number of other professions, is under attack for requirements that restrict membership in the profession. At present, the practice of psychology in all 50 states is limited by legislation to those who have met specific educational and training requirements, and these limitations, which sometimes restrict competition, have been upheld by the courts in order to regulate the profession for the benefit of the public. However, a critical proposition in the attack is that there is no evidence that any specific educational or training program or experience is related to professional competence. Without that evidence, restricting the practice of psychology is not only unfair but potentially in restraint of trade and in violation of antitrust legislation. Ironically, some of the same arguments used by psychology to achieve parity with psychiatry are now being used by master's-level psychologists, social workers, family therapists, and Doctors of Psychology (PsyD) and PhDs from unaccredited programs in order to gain access to the spoils of private practice. These attacks make it imperative that psychology begin to assemble a body of persuasive evidence of the value of specific educational and training requirements.

The notion that the skills on which credentials are granted are different from the skills most relevant to performance of the profession's duties is certainly not new to psychology. In 1979, Daniel Hogan, a lawyer and social psychologist, published a four-volume study called *The Regulation of Psychotherapists*, in which he concludes that

> the effectiveness of therapists is determined more by the presence or absence of certain personality characteristics and interpersonal skills than technical abilities and theoretical knowledge. (cited in Fallows, 1985, p. 65)

Hogan's conclusions that the skills that make a good psychotherapist are mainly common-sense human skills and that advanced technical training is irrelevant to positive therapeutic outcome illustrate the extreme, yet increasingly held view of education and training in the mental health professions in general and clinical psychology in particular—we are on the defensive.

Perhaps it needs to be said that there is no presumptive "right" to be a psychologist. There is a constitutional right to due process when public bodies make decisions affecting public welfare, but not everyone who is qualified, let alone everyone who would like to, has the right to become a psychologist.

Whether or not evidence for the effectiveness of clinical psychology's educational and training requirements can be developed in time to forestall the serious attacks now under way is uncertain. The task of producing such evidence is formidable and will not be quickly accomplished. The best hope for clinical psychology may lie in its ability to demonstrate that it has a systematic program for evaluation that will produce a regular, dependable flow of information by means of which to validate and improve its practices and requirements. It does not now have such a program.

Assumptions upon Which to Base an Evaluation Program

It is possible to develop a program by which educational and training practices and requirements can be evaluated, but even to approach this task requires some simplifying assumptions to help reduce the problem to manageable dimensions.

No final, simple answer is attainable. The profession of psychology and its practice are too diverse and too rapidly changing to make possible a definitive, unequivocal answer to the question as to whether its educational and training requirements are supportable. There are actually several professions within psychology, each with different aims, competencies, and styles of practice. Psychology is also in a state of flux with respect to its scientific base and demands similar elasticity of educational and training activities to ensure their responsiveness to the limitations and openings provided by the changing scientific base.

The task of evaluating educational and training activities is too vast to be accomplished by a frontal attack. The task will have to be broken down into relatively small subtasks and decisions made as to which to undertake first. Those decisions will almost certainly reflect a number of diverse factors ranging from strategic to methodological and practical concerns. The most important questions should be addressed first, and the most realisitic starting points identified. It is critical, however, that a systematic and comprehensive program of research be developed that avoids the risks of triviality and opportunism.

The problems involved in evaluating education and training are exceedingly complex, and it is difficult even to identify the goals of education and training. To specify the particular skills and outlook congruent with those goals is of an order of magnitude yet more difficult. The value of education and training may be demonstrable for some forms of practice but not for others. A particular type of educational program may quite successfully prepare people for some areas of professional activity but not for others. In order to establish criteria for performance, realism may occasionally have to be sacrificed. In other cases, the only solution may be to extrapolate substantially from what can actually be studied. The task of evaluating educational and training requirements will strain our capacities for synthesis of data and information.

The most serious problems with respect to credentialing and the validity of educational and training requirements seem to arise in clinical psychology. The crucial nature of clinical psychology's position has several origins. Clinical psychology is by far the largest specialty within psychology involved in independent practice—the professional activity that raises the greatest concerns. School, counseling, and industrial/organizational psychology are more likely to be practiced within organizations able to make informed decisions about the kinds of psychologists they wish to employ.

Problems arise when psychologists not trained in clinical psychology, or persons not trained in psychology programs at all, want the right to practice independently and to offer the same kinds of services as are offered by clinical psychologists. Clinical psychology is also potentially quite lucrative so that it is attractive as a field in which to work. Its status with respect to third-party payers is important because it both enhances the prospects for a good income and creates additional concerns about professional qualifications. Many clinical psychologists practice with an unusually high degree of independence, further raising concern about their qualifications and competencies. Psychologists in independent practice may have no supervision and little contact with their peers and even be largely divorced from their discipline and the professional contacts it affords. Finally, whether accurately or not, clinical psychologists are widely thought to deal with the most sensitive, readily damaged clientele of all the specialties. Clinical psychology is, therefore, we conclude, at the crux of the problem of evaluating education and training.

Another assumption is that the outcome of education and training in a profession is not simply an array of practices based on complex disciplined knowledge. Training must inculcate a set of beliefs, attitudes, and values that are conducive to a high level of personal and professional responsibility. Part of the definition of a professional has to do with the capability of that person to practice independently, a capability that must have as its basis a firm ethical sense, respect for clients, commitment to maintaining competence, and so on. Whether or not it can be taught, judgment is a fundamental capacity of the professional (Klemp, 1977). Knowing what to do, how, and when to do it (as well as knowing when not to) are all critical aspects of competence. These aspects of professional outlook and practice demand careful consideration in planning an evaluation of education and training. Moreover, the responsible, well-trained professional knows the limits of personal competence and accepts them.

In any human service occupation, the personal qualities of practitioners, over and above technical knowledge and skills, are likely to be critical determinants of effectiveness in practice. These qualities may not be readily assessed and may be difficult to modify. The opportunity to make accurate assessments of these qualities, to develop corrective measures for those that are alterable, and to counsel regarding alternative uses of talent is likely only in the context of an intensive and protracted training program. Training for professional practice, in order to fulfill its function of ensuring that practitioners have the personal qualities that are needed, may have to provide diverse occasions for observation, including those stressful to the trainee, and a depth of acquaintance that can only be achieved in intimate interaction over time. Training directed too narrowly toward technical skills, or failing to provide continuity of instruction and supervision, or limited in extent may fail in this critical selective function.

Although there is much discussion of specialties and subspecialties within psychology (Carboy & Curley, 1976; Noonberg & Page, 1982; Sales, 1985; Sechrest, 1985), we still assume that education and training are, and should be, preparation for the general practice of clinical psychology (Task Force on Future Directions, 1982). The demands and opportunities of professional psychology are sufficiently diverse and uncertain that to train clinical psychologists at the doctoral level too exclusively for any specialization seems unwise. A set of basic skills and an outlook common to clinical psychology as a professional specialty should be imparted in any educational and training program (Committee on Professional Standards, 1981). Further specialized training after the doctorate should, of course, also be evaluated, but the tasks are conceptually and empirically separable.

The assertion that training is oriented toward general practice is admittedly controversial in some quarters, but until there is a soundly conceptualized and restrictive system of specialization that precludes psychologists from practicing outside the areas of their training, it appears important that this assertion guide professional development. Virtually all other professions are characterized by initial training of a general nature, culminating in a professional degree, with any specialization and concomitant recognition achieved later. To date, clinical psychology has followed this model, and education and training should be evaluated from that perspective.

We must also assume that professional psychological services have some degree of effectiveness. Although there are controversies concerning this matter with regard to psychotherapy, for example, there are many reports showing psychotherapy to have some degree of efficacy. At the very least, we must begin to look at new and creative ways in which to measure, assess, and evaluate *all* professional services, especially psychotherapy, before we can realistically and effectively evaluate whether or not our training programs are properly preparing professionals for the delivery of those services. Also, the quality of professional services varies greatly from practitioner to practitioner, and to try to provide a definitive resolution of all the controversies would be an enormous task. It would also be advisable to conduct the evaluation of the effectiveness of psychotherapy in the context of other professions, because the practice of psychotherapy is not limited to clinical psychologists. Therefore, as a first step it is most feasible to focus on whether clinical psychologists do well what they are expected to be able to do as professionals.

Some Limitations for Evaluating Education and Training

Aside from the sheer magnitude and complexity of the task, there are other limitations on our ability to evaluate the efficacy of education and training. One of these, embarassing in the extreme, is that clinical psychology is an inadequately defined specialty. There is no universal definition of *clinical psychologist*, and there are many paths by which a person may become a clinical psychologist. Although some of these paths lack official sanction, those who take them often gain professional acceptance from third-party payers, referral sources, and other clinical psychologists of repute.

Another limitation to studying the education and training of clinical psychologists is that their activities are extremely diverse and not well-known. Just what do clinical psychologists *do*, anyway? They practice under diverse conditions and engage in a wide range of professional services from neuropsychological assessment to industrial/organizational consultation. Some practice in near isolation in small rural communities; others practice in urban group practices with scores of other health professionals. We really have only impressions of what clinical psychologists do, and until we know the kinds of activities and the amount of time that is spent on each, it will be difficult to know how to best train clinicians. Although the diversity of clinical psychology is one of its greatest strengths, it will make it difficult to evaluate the training and education of clinical psychologists.

Actually, the foregoing somewhat overstates the case for our ignorance concerning the activities of clinical and other professional psychologists. The 1983 report *Job Analysis of Licensed Psychologists in the United States and Canada* (Rosenfeld, Shimberg, & Thornton, 1983) provided a good bit of detailed, but curiously superficial, information. An intervention item, for example, was to "provide assistance to individuals regarding personal and organizational problems." The report showed that nearly all clinical psychologists engage in that activity, but the category is so broad as to be virtually meaningless. One needs to know whether some clients were suicidal, whether they came from lower- or middle-class backgrounds, how many were children, whether some had legal problems, and so on. Planning effective educational and training programs and then their evaluation is likely to be beyond us without much better knowledge about practice.

Further complicating the evaluation picture is that the skills, attitudes, and knowledge desirable at the entry level may not be those desirable after 10 years of practice. The Rosenfeld *et al.* (1983) report did not find important job activity differences by age or experience levels, but, again, the activity definitions were superficial. One suspects (even hopes), for example, that more severe cases would be seen by more experienced clinicians. It is ludicrous to expect that professional training could produce new clinicians as expert as older, more experienced ones; but if we cannot agree on an ideal of the experienced clinician, we will be unable to identify the characteristics of new clinicians that foretell competency and success. Although having to guess how a young psychologist will develop is discomforting, we assume that in any training program there is a compromise between the ideal of the experienced professional and the newly graduated entry-level PhD in clinical psychology.

Yet another serious limitation to the evaluation of education and training of clinical psychologists is that we simply do not have a very good understanding of what actually *happens* in clinical training. The APA has an accreditation procedure devised to produce *some* uniformity in clinical training, but it is in actuality only a verification that programs meet a minimum education and training standard. Otherwise, useful documentation of the training of clinical psychologists is scarce and may exist only at the level of the graduate school transcript for both the program and the individual. The fact that courses are required does not guarantee that they will be taken, and "usual" experiences are not universal. The outcome of the accreditation process is simply a binary conclusion of *accredited* or *not accredited*. Dumke (1986) makes the provocative suggestion that training programs should be graded according to their quality. Is clinical psychology ready to admit that it has some "B" and "C" programs?

Because there is such a close relationship between the training program and the internship, it is difficult to evaluate either in isolation. Most academic programs are planned with some assumptions about the internship experiences their graduates will have, and internship agencies in turn tend to select students with academic backgrounds that meet their needs. Therefore, a training program may neglect some aspects of clinical training because the internship is supposed to provide the experience, whereas another program has a completely different emphasis. The potential for gaps in training on one side or the other is evident, and the evaluation of any student or program would depend heavily upon whether it was carried out pre- or postinternship. One interesting possibility to get around this would be to compare graduates of regular programs with graduates of those programs with "captive" internships, that is, those programs that provide internship experiences that complement their academic programs. Perhaps the result would be that clinical psychologists from captive programs would prove to be more thoroughly trained, suggesting a national revamping of the relationship between academic graduate programs and internship agencies. There is certainly reason to believe that internship experiences may often be less than satisfactory (Tucker, 1970; Tucker & James, 1971).

In addition, there is likely to be a person-by-program interaction in selection for education and training. Students do not apply randomly to training programs, and programs do not select randomly from applicants. Consequently, it may be difficult to allocate education and training effects accurately to the two elements of person and program. In some sense, it may not seem to matter whether a program is successful because of good trainee selection or good training practices, but in terms of recommendations across programs, planning new programs, and monitoring program change, it matters a good deal. If, for example, a newly established program successfully attracted an initial group of high-quality students who made the program look good but whose capabilities could not be replicated year after year, initial conclusions about the program's quality might be misleading.

What Do We Want to Know about Education and Training?

We believe that a comprehensive program to evaluate education and training should be developed and directed initially toward professional psychologists at the entry level. The evaluation should come about through gradual, incremental accumulation of knowledge aimed at the critical issues the profession faces and applicable to the students now in training, with whom the future of the profession resides. What are some of the important beginning points of such an evaluation?

Current education and training must be documented at both program and individual levels. Methods of documenting as precisely as possible the experience of trainees in academic and practicum settings must be developed. One possibility is to ask the Education and Training Board of the APA to develop standard documentation forms for programs and students. Although the reporting requirements might seem formidable, they are not considered unusual by many other professions. Professional photographers, for example, rarely take a picture without recording the conditions, and pilots keep careful logs of each flight. Dentists and physicians record every patient contact, often in considerable detail. If training programs cannot document the detail in which students are exposed to information about biochemical aspects of mental disorder and if students cannot document the number of hours they have spent in group-therapy training, then the most basic documentation practices are absent.

The rationale for education and training activities needs to be evaluated and determined at the program level. Surveys of faculty, supervisors, program directors, and trainers are necessary (e.g., see Calhoun & Green, 1984) to determine the factors that enter into decisions about what to teach, what emphasis to provide, what skills to focus on, and what sequences to follow. We need to know the extent to which training and educational decisions are opportunistic or forced by circumstances and the effect of scientific and professional developments. The result would be a better understanding of the extent to which programs change by drift rather than deliberate planning.

A good beginning point for an inquiry about the rationale for a training program is to determine the structure of the faculty and how it has come to be that way. One suspects that the faculties of many psychological training programs have simply "grown like Topsy" without any teleological guidance. We believe that many, if not most, faculties in clinical psychology are not large enough to reflect well the structure of the field. We believe also that the vagaries of university funding, tenure rules, and pressures from other areas in departments are likely to have influenced the development and structure of clinical faculties. Suppose, for example, that the professor of radiology leaves a medical school. Is it imaginable that the dean would decide to transfer that "slot" to pediatrics or that the professor would be replaced with a newly graduated MD because of financial exigencies or that the faculty would elect to fill the position with an outstanding dermatologist as "the best person available?" Such things happen regularly in academic fields, including clinical psychology. A fundamental reason is that original failure ever to define the field and specify the faculty competencies *required* in it leaves the field defenseless when any crunch comes. We suspect, too, that the definition and specification process might expose many programs as inadequate and unbalanced.

We need to determine whether there are distinct types of training programs and what their characteristics may be. To the extent that programs differ in their aims and practices, different approaches to evaluation or outcome measures may be required. There are prevalent assumptions about types of programs such as behavioral versus psychodynamic, or research versus applied, but little is actually *known*. Within limits, programs should be evaluated in the context of their own aims, but those aims demand careful scrutiny (Dumke, 1986). On the other hand, to the extent that a set of skills, an orientation, and a fund of knowledge is to be expected of the professional psychologist, programs must be prepared to provide these no matter what their individual characteristics. A medical school, for example, may have an orientation that distinguishes it from others, but it may not neglect biochemistry or anatomy and retain its accreditation. Similarly, a clinical psychology training program might be characterized by an orientation toward therapy but should not neglect clinical assessment if that is among the core clinical skills expected of new doctoral students.

We need to determine what kinds of students enter what kinds of programs and the normal progression during training. Graduate students in professional psychology likely vary enormously in abilities, interests, and personal goals and therefore require different evaluation approaches. We were startled to hear recently a justification for a new professional program on one campus that would admit students with lower grades and test scores than those characteristic of an already established program. Surveys could easily be designed to determine differences among students across programs. These same surveys could determine whether there are systematic changes that occur during the years students spend in professional education and training activities. An example of such a survey is one (Goodman & Kahn, 1983) assessing attitudes of psychology graduate students toward research.

An attempt should be made to determine expected and desired entry-level skills of professional psychologists. A useful evaluation requires better understanding of what the newly trained psychologist should be expected to think, know, and be able to do. Again, surveys could help determine this, with respondents selected so as to represent potentially diverse views. As an example, Dana, Gilliam, and Dana (1976) attempted to determine what skills are expected and desired of psychology interns at the time of entry into internship programs. Expectations differed from one setting to another, but assessment skills were generally regarded as more critical than others. This type of job analysis for the entry-level psychologist should not focus exclusively on specific skills and knowledge but should also attempt to determine the crucial attitudes and judgment capabilities required for competent functioning. It should pay attention to the hazards of professional practice and those factors that help us avoid them. Ferguson (1976) believes that students should be prepared to accept the limitations of psychology, imbued with "regretful self-acceptance" as a basis for using those skills that can be taught.

After entry-level knowledge, attitudes, and skills have been described, more structured plans could be developed for their assessment. Entry-level skills may be more important than they seem initially. It appears that professionals do what they were trained to do and perpetuate these practices not only throughout their own careers but in their supervision of neophytes, making initial acquisition of the right skills and attitudes even more imperative. Among the most important of these may be a readiness for change and continuing professional development, balanced by a steadiness of view and judgment that discourages indulgence in professional fads and other inadequately tested practices.

Better information is needed about the career patterns of professional psychologists in order to design better evaluation strategies. For example, do clinicians in independent practice usually begin their careers in another clinical setting? Do clinicians who work with children specialize in that area or move into it gradually over a period of time? If they *do* specialize, *when* do they do it—predoctorally, postdoctorally, or in some other way? What proportion of professional psychologists are in part-time private practice, and what activities do they engage in the rest of their working day? Answers to these questions are prerequisties for a clear conception of entry-level professional skills and for a sense as to which additional skills should later be developed and how long all of this should take. Again, it seems as though surveys could provide reasonably satisfactory answers to these questions.

More information is also needed about the extent to which skills can become obsolete. If competence depends much more on judgment and problem-solving ability than specific knowledge and skills, it may be that the "half-life" of competence in professional psychology is much longer than is the case for professions more dependent on technique. On the other hand, emerging service needs may present problems for psychologists not trained to meet these needs (Jenson, 1979). How to sustain competence and develop skills to meet new needs are questions of fundamental importance to the task of evaluating and demonstrating professional competencies.

We need to discover the activities that clinical psychologist engage in, their frequency, and their clientele. In order to evaluate the relevance of education and training to the demands of the profession, we need more detailed information about what professional psychologists actually *do*. Who are their clients and what is the nature of these contacts, their hours, and conditions of work? In what other types of professional activities do they engage? Activity logs have been demonstrated to be a feasible route to describing the practices of physicians (Mendenhall & Abrahamson, 1973) and could be easily kept by a sample of psychologists recruited, and perhaps compensated, especially for the purpose.

Perhaps we can identify critical incidents in the practices of professional psychologists in which education and training played a role. One useful approach to evaluation might be to determine whether psychologists have experienced critical incidents (Flanagan, 1954; McDermott, McGuire, & Berner, 1976) that influenced their education and training. For example, a clinician might report an ethical dilemma for which he or she was well-prepared because of a seminar in ethical considerations in professional psychology. Another might have treated a case in a particular way because of similarities to a case handled on internship. Standard critical incident methodology could be used with samples of professional psychologists of different types to produce the data. Similar data could be obtained from supervisors of students and interns. Although incidents reflecting directly on the value of training may be rare, they may also be critical. The threat to quality of service may lie not so much in routine mediocrity as in occasional but highly damaging blunders. The medical dictum *primum non nocere* [First Do Not Harm] should also apply to the practice of professional psychology. Poor judgment and poor professional orientation may be more likely to produce occasional, spectacular blunders, whereas skill deficiencies may show up more often in routine practice.

Data on how professional psychologists know and define the boundaries of their competence could be useful in developing a program to evaluate education and training. Guideline 1.6 of the specialty guidelines for clinical psychology (Committee on Professional Standards, 1981) states that "clinical psychologists limit their practice to their demonstrated areas of professional competence" (p. 7). The text goes on to establish the basis for competence as "verifiable training and experience" and the extension of services "beyond the range of their usual practice." No such guideline can be very specific, but it seems important to know how clinicians and other psychologists come to identify their competencies and define the boundaries of those competencies. For example, a psychologist could have had ample training and experience with a particular problem, yet still sense a deficiency in his or her personal competence on other grounds. How much training and experience is sufficient surely differs from one professional to the next, and some would undoubtedly be bolder than others in generalizing the effects of their training and experience across age groups, problems, modalities, and so forth. Data on how psychologists define their competencies could be useful in developing a program to evaluate education and training.

An Initial Research Program

For psychology to evaluate its education and training requirements, even limiting the evaluation to clinical psychology, requires a comprehensive and multifaceted research program. Even to begin would require developing a variety of methodologies because we do not have either the measures or all the designs and methods of analysis eventually required for such an effort. The process of evaluating education and training will be iterative and dynamic, for initial results will be applied to improve subsequent evaluation and to change training programs. The evaluations will require a period of time that is so long that programs will be changing in the meantime anyway. The general evaluation model described by Tharp and Gallimore (1979) as *evaluation succession* could provide a useful basis for an effective plan for evaluating education and training because it allows for the evolution of a program based on feedback from evaluations..

One requirement of an effective evaluation plan must also recognize that people change over time, and the process and nature of these changes must be studied and integrated into the evaluation. If some educational experiences dispose persons toward more rapid and desirable changes, we want to know that. A comprehensive "developmental assessment" should consider the occurrence of changes over time and the factors that produce or stimulate those changes.

Those involved with training directly, especially the directors of clinical training, should be strongly encouraged to participate in the evaluation of the education and training of clinical psychologists. The views of internship centers as well as current practitioners should be sought because they are in a particularly good position to suggest what to look for in evaluating education and training.

Some types of training have a manifest or "face" validity that makes their evaluation uncomplicated or even uninteresting. For instance, virtually no one knows how to administer a complicated neuropsychological assessment battery without having been taught to do so; few persons know much about statistics without training. However, to extend the assumption of validity to applications of these skills that require *judgments*—when to use a technique and how to interpret the results—would be risky.

We could simply assume that education and training are better than no training at all, and focus our evaluation on how to improve what exists. This simplification is particularly appealing to the extent that improvement of instruction or supervision can be demonstrated to produce improved performance. Such a demonstration of training effectiveness seems achievable, however, only by first evaluating the status quo.

The evaluation of education and training now desirable, if not absolutely necessary, is well beyond anything performed for any profession to date. It will be extensive, intensive, and expensive, but the potential benefits are great. The undertaking is not without risks, for there is no guarantee that the results will be favorable to the field or that the prevailing wisdom will be validated. Psychology will simply have to trust that whatever credibility is jeopardized by exposure will be regained by the profession's candor.

Evaluation of Education and Training and Quality Assurance

There is some relationship between the issue of quality assurance in the profession and the evaluation of education and training of professionals. Quality assurance within psychology can be considered to begin with the selection of both students and the faculty to teach them. As a profession, we are reasonably careful about the persons we admit to training, and we are reasonably careful about the faculty hired to teach and train future representatives of the profession. Although there is little empirical basis for, and tremendous variability between, our selection practices, we suppose for commonsensical reasons that substantial variance in the output of training programs is accounted for by the variance in input. These selection procedures and selection pressures are of interest in their own right. In fact, it may be that the most important consequence of graduate training is the selection process itself. However, there is much variability in outcome to be explained, possibly by the specific features of an educational or training program, and the proposed evaluation and methodological designs should address training from a value-added question.

Another aspect of quality assurance related to education and training is the accreditation of training programs in clinical psychology. Again, there seems to be no empirical basis at all for accreditation as a way of enhancing quality of professional training; it is accepted on a commonsense basis. Accreditation may too often focus on resources rather than how they are used (Jacobson, 1986). Nonetheless, accreditation remains a powerful factor in determining internship placements and job offers for newly trained clinical psychologists.

During training, we also try to provide for appropriate socialization of students into the profession. We suggest role models, discuss ethics, and offer supervised practice in playing the professional role. We do not know just *how* effective our socialization is in enhancing quality of training and education, but it seems likely that improvements in socialization could be achieved with obvious results.

Another ongoing effort aimed at producing quality clinicians and common to nearly all training programs is standardization of practice. As professionals, we sense that there are right or better ways of doing things, and we strive to teach those ways to our students, to dampen their idiosyncracies, and even to persuade those already out of training to adopt and maintain reasonably standard ways of doing things. How much standardization we achieve is difficult to say, but it is probably not as much as we would prefer to think.

The process of selecting the students we admit to graduate study, the mechanism of APA accreditation of clinical psychology programs, as well as professional socialization and standardization of practice that begins during professional training are all ways in which clinical psychology has attempted to maintain and enhance the quality of training and education of clinical psychologists. Not a little perturbing, though, is the finding that the personality measures that are taught in clinical programs are not regarded as adequate for selection of clinical students (Stevens, 1981).

Need for Proximal Measures of Performance

An evaluation of education and training requirements will depend upon devising satisfactory performance measures feasibly obtained at the level of the individual practitioner. Feasibility, however, is to a considerable extent a function of the evaluation plan. Design options could include a mix of interrelated studies that would yield questionnaire and biographical data on relatively large numbers of persons while simultaneously permitting more intensive study of smaller samples. That a particular measurement approach is expensive or administratively and logistically difficult should not rule it out of consideration. Implementing several approaches in a coordinated way might well produce a pattern of persuasive results despite the limitations of individual studies (e.g., small sample sizes). In the long run, the evaluation of education and training will depend on many research efforts, varying in size and complexity from large-scale surveys to small studies of specific activities. The conclusions reached will be a synthesis of these findings rather than a single number.

A first step in developing ways to assess the effects of education and training would be to survey training programs in clinical psychology, including internship programs, about their ways of assessing their own students and trainees. Although their methods might not be sophisticated or systematic, such a survey could reveal what the programs themselves consider to be important and assessable knowledge and skills. It might also yield interesting and even novel ideas about how to assess neophyte professional psychologists.

In particular, we need to find ways to assess crucial capacities in the areas of clinical problem solving and judgment as distinguished from skills (Klemp, 1977; Menges, 1975). Without underestimating the difficulty of measuring clinical skills and knowledge, assessing good judgment and problem solving seems even more formidable. No other profession appears to have solved this problem, for there are apparently no dependable assessment paradigms. Medicine is clearly ahead of psychology in this regard, however (Tonesk, Chapter 8 in this volume).

Of course, a profession could attempt to assess performance at many different levels, but the two most obvious are minimal adequacy and excellence. Certification and licensure are meant to assess candidates to ensure that they meet at least minimal standards of adequacy, and nothing beyond that is to be inferred from a successful outcome. Similarly, accreditation is usually focused on minimum standards, a level that may not be sufficient for instilling confidence in a profession (Dumke, 1986). Higher standards are entailed in examinations leading to diplomate status or similar recognition; awarding such recognition implies that services provided by the professional will be of excellent quality. There are few examinations for professionals that certify quality in between these two extremes, although the American Board of Professional Psychology has considered a proposal to certify at the "journeyman" level, presumably a status somewhere between minimal and excellent, perhaps "excellent for a beginner."

The level at which to assess skills and therefore to make statements as to quality of performance is not a decision to be taken lightly. Choosing to assess at a minimum competence level implies that anyone lacking the prescribed education and training will probably fail to meet even those minimum standards. This, in turn, implies an increased possibility that persons with nonstandard training might meet these standards. On the other hand, the decision to assess professionals at a higher standard of performance runs the risk that a substantial proportion of persons trained in acceptable programs will not meet the standard, and the decision as to the appropriate performance level at which to assess should be thought through carefully before a major assessment is mounted.

A wide range of performance measures of professional psychologists should be considered and tested. We should not foreclose any possibilities at present, but explore at least the following:

Self-Report Measures. Although they are obviously open to distortion, self-report measures may be useful (Fuhrmann & Weissburg, 1978). Self-report is the most efficient way to obtain much biographical information and is particularly useful for identifying persons who are true outliers in their attitudes and practices. Some isolated practitioners may have no social comparison groups by means of which to measure their own deviance, and many others, although deviant, are sufficiently persuaded of their convictions to report accurately. In reviewing self-evaluations of ability across a wide range of fields and skills, Mabe and West (1982) concluded that self-evaluation relates reasonably well to other measures of performance within some limits that could be met in the types of evaluation studies envisioned here. Specifically, self-evaluation is likely to be relatively accurate when (a) raters expect their own evaluations to be compared to other measures; (b) the raters are experienced with self-evaluation; (c) raters are guaranteed anonymity; and (d) instructions emphasize comparison with others.

Reputational Measures. In many studies of performance in other fields, reputational measures have been found valuable. It is likely that most professional psychologists have a reasonably clear idea about the nature and adequacy of the practices of their local peers. If not, this may indicate something important about the relative positions within the socioprofessional structure of those involved. The question whether professionals are willing to rate their peers may be raised, but it is an empirical question, and because such ratings have been widely used, the answer is probably yes if confidentiality is assured.

Supervisor's Ratings. Obtaining supervisor's ratings of clinicians' performance is another possibility. Such ratings are seldom especially discriminating because of the conditions under which they are made, but in the context of a research project, they could be substantially improved and become a valuable source of information (Cormier & Bernard, 1982). Ratings by internship and postdoctoral supervisors could be especially useful because they are less likely to show the halo effect often emanating from academic performance. Moreover, ratings by clinical supervisors would be more likely to assess capacities for judgment and problem solving than many alternative sources of information.

Work Samples. Work samples are difficult to obtain for large, random samples, but may be useful (Irby, Evans, & Larson, 1978) even if samples are limited in size. The possibility of exploiting existing data sets that are in fact work samples of a sort should not be overlooked. The APA Civilian Health and Medical Program of the Uniformed Services (CHAMPUS) project, for example, resulted in a large set of treatment reports filled out by providers and reviewed by peers. CHAMPUS and other third-party payers, including insurance companies, might be willing to provide data at the group level. For example, the names of 300 providers of one type and 300 of another could be sent and the organizations simply asked to indicate with how many providers from each set they have experienced which kinds of problems. Consultations with the American Board of Professional Psychology (ABPP) staff and examiners might produce useful clues as to the types of work samples most revealing of critical information. With small samples of clinicians, it might be possible to videotape real or simulated clinical encounters that could be judged for adequacy of performance (Maatsch & Gordon, 1978).

On a limited basis, site visits to educational and training programs could help determine, as a sort of work sample, what goes on in training and provide a way to observe trainees in actual work settings. Observation rather than interviewing as a method for determining the quality of activity would be emphasized.

Both the ABPP and the American Association of State Psychology Boards are attempting to improve assessment of the knowledge and skills of professional psychologists. From the standpoint of cost-effectiveness, more active participation in those efforts by any other group, especially one evaluating training, would appear highly desirable. In fact, to the extent that better performance measures for clinical psychologists would be in the interests of psychology and that subspecialty, APA and clinical psychology groups should consider subsidizing these efforts directly.

Retrospective Studies. Some useful information might be obtained at low cost through retrospective studies of persons now practicing in the field whose backgrounds differ with respect to education and training. Archives and data tapes already available could be examined. The *APA Directory*, for example, provides information about highest degree, field of degree, the university granting the degree, and the date of award. Those data could then be linked to later employment history, fields of interest, and so on. *The National Register of Health Service Providers in Psychology* is a similar archive from which useful information could be drawn at relatively little cost. State Professional Standards Review committees might be willing to discuss problems they have had and whether these have stemmed from deficiencies in education and training. Because ethics violations may stem as much from poor judgment as from wickedness, examining the APA archives concerning those charges might be useful. A report on ethics cases in one state (Butler & Williams, 1985) indicated that all founded charges involved psychologists who were not graduates of accredited programs, and in only one case was the culprit identified as a clinical psychologist. Undoubtedly there are many other sources of data to be discovered and usefully employed. These opportunities, both relatively inexpensive and rapid in payoff, should not be overlooked.

Failing Performance. Another type of study that could be undertaken relatively inexpensively and rapidly is a study of those persons who have failed in their employment, especially their initial jobs. By failure is meant performance that proved unsatisfactory. The study could be undertaken by methods similar or identical to those for the critical incident studies. The aim would be to determine the extent to which inadequate training or education could be clearly identified as a factor in poor job performance. Could therapeutic successes and failures be identified for which a strong case could be made that the outcome depended upon education and training? Such approaches might help determine the relative importance of a program's function of screening out the obviously inadequate, compared to the value it adds by training. The screening-out function of programs suggests it is advisable to study "failure" at every level, that is, during graduate school and the internship as well as in later employment. Moreover, because self-selection might also be a factor, those who voluntarily drop out, either out of school or a job, should also be studied.

Research Designs for Comparison Groups

Because no one is randomly assigned to education and training programs in professional psychology, it will be necessary to develop the strongest possible nonequivalent control group designs. The plural of design is used because clearly no one comparison or type of data will be sufficient. There appear to be four critical points at which to assess performance, whether by one or more of the means already discussed, or by other means yet to be developed. These points are early in academic training, later in academic training (preinternship), postinternship, and during the first job. "Value added" for academic training would be reflected by changes in performance between the early and late academic points. Value added by the internship would be reflected by comparing late academic performance to post internship performance. Value added by the initial job experience would be reflected in changes occurring between the postinternship and first employment.

There are several groups against whose performance professional psychologists could be evaluated. These comparisons would cast light on various aspects of the value-added question and help to rule out rival hypotheses such as maturation and deselection of the inept. Comparing trainees in PhD clinical programs to those in PsyD or practitioner-oriented programs could show something about the effects of differential emphasis on research and practice in training. Comparisons could also be made of students in programs thought to differ substantially in quality. Because our interest is in value added from one critical point to the next, a student's initial performance level would not be critical unless there was a student ability-by-training interaction or unless measures taken during internship or employment found that low standards for entry into some programs caused inadequate final performance. The latter outcome would suggest that the type of program helps ensure selection and retention only of competent persons. It might be possible to compare students in other areas of psychology, such as counseling or school psychology, but it is not clear that this would be especially revealing because there is much overlap in trainee experiences. However, comparison between early and late academic periods of students in clinical psychology programs and those in other academic psychology tracks not intended to be clinical (e.g., social and personality psychology) could prove useful for assessing the effects of education and training with groups that are closely equivalent in terms of initial selection criteria.

Two types of master's-level practitioners are often identified: terminal master's psychologists and terminated master's psychologists. The former will have been in programs deliberately designed to be terminal and, presumably, to possess professional integrity. The terminated master's psychologist is a student who voluntarily or otherwise dropped out after earning the master's degree from a program intended to train doctoral-level persons. These students may not have completed a program with any plan or integrity. Because terminal MA students can be identified at the beginning of their academic careers, they can be compared to clinical psychology doctoral students early and perhaps later in their academic work, and at the conclusion of any internship or other practice experience. In many ways, the terminal and terminated master's comparison groups are the most critical from the standpoint of validating education and training because these persons are among the most vociferous and numerous of those objecting to doctoral-level prescribed educational and training requirements. Perlman (1985) has reported one such comparison.

Comparisons of professional psychologists with psychologists in other areas, especially social and personality psychology, would have application in determining the specific effects of professional training as distinguished from general academic training, selection pressures, maturation, and so on. These comparisons could be made both early and late in academic training and after some time in first employment. It might also be revealing to compare professional psychologists with nonpsychologists at the time of first employment to determine the extent to which clinical skills are specific to training in that field. Comparisons of interviewing skills, for example, could be made between professional psychologists and physicians, lawyers, nurses, salespersons, and others.

Evaluation of Education and Training in Other Professions

As the chapter by Tonesk (chapter 8 in this volume) shows, medicine has been active in pursuing the evaluation of its students and, to some extent, of their training, but medicine is not alone in the enterprise. Nursing (Engelgau, 1985) planned a study of some of its highly regarded training programs in order to try to determine what elements characterize high quality programs. A mechanism also exists to evaluate the performance of Certified Public Accountants ("President of national CPA group," 1984), an activity carried out by the American Association of CPAs. Psychology may have much to learn from other professions and some catching up to do.

Research in Other Professions. Although the evaluations proposed here are more intensive and extensive than any previously undertaken, other fields and professions have attempted numerous evaluations, some courageous to the point of daring, many beyond what has yet to be attempted in psychology. A very important task for those undertaking a comprehensive evaluation of professional psychology would be to review and integrate previous attempts to evaluate professional education and training (Morgan & Irby, 1978). The instances that exist may be informative, and their careful study could help anticipate pitfalls to be avoided or endured. We have not attempted a comprehensive review of evaluations, but a few examples illustrate the kinds of things that have been done and where they could lead.

As its age and critical position in the human services delivery system would predict, the medical profession has probably been the focus of more evaluation attempts than any other. (It has, of course, also been better funded than other professions.) The Flexner (1910) report is, in fact, the archetype of professional evaluations. However, it has not been truly prototypical because, except for the Geiss (1926) report on dentistry, it has never been replicated. Nonetheless, psychology would do well to study the experience of professional medicine in self-study and evaluation.

One of the earliest and most comprehensive attempts to evaluate a specific program began at Western Reserve Medical School with the development of a new curriculum in 1952 (Williams, 1980). The evaluation was at best only partially successful but nonetheless revealing.

The evaluation foundered in part because the curriculum continued to change and evolve over the years. Another problem, however, was the lack of adequate outcome measures. But most instructive is the lesson to be learned from the fact that the faculty, perhaps unintentionally, came to accept student performance on the National Board of Medical Examiners examination as a criterion of quality. That drift into decision was critical for the Western Reserve Medical School, for their curriculum was originally directed toward goals quite different from high scores on the national board exams. However, declining student scores on the exams resulted in pressures to alter the curriculum to regain lost ground and prestige. The experience of the Western Reserve medical faculty suggests that professional psychology should hesitate to commit itself too soon or too strongly to any single examination system, for such a commitment can distort the education and training process.

A different and rather daring evaluation of medical practice was undertaken by Peterson and his associates (Peterson, Andrews, Spain, & Greenberg, 1956) in North Carolina. These investigators stationed observers in the offices of general practitioners in North Carolina to observe and rate their performances. The observers were by no means lenient because a substantial number of physicians were judged to be inadequate in many respects. Of special importance is the fact that the quality of their practice was related to their performance in medical school across all areas of practice, but the relation held only for younger (ages 28–35) physicians; apparently the effects of medical training wash out over a period of years. Also interesting was that the quality of practice was related to the length of training specifically in medicine, as opposed to surgery or obstetrics, suggesting that the type of medical training is important. Of more than passing interest is that in 1974 the American Board of Psychiatry reinstituted an internship in general medicine as part of the requirement for board certification (Crowder & Roback, 1981). Physicians with higher practice ratings also tended to subscribe to more journals and to own more common laboratory equipment, perhaps indicating that better physicians try harder to "keep up." On the other hand, there was no evidence that postgraduate (continuing) education had any effect on physician performance. More recently, McCarberg (1981) has concluded that the effects of continuing education on medical practice remain uncertain, but some studies have shown positive effects, even if mostly equivocal. We must, of course, bear in mind that Peterson's findings are now nearly 30 years old and so should be treated with caution. Nonetheless, the example set by Peterson's use of observers represents a challenge whose findings support the hope that the effects of education and training on practice are identifiable.

Peterson and his associates (Peterson, Lyden, Geiger, & Colton, 1963) studied the relationship between medical school aptitude (MCAT scores), performance in school, and later career choices. They found small but consistent relationships indicating that lower aptitude students did less well in school, more often took rotating (general practice) internships in less prestigious hospitals, were less likely to take residencies, spent less time in residencies, and more often ended up in general practice. Schumacher (1964) also found that students with low MCAT scores tended to go into general practice. He also found that those students placed a higher value on the practical application of knowledge and did not have as great a need to exercise leadership as their classmates. Whether those findings have any relevance or application to professional psychology is not known, but they are provocative. Richards, Taylor, and Price (1962) found a positive correlation between the letters of evaluation of medical interns by staff members and the students' grades in courses in the clinical years of medical training, but not as large a correlation with grades in preclinical courses. Considerably more overlap seems likely between clinical courses and internships than for more academic courses. We suspect these findings would be replicable for training in professional psychology.

Peterson *et al.* (1956) found quality of practice related to length of training specifically in medicine, as opposed to training in a specialty. Gonnella and Veloski (1982) also found that residents in medicine do better on Part III of the National Board Examination than residents in more specialized areas of medicine, even when performances are corrected for the ability levels indicated by performance on Part II. The Part III examination is a 1-day examination designed to measure clinical competence especially as manifested in the use of medical knowledge to solve clinical problems. It is tempting to suppose that these findings, too, have direct relevance for training in professional psychology.

The first step in any evaluation of a training program is to specify training objectives (Irby, Evans, & Larson, 1978), for which a task analysis and definition of required skills is a valuable prerequisite. The American Board of Pediatrics (1974) performed an analysis of tasks involved and skills required for pediatrics, a field at least as complex as professional psychology. The essential competencies of child psychiatrists were identified by means of a critical incidents study (McDermott, McGuire, & Berner, 1976). LaDuca, Engel, and Risley (1978) took a somewhat different approach, called the *professional performance situations model*, and were able to identify entry-level competencies for occupational therapists, clinical dieticians, and medical laboratory scientists. Obviously these latter occupations are not equivalent to clinical psychology in tasks and responsibilities, but the approach may be worth considering.

In 1973, a report was issued on the evaluation of education in optometry (Havighurst, 1973). Although the evaluation was global rather than directed toward the value of specific educational and training experiences, the report has some relevance. In particular, it found that the optometric curriculum should be strengthened in the areas of opthalmic pharmacology and pathology, public and community health, and social and behavioral sciences, as these relate to vision. The clear implication of the report is that these areas were relatively neglected and that professional performance was likely to suffer on that account. The report did recommend a number of areas for study, but education and training practices and requirements were not among them.

An aspect of legal training comparable to psychology is *clinical legal education*, which has similarities to the internship. According to Cecil (1979), skills training is the most commonly cited justification for clinical training of law students. Surveys of attorneys and graduates of law schools (Baird, 1979; Dunn, 1969) indicate that they believe their preparation for professional work would have been improved by more practical experience with law and the courts. Cecil was fortunate enough to have access to a law school program in which, because there were more students who wanted clinical training than could be accomodated, a lottery was used to decide which students to admit. Attorneys who participated in the clinical program showed substantially greater satisfaction with the adequacy of their legal education than did attorneys not admitted to the program. Cecil's analysis indicated that the results could not be accounted for either by response bias or demoralization of those not selected. However, clinical legal training had little if any effect on the areas students chose for legal practice, that is, public versus private service. Neither did clinical training appear to affect their sensitivity to ethical issues. Cecil notes that previous studies also indicated that legal training had little impact on ethics or professional responsibility. There is no consensus, however, on the value of clinical legal training.

The studies cited here by no means exhaust the attempts to evaluate education and training in other professions. An exhaustive survey would be an unrealistic aspiration, but if an evaluation of training in any area of psychology is to be undertaken, the attempt to tie that work with what has already been done in other fields would be most worthwhile. It could reveal both similarities and differences between psychology and other professions, which are valuable in understanding psychology and its subspecialties as professions.

Research on Professional Psychology. The body of literature on psychology as a profession is by now voluminous and cannot be adequately surveyed here. Most is not particularly relevant to the value of education and training in any case. However, it again seems essential that the effort to evaluate education and training in psychology be tied to what has already been done. We will point to some of the more obviously relevant work, discussing how it bears generally on evaluation of education and training, and then discuss efforts specifically having to do with development of methods to assess performance.

Catterall (1973) developed a list of abilities that could be considered entry-level competencies for school psychologists. The list included such areas as assessment, intervention strategies, counseling, consultation, parent education, and written communications skills. Although Catterall's list has been criticized (Bennett, 1980) on the grounds that the criteria for evaluating the competencies are often questionable, the list does demonstrate the feasibility of such a project. There are no obvious reasons why it could not be done for professional psychology.

Past surveys of clinical psychologists (Norcross & Prochaska, 1982a, b) and psychotherapists (Prochaska & Norcross, 1983) indicate extensive involvement in psychotherapy by both groups, with nearly 90% of the clinicians and 99% of the psychotherapists claiming psychotherapy as professional activity. Psychotherapy was said to take up about 35% of the time of clinical psychologists and about 55% of the time of those identified as psychotherapists. Individual therapy accounted for nearly two thirds of the time performing psychotherapy. The sample of clinical psychologists reported somewhat more involvement than the psychotherapists in assessment, teaching, supervision, research, consultation, and administration. Of special interest is the fact that relatively *inexperienced* clinicians reported greater involvement in psychotherapy, assessment, and research; and Perlman (1985) found that master's-level clinicians had somewhat greater involvement in psychotherapy than PhDs. Sixty-three percent of the clinical psychologists and 80% of the psychotherapists regarded themselves as primarily clinical practitioners, whereas only 17% and 10%, respectively, claimed to be academicians.

In general, these psychologists reported that they were quite satisfied with their career choices, although 10% of the clinical sample reported themselves unhappy. Only 18% reported any dissatisfaction with their training, and only 15% reported dissatisfaction with their internship experiences. The major suggestions made for improving training were to provide more supervised experience under skilled clinicians, more emphasis on therapy and clinical techniques, and a "more relevant" approach to training.

A study of the graduates of PsyD training programs (Peterson, Eaton, Levine, & Snepp, 1980) produced similar findings with regard to extensive involvement in individual psychotherapy. The PsyD graduates were, however, even less likely to be involved in research or to be dissatisfied with their training; only 2% reported any dissatisfaction with their professional training.

These studies, which contain much more information of potential value, offer at least some clues as to the directions that initial evaluation programs should take. Task analyses will eventually show that individual psychotherapy absorbs the greatest amount of time, but the range of additional activities is great and indicative of considerable complexity. Moreover, more detailed information will be needed about the nature of therapeutic practice and clienteles served. These professionals report being fairly to highly satisfied with their training, and, as might be expected, focus their suggestions for improvement on more intensive clinical involvement.

Evaluation of Education and Training in Psychology. The concerns of a clinical faculty in evaluating medical students and the recent emphasis on a systems approach (Tonesk, Chapter 8 in this volume) suggest some potentially valuable approaches for improving evaluative practices in professional psychology. Despite the questioning of the "medical model" in conceptualizing the area of service for psychology, education and credentialing of clinicians are still more akin to medicine than to teaching and law. With the few recent exceptions mentioned earlier using legal clinics as a training device, the legal profession has relied almost exclusively on evaluating the quality of a lawyer's preparation through bar examinations. Beyond admission to the bar, whatever else differentiates good lawyers from bad lawyers—good judgment, ethical responsibility, and so on—is left to be sorted out by the marketplace. The inherently adversarial system of law practice insures that the work of nearly every lawyer invariably falls under the scrutiny of another. Such a peer review system is not built into medicine or other health service professions. Nor is there a built-in institutional umbrella in these professions as there is in teaching. A certified teacher continues to bear scrutiny through hiring, supervision, and promotion, and thus the responsibility to the public for the inadequacy of formally credentialed teachers is shared between the training program that prepares them and the educational institution that sanctions their functioning.

By contrast, most physicians and other health professionals, including clinical psychologists, function as independent practitioners, accountable directly to clients who are generally ill-positioned to assess the quality of their services. There is also the parallel of the importance of personal *qualities* that seem related to successful clinical work. These "humanistic" qualities, although unquestionably important in medical practice, may be nothing less than critical in professional psychology. Beyond these basic qualities of compassion, empathy, integrity, and respect for the patient, there are numerous personal *competencies* required for effective clinical performance in the delivery of both medical and psychological services. Among these are the ability to make decisions in the face of ambiguous or incomplete data, a keen awareness of the context within which presenting problems exist, a sense of proportion between means and ends, and an ability to act appropriately in situations involving conflicting expectations or ethical principles.

The assessment of such qualities challenges all health educators, but it is most challenging to the training and evaluation of professional psychologists who, on the one hand, expressly study human personality and behavior, and on the other, educate clinicians to work in a profession in which these competencies are more critical than in most others.

Although there have been few comprehensive attempts to evaluate education and training in psychology by means of formal research designs, many aspects of education and training have been evaluated or related to some outcome variables in one way or another. These efforts should be systematically reviewed. There have been, for example, comparisons of outcomes achieved in therapy by professionals and paraprofessionals. Although these comparisons were probably undertaken primarily to show that paraprofessionals can be safely and effectively utilized, to the extent that the results do not clearly favor professionals, they have some bearing on the specific value of professional education and training. Durlak (1979) reviewed the comparisons between professionals and paraprofessionals and by a "scorecard" approach discovered that in 42 comparisons across a variety of types of services, roughly half of the volume of which was individual or group therapy, paraprofessionals had better outcomes in 12 comparisons and were equal in 28 others. In only 2 comparisons did the professionals perform better. Other findings, such as those of Strupp and Hadley (1979), comparing outcomes achieved by trained psychotherapists with those of persons whose education was of a similar level but in nontherapeutic fields, also show no evidence of the value of education and training specifically in psychotherapy. Similarly, reviews of literature on experience in the practice of psychotherapy show no clear-cut advantages for the experienced psychotherapist (Parloff, Waskow, & Wolfe, 1978). Although these findings should not be taken as conclusive evidence against the value of education and training and the legitimacy of their requirements, they do represent a challenge for professional psychology.

Efforts to develop procedures or devices for assessing the skills and professional attitudes of professional psychologists have not been extensive, but examples of the kinds of things that could be done do exist. It may be helpful to illustrate these as a guide to further efforts.

Empathy is widely regarded as a critical element in the practice of clinical psychology. Although empathy itself is not a skill, the ability to communicate empathy is. Truax (1966), an early investigator of empathy, developed ways to measure it (but see Parloff *et al.*, 1978). Since that time, the literature on empathy in counseling and psychotherapy has grown substantially, and the concept has become current in nursing and medicine as well (e.g., Dimatteo & Taranta, 1979; Kalisch, 1971). Kagan (1975), in particular, has pioneered the development of materials and procedures to engender and communicate empathy.

Clinical problem solving is another important clinical skill that has been a focus of assessment efforts. Berven and Scofield (1980a) reviewed the literature on standardized simulations of clinical situations, which have had considerable use across a variety professions. The "In-Basket Test" (Fredericksen, Saunders, & Wand, 1957) was an early example of a problem simulation device, developed for assessing managerial skills but adaptable to a variety of problems. Problem simulations have a fairly long history in medicine also. Berven and Scofield (1980b) reported on a computer-based simulation for clinical problem solving. The flexibility of problem simulations makes them highly attractive as potential instruments to evaluate education and training. Although some simulations are not feasible for use with large numbers of persons in scattered geographic locations, the paper-and-pencil and computer varieties could be adaptable to almost any purpose.

Stricker (1982) reported on the development of a new measure of interpersonal competence utilizing videotaped stimulus scenes and both tape-recorded and written responses. Responses are scored for effectiveness, originality, and accuracy. The three scores are all judged and have demonstrated internal consistency. Of interest is the fact that psychology majors score higher than other students, and students who had completed even one psychology course scored higher than students who had not.

The assessment procedures discussed here do suggest that it should be possible to get some useful information about performances of trainees in and graduates of different programs. To the extent that individuals with different amounts of training perform differently on such measures, one could conclude that their training had a specific effect at least on some skills. Because these skills are valued by the profession and probably are necessary for efficacious delivery of services, the case for education and training would be strengthened.

CONCLUSIONS

The evaluation of educational and training requirements should not begin with the presumption that current practices are inadequate or ineffective. They may, in fact, be developing highly competent, effective practitioners to a degree unmatched by any markedly different alternatives. On the other hand, the evaluation should also be planned and carried out so that improved education and training is a likely outcome. The evaluation should be formative as well as summative in a meaningful way.

The evaluation plan must be realistic if it is to receive professional and financial support. An evaluation plan so abstract and general as to defy implementation or so grandiose as to elicit derision will not serve us well, but neither will an evaluation plan that invites the charge of irrelevance or triviality. It is for these reasons that we believe that the evaluation should begin by examining sets of data collected relatively easily from samples of new or recent doctorates. The difficulty of separating the influence of academic and internship programs probably means that, at least for now, the latter must be included in the initial plan.

It is critical, however, that any evaluation program be conceived and accepted in its entirety. A piecemeal evaluation would be unpersuasive and lead nowhere in the long run. Such a plan would not be likely to convince policymakers that professional psychology is serious about self-evaluation. A comprehensive, long-range program might persuade policymakers that it is reasonable to accept the status quo for the present, forestalling drastic changes in legislation and regulation that could prove disastrous for professional psychology and be inimical to the public interest.

REFERENCES

American Board of Pediatrics. (1974). *Foundations for evaluating the competency of pediatricians*. Chicago: Author.

Baird, L. (1979). A survey of the relevance of legal training to law school graduates. *Journal of Legal Education, 29*, 264–294.

Bennett, R. E. (1980). Methods for evaluating the performance of school psychologists. *School Psychology Monograph, 4*, 45–59.

Berven, N. L., & Scofield, M. E. (1980a). Evaluation of professional competence through standardized simulations: A review. *Rehabilitation Counseling Bulletin, 23*, 178–202.

Berven, N. L., & Scofield, M. E. (1980b). Evaluation of clinical problem-solving skills through standardized case-management simulations. *Journal of Counseling Psychology, 27*, 199–208.

Butler, R. W., & Williams, D. A. (1985). Description of Ohio State Board of Psychology hearings on ethical violations: From 1972 to the present. *Professional Psychology, 16*, 502–511.

Calhoun, J. F., & Green, C. (1984). Perspectives of psychology training clinics from training and clinic directors. *Professional Psychology: Research and Practice, 15*, 371–378.

Carboy, J., & Curley, J. F. (1976). A new training model: Professional child psychology. *Psychology in the Schools, 13*, 152–156.

Catterall, C. D. (1973). A competency-based school psychology internship. *Journal of School Psychology, 11*, 269–275.

Cecil, J. S. (1979). *The impact of clinical legal education on skills training, career choice, and appreciation of ethical issues in the practice of law.* Unpublished doctoral dissertation, Northwestern University.

Committee on Professional Standards. (1981). *Specialty guidelines for the delivery of services.* Washington, DC: American Psychological Association.

Cormier, L. S., & Bernard, J. M. (1982). Ethical and legal responsibilities of clinical supervisors. *The Personnel and Guidance Journal, 60*, 486–491.

Crowder, M. K., & Roback, H. B. (1981). The internship year in psychiatry: A status report. *American Journal of Psychiatry, 138*(7), 964–966.

Dana, R. H., Gilliam, M., & Dana, J. M. (1976). Adequacy of academic-clinical preparation for internship. *Professional Psychology, 7*, 112–116.

Dimatteo, M. R., & Taranta, A. (1979). Nonverbal communication and physician-patient rapport. *Professional Psychology, 10*, 540–547.

Dumke, G. (1986, January 15). Accrediting: The weak link in education reform. *Chronicle of Higher Education*, p. 5.

Dunn, R. E. (1969). Legal education and the attitudes of practicing attorneys. *Journal of Legal Education, 22*, 220–226.

Engelgau, D. (1985, January 30). Notes on health schools. *Chronicle of Higher Education*, p. 3.

Fallows, J. (1985, December). The case against credentialism. *The Atlantic*, pp. 49–67.

Ferguson, K. G. (1976). Graduate training in clinical psychology: A further critical evaluation. *Ontario Psychologist, 8*, 31–33.

Flanagan, J. C. (1954). The critical incident technique. *Psychological Bulletin, 51*, 327–358.

Flexner, A. (1910). *Medical education in the United States and Canada: A report to the Carnegie Foundation for the advancement of teaching* (Bulletin No. 4). New York: Carnegie Foundation.

Fredericksen, N., Saunders, D. R., & Wand, B. (1957). The in-basket test. *Psychological Monographs, 71* (9, Whole No. 438).

Fuhrmann, B. S., & Weissburg, M. J. (1978). Self-assessment. In M. K. Morgan & D. M. Irby, (Eds.), *Evaluating clinical competence in the health professions* (pp. 139–150). St. Louis: C. V. Mosby.

Geiss, W. J. (1926). *Dental education in the United States and Canada.* New York: Carnegie Foundation for the Advancement of Teaching.

Gonnella, J. S., & Veloski, J. J. (1982). The impact of early specialization on the clinical competence of residents. *The New England Journal of Medicine, 306*, 275–277.

Goodman, K., & Kahn, M. (1983). Psychology graduate students' attitudes toward research: A national survey. *Teaching of Psychology, 10*, 139–143.

Havighurst, R. J. (1973). *Optometry: Education for the profession*. Washington, DC: National Commission on Accrediting.

Inspector General of Health and Human Services (1986). *Report on the training and practice of physicians in the United States*. Washington, DC: Department of Health and Human Services.

Irby, D. M., Evans, J., & Larson, L. (1978). Trends in clinical evaluation. In M. K. Morgan & D. M. Irby (Eds.), *Evaluating clinical competence in the health professions* (pp. 20–29). St. Louis: C. V. Mosby.

Jacobson, R. L. (1986, January 22). Accrediting council seeks bigger role for agencies. *Chronicle of Higher Education*, p. 2.

Jenson, R. (1979). Competent professional service in psychology: The real issue behind continuing education. *Professional Psychology, 10*, 381–389.

Kagan, N. (1975). Influencing human interaction: Eleven years with IPR. *Canadian Councellor, 9*, 74–97.

Kalisch, B. J. (1971). An experiment in the development of empathy in nursing students. *Nursing Research, 20*, 202–211.

Klemp, G. O. (1977). Three factors of success. In D. W. Vermilye (Ed.), *Relating work and education* (pp. 102–109). San Francisco: Jossey-Bass.

LaDuca, A., Engel, J. D., & Risley, M. E. (1978). Progress toward a general model for competence definition in health professions. *Journal of Allied Health, 7*(2), 149–156.

Maatsch, J. L., & Gordon, M. J. (1978). Assessment through simulations. In M. K. Morgan & D. M. Irby (Eds.), *Evaluating clinical competence in the health professions* (pp. 123–138). St. Louis: C. V. Mosby.

Mabe, P. A., III, & West, S. G. (1982). Validity of self-evaluation of ability: A review and meta-analysis. *Journal of Applied Psychology, 67*, 280–296.

McCarberg, P. (1981). The efficacy of continuing education. In D. S. Falk, N. W. Weisfeld, & P. McCarberg, (Eds.). *A report to the National Commission for Health Certifying Agencies: To assure continuing competence*. Washington, DC: Department of Health and Human Services.

McDermott, J. F., McGuire, C. H., & Berner, E. S. (1976). *Roles and functions of child psychiatrists*. Evanston, IL: American Board of Psychiatry and Neurology.

Mendenhall, R. C., & Abrahamson, S. (1973). The practical utility of log-diaries in describing physician activities. In *Proceedings of the Twelfth Annual Conference on Research in Medical Education*. Washington, DC: Association of American Medical Colleges.

Menges, R. J. (1975). Assessing readiness for professional practice. *Review of Educational Research, 45*, 173–207.

Morgan, M. K., & Irby, D. M. (Eds.). (1978). *Evaluating clinical competence in the health professions*. St. Louis: C. V. Mosby.

Noonberg, A. R., & Page, H. A. (1982). Graduate neuropsychology: A later look. *Professional Psychology, 13*, 252–257.

Norcross, J. C., & Prochaska, J. O. (1982a). A national survey of clinical psychologists: Characteristics and activities. *The Clinical Psychologist, 35*(2), 5–8.

Norcross, J. C., & Prochaska, J. O. (1982b). A national survey of clinical psychologists: Views on training, career choice, and APA. *The Clinical Psychologist, 35*(4), 3–6.

Norcross, J. C., & Stevenson, J. F. (1984). How shall we judge ourselves? Training evaluations in clinical psychology programs. *Professional Psychology, 15*, 497–508.

Parloff, M., Waskow, I., & Wolfe, B. (1978). Research on therapist variables in relation to process and outcome. In S. L. Garfield & A. E. Bergin (Eds.), *Handbook of psychotherapy and behavior change: An empirical analysis* (2nd ed., pp. 233–282). New York: Wiley.

Perlman, B. (1985). A national survey of APA-affiliated Master-level clinicians: Description and comparison. *Professional Psychology, 16*, 553–564.

Peterson, D. R., Eaton, M. M., Levine, A. R., & Snepp, F. P. (1980). Development of Doctor of Psychology programs and experiences of graduates through 1980. *The Rutgers Professional Psychology Review, 2*, 29–34.

Peterson, O. L., Andrews, L. T., Spain, R. S., & Greenberg, B. G. (1956). An analytical study of North Carolina general practice, 1953–54. *Journal of Medical Education, 31*(12, Pt. 2).

Peterson, O. L., Lyden, F. J., Geiger, H. J., & Colton, T. (1963). Appraisal of medical students abilities as related to training and careers after graduation. *The New England Journal of Medicine, 269*, 1174–1182.

President of national CPA group, Bernard Z. Lee, now audits his profession. (1984, January 30). *Houston Digest*, p. 6.

Prochaska, J. O., & Norcross, J. C. (1983). Contemporary psychotherapists: A national survey of characteristics, practices, orientations, and attitudes. *Psychotherapy: Theory, Research, and Practice, 20*, 161–173.

Quick, S., Robinowitz, C., & Wilson, P. (1981). Results of the 1976 APA Self-Assessment Program. *American Journal of Psychiatry, 138*(12), 1587–1591.

Richards, J. M., Jr., Taylor, C. W., & Price, P. B. (1962). The prediction of medical intern performance. *Journal of Applied Psychology, 46*, 142–146.

Rosenfeld, M., Shimberg, B., & Thornton, R. F. (1983). *Job analysis of licensed psychologists in the United States and Canada*. Princeton, NJ: Center for Occupational and Professional Assessment, Educational Testing Service.

Sales, B. (1985). Specialization: Past history and future alternatives. *The Clinical Psychologist, 38*(3), 49–52.

Schumacher, C. F. (1964). Personal characteristics of students choosing different types of medical careers. *Journal of Medical Education, 39*, 278–288.

Sechrest, L. (1985). Specialization: Who needs it? *The Clinical Psychologist, 38*(1), 1–3.

Sechrest, L., & Hoffman, P. (1982). The philosophical underpinnings of peer review. *Professional Psychology, 13*(1), 14–18.

Stricker, L. J. (1982). Interpersonal Competence Instrument: Development and preliminary findings. *Applied Psychological Measurement, 6*, 69–81.

Strupp, H. H., & Hadley, S. W. (1979). Specific versus nonspecific factors in psychotherapy: A controlled study of outcome. *Archives of General Psychiatry, 36*, 1125–1136.

Task Force on Future Directions. (1982). Report, Division 12 of The American Psychological Association. Washington, DC: Author.

Tharp, R. G., & Gallimore, R. (1979). The ecology of program research and evaluation: A model of evaluation succession. In L. Sechrest, S. G. West, M. Phillips, R. Redner, & W. Yeaton (Eds.), *Evaluation Studies Review Annual* (Vol. 4, pp. 39–60). Beverly Hills: Sage Publications.

Truax, C. B. (1966). Therapist empathy, warmth, and genuineness and patient personality change in group psychotherapy: A comparison between interaction unit measures, time sample measures, and patient perception measures. *Journal of Clinical Psychology, 22*, 225–229.

Tucker, R. C. (1970). Strangers in paradise. *Journal of Consulting and Clinical Psychology, 34*, 140–143.

Tucker, R. C., & James, S. A. (1971). Note on "Strangers in paradise," or telling it like it isn't. *Journal of Consulting and Clinical Psychology, 37*, 304.

Turkington, C. (1986, January). Despite many models, basic questions remain. *APA Monitor*, p. 14.

Williams, G. (1980). *Western Reserve's experiment in medical education and its outcome.* New York: Oxford University Press.

2

Program Evaluation

Defining and Evaluating Quality

ALVIN G. BURSTEIN

NOMINAL AND ORDINAL ASPECTS OF QUALITY

The educational enterprise is not notable for a wealth of research or a strong theoretical base. It is especially ironic that this is true for psychology education as well. The observations in this chapter are thus based not on research but on almost 25 years of involvement in graduate school and internship program development in clinical psychology and on almost 15 years of involvement with psychology program evaluation through the American Psychological Association (APA), its Education and Training Board, and its Accreditation Committee.

The word *quality* has two meanings that, in the context of program evaluation, are often confused. One meaning is "degree of excellence," an ordinal judgment that ranks programs in terms of a good/bad dimension or classifies them in terms of such a dimension (e.g., above or below average). The second meaning of quality is "essential character," a nominal judgment that classifies or distinguishes programs in terms of some criterion feature or features. For example, one might distinguish applied psychology programs or human services programs or clinical

ALVIN G. BURSTEIN • Department of Psychology, University of Tennessee, Knoxville, TN 37996-0900.

programs. These nominal distinctions present major problems, however, and some of the most common can be questioned. For example, is classroom teaching considered applied psychology, or is it a human service? Are the differences among programs called "clinical" greater than the differences between (some) clinical programs and (some) counseling programs?

The Education and Training Board of the APA has a policy of requiring programs seeking accreditation to define explicitly the model of training offered. Although the justification is not an explicit one, that policy can be understood best as a recognition of the ambiguities of the current nominal categories (or taxonomy) used in describing psychology programs. Given some of the purposes of evaluation discussed later (e.g., providing information to consumers) and given the taxonomic ambiguities, the ability of a program clearly and accurately to define its nature becomes a generally desirable characteristic and an index of quality in the ordinal sense. To put it another way, it is operational policy for APA to assume that a high-quality program of any sort must be able to say what kind of program it is.

The ability to specify a program's essential character becomes even more important because, although some education and training components are seen as nonspecific (e.g., the ability to attract talented students), others may be goal-specific. For example, wisely or not, substantial course work in psychopathology is often thought of as more central for programs in clinical psychology than for programs in counseling or school psychology. Judgment of the adequacy or excellence of a specific program therefore may not be possible in the absence of a clearly and accurately articulated statement of its goals, and the dual meanings of "quality" become mutually relevant.

FUNCTIONS OF EXTERNAL EVALUATION

Evaluations of program quality, if carefully done, can be expensive. Current APA accreditation fees for a graduate program will exceed $4,000 over a routine 5-year cycle. The cycle includes a 2-day, 3-person site visit, committee review, a 4-year period of staff monitoring of annual reports, and the prorated costs of anticipated appeals. Because cost of the activity is subsidized at the 25% level by membership fees, the actual cost is probably closer to $5,500. Despite this high cost, when a proposal was made to abandon the accreditation activity, as was done some 15 years ago, the programs indicated their willingness to pay increased costs. A less dramatic indication of the perceived cost-effectiveness of accreditation is the ever-increasing number of programs that seek, earn, and wish to retain accredited status, that is, who wish to be involved in an admittedly expensive program of external evaluation.

Why is this evaluation activity valuable? A number of overlapping useful purposes are served by external evaluation: program development, information to regulatory/funding agencies, information to applicants, and the muting or rational resolution of internal organizational conflict. Preparing for external evaluation usually involves articulating the program's goals and preparing to demonstrate that those goals are, to a reasonable degree, being achieved. Such a program review provides the occasion for improving the program's function, either by modifying goals or indicating the need for corrective activities. In that sense, external review serves a program development function, that is, it ensures the clarification of a program's goals, of relevant strategies for goal achievement, and of implementation strategies.

Program development in turn serves at least two purposes, one of them external, the other internal. Both nominal and ordinal considerations of quality can define "essential" parameters of a given educational enterprise. The presence of these parameters can then serve as the basis for defining or designating minimally acceptable programs (standard setting). If the designation is public, then graduation from a designated program can serve as a qualifying credential either to the public at large or to other interested parties such as professional associations, licensing boards, or insurance companies. In other words, public external evaluations of program quality can serve as a control function by legitimizing the graduates of programs. Sociologists who study professions (e.g., Elliot, 1972; Strauss, 1975) argue that one criterion of a profession is the ability to control entry or membership into its ranks; in that sense, evaluation mechanisms qua control devices serve an essential function for psychology qua profession.

An internal effect of program development is the establishment of a consensus among program faculty about educational processes and goals. The pressure to develop an articulated model or stated intention, the need to plan explicitly, and the opportunity to justify values and goals to interested others can have the effect of transforming a collection of educators into a community with a shared educational purpose. In the presence of such a shared goal, peripheral intragroup conflicts can become muted, and rational working relationships can be facilitated.

A second purpose served by external evaluation has to do with resource allocation. Most educational programs exist within a larger organizational matrix—for example, a department of psychology that must compete for resources within a college of liberal arts. When, as is most often the case, the evaluation activity is sanctioned by higher levels of administration, that sanction obligates the larger organization to find the resources to meet the standards of quality invoked. Quality standards and external peer recommendations become very weighty considerations in the pursuit and allocation of organizational resources. Of course, this potential can have negative consequences as well. Sufficient criticism by external evaluators can provide a rationale for discontinuing a program. In fact, some negative consequences of this sort are probably necessary to maintain the credibility of the evaluation process.

Finally, of course, public evaluation of program quality can be of use to the applicant population choosing programs to which to apply. Not only are listings of "approved" programs often considered to be listings of higher quality programs, but in a market in which each high-quality student is sought after by many programs, an index of approval such as accreditation acquires additional worth. Even more useful information might result if programs made evaluation reports available to prospective applicants. Such a practice might shift attention from overly broad categories (approved/not approved; clinical/counseling) to more meaningful specifications of theoretical and technical orientation, size of student body, faculty quality, and the like.

EVALUATION OF OUTPUT

A key question in evaluating quality is that of the intended product. As has been already observed, current psychology program taxonomies focus on labels that are person-specific. Programs produce social psychologists or physiological psychologists, and so forth. The problem with this view is that the range of activities performed within each category of psychologist varies widely. Some social psychologists are undergraduate teachers, some are researchers, some are consultants, some are switch-hitters. An alternative to the-person-as-product approach is to conceptualize that that is to be taught to the person. The advantages of giving consideration to those things that are to be learned, as opposed to the learner, is that the various modes of instruction and/or assessment may be better suited to different objects of knowledge. In graduate psychology programs, the objects of knowledge can be considered to exist at four levels: facts, theories, skills, and attitudes.

Perhaps the most conventional view is that "facts" are the basic data of psychology, that the purpose of instruction is to convey them, and the purpose of research is to discover them. A student's mastery of facts is easily assessed using multiple choice or short-answer examinations, and the overall performance of an appropriate body of students would become an index of a program's success at imparting knowledge. At first blush, the notion of basic, factual data is appealing. Knowledge of statements such as "the rate of cure for psychotherapy does not exceed the spontaneous remission rate" or "the conditions of learning are contiguity, exercize, practice, effect, belonging, intensity, recency, and primacy" or "recognizing is easier than recalling" appear relevant, unambiguous, and testable. Unfortunately, the search for basic facts is as elusive as the search for basic perceptions. Finding that a particular rodent leaped from a specific jumping stand on a well-defined occasion seems less important than the implications of that reality. The multiplication of reported studies, the increasing number of journal pages printed, and lengthening publication lags argue for an ever-enlarging domain of data. As the number and variety of established psychological facts increase, the difficulty of adequately sampling the domain(s) increases as well. In consequence, measures of program quality that involve measurement of imparted facts also become increasingly problematic.

The problems of measuring factual knowledge might be thought to enhance the value of theory or the general laws or principles derived from observed facts. Unfortunately, psychology has not developed general theories that command universal or general assent. For that reason, attempts to measure a program's quality on the basis of its ability to impart theoretical sophistication must either permit the program to define its theoretical orientation, an option relevant to the nominal definitions of program quality defined previously or, alternatively, should focus on sophistication about means of theory building and theory testing. In other words, the second alternative implies that high-quality programs might be expected to acquaint students with the whole array of empirical techniques that psychologists have employed, the types of problems that have been attacked by each technique, the theoretical yield(s), and the ensuing practical applications. Many of the most convenient and familiar means of assessing knowledge, for example multiple choice or short-answer tests, do not lend themselves to assessing this kind of sophistication. Power tests, such as papers, essays, or oral examinations are more likely to be satisfactory but involve problems of grader subjectivity and comparability of tests. Newer, interactive computerized problems also may prove to be useful.

This second view of theoretical sophistication implies that a criterial skill for some or all psychologists is theory building, and further suggests that a program's quality might be defined, not by its ability to impart facts alone or theory alone, but by its ability to teach people to do the things that psychologists are expected to do—including theory building. Some skills are obviously specialty-specific; others may be generic. I would argue that the one skill generic to all psychologists is that described already: the ability to develop and evaluate theory. This view basically is an endorsement of the centrality of research training in the education of psychologists but is one that involves a broadening of the conception of what is centrally involved in "doing research" and of developing means of assessing the skill. Means that have been used are work samples of the kind that a dissertation or other scholarly writing might represent. It would clearly be appropriate for the evaluators of a graduate program in psychology to read a sample of the dissertations produced.

Other skills are specialty- or subspecialty-specific, involving especially detailed knowledge of certain empirical techniques and/or knowledge of ways of assessing factors relevant to a particular kind of problem situation and the most appropriate ameliorative methods.

A fourth kind of knowledge that programs might be expected to impart is attitudinal. Separate from knowledge of specific facts or theories and distinct from specific capabilities or skills is the system of values or attitudes inculcated by the educational system. Membership in any profession involves embracing a value system. I believe that exploitative or corrupt educational systems impart unfortunate attitudes of cynicism and suspicion, whereas desirable attitudes of commitment to the scientific enterprise of psychology, a fiduciary commitment to students, research subjects, and patients, and a collegial regard for the opinions of one's peers can be induced by example if not by exhortation. The effectiveness with which a program imparts appropriate attitudes can be indexed in various ways: choice of career lines, professional involvement, peer awards, or, negatively, ethical and/or legal violations.

EVALUATIONS OF PROCESS

Although output measures of a program's success at imparting knowledge are possible, they are not without problems. Many are indirect indexes, and consensus about the relative importance of various kinds of objects of knowledge, for example facts versus attitudes, is lacking. For that reason, attention is often given to evaluating the educational process rather than its product (knowledge imparted, either factual, theoretical, practical, or attitudinal) and to process issues such as student and faculty quality, and the like.

The traditional modes of instruction are the classroom, the laboratory, and the apprenticeship. Each has appropriate objectives and major variations. Classroom teaching includes reading that the student does in preparation for formal classes. Classes can be seminars, characterized by student presentations and interactive discussion, or lectures where the material that has been read is augmented, evaluated, analyzed, and/or integrated by the lecturer. Both theoretical and factual material are effectively presented in written material; the lecture itself or seminar discussion is best suited to the presentation of theory or the analysis of the meaning of data. A relevant question for evaluators is whether a program requires and has available readings that expose the students to appropriate facts and theories and offers lectures or seminars that elaborate on the material read.

The term *laboratory* is applied to two different kinds of settings relevant to education. A laboratory can be a place where experiments are done—where "facts" are determined. The term *laboratory* is also applied to a controlled setting in which particular skills are demonstrated and/or practiced. These skills can be computational (e.g., a statistics laboratory), diagnostic, or therapeutic. Research skills can be practiced *in vivo* (a laboratory in the first sense) or by means of trivial problems pursued for heuristic purposes rather than on their own merit (a laboratory in the second sense).

When human services skills are being practiced, the term *supervisor* is often used to denote a laboratory instructor. This usage, though common, introduces a confusion between two senses of the term *supervisor*. One sense refers to overseeing work for the purpose of providing formative or summative feedback to the person learning the skill. This function is basically an educational one. The second sense refers to a boss, foreman, or overseer who takes personal responsibility for the work produced by a supervisee. In this second sense, the supervisee is not primarily a student or learner but a worker who multiplies the supervisor's efforts. These two usages can be confusing in licensing laws that refer to the educational function by requiring "supervised" experience as an educational prerequisite for licensure and at the same time requiring psychological technicians to be "supervised" in the second sense. The confusion leads to the argument that it is unfair not to recognize when a supervised technician has learned to practice independently or to arguments that a laboratory instructor is "responsible" for the quality of work done by a student who may be at a very low level of competence and who is being graded.

Apprenticeships are similar to laboratories in that the object is the learning of a skill. Reading courses or tutorials can be considered apprenticeships in scholarly evaluation of written material, and research training is often in the apprenticeship mode. Internship training in human services skills is another clear example of apprenticeship. Any apprenticeship involves a "master," one who functions in both the supervisory senses described previously—teaching the supervisee and being responsible for the product. Apprenticeships have the advantage of involving the student in "real-life" problems but with the hazard that such problems may not contribute maximally to the student's needs, being too complex or too simple, or insufficiently varied. Apprenticeships also involve close and singular relationships with the supervisor, both because the responsible supervisor must be unambiguously identified and because the inculcation of values and attitudes occurs most effectively in close personal working relationships. When one wishes to emphasize the personal, value-imparting nature of an apprenticeship, it is often called a *mentorship*. If a program's ability to impart appropriate ethical or personal values is to be evaluated, close attention should be paid to the presence and quality of apprenticeships or mentorships.

In the literature describing psychology education, little explicit attention has been paid to the previously described range of educational modalities and to the assessment of the educational goals most appropriate to each—a topic that might merit careful study. The distinction sometimes made between "education" and "training" is an attempt to differentiate teaching modalities, but it is quite crude and usually includes the assumption that education is "nonapplied" and that training is human services oriented. As has been pointed out, research and scholarly skills as well as human services skills can be learned in an apprenticeship training mode, and imparting some important elements of human services skills can involve classroom discussion of theoretical issues (e.g., theory of technique courses). In any case, programs having at their disposal the whole range of instructional modes—classroom experiences (including readings), laboratories, and apprenticeships—and showing evidence of attempting to match modes and objects of instruction are assumed to have at least potential quality in graduate education in psychology.

Other, perhaps more familiar, process measures of program quality have to do with student and faculty characteristics. Clearly, the quality of the graduate produced is in part a function of the quality of the students attracted, and one generic index of program quality (in the ordinal sense) is its ability to attract talented students.

Faculty quality is seen as relevant, too, in both a nominal and ordinal sense. In the nominal sense, a program training in a particular model should have faculty trained in that mode. In the ordinal sense, a well-regarded faculty should have more to teach, and the conventional (although debatable) indexes of academic status—publication in prestigious journals, professional awards, scholarly citation—become relevant in program evaluation.

A more vaguely defined set of faculty characteristics with a presumptive historical relationship to program quality is now being challenged on both explicit and implicit levels. Prior to the 1950s, doctoral education in psychology almost invariably occurred in liberal arts departments of psychology, as distinct from professional schools. This circumstance implied several other characteristics: a resident faculty with undergraduate teaching responsibilities whose salary, promotion, and tenure were largely dependent on published research, a course of studies that included "outside" requirements and electives—that is, studies in fields other than psychology—and perhaps, most important, a budget justified on the basis of educational activities.

The first challenge to this model was the recognition, embodied in what is called either the Shakow model or the Boulder model, that doctoral education in human services should include training in human service settings analogous to medical internships and residencies. Shakow's central concept (Shakow, 1976) was of a partnership between universities and affiliated agencies for the purpose of training initially clinical, then counseling, and finally school psychologists. Although full partnership in the sense of mutually planned and executed educational programs never materialized, a central and irreducible role for field training and the importance of applied credentials for some of the human services faculty had been established firmly. Thus the assumption that only university faculty were good teachers for human services psychologists was questioned.

Professional schools of psychology constitute a more profound and radical challenge, especially when they are not university based. The challenge is radical because it stems from both philosophical and fiscal considerations. The core philosophical consideration is the notion that education of human services psychologists is best done at the hands of other human services psychologists rather than in "departments" of psychology where educational mandates can be imposed by "alien" basic science faculty to whom the human services faculty and students are accountable. It is not a political triviality that in professional schools of medicine the large clinical departments (medicine and surgery) most powerfully define the curricula and that medical school basic science departments often are budgeted through clinical departments.

The basic philosophical question is this: Does the doctoral education of human services psychologists benefit in major ways from ready access to "academic" psychologists and to academic departments other than psychology? That such students require some teaching from practitioners is assumed by the Shakow model. The further and more radical question is whether such students need "basic science" courses, and if they do, is that basic science best taught by basic scientists or by human services practitioners?

The fiscal issue is clearest when one considers the challenge posed by professional schools that are not university related. The belief that universities give higher priority to educational than to fiscal considerations was expressed in Robert Hutchins's well-known quip, "A university that doesn't lose a million dollars a year isn't worth its salt." Lacking educational endowments and legislatures with statutory commitments to education, private entrepreneurial professional schools cannot tolerate negative cash flow and must, as a condition of survival, give primary consideration to cost control. In a university setting, a full-time, tenured faculty with a low teaching load is assumed to reflect quality. Private professional schools are impelled by fiscal considerations to avoid tenure and to pay part-time faculty on a piecework basis for courses taught. To the extent that these faculty are involved in other piecework activities, it is in their financial interest to minimize their indirect teaching time (office hours, preparation) in order to maximize their income, but, arguably at the expense of the quality of their teaching. Even university-based professional schools can feel this pressure, if their budget is partly generated by service activities performed by faculty—or by students. For example, medical schools, once heavily subsidized by the federal government, are now expected to provide one fourth or more of their operating budgets from patient fees and to increasingly press faculty and students to perform fee-generating services even when these do not have a clear educational function.

It is clear that professional schools pose a radical challenge to the conventions of university teaching and to the Shakow model. Whether this challenge will be evaluated on the basis of the quality of the respective products (in either sense of quality) or settled by marketplace considerations that make professional schools, with their higher tuition, less desirable to a shrinking pool of graduate applicants remains to be seen.

Central to most university education is the notion of a residential faculty and student body. The core assumptions are that collegial accountability fosters high-quality instruction; that close, individual faculty–student bonds (mentorships) as described previously are crucial to important aspects of graduate education; and that peer–student relationships as well as faculty–student relationships provide a basis or template for later collegiality that is essential for later scholarship, research, or applied practice of high quality. "Universities without walls" whose faculty do not assemble to consider, debate, and evaluate educational policy and practices but rather who contract to perform specific educational functions for isolated students are a radical departure. Ideally, a student might travel to expose himself or herself to a highly individual array of mentors. More typically, such students try to collect an education as an ancilla to other, more compelling activities. Further problems can be generated by the difficulty of monitoring geographically distant educational activities performed by individuals with a tenuous tie to the sponsoring institution, a tie that competes with other ongoing loyalties.

It is not surprising that "open universities" have met with some skepticism at the hands of their more conventional sister universities. Nevertheless, they are a prologue to even more radical challenges to the concept of a resident faculty and student body: telecommunication and computer-augmented education. Not only do interactive video facilities provide potential means of linking geographically distant faculty and students, but interactive computer programs can provide simulated research on human services problems with almost infinitely variable feedback possibilities.

The impact of these developments and the impact of computerized data banks on hard-copy libraries is indeterminate now but will be massive in the long run. At the worst, we will see either faddish endorsement of technical novelty or cranky insistence on traditional ritual. At best, we will see exploration and increasing refinement of the specific benefits and shortcomings of specific educational modes and mechanisms. For example, interviewing can be taught by lecture, demonstration, review of videotapes, process notes, or summary notes. Each modality has its own merits. Lecture can impart general principles of technique; demonstration can illustrate these; videotape review can enhance self-awareness—and self-consciousness; process notes can enhance memory; summary notes can develop the capacity to conceptualize the process, and so forth. Nevertheless, some programs seem committed to pursuing the latest technical innovation as the "best" educational technique, without regard to the needs of the specific student at a specific time. Access to and rational use of the wide range of educational modalities is an index of ordinal quality. In reviewing the special advantages of various educational modes, the relationship between imparting of values and close mentorships must be kept in mind, and the role of value induction in graduate education given due weight.

One of the most vexing tensions in the evaluation of doctoral psychology programs is that that exists between the values associated with innovation and freedom, on the one hand, and those associated with credentialing and control, on the other. Some state licensing laws mandate graduate courses in specific areas, and APA's accreditation criteria require that accredited programs show how they demonstrate competence in a variety of foundation areas (APA, 1980).

Such requirements are strongly objected to, sometimes on the grounds of academic freedom, sometimes on the grounds of chilling innovation. Objections based on academic freedom are poorly grounded. Academic freedom has to do with an individual professor's right to teach what he or she believes to be scientifically true without fear of loss of job or salary and privately to embrace political and moral views of his or her own choosing. Academic freedom is the polar opposite of McCarthyism, which held that "known communists" should not be employed and that "un-American" points of view should not be taught. An individual professor's academic freedom is not infringed by educational requirements, for example, that doctoral students take a foreign language or do doctoral research or have an internship. In fact, inherent in the notion of an academic program is that of a specified sequence of academic experiences. Although a *student's* freedom is obviously reduced by any academic requirements, the assumption is that the student and the public gain by the restriction.

The objection that requirements of this sort dampen innovation is better grounded, but only if it is understood that innovation is not an unmitigated good. Some changes can be for the worse. Balancing the considerations involved may be simplified by distinguishing between a program and a field of study. The former is characterized by a well-defined sequence of academic experiences, the latter, by a central concern or interest that is explored in highly varied ways by different students. Hence one might expect *programs* in clinical psychology to be subject to a higher degree of specification than fields of study such as physiological psychology or neuropsychology or child psychology. *Programs* should also demonstrate sensitivity to the merits of both change and stability. A generic condition of ordinal quality should be the ability to record their changes over time, to demonstrate the educational grounds for the changes adopted as well as the means for evaluating the effects of the changes.

METAEVALUATION

A discussion of the evaluation of quality in graduate education would not be complete without some consideration of the indexes of quality in evaluation activity. From a nominal point of view, are they summative or formative? Either is legitimate, but their respective purposes should not be confused. For example, currently the APA stipulates that the accreditation team's recommendation about accreditation be revealed to the evaluated site *before* the site responds to the findings of the report. This policy is justified from the view of accreditation as summative and requiring full disclosure at every point. Unfortunately, not requiring the evaluated site to take a position about the merit of the findings in the report distinct from the accreditation recommendations in the report may well lessen the educational, formative, program development impact of the report.

Do the evaluation mechanisms serve the various institutions that support them: educational institutions, the public at large, students, governmental bodies, and the profession at large? Do the evaluation mechanisms express the values of collegiality, community, and social responsibility? Answers to these questions can constitute an evaluation of evaluation activity.

FINAL COMMENTS

Three concluding comments about program evaluation are in order. The first is a historical one—an antidote to inaccurate rhetorical allusions to two educational pioneers: Flexner and Shakow. Flexner was a nonphysician (who took an eventual master's in psychology) who carried out a highly consequential study of medical education in the United States and Canada for the Carnegie Foundation (Flexner, 1910). The problem, he found, generated by a plethora of entrepreneurial medical schools, was too many, poorly trained physicians. The solution was more fully to specify the content of medical education (e.g., 2 basic science years, 2 clinical years, and an internship) and to foster increasing university involvement in medical education. The result was a beneficial reform in medical education but one that by the 1980s had generated new problems: too many specialist physicians and a strangulation in effective medical education (Burstein, 1982).

The problem Shakow found was very different: too few psychologists to meet the 1950 demands of society and psychology education dominated by the university. The Shakow (or Boulder model) for the education of human services psychologists has been a success in that universities, internships, and practicum settings are now linked in a network that has multiplied the production of well-trained human services psychologists. That beneficial reform has produced, again not surprisingly, some new problems: an American Psychological Association highly committed to meeting the needs of human service-oriented psychologists but at the expense of increasing disaffection among their academic counterparts, the attenuation of research training, and a looming overproduction of human services psychologists. These problems will not be solved by the adoption of rigid codifications of psychology education, even if those are described as the recommendations of a "Flexnerlike commission" and presented as educational reform.

A second comment has to do with the erroneous identification of human services psychology and applied psychology. Too often, clinical, counseling, and school psychology are taken as the prototypes of applied psychology, with applied psychology typically understood as a post-World War II phenomenon. In point of fact, psychology in the United States from its earliest days has been coextensive with applications and utility. H. L. Hollingworth did applied research for Beechnut chewing gum and Coca-Cola, and J. B. Watson "sold" his behavioral expertise to the end of popularizing smoking among women.

Whatever the social merit of gum chewing, drinking soft drinks, and smoking, Hollingworth, Watson, and many other psychologists were applying psychology—for money. William James's pragmatism is a philosophical statement that truth—including psychological truth—is what works.

The equation of applied psychology with issues of treatment and cure has had unfortunate consequences. The involvement of psychologists in public school education, initially an expression of pragmatic interests like those of Thurstone in the educational process, has lately become overidentified with quasi-medical issues of diagnosis and treatment. One hopes that the current involvement of psychologists in health issues will avoid a similar fate. In any case, the notion of a university-bred psychology with real-world implications (though obviously not foreign to the Frenchman Binet) has been a special expression of Yankee genius, and for United States psychology to evaporate from the university—or to be confined by it—would be an unfortunate loss.

This leads to a third comment in the form of a dual question. What role will the university play in the education of psychologists, and what role will psychologists play in university education? We have tended to regard as good undergraduate psychology programs those that teach what has been regarded as desirable for psychology graduate students to know. As academic employment for psychologists shrinks and the foreseeable needs for human services psychologists level off or decline, such a definition is less relevant because there will be fewer graduate students in psychology. Rather we should be asking what relevance undergraduate psychology teaching can have for a liberal arts curriculum and for curricula in nonpsychology professions like business, law, engineering, and the health professions. Exploring those needs will define the pragmatic interests of the next generation of university psychologists. Ignoring those questions will lead to a psychology irrelevant to the "main campus" and best suited to a professional school setting.

The role of the university in the training of psychologists is a function of one's view of psychology as an intellectual enterprise or human service. If one views psychology as an intellectual enterprise, albeit a pragmatic one, then the centrality of empirical training and the exposure of students to a wide variety of intellectual approaches and to sister disciplines cannot be denied, and the relevance of such factors to excellence must be given due weight.

REFERENCES

American Psychological Association. (1980). *Committee on accreditation, accreditation handbook* (rev. 1983). Washington, DC: author.

Burstein, A. G. (1982). The system is failing, but the students are getting the "F's." *Pharos, 45*(2), 30–34.

Elliot, P. R. C. (1972). *The sociology of the professions*. New York: Herder.

Flexner, A. (1910). *Medical education in the United States and Canada: A report to the Carnegie Foundation for the advancement of teaching* (Bulletin No. 4). New York: Carnegie Foundation.

Shakow, D. (1976). What is clinical psychology? *American Psychologist, 31*(8), 553–560.

Strauss, A. (1975). *Professions, work and careers*. New Brunswick, NJ: Transaction Books.

3

Work Samples and Simulations in Competency Evaluation

ANN HOWARD

INTRODUCTION

The evaluation of student competence in clinical training is part of the broader issue of competency evaluation across a variety of professions. Many disciplines have similar needs to evaluate the application of skills as distinct from levels or scope of knowledge. Work samples and simulations offer alternative measurement methods to paper-and-pencil testing that can well be applied to skill application. The usefulness of such methods for evaluation of interactive skills is particularly appropriate to clinical training.

This general discussion of the advantages and disadvantages of work samples and simulations for competency evaluation cites many examples that point to their usefulness in clinical training. Application to student samples is illustrated by the simulations used for medical

From "Work Samples and Simulations in Competency Evaluation" by Ann Howard, 1983, *Professional Psychology: Research and Practice*, pp. 780–796.

ANN HOWARD • Human Resources Research, American Telephone and Telegraph Company (AT&T), 550 Madison Avenue, New York, NY 10022.

students in Scotland (Harden & Gleeson, 1979). For school psychology, there is the example of the competency model developed by the State of Washington (Shoemaker & Splitter, 1976) and the hypothetical examination suggested by Miller and Engin (1974). Other models in the clinical domain include the oral examination and videotape exercises used by the American Board of Psychiatry and Neurology and the prototype of an assessment center developed by the American Board of Professional Psychology (ABPP).

There are, of course, disadvantages to the use of work samples and simulations for evaluations of competency. Yet the administrative complexities described here for postgraduate, professional competency evaluation are considerably lessened in a training situation. At the same time, the advantages remain strong.

PSYCHOLOGY'S EVALUATION OF ITSELF

Various boards that grant credentials, such as the state licensing boards, the ABPP, and other nonstatutory boards, face the problem of evaluating professional competence to practice psychology. Unfortunately, such groups have yet to take advantage of the expertise in psychological measurement of those professionals they attempt to certify. The national licensing examination (Examination for Professional Practice in Psychology, or EPPP) is a knowledge-based paper-and-pencil test that measures psychological background rather than competence to practice psychology. Oral examinations or essays may be used by licensing boards to focus on practice, but they lack the standardization of the EPPP. The ABPP examination relies on work samples brought in by candidates, but it also lacks standardization; reliability and validity remain unchecked. Other boards have experimented with measurement methods but have so far failed to establish their reliability and validity for the evaluation of competence. In evaluating itself, psychology has not stood up to its own standards.

This article offers one step toward improving that record by looking at the accumulated evidence for and against the use of work samples and simulations for competency evaluation. Evidence and examples are drawn from two primary sources: the use of such tools for competency evaluation in various professions (often with the advice and consultation of psychologists) and the experience in personnel selection of many industrial/organizational psychologists.

HISTORY AND RATIONALE

Historically, the personnel selection literature has been dominated by the use of paper-and-pencil tests. This trend was promulgated during the two world wars, when general intelligence tests and later multiple-aptitude batteries proved to be expedient ways to select military personnel (Anastasi, 1982). One deviation from this genre was the work directed by Henry Murray for the Office of Strategic Services (OSS), which used assessment center methods, including extensive simulations, to select espionage agents (OSS, 1948). But, as the work was extended to include tests of specific aptitudes, personality characteristics, and interests, it was the quick and economical paper-and-pencil methods that primarily appealed to later military and industrial test usage.

In a classic article, Wernimont and Campbell (1968) pointed out that the standard validity model was thus tied to the use of tests as "signs" or indicators of predispositions to behave in certain ways; they suggested it would be more fruitful to focus instead on "samples" of behavior. Their proposed behavior-consistency model was based on the axiom that the best predictor of future performance is past performance. Hence it should be advantageous to select or develop predictor measures that would be as close to the criterion as possible. For example, it has been shown that one of the best predictors of achievement in a certain activity is biographical data that assess previous achievement on similar types of activities. If a candidate responds affirmatively to an item like "I built a plane that flew," this is good evidence of future success as an aeronautical engineer.

Another example mentioned by Wernimont and Campbell (1968) was the simulations used in management assessment programs. These simulations derived from Douglas Bray's initiation in 1956 of the Management Progress Study at AT&T, in which the assessment principles of the OSS center were adapted for managerial selection (Bray, Campbell, & Grant, 1974).

That work samples or simulations might also have higher predictive ability than do paper-and-pencil tests for measuring professional competence has not been overlooked by other professions. In the medical field, grades in premedical and medical schools as well as medical aptitude and achievement tests have been found to be poor substitutes for later measures of physician attributes and performance (Albo, Taylor, & Page, 1982). For example, among residents in anesthesiology, the correlation of a newly developed on-the-spot work sample test of the administration of spinal anesthesia proved to correlate only .20 with a multiple-choice knowledge test of the procedure, which confirmed the belief that not all residents who can answer test questions about a skill can also perform that skill well (Miller, 1982).

Before evaluating the demonstrated advantages and disadvantages of work samples and simulations, some definitions and examples are in order.

DEFINITIONS AND EXAMPLES

Work samples and simulations are both types of performance tests, or standardized measures of behavior, whose primary objective is to evaluate what one can *do* rather than what one *knows* (Cascio & Phillips, 1979). In a *motor* test, the task is a manipulation of things, such as tracing a complex electrical circuit, operating a sewing machine, repairing a gear box, making a tooth from plaster, or driving an automobile. *Verbal* tests, in contrast, are problem situations that are primarily language oriented or people oriented. For example, a technical magazine editor's test may evaluate writing skill, choice of picture headlines, layout, story organization, and design. Similarly, students in optometry school might have a test of graph reading and interpolation (Asher & Sciarrino, 1974).

A *work sample* is an example of one's work, job, or profession. ABPP has used several types of work samples in its clinical, counseling, school, and industrial/organizational (I/O) psychology examinations. In *site visits* the examining committee goes to the workplace and observes the candidate at work, such as interacting with patient, boss, or staff, or planning a research study. In the *advance preparation* work sample, the candidate brings in an example of his or her completed work, such as a transcript or videotape of therapy or an I/O psychologist's plan for organizational development with analyses of results, charts, and reports used to present the findings to management and recommendations for the organization. An *on-the-spot* work sample requires the candidate to demonstrate his or her competency in a situation parallel to that at work, such as performing a screening interview on a patient, who is made available at the examination.

A *simulation* is also a work sample but a simulated one—an imitative representation of one's work. Although many varieties of simulations are available, examples of some of the more common ones follow.

A *business game* simulates important aspects of business operations for small groups of participants. For example, in the Management Progress Study's Manufacturing Problem, a manufactured product is represented by tinker toys that can be built into models of different complexity (a man, top, wagon, ladder, or airplane). A group of six people being assessed must buy parts, decide what to manufacture, and sell finished products as market conditions change (Bray *et al.*, 1974).

A *leaderless group discussion* is usually conducted with small groups of about six people and presents topics to get the group to interact. Individuals thereby demonstrate such characteristics as leadership skills, persuasiveness, or behavior flexibility. Assigning roles may create a competitive environment.

A *written simulation* can help evaluate the problem-solving ability of a candidate. For example, an I/O psychologist might get a request from a fictitious boss to make a proposal for a staffing program that must operate under specified constraints, such as the available labor market or company policies.

First applied to managerial jobs, the *in-basket* exercise presents a candidate with written materials supposedly from a manager's in basket. It may include memos, letters, telephone messages, vouchers to be signed, and reference materials such as an organization chart or statements of personnel policies. The candidate must respond to the group of problems as if he or she had assumed that manager's role. The in-basket exercise typically includes a follow-up interview in which an assessor can explore rationales for decisions and also evaluate some interpersonal skills.

The in-basket exercise can be adapted to professions other than management. For example, an assessment center that evaluates pharmacists presented material on a hypothetical pharmacist's in basket, which required the candidate to deal with such diverse topics as personnel problems, customer-related issues, drug selection, and general pharmacy management (Silzer, 1978). A hypothetical examination for school psychologists (Miller & Engin, 1974) used an in-basket format to present daily problems by mail but added the complexity of interrupting the procedure with a simulated telephone call (accomplished with earphones). The voice on the telephone said, "This is Principal Jones. I have a kid in my office acting real queer. He won't answer me and stares off in the distance like he doesn't know where he is. Can you come right away?" The candidate's decision of whether or not to go, questions asked the principal, and suggestions made are all evaluated for professional competency.

The practical examination of the American Board of Dermatology has made extensive use of films, slides, or videotapes because theirs is a highly visual profession. Aspirants answer questions about projected slides and also use a microscope to examine sections (Hurley, 1982).

ABPP recently developed a clinical psychology prototype examination based on an assessment center model that presents videotaped vignettes of patient–therapist interactions. The candidate is required to discuss the problem presented, how the therapist was handling it, the next steps in the therapeutic process, and overall recommendations for treatment.

The hypothetical school psychology examination (Miller & Engin, 1974) proposed films of incidents such as an irate parent claiming the candidate tested his son without permission or a group of filmed teachers who think that failure of children to learn is the responsibility of the home, the community, or the social milieu, but never of the teacher.

Both the candidate and an examiner or an actor are often involved in *role plays*. For example, in a study selecting an employment interviewer, the candidate had to role play a telephone interview with a hiring supervisor who had supposedly screened two applicants for a job and wanted to hire the lesser qualified one (Ofsanko & Paulson, 1977).

In the *oral fact-finding exercises*, the examiner acts as a resource person from whom the candidate must extract the relevant information to deal appropriately with the presented problem. In the ABPP clinical psychology assessment prototype the candidate is given a brief description of a client and a therapist and is asked to seek out additional information, arrive at an evaluation of the patient's problem, and suggest future therapeutic tactics. All responsibility for structuring and timing the interview rests with the candidate, who must make an oral presentation of conclusions to the examiners at the end of the fact-finding phase. Following this step, the examiners question the candidate to probe for such things as quality of reasoning and ability to defend conclusions.

Although there are various types of work samples and simulations, they can be broadly considered together as performance tests to evaluate their advantages and disadvantages.

ADVANTAGES OF PERFORMANCE TESTS

The advantages of performance tests are particularly evident when they are compared to the multiple-choice variety of paper-and-pencil tests.

Application of Skills

Performance tests can measure the application of skills, that is, not just what one knows about how something should be done but whether one can effectively apply that knowledge. This differentiation of knowledge from skill application is reflected in the medical model of competency evaluation, in which national boards measure knowledge for the purpose of licensing, but specialty boards measure both knowledge and clinical competence in the different medical specialties.

One popular use of simulations to measure skill application is the sequential model of patient management. The candidate may be presented with a problem, such as that of a 50-year-old woman executive who develops severe abdominal pain during a board of directors meeting. To indicate the first step taken, the candidate must select one alternative mode of action from about six presented, such as obtaining further history, ordering tests, or hospitalizing the patient for immediate surgery. That choice would lead to a programmed outcome, such as test results, followed by another choice point, and so on until the patient reaches a final outcome. The intellectual process needed to work through such a patient-management problem reportedly "feels more like" the process of clinical judgment a physician uses when caring for patients and is qualitatively different from that process used in objective tests (McGuire & Babbott, 1967).

The American Dental Hygienists' Association (ADHA) developed a test that focuses on application of skills for the licensing process. Applicants must demonstrate data gathering and charting skills, conduct an oral prophylaxis, and demonstrate radiography skills (ADHA, 1978).

The examination in pharmacy mentioned earlier (Silzer, 1978) incorporated ethical principles into its evaluation of the application of professional skills. The participant was presented with a number of audiotaped and written case situations related to ethical practices and professional standards. The participant was asked to decide how each situation should be handled and, more important, what aspects needed to be considered when making each decision.

In the hypothetical school psychology evaluation, a candidate who sees a film of a small boy has to administer a Wechsler Preschool and Primary Scale of Intelligence to him; the child's oral responses are generated by computer on audiotape. After being tested and reviewing a 10-minute film of the boy's classroom behavior and a written report from his teacher, the candidate must write a short predictive report and make two alternative plans for the child (Miller & Engin, 1974).

Interactive Skills

Another strong advantage of work samples and simulations is their ability to measure interactive skills, such as with a patient, a client, company management, or a school child. To illustrate the importance of such measures, in a competency model developed by the State of Washington for school psychology (Shoemaker & Splitter, 1976), certification of counseling skills required that the applicant demonstrate the ability to develop an atmosphere and relationship that stimulates open communication. Specifically, the applicant must demonstrate effective use of (a) minimal encouragement for the client to talk, (b) silence, (c) open-ended questions, and (d) a focus on the client's content without introducing irrelevant data. Obviously, it is impossible to measure such competencies by paper-and-pencil methods.

A simulated office oral examination was used by a group of family physicians in Canada to evaluate interactive skills (Lamont & Hennen, 1972). Each candidate had to interview three simulated patients who were instructed to portray an individual with a problem commonly encountered in family practice, such as learning of a positive Pap test result. Twelve actors from an amateur theatrical group were typecast as the patients while examiners observed from behind a one-way window.

Detachment of Stress from the Examiners

Another advantage of performance tests is that it is possible to measure reactions under stress while detaching the imposition of stress from the interviewers. This makes the exam more palatable to both the examiner and the examinee. For example, in the assessment for an employment interviewer (Ofsanko & Paulson, 1977), the candidate role played an employment interviewer who rejects a hostile applicant for company employment; the simulated applicant provided the stress and suffered the consequences.

Content Validity

It is readily apparent that content validity is much easier to establish for performance tests than for paper-and-pencil tests because the latter are only signs of behavior. If the performance test is a sample of the job, it can be directly related to a job analysis.

Predictive Validity

The rationale for using performance tests rests on the assumption of greater predictive validity. One might be hard pressed at the present time for definitive, conclusive evidence of this point, given the multiple variations in validity studies that can affect the outcome, for example, selection of sample, tests, and criteria. Yet several hypotheses have been advanced to account for greater predictive validity of complex work sample tests. Four of these were summarized by Asher and Sciarrino (1974): (a) The *point-to-point hypothesis* suggests that the more points in common between predictor and criterion space, the higher the validity coefficient. (b) A classic approach to test construction is to factor analyze skills into aptitudes or traits, pattern these into composites with multiple regression methods, and measure the aptitudes or traits involved. The *interaction hypothesis* suggests that a complex task may elicit an interaction effect among aptitudes that may not be additive, so that the criterion is poorly predicted with an additive model based on measures of single aptitudes or traits. (c) The *work methods hypothesis* suggests that a miniature work sample test may elicit realistic work methods or habits that individuals use to solve specific problems, which in turn may account for more individual differences than the basic aptitudes. (d) The *transfer-of-experience hypothesis* suggests that a work sample may be sorting those with progressively more criterion-related experience. Another rationale for superior predictive validity of work sample tests is the *motivation hypothesis*. That is, candidates may be more interested in and motivated for a work sample test than for a paper-and-pencil test (Gordon & Kleiman, 1976).

Less Adverse Impact

Evidence is accumulating that performance tests have less adverse impact against minority group members than do paper-and-pencil tests. Recent reports that blacks score 100 points lower than do whites on the Scholastic Aptitude Test ("100-Point Lag," 1982) highlight some of the ubiquitous problems with paper-and-pencil tests.

In AT&T's Management Continuity Study, large race differences were found in the paper-and-pencil School and College Ability Test; however, the in-basket exercise showed much less adverse impact, and performance in group discussions showed almost none (Bray & Howard, 1983). Likewise, in a study of 87 metal trades apprentices, Schmidt, Greenthal, Hunter, Berner, and Seaton (1977) found all five subtests of a content-valid Machine Trades Achievement Test showed majority/minority differences compared to only one of three scores in a specially developed performance test that required completing a workpiece with oral instructions. Cascio and Phillips (1979) found no evidence of adverse impact when white, black, and Latin groups were compared on 11 motor performance tests and 10 verbal performance tests that the Miami Beach, Florida, city government used.

DISADVANTAGES OF PERFORMANCE TESTS

In spite of the long list of advantages, there are a few serious disadvantages of work samples and simulations for competency evaluation.

Costs

Initial development costs for work samples and simulations can be high. Aside from the expense of such things as actors and videotapes, a variety of forms, checklists, and rating scales must be developed to use the tools properly. Revisions and parallel tests are also expensive to develop, although test security is not as big a problem for performance as it is for paper-and-pencil tests, in which items must be continually developed (Cascio & Phillips, 1979). A candidate might know in advance he or she will be questioned about a paranoid case in a performance test but still not handle it well or be able to answer examiners' questions about what he or she did.

Administrative Complexities

Additional costs and complexities come from the need for examiners. Their training, preparation time, and administration time can be both costly and demanding. With a high volume of candidates, such as those who want to be licensed, these problems can be difficult though not impossible to solve. A poor examiner can also ruin a performance test because he or she may not be able to elicit or evaluate the behavior needed. The more the exam is preset, the easier it is to take care of examiner deficiencies.

Byham (1982) offered several solutions to reduce the administrative complexities and costs of multiple performance tests used in competence evaluation. Training can be shortcut by developing specialists in each exercise, rather than by training all examiners on all exercises, and by using home study programmed instruction. Data collection can be done by videotape and shipped off to the exercise specialists rather than by paying their expenses to travel to a central location. Data can also be integrated mathematically rather than requiring face-to-face integration sessions with examiners.

Range of Knowledge

Work samples and simulations are not particularly good for measuring a candidate's range of knowledge. Competent examiners could ask a wide variety of questions about a work sample, relating it to many aspects of a field, but the examiners may not know enough to do so or may lack the appropriate questioning skills.

Reliability

Time limitations may result in too few examples for performance tests, whereas paper-and-pencil tests can offer a wide selection of items. This may require a series of short simulations rather than only one or two long ones. In the oral exam of the American Board of Otolaryngology (Reed, 1982), each candidate has four 1-hour examinations with different examiners. Because each examiner has four simulated patient protocols (consisting of X rays, glass microscopic slides, photomicrographs, patient photos, endoscopic photos, audiograms, etc.), each candidate is presented 16 protocols.

Another medical example, geared both to short simulations and the accommodation of large groups of candidates at once, is the Objective Structured Clinical Examination used with medical students in Scotland (Harden & Gleeson, 1979). Students rotate among 20 or so stations, spending a specified time at each, and moving on to the next station on a bell signal. At each procedure station, the student has a task to perform, such as examining the abdomen, and at each question station, the student responds to inquiries on the basis of information he or she has obtained at the previous station. Students are asked to demonstrate a variety of skills or knowledge, such as taking a brief history, testing a patient's hearing, explaining how to self-administer an insulin injection, telling a wife her husband has just had a myocardial infarction, responding to questions about surgical instruments, or examining urine specimens.

In addition to inadequate sampling of the relevant performance domain, unreliability can be created by the use of ratings to judge performance on work samples and simulations. Ratings are often thought of as unreliable measurement methods, although some researchers, such as Livson (1973), defend the practice as the only workable means for quantifying naturalistic samplings of behavior over a wide range of situations. One problem with ratings is that they are subject to constant errors such as halo, central tendency, and leniency. Various training methods have been used to correct for these errors, with some success (Borman, 1979; Ivancevich, 1979; Latham, Wexley, & Pursell, 1975), although the effects may not be long lasting without additional instruction. Yet accuracy of ratings depends on more than eliminating these common errors, and attention should also be paid to having specific definitions for rating scales, increasing rater knowledge of performance standards and particular rating formats, and improving raters' observational skills (Anastasi, 1982; Borman, 1982).

In assessment centers, management examiners must be taught to observe and record behavior, categorize behavior, and rate behavior on agreed-on dimensions; careful attention to standardized training can help ensure greater reliability among raters in each step of the process. Byham (1982) makes extensive use of such tools as videotapes and films, programmed instruction, demonstrations, and certification in assessor training. Although formal research on the effects of assessment center training is sparse, one small study did show that ratings gathered before and after a 24- to 48-hour training program decreased substantially in range and standard deviation (McConnell & Parker, 1972).

The design of a work sample or simulation can also incorporate procedures that will augment interrater reliability. Considerable attention was paid to this aspect in the design of the on-site work sample examination for licensing dental hygienists (ADHA, 1978). Examiner stations and assistants were standardized as much as possible, and examination forms for candidates and examiners were tailored to precisely record all results. Examiners apply a uniform sampling formula, randomly varied across candidates, to examine the same seven teeth and tooth surfaces per candidate. Two examiners independently rate candidate performance, compare their findings, and validate any discrepancies found. Similar consensual validation techniques are used with dimension ratings in assessment centers.

In situations in which attention has been paid to the training of raters or to the standardization of procedures, reliability of ratings can be at an acceptable level. For example, in the Berkeley Guidance Study, ratings of personality characteristics by a Q sort applied to data from multiple sources and measuring instruments over a 16-year developmental span produced a mean interrater reliability coefficient across two raters of .86 (Livson, 1973). Similarly, assessment center research has found agreement among raters consistently over .80 for certain dimensions, such as planning and organizing and decision-making skills, communications effectiveness, initiative, and leadership. Less agreement has been found for some stylistic or intrapersonal attributes, such as resistance to stress or inner work standards (Thornton & Byham, 1982). Yet the issue of interrater reliability should not be taken lightly, and careful attention to rater training and procedural standardization should be considered essential if ratings are to be used.

WORK SAMPLES VERSUS SIMULATIONS

Work samples and simulations were considered together when their advantages and disadvantages were assessed relative to paper-and-pencil tests. But these different types of performance tests can also fade or shine when compared with each other. The following comments focus on the weakness of each particular method relative to the others.

Work Samples

Site Visits. Site visits may produce work samples that are not representative of the whole content of the job. Moreover, they may not provide any resolution or finished product because this is unlikely in a single day. What may be shown to the examiners could, in fact, be trivial, and there is considerable expense involved in getting each committee to each examinee's workplace.

Advance Preparation. Given the prerogative of preparing a work sample in advance, the candidate has unlimited preparation time, and the outcome is likely to be considerably more than a representative sample of the person's work. Moreover, what is presented may not be solely the work of the candidate. Examiners may also struggle with samples that are too narrow and specific and that do not lend themselves to much questioning. It may be difficult to evaluate the quality of something that is too focused relative to the general expertise of the examiners.

On the Spot. Compared to site visits and advance preparation work samples, an on-the-spot work sample may not be very representative of the person's job or be content valid. Moreover, the examiners cannot control the content or level of difficulty, as when a patient is brought in for a screening interview. The dental hygienists' examination (ADHA, 1978) does make two efforts to compensate for variable difficulty level. The candidate's assignment is adjusted to the patient's condition, so that prophylaxis is required for only one quadrant for patients with heavy deposits but for two quadrants for those with medium calculus. This still does not equalize the situations because the amount of calculus affects the difficulty of subgingival scaling, so performance levels and allowable errors are also adjusted.

On-the-spot work samples are not as reliable as simulations because real patients or clients differ for each candidate; with simulations the same stimulus can be provided for each, and comparisons can also be made across time. A further problem with on-the-spot samples is that the patients may not be treated well. A therapist-candidate is likely to be tense, and even if not, he or she may uncover psychopathology and then never see the patient again (Morgenstern, 1972).

Simulations

A problem with the use of videotaped simulations is that there is no opportunity to measure interactive skills, an important domain for psychology. An alternative is to use actors, although they will be subject to some differences in stimuli from different candidates. However, this approach still seems preferable to the use of a completely different case per subject in a work sample.

Although the consistency provided by simulations may enhance reliability, it may also create boredom. At the same time they require more examiner preparation time because real work samples, especially those that are on-the-spot, use "seat-of-the-pants" questioning. Simulations usually involve an extensive training manual, which examiners must learn well. Nevertheless, there generally seem to be more advantages and fewer problems with simulations than with the various types of work samples.

An Experimental Contrast in Psychiatry

The American Board of Psychiatry and Neurology has traditionally evaluated competence by a written exam that tests basic knowledge, taken while a candidate is still in residency, and an oral exam given three places and times each year. Two hours of the oral exam are in clinical psychiatry and 1 hour is in neurology; half of each exam involves the examination of a patient, and the other half of the exam involves the testing of the candidate by the examiners. A problem with the oral exam has been the lack of standardization in patient selection and assignment; in live oral exam some candidates got "easy" patients and others got "difficult" ones. The standardized questions used with the videotape also reduced the possibility of gross error by the examiners (Naftulin, Wolkon, Donnelly, Burgoyne, Kline, & Hansen, 1977).

Another finding from this comparison was that the outcomes were not correlated because the two types of examinations were not really covering the same thing. The videotape helped evaluate the candidate's observational and listening skills, deductive reasoning, clinical formulations, differential diagnoses, and treatment plans based on someone else's examination. But the oral procedure demonstrated the clinical examination of a patient and abilities to establish rapport, elicit a relevant data base, conduct an orderly examination, and interact professionally with a "suffering human being" while exhibiting empathy and understanding (Scheiber, 1976). What had been demonstrated was that the type of simulation selected was more useful for the evaluation of some competencies and the work sample was more useful for others.

The moral of this story seems to be that one examination or exercise cannot be expected to do everything in competence evaluation. The current exam of the American Board of Psychiatry and Neurology includes both a work sample and a simulation—interviewing live patients during 1 hour and viewing videotaped interviews during the second hour (Small, 1982).

CONCLUSIONS AND DISCUSSION

The lesson from the psychiatrists' comparison of work samples with simulations can be extended to the entire thrust of this chapter. As measurement experts can attest, the evaluation techniques selected must be relevant to the objective being measured. In fact, the selection of techniques should depend as much on the goals of the measurement situation as on the technical qualities of the techniques, such as validity, reliability, and ease of administration, scoring, and interpretation (Gronlund, 1965).

Performance tests have many decided advantages over paper-and-pencil tests for competency evaluation, including the ability to measure the application of skills and interactive skills and to do this while detaching the imposition of stress from the examiners. They are also highly acceptable because of their easily established content validity, possibly greater predictive validity, and less adverse impact against minority groups. Suggestions have been made to diminish some of their serious disadvantages, such as costs, administration complexities, and unreliability.

The remaining disadvantage, the relative inability of work samples and simulations to tap a range of knowledge, cannot be easily overcome. Rather than force work samples and simulations to serve this purpose, a better solution would be to include a paper-and-pencil test of knowledge in competency evaluations and use peformance tests to accomplish the many other important goals. As Bray (1982) pointed out, various types of exercises can be combined in an assessment center model, using dimensions to represent the characteristics one desires to measure and to help conceptualize and synthesize the behavior observed in the various exercises.

To relate these conclusions to the profession of psychology, let us first review the goals and procedures of the two major components of the present system for evaluating competence. At the licensing or certification level, the states attempt to evaluate minimal competency, usually in the generic field of psychology, to determine who should have the privilege of practicing psychology and using the title "psychologist." Large numbers of persons are processed annually, and the EPPP examination serves to screen out those without proper psychological knowledge. The boards do not have such a systematic method for determining competency in the actual practice of psychology. Oral examinations, interviews, or essay tests may attempt to get at what individuals do, but these procedures differ by state.

At the other end of the credentialing spectrum is the ABPP. With this nonstatutory method, the profession attempts to determine excellence in the practice of psychology in given specialties. Small numbers of persons are processed—of those persons in clinical, counseling, school, or I/O psychology listed in the 1981 APA directory, only 6 1/2% are diplomates compared to 75% who are licensed (Howard, 1982). The ABPP examination has no formal or comprehensive test of knowledge and relies heavily on an unstandardized, prepared-in-advance work sample to evaluate competence in practice. There is often an on-the-spot work sample (a client to be interviewed) as well.

How then could the present system be improved to evaluate competency in psychology incorporating the best of the techniques discussed in this article? Beginning with the licensing process, it appears that the EPPP serves the important role of weeding out total incompetents on the basis of knowledge of the broad-based foundation of the profession. Research has shown the EPPP's relationships to other indexes of acquiring such knowledge, such as the number of psychology courses taken and having a PhD degree in psychology (Carlson, 1978). Yet surveys of psychologists have also made it clear that some roles performed in practice are not measured best by the multiple-choice examination (Schoon, 1982). Determining who is competent to apply the knowledge of psychology is thus a more complex matter.

One problem is that the licensing boards usually consider psychology in a generic sense, which has the advantage of providing a cohesive picture of one profession, not a cluster of technical specialties. At present, a job analysis of the "job" of psychologist is being undertaken by the Educational Testing Service (ETS), sponsored by the American Association of State Psychology Boards, to determine if this generic concept is appropriate or whether there are clearly defined specialties within the profession that should be treated somewhat differently in the licensing process. Even if it is concluded that the profession can be treated as a whole with respect to its fundamental body of knowledge, it is difficult, perhaps impossible, to conceive of a generic *practice* of psychology. Nor, then, is there likely to be developed a generic work sample or simulation of the practice of psychology without attaching such practice to the content domain of a specialty. Although one might conceive of generic dimensions of practice, such a oral fact finding or technical translation, how would one measure them without making use of the content of a particular specialty? One must understand the technical content to translate it. Similarly, getting the facts about the manifestation of a particular form of psychopathology does not mean one would be able to get the facts about the flow of communications in a business organization and vice versa.

One possibility is to forgo any attempts to measure competency to practice at the licensing level and leave that process to nonstatutory boards in the relevant specialties. This option may not provide the kind of public protection expected of licensure. Another possibility is to treat practice on an individual level and require a prepared-in-advance work sample based on the 1 or 2 years of supervised experience required for licensure. However, this would suffer from the same lack of standardization as does the ABPP work sample. A third alternative, measuring competency to practice psychology at the licensing level, would seem to require some kind of examination in a specialty, which is an official undertaking in only a few states.

An issue in specialty examination is the definition of what a specialty really is, a recognition program with which both APA and ABPP are grappling at present. Yet a semispecialized model may be sufficient at the entry level of the license. This would permit testing for some basic practice competencies without bogging down in the finer details of specific specialties. For example, there might be a "health care" specialty or an "organizational" specialty. The latter should not be mentioned without acknowledgement that the I/O psychology division of APA has taken the position that I/O psychologists shoudl not ordinarily have to be licensed (APA, 1981). A full discussion of this issue is beyond the scope of this article (cf. Howard & Lowman, 1982), but as a practical matter, elimination of this group would greatly relieve the problem of heterogeneity among practice specialties at the licensing level.

Within the framework of a semispecialized licensing process, candidates passing the first hurdle of the EPPP could go on to a second practice phase of the examination; keeping the EPPP as a first hurdle would reduce, with a subsequent cost savings, the number of candidates taking the next phase. To promote fairness and maximize resources, the practice part of the exam should be a standardized, nationally developed test of the application of psychological skills in a few broad specialty areas. The technology of work samples and simulations could be applied in ways that would permit testing large numbers of people for a relatively low cost.

Although performance tests could be incorporated in the oral examination for licensure that explores practice areas, theoretically it should be possible to design exercises that could be simply and objectively scored and eliminate entirely the need for examiners, an advantage over the present system with respect to administrative requirements. For example, a series of videotaped therapy or organizational consulting sessions could be viewed en masse and answers to questions recorded in a paper-and-pencil multiple-choice format. Ethical dilemmas could be incorporated into such videotapes or evaluated in a series of vignettes presented in an in-basket format. To respond to some of the issues, the examinee would have to construct additional questions; others could be decided on the evidence presented. Scoring could be structured so that an administrator could do it. An assistant could also administer an oral fact-finding exercise in a health care or organizational setting, using a checklist to record items pursued or overlooked and a predetermined evaluation scheme for types of solutions proposed by the candidate.

One type of exercise not included in the preceding plan is one to measure interactive skills. This would be best done by having actors role play clients with various problems while examiners observed and rated the candidate interactions. To do this, finances would be needed to support the actors, and examiners would also have to be on the spot. However, this may be impractical at the licensing level, where it may be more reasonable to concentrate on the application of knowledge in a practice setting.

The major hurdle to developing such a scheme for the practice part of a licensing examination would be the cost of the initial development of exercises. Because the construction of items for the EPPP has been accomplished by many volunteers from the profession, presumably it should also be possible to use this source for the creative construction of exercises. Expenses for materials such as videotapes and rating forms could be supported by licensing fees, just as money was raised by increasing licensing fees to support the ETS job analysis.

The evaluation of competence to practice in particular specialties, in more than the minimal sense required for licensure, could be accomplished by a series of boards much like those in the various medical specialties. Although ABPP has to some degree attempted to fill this role, it would need broader acceptance by psychologists and would need to branch into additional specialties. This latter step is currently under way as an outcome of the conference described here. The concept, also developed at the conference, of ABPP as an umbrella organization for multiple boards is promising.

For an evaluation process by a board to be effective in measuring specialty competence, a first step would be to tap sufficient knowledge in the specialty—that is, to develop an EPPP for each specialty. This would be particularly beneficial in a field like I/O psychology, in which one half of those PAP members claiming it as a major field to not have a degree in I/O psycology (Howard, 1982). A knowledge test used by the board as a first hurdle could certify equivalency to the specific degree for those making legitimate field changes and save the expense of further examination of those who do not meet this essential first criterion.

In a complete examination of competence to practice in a specialty, examiners would be important and so, therefore, would be their training. Programmed instruction could provide an important component in such training, and examiners could be made specialists in the interpretation of certain exercises. The exercises themselves should be mostly simulations and include such techniques as videotapes, in baskets, oral fact-finding exercises, and role plays by actors to determine interactive skills. In many cases the simulations could be administered by an assistant and written materials sent to the examiners for evaluation. Even the role play of interactive skills could be recorded or videotaped if that were less expensive than bringing the examiners to the examination place. Each examiner could evaluate and report performance on his or her special exercise, and data could be pooled mathematically or consensually by a telephone conference call. The exercises could be administered in only a few locations at certain times of the year to handle larger numbers and contain costs.

One factor that has not been addressed in any of this discussion is how to measure the impact of the psychologist's practice on his or her client. This may represent the ultimate criterion of competency, but for the most part the profession has been unable to measure it well. Perhaps one step in this direction might be a prepared-in-advance work sample that incorporates some statistics on, for example, how the organization or its employees fared or how many patients improved as a result of the candidate's practice. These kinds of ultimate criteria would be more appropriate at the ABPP or the board level than at the entry licensing level, when the data may not have matured, although they might play a role in any relicensing or recertification procedures.

Whether or not it is feasible to have the kinds of models described here, the potency of work samples and simulations for competency evaluation has been clearly demonstrated. They should be seriously considered in some form for the evaluation of the competency of psychologists. It is disheartening to note that tools and methods developed and evaluated within psychology are being applied in other professions long before they are applied to our own.

REFERENCES

Albo, D., Jr., Taylor, C. W., & Page, B. (1982). Evaluating the performances of resident-physicians against the target of excellent physicians in practice. In J. S. Lloyd (Ed.), *Evaluation of noncognitive skills and clinical performance* (pp. 113–125). Chicago: American Board of Medical Specialties.

American Dental Hygienists' Association. (1978). *Dental hygiene clinical evaluation for state licensure*. Washington, DC: U.S. Department of Commerce.

American Psychological Association, Committee on Standards for Providers of Psychological Services. (1981). Specialty guidelines for the delivery of services by industrial/organizational psychologists. *American Psychologist, 36*, 664–669.

Anastasi, A. (1982). *Psychological testing* (5th ed.). New York: Macmillan.

Asher, J., & Sciarrino, J. A. (1974). Realistic work sample tests: A review. *Personnel Psychology, 27*, 519–533.

Borman, W. C. (1979). Format and training effects on rating accuracy and rating errors. *Journal of Applied Psychology, 64*, 410–421.

Borman, W. C. (1982). Evaluating performance effectiveness on the job: How can we generate more accurate ratings? In J. S. Lloyd (Ed.), *Evaluation of noncognitive skills and clinical performance* (pp. 179–193). Chicago: American Board of Medical Specialties.

Bray, D. W. (1982, October). *Combining heterogeneous data in competence evaluation*. Paper presented at the Conference on Professional Competence Evaluation. American Board of Professional Psychology, Washington, DC.

Bray, D. W., & Howard A. (1983). The AT&T longitudinal studies of managers. In K. W. Schaie (Ed.), *Longitudinal studies of adult psychological development* (pp. 266–312). New York: Guilford Press.

Bray, D. W., Campbell, R. J., & Grant, D. L. (1974). *Formative years in business*. New York: Wiley.

Brugnoli, G. A., Campion, J. E., & Basen, J. A. (1979). Racial bias in the use of work samples for personnel selection. *Journal of Applied Psychology, 64*, 119–123.

Byham, W. C. (1982, October). *Developing examiner skills in competence evaluation*. Paper presented at the Conference on Professional Competence Evaluation, American Board of Professional Psychology, Washington, DC.

Carlson, H. S. (1978). The AASPB story: The beginning and first 16 years of the American Association of State Psychology Boards, 1961–1977. *American Psychologist, 33*, 486–495.

Cascio, W. F., & Phillips, N. F. (1979). Performance testing: A rose among thorns? *Personnel Psychology, 32*, 751–766.

Gordon, M. E., & Kleiman, L. S. (1976). The prediction of trainability using a work sample test and an aptitude test: A direct comparison. *Personnel Psychology, 29*, 243–253.

Gronlund, N. E. (1965). *Measurement and evaluation in teaching*. Toronto, Canada: Macmillan.

Guion, R. M. (1978). Scoring of content domain samples: The problem of fairness. *Journal of Applied Psychology, 63*, 499–506.

Harden, R. M., & Gleeson, F. A. (1979). Assessment of clinical competence using an objective structured clinical examination (OSCE). *Medical Education, 13*, 41–54.

Howard, A. (1982, January). *Who are the industrial/organizational psychologists? An analysis of data from the 1981 APA Directory survey*. Report prepared for the Executive Committee of APA's Division of Industrial and Organizational Psychology (Division 14).

Howard, A., & Lowman, R. L. (1982, January). *Licensing and industrial/organizational psychology: Background and issues*. Report prepared for the Executive Committee of APA's Division of Industrial and Organizational Psychology (Division 14).

Hurley, H. J. (1982). The Part II certifying examination in dermatology: An assessment of interpretive skills. In J. S. Lloyd (Ed.), *Evaluation of noncognitive skills and clinical performance* (pp. 43–50). Chicago: American Board of Medical Specialties.

Ivancevich, J. M. (1979). Longitudinal study of the effects of rater training on psychometric error in ratings. *Journal of Applied Psychology, 64*, 502–508.

Lamont, C. T., & Hennen, B. K. E. (1972). The use of simulated patients in a certification examination in family medicine. *Journal of Medical Education*, 789–795.

Latham, G. P., Wexley, K. N., & Pursell, E. D. (1975). Training managers to minimize rating errors in the observation of behavior. *Journal of Applied Psychology, 60*, 550–555.

Livson, N. (1973). Developmental dimensions of personality: A life-span formulation. In P. B. Baltes & K. W. Schaie (Eds.), *Life-span developmental psychology: Personality and socialization*. New York: Academic Press.

McConnell, J. J., & Parker, T. (1972). An assessment center program for multiorganizational use. *Training and Development Journal, 26*, 6–14.

McGuire, C. H., & Babbott, D. (1967). Simulation technique in the measurement of problem-solving skills. *Journal of Educational Measurement, 4*, 1–10.

Miller, E. V. (1982). Performance checklist to evaluate anesthesia skills. In J. S. Lloyd (Ed.), *Evaluation of noncognitive skills and clinical performance*. Chicago: American Board of Medical Specialties.

Miller, J. N., & Engin, A. W. (1974). Performance-based school psychology certification: Situational response testing. *Psychology in the Schools, 11*, 422–424.

Morgenstern, A. L. (1972). A systematic approach for oral board examinations in psychiatry. *American Journal of Psychiatry, 129*, 54–58.

Naftulin, D. H., Wolkon, G. H., Donnelly, F. A., Burgoyne, R. W., Kline, F. M., & Hansen, H. E. (1977). A comparison of videotaped and live patient interview examinations and written examinations in psychiatry. *American Journal of Psychiatry, 134*, 1093–1097.

Office of Strategic Services Assessment Staff. (1948). *Assessment of men*. New York: Rinehart.

Ofsanko, F. J., & Paulson, C. C. (1977, February). Who interviews the interviewer—and how? *The Personnel Administrator*, 27–29.

100-point lag found in black's S.A.T. scores. (1982, October 5). *The New York Times*, p. A21.

Reed, G. F. (1982). The use of visual materials in the evaluation of interpretive skills. In J. S. Lloyd (Ed.), *Evaluation of noncognitive skills and clinical performance*. Chicago: American Board of Medical Specialties.

Scheiber, S. C. (1976). Board certification in psychiatry: An eye toward the future, *Psychiatric Forum, 6*, 22–25.

Schmidt, F. L., Greenthal, A. L., Hunter, J. E., Berner, J. G., & Seaton, W. (1977). Job sample vs. paper-and-pencil trades and technical tests: Adverse impact and examinee attitudes. *Personnel Psychology, 30*, 187–197.

Schoon, C. (1982, October). *Update on activities by the Professional Examination Service*. Paper presented at the Conference on Professional Competence Evaluation, American Board of Professional Psychology, Washington, DC.

Shoemaker, J. T., & Splitter, J. L. (1976). A competency-based model for counselor certification. *Counselor Education and Supervision*, 267–274.

Silzer, R. F. (1978, August). *Competency assessment: Use of performance rating scales and assessment centers*. Paper presented at the meeting of the American Psychological Association, Toronto, Canada.

Small, S. M. (1982). Evaluation methodology for the oral examination of the American Board of Psychiatry and Neurology. In J. S. Lloyd (Ed.), *Evaluation of noncognitive skills and clinical performance* (pp. 33–41). Chicago: American Board of Medical Specialties.

Thornton, G. C., III, & Byham, W. C. (1982). *Assessment centers and managerial performance*. New York: Academic Press.

Wernimont, P. F., & Campbell, J. P. (1968). Signs, samples, and criteria. *Journal of Applied Psychology, 52*, 372–376.

4

Current Status of Training Evaluation in Clinical Psychology

JOHN F. STEVENSON and JOHN C. NORCROSS

INTRODUCTION

Urgency of the Issue

Clinical psychology has matured to a stage at which it is both possible and necessary to evaluate its training activities. The need to evaluate training process and outcome has become particularly intense at this time of declining federal support, shrinking job market, and increasing demands for demonstration of professional competence as well as documentation of special skills imparted by training programs. More locally, training can be directly improved by formative feedback, and students can be socialized to understand and appreciate quantitative evaluation efforts.

The competence of our graduates and, indeed, the adequacy of our clinical training are typically assumed rather than verified (Malouf, Haas, & Forah, 1983). Although the majority of clinical graduates express

JOHN F. STEVENSON • Department of Psychology, University of Rhode Island, Kingston, RI 02881. **JOHN C. NORCROSS** • Department of Psychology, University of Scranton, Scranton, PA 18510.

some degree of satisfaction with their graduate education (Garfield & Kurtz, 1976; Norcross & Prochaska, 1982b; Walfish, Kaufman, & Kinder, 1980), the quality of contemporary training in clinical psychology is not assured. Recent national surveys of clinical psychologists reveal that practical clinical training is perceived as the most important, and often least adequate, component of graduate education (Garfield & Kurtz, 1976; Norcross & Prochaska, 1982b). Several authors (cf. Kalafat & Neigher, 1983; Robertson, 1985) have reviewed studies underscoring the inadequacy or irrelevancy of clinical training with respect to preparing graduate students to be competent practitioners. Many observers (cf. Autor & Zide, 1974; Dana, Gilliam, & Dana, 1976; Rice & Gurman, 1973; Robertson, 1984) have also noted a widening gap between academic knowledge and clinical skills among incoming interns, whose preinternship preparation in psychotherapy and assessment skills is frequently seen as deficient by internship directors (Shemberg & Keeley, 1974; Shemberg & Leventhal, 1981).

Clinical training in an academic environment is often just that—academic—long on teaching by exposition and short on teaching by practice (Robertson, 1984). Haley (1976) observed that

> until quite recently, a therapist could graduate from a clinical training program and be considered trained even though none of his teachers had observed him do therapy or even conduct a single interview. . . . Even more curiously, the student's success or failure with cases was never examined. (p. 169)

Grant and Anderson (1977) provided a helpful list of criteria to apply in order to decide when to evaluate training. These criteria make an eloquent case for the evaluation of training in clinical psychology:

1. Training is expensive. The cost of training PhD-level clinicians is quite high, involving an average of 6 years (Norcross & Prochaska, 1982a) and extensive individual supervision.

2. Training is a continuing effort. Unlike some other educational efforts, clinical training is an ongoing and evolving mission.

3. Graduates' activities are crucial to the "health, well-being, or safety of others." Clinical psychologists function as direct-care providers, administrators, trainers, and researchers within virtually all service delivery systems.

4. Evaluation results can affect decisions. Collective experience and wisdom have shown that training evaluation can be conducted in ways that will influence policy, program, and training decisions.

5. There are personnel interested and informed enough to conduct evaluations. Clinical training sites are endowed with an abundance of professional and professionals-in-training with applied research skills and incentives to conduct evaluation research. Indeed, psychologists

constitute the majority of practicing evaluators (Flaherty & Morell, 1978; Korn, Keiser, & Stevenson, 1982).

These criteria, local considerations, national priorities, and external demands attest to the need for systematic evaluation of clinical psychology training programs. Neither clients nor the public are equipped with the requisite skills and perspectives to evaluate professional training and competence. As a consequence, it has become imperative to examine our own training and competence, lest they be evaluated for us by others (Albee & Kessler, 1977). Responding to these pressures, the American Psychological Association (APA) created the Task Force on Education, Training, and Service in Psychology. They ominously concluded that

> the time is already late for psychology. Whether evidence for the effectiveness of its educational and training requirements can be developed in time to forestall the attacks now under way is not certain. The best hope for the profession may be in its ability to demonstrate that it has a serious, systematic program for evaluation that will produce a regular, dependable flow of information by means of which to validate and improve its practice and requirements. (APA, 1982, p. 2)

Moreover, the most serious problems regarding the validity of educational and training requirements in psychology seem to arise in clinical psychology. The crucial nature of clinical psychology's position has several origins, including the fact that it is the largest specialty within psychology; it is the most involved in independent practice; it is potentially the most lucrative; its practitioners have an unusually high degree of independence; and they deal with the most sensitive and damaged clientele. The Task Force *Summary Report* (APA, 1982) states that "clinical psychology is, therefore, we conclude, at the crux of the problem of evaluating education and training" (p. 5) and "the place to start" (p. 4).

Unfortunately, we need to start at the beginning as little systematic evaluation of clinical training has been undertaken (Bernstein, 1982; Garfield, 1977; Matarazzo, 1978). Edelstein & Brasted (1983, p. 50) have called training evaluation "perhaps the most important and most overlooked issue in clinical training." Ford (1979, p. 113), in his review of research on training counselors and clinicians, concluded that "most counselor/clinician training programs have not evaluated their impact on trainees, nor their trainees' impact on clients, in any systematic and valid fashion." Korman (1974, p. 445), in his synopsis of the Vail Conference, noted that

> considering the financial cost and human effort represented by professional education, there has been a curious lack of concern over product and program

evaluation. . . . Its absence is all the more remarkable in a discipline that prides itself on its expertise in evaluation research.

Scope of the Chapter

In what follows, we examine evaluation models, designs, and measures as they relate to professional training in clinical psychology. This chapter is *not* intended as a review of current training methods nor as a statement of desirable clinical skills and competencies. Rather, we examine several of the most salient measurement approaches and theoretical issues pertinent to clinical psychology. The term *clinical* is applied generically to all professional help-providing activities; however, our chapter and research is on American doctoral-level clinical psychology training.

Throughout the chapter a critical distinction is maintained between "clinical competence/quality assurance" and "clinical training (or program) evaluation." Although the two terms are frequently and erroneously consolidated, the former is concerned with determining the competence of individual trainees in various clinical skills and in documenting the quality of service provision (cf. Bent, 1982; Cohen, 1983; Sechrest & Hoffman, 1982). Clinical training evaluation, or program evaluation (cf. Edelstein & Brasted, 1983; Levy, 1983), is admittedly related to the former but is concerned with assessing the effectiveness, efficiency, and relevance of a given clinical training program in part or in whole (Norcross & Stevenson, 1984).

We begin, then, with a discussion of current issues that affect definitions of training evaluation in clinical psychology. We go on to present results from national surveys of clinical psychology training clinics, graduate programs, and predoctoral internships concerning their training evaluation practices. Current efforts to specify and measure clinical competence are described with particular emphasis on conceptual and measurement considerations. Next, we discuss approaches to assessing training processes. Finally, on the basis of our review and our own experience, we offer several directions for the future of training evaluation in clinical psychology.

DEFINING EVALUATION QUESTIONS

For the reader who has had little exposure to the evaluation research literature, the issues in evaluating clinical psychology training may seem straightforward. Pick one or more measures of clinical competence, assess competence before and after training, and *voilà*—either training has improved competence or it has not. To get somewhat fancier, maybe it would be helpful to compare two or three competing "models" for clinical training to see which works best. This seemingly straightforward enterprise is akin to the one envisioned by early generations of psychotherapy researchers. For a host of reasons, the task is not so easy as it looks. Schacht (1984, p. 26) helps to make this point by taking the psychotherapy research analogy one step further to pose the question: "What training, by whom, is most effective with which student, who is acquiring which specific knowledge or competency, under which set of circumstances, and at what cost?" Several of the issues underlying decisions regarding the framing of training evaluation questions are reviewed in the following pages.

Variations in Perspectives and Purposes

Evaluation questions are necessarily posed in a political context (Weiss, 1972). Whose questions are we attempting to answer when we design and conduct evaluations of clinical training in psychology? As the introduction to this chapter has noted, there are a series of pressing reasons for evaluating training—but they need not all converge on the same questions. From within the profession of psychology, there are those who wish to document and justify the special training and competencies of psychologists (APA, 1982; Korman, 1973). Others, both within and outside the field, wish to assure consumers and third-party reimbursers that only those trained to practice in a competent and ethical fashion will be licensed to do so (Albee & Kessler, 1977). Stern (1984) points to the "political-economic" context for conceptualizing training, and this agenda can be extended to the evaluation of training as well. Evaluation questions, designs, and measures may be intended to define and defend the profession.

On the other hand, evaluation questions can be oriented toward the improvement of training processes, either by controlled studies of carefully specified alternative training techniques (e.g., Ford, 1979) or by naturalistic exploration of ongoing training at the local level (e.g., Stevenson & Norcross, 1984). The more the emphasis is on improving training, the more important becomes description of the training process and components, measures of change rather than measures of attributes, and establishment of links between training processes and outcomes. Particularly for trainers at the local level, the questions are likely to be practical ones, concerned with incremental changes in local policies and practices.

Current and former students, as consumers of training, may wish to pose some questions of their own regarding the costs and benefits of training. Their questions may place more emphasis on consumer satisfaction, the climate in which training is conducted, and the fit between training and their career objectives (Stevenson, Norcross, Nash, & Grebstein, 1985; Walfish *et al.*, 1980).

The political context for evaluation of clinical training is also important from another standpoint. As Shadish (1984) points out, ideological issues can powerfully affect the role of evaluation in policymaking. Although one can argue with Shadish's conclusion that the premises of evaluation research designs should reflect the dominant ideological stance of policymakers, it is unwise to ignore the lessons he draws from the history of policy-oriented evaluation in mental health.

At local, state, and national levels, evaluators of clinical psychology training must operate in the context of the preferences and prejudices of those who will use the data. An experimental training model might, for example, deemphasize supervised outpatient psychotherapy with an experienced PhD clinician as the supervisor and place more weight on (a) self-paced texts, (b) videotape models, (c) simulated therapy with peer feedback, (d) structured client feedback, and (e) advanced training in supervision as peer feedback provider. Such a shift in emphasis might have much to recommend it, including reduced costs associated with less intensive use of high cost supervision. Despite substantial evidence for the value of several of these "experimental" training procedures, however, there is little sign of their adoption within clinical psychology PhD programs (Ford, 1979). This may not be simply a case of tradition resistant to change. Other innovative training procedures, such as live supervision with a telephone link, may be much more readily assimilated into conventional training programs. Ideological premises seem likely to affect research designs, perceptions of results, and responses to the evidence. Those selecting evaluation questions may wish to take this into account.

On a more optimistic note, it is also important to see evaluation research as a theory-testing enterprise (Chen & Rossi, 1983; Gottfredson, 1984). In evaluating clinical training it will be of great value to clearly articulate the theoretical relationships between training activities and clinician competencies (Levy, 1983; Schacht, 1984). Stern (1984) makes a useful contribution to a needed literature on the translation of alternative educational philosophies into curriculum and objectives. Internal and external pressures for evaluation may provide the impetus for more explicit and detailed development of conceptual foundations for training.

Variations in Training Context

Training in clinical psychology is not a well-defined and uniform entity. This diversity has several important implications for the evaluation of training and poses some special challenges.

First, this diversity provides competitive energy to fuel evaluation efforts. The debate over the proper goals for predoctoral training and the best means to achieve these goals are very much with us (Peterson, 1985; Stern, 1984; Strupp, 1975; Strupp & Schacht, 1984). So-called "traditional" training programs (Edelstein & Brasted, 1983; Ford, 1979) emphasize a rigorous scientific knowledge base, research skills, and clinical skills often acquired within a department clinic (Serafica & Harway, 1980; Stevenson, Norcross, King, & Tobin, 1984) and through the internship, where outpatient psychotherapy skills are most emphasized and most sought (Edelstein & Brasted, 1983; Steinhelber & Gaynor, 1981). The goals of this training are vague; the relative weights on content, research, and clinical skills probably vary widely (Peterson, 1985), and the degree of implementation of the "Boulder model" in these programs is open to question (Henry, 1984). Professional school training is seen as placing greater emphasis on the acquisition of a broad range of practitioner-relevant knowledge and skills, includes the same core content required by the APA, and may or may not place less emphasis on research skills (Peterson, 1985; Stern, 1984). Organizationally, professional schools may be free-standing, may have higher student-to-faculty ratios, and may make more extensive use of adjunct and part-time faculty.

Cutting across these two programatic contexts for training are varying orientations toward the methods for training. Strupp (1981) argues for training within a consistent, unifying theoretical model that can guide clinical and research processes—he explicitly rejects theoretical eclecticism in training programs. Schacht (1984) is a proponent of competency-based clinical education, with training in a specified set of skills provided, measured, and explicitly tied to licensure requirements. Stern (1984) and Henry (1984) endorse training methods that foster flexible, creative, cognitive problem-solving skills, skills that are seen as underlying the more focused learning necessary for competency in specific and scientific clinical endeavors.

These differences of opinion regarding training means and ends provide grist for the mill of those interested in evaluating training. But beware—the issues are complex. Broad distinctions in training context (e.g., psychology department versus professional school, PsyD versus PhD) really tell very little about actual training practices (Edelstein &

Brasted, 1983; Peterson, 1985). In fact, we know very little about what is going on within clinical training programs (APA, 1982). There is probably as much variation within any major category of training model as there is between models. Therefore, it is unwise to compare models as though we know what they represent. From this vantage point, Shemberg and Leventhal's (1981) use of internship directors' ratings as a basis for comparing PhD interns with PsyD interns is not very informative, despite their commendable attempt to shed light on the issue.

To some extent, alternative training models and methods do suggest different training goals, and this can be helpful in designing evaluation studies by clarifying directions for developing dependent measures. However, those operating within a particular framework are likely to assert their goal measures as universally appropriate. Finally if, as Henry (1984) asserts, the Boulder model has never really been implemented, it seems premature to conduct a comparison of the major models. Several of these problems point to the same conclusions: (a) better means of program description are as essential as competency measures; (b) training methods and components are more promising for evaluation than are training models as currently implemented; and (c) theories that articulate training processes and outcomes can enhance framing meaningful evaluation questions.

Design Alternatives and Research Agendas

Another source of complexity is the range of alternative research strategies for evaluating clinical training. Controlled experiments, with random assignment of subjects to conditions, may be quite useful for comparing two precisely defined methods for training a specified skill. However, when training processes, competencies, and the links between them are difficult to specify, we may find alternative methodologies preferable. Several research agendas and the methods associated with them are described here to illustrate the range of choice.

At the local level, self-change, accountability, and demonstration of efficacy of specific training techniques are likely purposes for evaluation. Stevenson and Norcross (1984) describe a formative, process-oriented approach to local evaluation intended to aid self-change. The emphasis is on continuous feedback over time from various "stakeholders." Outcome data are linked to training process description and evaluation. Some of these data also serve an accountability function, providing a description of how well the program process meets certain expectations as well as how competencies look following training. It is also possible to conduct experimental and quasi-experimental studies at the local level to compare particular training techniques (e.g., forms of supervision), components (e.g., feedback), or modalities (e.g., family therapy and individual therapy). Ford (1979) provides a detailed summary of published examples of this approach. Much of the evaluation done at the local level is formative—that is, it is intended to incrementally improve training. APA accreditation reviews, however, have summative as well as formative purposes. Conclusions are drawn as to overall program viability.

Beyond the local level, what we have at the moment are mainly recommendations for evaluation and a few surveys of former students and internship directors. The report of the APA Task Force on Education, Training, and Service in Psychology (1982) calls for initial development of descriptive systems for documenting and classifying local training activities, measures of expected entry-level competencies, and descriptions of career patterns and roles of clinical psychologists. Recommended research designs use multiple nonequivalent treatment groups and longitudinal, repeated measures to assess "value added" by several stages in training (preinternship, first job), comparing alternative training models (PhD versus PsyD) for clinical psychologists as well as comparisons with other professional fields, nonclinical psychology, and master's degree programs in clinical psychology. One seeks in vain for the definitive experiment that will demonstrate unequivocally that a certain form of training will produce competent clinical psychologists at a lower cost than other training systems. Instead, one finds descriptive and quasi-experimental methods suitable for the complex set of questions posed by those who have a stake in the training of clinical psychologists.

Constructing the Clinical Psychologist

A final source of difficulty in framing evaluation questions is the debate regarding the desirable consequences of training. In order to measure competencies we need consensus on the content, limits, and level of competence expected to result from training. This we do not have. The previous discussion of alternative training models has suggested some of the issues. Although there is widespread agreement that practitioner skills are essential and are often not effectively provided by traditional clinical training programs (Shemberg & Leventhal, 1981), ways of construing these skills vary. Mastery of knowledge relevant for a wide range of clinical applications may seem an obvious aspect of competence, but Stern (1984) challenges this. To what extent is a cognitive approach to clinical problems a more important objective for predoctoral training than either broad knowledge or broad technical competence? If personal qualities that have little to do with training are at least as important as anything gained from training, as Strupp (1981) suggests, then we seem to need a personality measure with scales like "psychological mindedness" and "basic decency." On the other hand, perhaps we should use job analyses to define a set of essential competencies for the practicing clinical psychologist (Schacht, 1984). What of the growing trend toward extreme specialization of skills (Edelstein & Brasted, 1983)? How will we ever arrive at a single list of competencies?

Even the empirical methods for identifying necessary competencies are at issue (Peterson & Bry, 1980). Asking former students what they are currently doing and what they wish they had been taught produces interesting but somewhat inconsistent results (Norcross & Prochaska, 1982a,b; Steinhelber & Gaynor, 1981; Walfish *et al.*, 1980). It appears that former students may dislike some aspects of their jobs and rue their training in the skills relevant for these aspects of their jobs (e.g., testing). On the other hand, former students may value the skills they received in training, yet report the need for other skills in their current professional roles (e.g., administration, supervision). Asking supervisors to generate and apply a list of defining attributes of competent clinicians (Peterson & Bry, 1980) leads toward the personal qualities endorsed by Strupp (1981). Conducting job analyses has been recommended by the APA Task Force on Education, Training, and Service in Psychology (1982) and undertaken by Rosenfeld, Shimberg, and Thornton (1984). Although this seems a very useful step, it does not address the questions of what role clinical psychologists would like to play and in what direction the profession should be moving. Are administrative and testing skills essential? What about competence in providing indirect services, for example, training paraprofessionals, designing social ecologies, coordinating self-help programs? And again, what of the relatively new specializations emerging in the field?

The definitions of competence we select will not only be used in the development of measures—they will represent the profession's self-definition. We had best proceed thoughtfully and cautiously.

The issues raised in this portion of the chapter challenge us in current efforts to evaluate the training of clinical psychologists. They help to account for the slow progress in the state of the art. In subsequent sections we will examine in more detail the state of the art as currently practiced, with some suggestions for forward movement.

NATIONAL FINDINGS ON TRAINING EVALUATION PRACTICES

> A first step in developing ways to assess the effects of education and training would be to survey training programs in clinical psychology, including internship programs, about their ways of assessing their own students and trainees. Although their methods might not be sophisticated or systematic, such a survey could reveal what programs themselves consider to be important and assessable knowledge and skills. It might yield interesting and even novel ideas about how to assess neophyte clinical psychologists. (APA, 1982, p. 23)

This task force's recommendation foreshadowed our survey efforts and results. We have conducted national studies of psychology training clinics (Stevenson & Norcross, 1985), clinical psychology graduate programs (Norcross & Stevenson, 1984), and predoctoral internship programs (Norcross, Stevenson, & Nash, 1986) concerning the procedures, practices, and problems associated with clinical training evaluation. This section reviews the methodologies, findings, and conclusions of these three national surveys.

The extant literature provided little hard data or reasons for optimism. Concerning psychology training clinics, Serafica and Harway (1980) found that 54% of responding sites had completed evaluations, but only 7% had an available report of the results. Concerning clinical psychology graduate programs, Levy (1983) discerned that the 11 programs he informally surveyed did not systematically use individual student evaluations in the assessment of their training programs. In a similar vein, Edelstein (1982) reported that most clinical directors indicated that clinical practicum training was evaluated, typically by rating scales directed at various clinical skills, but none of the evaluation instruments appeared to have been validated. Internship programs have not fared any better; in one survey (Miller, 1977), less than 30% of the internship sites used any form of quantitative data in the evaluation process. The remaining literature consisted primarily of graduates' retrospective evaluations of their training (e.g., Khol, Matefy, & Turner, 1972; Kirchner, 1969; Rosenkrantz & Holmes, 1974; Steinhelber & Gaynor, 1981; Stout, Holmes, & Rothstein, 1977; Tucker, 1970; Walfish *et al.*, 1980; Weiss, 1975).

Methodology

The first survey (Stevenson & Norcross, 1985) was designed to determine the scope, nature, and impact of both training and treatment evaluation conducted in psychology training clinics. The present discussion concerns only training evaluation. The questionnaire was mailed to the 131 members of the Association of Directors of Psychology Training Clinics (ADPTC), producing a 66% total response rate and a 56% usable response rate. The 74 usable responses were all from PhD psychologists who directed training clinics, located in 33 states and heterogeneous in size and composition.

The second survey (Norcross & Stevenson, 1984), building on the first, was conducted to examine the training evaluation practices of APA-accredited doctoral programs in clinical psychology. Sixty-seven surveys (61%) were returned from the 109 members of the Council of University Directors of Clinical Psychology. The 62 usable questionnaires represented responses from one half of the 124 doctoral programs then holding APA accreditation in clinical psychology.

The third survey (Norcross *et al.*, 1986) was designed to assess the training evaluation practices of American internship programs and to provide comparisons to findings from the first two studies. The questionnaire was mailed to directors of the 268 APA-accredited predoctoral internship programs in clinical and counseling psychology. Sixty-seven percent or 179 of the questionnaires were returned complete from directors of internships, which were demographically representative of the APA-approved programs listed in the Association of Psychology Internship Center (APIC) *Directory* (Kurz, Fuchs, Dabek, Kurtz, & Helfrich, 1982).

The questionnaires were modified to suit the particular training site but were generally similar in content in order to permit comparisons across the three sites. Each questionnaire, four to five pages in length, consisted of items (a) to assess the current use of informal and formal training evaluation procedures; (b) to gauge the relative impact of these procedures in forming an overall impression of the quality of the clinical training; and (c) to delineate the major obstacles in conducting clinical training evaluation.

Training Evaluation Procedures

Reacting to our first survey, 46 (62%) of the 74 responding psychology training clinics reported that they had quantitatively evaluated clinical training effectiveness *at some time*. Of these, 16 were described as part of a time-limited study, and 20 were described as an ongoing part of clinic operation. At the time of the survey, 61% of the clinics were routinely collecting and aggregating data to evaluate training effectiveness.

But how are they evaluating their training? The vast majority of these clinics reported using both verbal (91%) and written (82%) supervisors' evaluations with somewhat fewer (67%) using supervisors' quantitative evaluations of supervisees. Similar figures have been presented by Tyler and Weaver (1981) as well as Hess and Hess (1983). However, less than a third of the clinics reported employing pre-post factual knowledge tests, pre-post analyses of therapy sessions, or analyses of responses to simulated cases in their training evaluation program.

For our second survey, we enlarged on these findings, and adopted a schema proposed by the APA Task Force on Education, Training, and Service in Psychology (1982). We identified 35 possible training evaluation procedures, classified into five superordinate categories: informal qualitative measures; formal aggregated measures; formal comparative designs; posttraining measures; and program-focused measures. Directors of clinical training were asked to indicate whether they routinely, occasionally, or never used each procedure to evaluate their programs. For any procedure employed (i.e., routinely or occasionally), they also rated the degree of importance (1 = not important to 5 = very important) attached to these procedures in forming an overall impression of program quality and in making program decisions. The reported utilization and importance of these clinical training evaluation procedures are summarized in Tables 1 through 5 for the responding graduate programs, internship sites, and in a few instances, training clinics.

Table 1. Use and Importance of Informal Qualitative Measures

Percentage use				Importance rating[a]	
Intern programs	Graduate programs	Training clinics	Measure	Intern programs	Graduate programs
99	95	—	Your own impressions of students' growth	4.3	3.9
99	95	91	Supervisors' verbal evaluations of students' clinical work	4.4	4.1
100	90	—	Your impressions of students' satisfaction with the program	4.2	3.6
82	84	—	Subjective contrast of your program with others with which you are familiar	3.2	2.9
91	86	—	Reputation of your training program	3.8	3.5
87	87	—	Reputation of your former students among their professional peers	3.8	3.9

[a]Importance ratings are based on a 5-point Likert-type scale (1 = not important to 5 = very important).

Table 2. Use and Importance of Formal Aggregated Measures

Percentage use				Importance rating[a]	
Intern programs	Graduate programs	Training clinics	Measure	Intern programs	Graduate programs
93	92	82	Written evaluations of students by clinical supervisors	4.6	4.5
61	60	—	Numerical ratings of students by clinical supervisors.	3.9	4.1
34	47	—	Measures of clinical problem-solving skills (e.g., simulated cases)	3.5	3.3
45	26	—	Students' self-ratings of ability	3.5	3.0
8	13	—	Simulated licensure examination	2.7	3.3
8	—	—	Simulated ABPP model exam	3.3	—
14	58	16	Tests of factual knowledge (outside of specific course/seminar requirements)	3.0	4.2
55	58	—	Systematic evaluation of videotaped therapy sessions	3.7	3.9
76	69	—	Systematic evaluation of case presentations	4.1	3.8
85	81	—	Systematic evaluation of written clinical reports	4.3	4.0

[a]Importance ratings are based on a 5-point Likert-type scale (1 = not important to 5 = very important).

Informal qualitative procedures (Table 1) appear to be employed extensively in all training programs; all of the measures are used by at least 82% of the programs. Personal impressions of trainees' growth and supervisors' oral evaluations of clinical work, for example, are reportedly employed by over 90% of the training sites.

With the exception of supervisors' written evaluations, formal aggregated measures of training evaluation are used less frequently than those in the former category (see Table 2). Several of the procedures in this category—measures of problem solving skills, students' self-ratings of ability, simulated licensure or ABPP exams—are used by less than half of the sites. It is interesting to note that systematic evaluation of

Table 3. Use and Importance of Formal Comparative Designs

Percentage Use			Importance ratings[a]	
Intern programs	Graduate programs	Measure	Intern programs	Graduate programs
29	26	Longitudinal (e.g., pre-post training) within-group comparison	3.5	3.2
26	39	Cross-sectional comparison of new students with those who have already received training	3.1	2.8
6	19	Formal comparison to students in other programs	2.3	2.8

[a]Importance ratings are based on a 5-point Likert-style scale (1 = not important to 5 = very important).

Table 4. Use and Importance of Posttraining Measures

Percentage use			Importance ratings[a]	
Intern programs	Graduate programs	Measure	Intern programs	Graduate programs
67	95	Quality of internships that students obtain	3.5	4.0
20	24	Systematically obtained feedback from employers	3.3	3.1
48	52	Rate of successful certification/licensure of former students	3.6	3.2
36	—	Proportion of former students holding formal leadership positions (e.g., officer, committee chair) in professional organizations	3.2	—
15	90	Proportion of former students achieving ABPP diplomate status	3.2	3.2
24	—	Publication rate of former students	3.1	—

[a]Importance ratings are based on a 5-point Likert-type scale (1 = not important to 5 = very important).

Table 5. Use and Importance of Program-Focused Measures

Percentage use			Importance ratings[a]	
Intern programs	Graduate programs	Measure	Intern programs	Graduate programs
80	89	Quantitative evaluation of didactic training by students (e.g., seminar/course evaluations)	4.2	4.1
81	74	Quantitative evaluation of supervisors by supervisees	4.4	4.2
83	73	Systematic site visits to evaluate training	4.3	4.1
73	45	Quantitative ratings by students of program effectiveness	4.3	3.7
87	76	Type and number of seminar/course offerings	4.0	3.6
76	53	Student quantitative satisfaction with clinical training	4.2	3.7
51	26	Quantitative ratings by former students of program effectiveness	4.0	3.4
39	23	Quantitative ratings by faculty of program effectiveness	3.8	3.0
100	92	APA Accreditation Report	4.5	4.3
99	—	Program planning activity with intern input	4.3	—

[a]Importance ratings are based on a 5-point Likert-type scale (1 = not important to 5 = very important).

"clinical products" or work samples—written reports, case presentations, and videotaped therapy sessions—are used in direct proportion to the general availability of the product. That is, reviews of clinical reports are used most frequently (85%, 81%), case presentations next most frequently (76%, 69%), and videotaped sessions least frequently (55%, 58%).

The three procedures representative of formal comparative evaluation measures (Table 3) seem to be infrequently employed. Longitudinal within-group, concurrent between-group, and cross-program comparisons are not particularly favored by either intern or graduate programs.

Posttraining evaluation measures (Table 4) were not employed very extensively either with the exception of internship/first-position quality. Approximately half reported that the rate of successful certification/licensure of former students was used to evaluate training; fewer used the proportion of students achieving ABPP diplomate status or professional leadership positions.

The final category (Table 5) consisted of program-focused procedures to evaluate clinical training. Here, practically all graduate and intern programs relied on the APA accreditation report as evidence for training effectiveness. In both graduate and intern programs, faculty/supervisors' ratings of clinical program effectiveness were used less frequently than students' ratings during training or after graduation.

By way of summary, the tables group sources of evidence for training quality on the basis of three dimensions: (a) focus of evaluation (aggregating performance indicators for individuals versus assessing the training program directly); (b) type of evaluation data (qualitative vs. quantitative); and (c) method of data collection (impressionistic vs. systematic). Without exception, results of these three studies indicate that current clinical evaluation practices heavily favor student-focused, impressionistically collected, qualitatively oriented sources of evidence to judge their training enterprise (see Stevenson & Norcross, 1984). Across the five categories, informal, qualitative procedures were utilized the most and the formal, quantitative procedures the least. Within categories, qualitative feedback was invariably more prevalent than quantitative ratings of the identical phenomenon.

The immense variability in evaluation procedures and the reliance on informal qualitative sources of evidence bespeak the preparadigmatic stage of training evaluation in American clinical psychology. It is evident that virtually all clinical training programs are engaged in some type of evaluation, perhaps more than previous findings have implied. However, it is also evident that many programs are functioning with good intentions but deficient performance in response to APA accreditation requirements for "an explicit, comprehensive system for evaluation" (APA, 1983, p. 8).

Although reliance on "fuzzy-headed, tender-hearted" data to evaluate clinical training is not to be recommended as the sole basis for judgment, it needs to be placed in a proper context. There are at least three reasons not to be disheartened by the prevelant subjective and qualitative emphasis. First, these findings suggest that most clinical programs systematically collect some written formal evaluation data, such as supervisors' written evaluations, numerical ratings, and course/seminar evaluations. Thus the majority possess multiple sources of evaluation data—qualitative and quantitative, impressionistic and systematic—on which to judge their training effectiveness. Second, these clinical psychology training programs do not appear to be vastly different from other training programs. Of 142 training programs *for which an evaluation had been publicly reported*, Ball and Anderson (1975) found that 70% had been formally evaluated and the remainder informally evaluated. The evaluation objectives usually revolved around program improvement rather than assessment of program impact. The typical *formal* evaluation consisted of administering questionnaires or conducting interviews. Against this backdrop, the preponderance of clinical programs appear to do at least as well in their training evaluation. Third, the paucity of appropriate training evaluation technology and the absence of precise training evaluation standards (APA, 1982; Levy, 1983; Norcross & Stevenson, 1984) have contributed to the development of this problematic condition, and these shortcomings can be rectified.

Evaluation Impact

In the first survey, one broad question asked the clinic directors to make judgments about the impact of quantitative training evaluation on clinic operation and policy. Of those 45 sites in which training evaluation was conducted, 19 (42%) reported significant influence on policy. Three significant correlates of evaluation impact were subsequently identified. For one, conducting the evaluation as a routine part of the clinic operation was more likely to influence decisions than was a specific, time-limited study. For another, internal and clinic-generated financial support for evaluation activities was more likely to lead to policy impact than was support from university or other external sources. This correlate is congruent with the frequent lesson that the internal commitment of relevant policymakers is a central influence on the impact of findings (e.g., Cohen, 1977; Patton, 1978). For still another, the total number of training outcome measures employed was positively associated ($r = .45$) with policy impact.

In the second and third surveys, respondents rated the impact of each specific evaluation measure that they employed in their programs. As shown in the preceding tables, the top five measures in terms of rated importance were supervisors' written evaluations, the APA accreditation report, students' evaluations of supervisors, supervisors' evaluations of students, and students' quantitative ratings of program effectiveness.

Notable by their low mean impact ratings were formal comparative designs. The comparative approach tends to yield minimal information about training in any given program and to be fraught with methodological and statistical problems. In addition, adequate comparisons are time- and money-consuming endeavors with questionable payoffs and risky consequences. An internal "formative" approach, in contrast to an external "summative" evaluation, may be most appropriate under these circumstances.

Consistent with the mean impact ratings, when asked to spontaneously nominate two indexes that they would recommend to other programs on the basis of their experience, internship directors' single most recommended measure of training evaluation was intern feedback (n = 99 of 221 total nominations), preferably structured and anonymous. Respondents also frequently nominated supervisor/faculty evaluations of interns (n = 46), training consultation site visits (21), and follow-up of interns (17).

Evaluation Obstacles

If training evaluation is so critical to clinical psychology on the local, state, and federal levels, then why is not everyone evaluating their clinical training? To begin to answer this question in our first study we had clinic directors list the three biggest obstacles to meaningful evaluation research in their sites. Table 6 presents the coded replies and their frequencies.

As seen there, the most common responses concerned time restraints followed by staff apathy/disinterest, technological limitations, and inadequate funding. Grouped into more generic categories, resource problems (n = 52) and staff resistance (n = 47) clearly emerged as the most intractable obstructions, at least relative to ethical difficulties and technological limitations.

Directors of clinical psychology graduate programs and internship programs were asked to indicate the seriousness of these 12 problems in our second and third surveys. They rated each problem on a 5-point Likert-type scale (1 = very serious obstacle to 5 = not an obstacle). The mean ratings are presented in Table 6. The five worst obstacles in conducting meaningful training evaluation in both sites were time restraints, inadequate methods and measures, lack of personnel, transience of students, and insufficient funding. The pattern across studies underscores the fact that overt staff resistance and theoretical disparities are not seen as largely to blame. Rather, with the exception of inadequate technology, the failure to evaluate training is attributed to the same reasons for many of our deficiencies—lack of time, people, and money.

Table 6. Problems in Evaluating Training

	Mean rating[a]		Frequency
Problem	Intern programs	Graduate programs	Training clinics
Time restraints	2.7	2.8	28
Inadequate funding	3.4	3.4	15
Lack of personnel	3.1	3.1	9
Transience of students and problems with follow-up	3.3	3.2	—
Heterogeneity of students	4.0	4.0	—
General apathy and disinterest	4.0	3.6	20
Student resistance, noncompliance	4.2	4.1	—
Faculty resistance, noncompliance	3.8	3.8	12
Philosophical and theoretical disparities among faculty	4.2	4.1	12
Lack of belief in the value of research evidence for this purpose	3.9	3.9	3
Ethical consideration	4.3	4.2	2
Inadequate evaluation methods and measures	3.0	3.0	19

[a]Based on a 5-point Likert-type scale (1 = very serious obstacle to 5 = not an obstacle).

To sum up, problems in evaluating training are ascribed to the 3 r's: resources (e.g., time restraints, inadequate funding, lack of personnel); resistance (overt and covert disinterest, apathy, noncompliance); and rigor (technological limitations, problems with follow-up, inadequate measures). To varying extents, all three are of our doing (and potentially undoing); perhaps they are even self-inflicted.

Setting Variations

Any discussion of prevalent practices and problems requires an examination of individual or site differences. We compared the reported utilization percentages and mean impact ratings of the evaluation measures for APA-accredited clinical psychology doctoral programs (n = 62), internship programs (n = 179), and where possible, psychology training clinics (n = 74) to explicate meaningful setting variations.

Inspection of Tables 1 through 5 yields considerable convergence in training evaluation designs and measures across settings. Overall, only 6 of the 31 direct comparisons revealed any substantial differences between graduate and internship programs, operationally defined as a difference of at least 10% in utilization and .5 in mean impact rating.

Graduate programs employed tests of factual knowledge more frequently (58% vs. 14%) and accorded them more importance (4.2 vs. 3.0) than internship programs. On the other hand, internships more frequently employed and ascribed more impact to trainees' ratings of abilities (45% vs. 26%, 3.5 vs. 3.0); trainees' ratings of program effectiveness (73% vs. 45%, 4.3 vs. 3.7); trainees' quantitative satisfaction with training (76% vs. 53%, 4.2 vs. 3.7); former trainees' ratings of program effectiveness (51% vs. 26%, 4.0 vs. 3.4); and faculty rating of program effectiveness (39% vs. 23%, 3.8 vs. 3.0). Thus the academically oriented graduate programs are more involved with evaluation of didactic knowledge, whereas the briefer but clinically oriented internship programs are more involved with student and former student perceptions.

The marked similarities in the utilization and importance of training evaluation procedures between these various programs suggest that site variation is limited. Even the problems encountered in trying to conduct useful evaluations are quite similar, as mentioned in the previous section. One major implication of this finding, to be explored more fully later, is that improvements in explicit criteria, standardized measures, and sensitive designs should equally benefit all psychology training programs in evaluating their clinical training.

SPECIFICATION AND MEASUREMENT OF CLINICAL COMPETENCE

In clinical psychology training, definitions of competence are typically vague (Korman, 1973; Levy, 1983; Peterson & Bry, 1980). Neither the APA nor most individual training programs have managed to get beyond specifying a list of required experiences for students, leaving desired outcomes from these experiences undefined.

Defining professional competence is an obvious first step in developing valid measures to be used in the evaluation of clinical training. Because this first step has frequently been ignored, competence has remained a nonspecific construct with many possible meanings depending on the context in which it is used. The vagueness of the construct has resulted in a lack of conceptual and definitional clarity and inadequate construct validity in methods used for assessing it. Until the meaning of competence in clinical psychology is adequately specified and more valid methods have been devised for measuring it, there can be no firm basis for differentially evaluating clinical training (Koocher, 1979; Stern, 1984).

Earlier sections of this chapter have pointed out some of the issues and dilemmas confronting the neophyte definer. Underlying many of these issues are fundamental ideological debates regarding the nature of the clinical psychology enterprise and the mental health treatment enterprise (Edelstein & Brasted, 1983; Ford, 1979; Korman, 1973; Levy, 1983). We are, for example, at the very beginning of understanding the contribution of therapist variables to successful psychotherapy (cf. Lambert & Bergin, 1983; Parloff, Waskow, & Wolfe, 1978). At this stage it seems more profitable to (a) develop clearer statements of the theoretical premises guiding training (divergent as these may be); (b) construct measures of competence that directly reflect the theoretically implicated variables, using the most appropriate sources and procedures; and (c) cover enough ground to make comparisons among training programs and models possible. Without careful linkages between theory and measurements, we are unlikely to understand the implications of empirical results in ways useful for improving training.

In subsequent portions of this section, we will examine some of the methodological problems in current measurement (linking them to definitional issues), briefly review current strategies for assessment of competence, and finish on a note of pragmatic optimism.

Methodological Considerations

Because other chapters in this volume (e.g., Berven [Chapter 9] and Hirschenberger, McGuire, & Thomas [Chapter 13], devote extensive coverage to these issues, they will be presented only briefly here. As Albee and Kessler (1977), Ford (1979), Howard (1983), and Scofield and Yoxtheimer (1983) have pointed out, the most serious problem is one of *validity* for measures of clinical competence. Until clear relationships between clinical activities and client improvement are identified and/or a consensual definition of the competent clinical psychologist is achieved, we are on shaky footing whenever we assert that our measures are valid. "Measuring clinical competence is easy, or difficult, or impossible, depending primarily on the reliability and the specificity of the criterion" (Albee & Kessler, 1977 p. 505).

There are three quite different traditions for operationally defining and validating competence, each of which has important limitations. The Rogerian tradition emphasizes the importance of interpersonal stylistic skills in creating a facilitative interpersonal relationship (cf. Rogers, 1957; Truax & Carkhuff, 1967) and relies on measures such as Barrett-Lennard's (1962) Relationship Inventory and Carkhuff's (1969) Scales.

These two measures employ client ratings and observer ratings, respectively, of therapist interpersonal behavior in therapeutic encounters. Both are based on the premise that empathy, warmth, and genuineness on the part of the psychotherapist are necessary conditions to bring about client change. Evidence for the validity of this premise is modest but extensive (cf. Patterson, 1984; Truax & Mitchell, 1971), principally in therapeutic encounters involving "counseling" with relatively intact clients coping with relatively nonspecific symptoms. Strupp (1984) also provides validating evidence for the importance of stylistic qualities of the therapist in affecting client outcome.

A second tradition for operationally defining clinical competence is the behavioral approach (cf. Ford, 1979; Krasner, 1969; Kratochwill & Van Someren, 1984). Operant and social learning techniques are used to teach specific, situationally grounded behaviors, such as assessment interviewing skills. Measures of competence are derived directly from the specific learning task in the form of the discrete behaviors toward which training is directed, perhaps in the form of behavior checklists. These measures are rarely checked for generalizability over time and beyond the training situation (Ford, 1979), nor have they been validated against client improvement.

A third tradition for operationally defining clinical competence is loosely associated with the psychodynamic perspective. Supervisory ratings of global competence or of more specific items like "deals effectively with negative transference" (Buckley, Conte, Plutchik, Karasu, & Wild, 1982) may be employed, based on the supervisor's belief in the mastery of certain therapeutic tactics as essential for effective clinical work. Most of these tactics have not been validated against client improvement. When rating dimensions are derived empirically from supervisors' characterizations of competent students, the dimensions that emerge sound closer to personality attributes than to trainable skills (Peterson & Bry, 1980).

A newer approach for establishing validity is a cognitive information-processing perspective, most closely associated with the ideas of Stern (1984). A major challenge for developers of competency measures is to identify appropriate correct answers that go beyond factual knowledge and are based on something more than local preferences. In psychiatry it appears that diagnostic decisions and accompanying (pharmacological) treatment decisions are becoming more reliable and consensual (Longabaugh, Stout, Kriebel, McCullough, & Bishop, 1986). This opens opportunities for investigators of psychiatric training to evaluate training processes in terms of trainees' ability to arrive at correct decisions regarding diagnosis and treatment (e.g., Nurcombe & Gallagher, 1986). Whether a wide spectrum of expert clinical psychologists will be able to find consensus on "correct" assessment and treatment decisions remains to be seen. It is also not clear whether clinical psychology trainers conceptualize their mission as training in accurate decision making; this seems a distinct perspective from the Rogerian, behavioral, and psychodynamic traditions.

This attempt to organize approaches to validity into three or four camps is clearly an oversimplification. Measures can be classified by content (knowledge, skill, attitudes, personality characteristics), scoring method (scaled ratings, behavior frequencies, multiple choice), behavior sampled (real therapy, simulation, paper-and-pencil test), and source of evidence (observer, client, peer, trainer, self). For each of these categories, issues associated with face, content, criterion, predictive, and construct validity can be discussed. Throughout discussions of this sort (Ford, 1979; Scofield & Yoxtheimer, 1983) certain themes recur. Validity evidence is in short supply, and "there is little evidence that any of these scales have validities that broadly generalize to real clinicians performing actual professional tasks" (Scofield & Yoxtheimer, 1983 p. 417). Defining the content domain of clinical competence is difficult. Selecting criteria short of client improvement is open to immediate question. When conventional psychometric standards for validity are applied, current measures can be readily faulted.

Theoretical and practical problems, which pose a major impediment in establishing the validity of competency measures, are somewhat less overwhelming for reliability. Here it appears that a number of measures can successfully meet psychometric standards, although this has frequently not been demonstrated in reported studies using these measures (Scofield & Yoxtheimer, 1983). Interjudge agreement, test–retest stability, and internal consistency have been found for some measures, though not for a number of others. As Howard (1983) has summarized, there are well-developed strategies for improving reliability (e.g., anchoring ratings, training judges, analyzing items) that can overcome problems in this area at an acceptable cost. Some sources of data appear to be less likely to have demonstrated any form of reliability (supervisors' ratings and self-evaluations), whereas others have been more carefully developed (client and observer data) (Ford, 1979; Scofield & Yoxtheimer, 1983).

For purposes of evaluating clinical training, it is also important to examine three other characteristics of competency measures: (a) sensitivity to training impact; (b) differential sensitivity to specific training components; and (c) clinical interpretability of measured levels of posttraining performance. Some approaches to measuring clinical competence, notably that of Peterson and Bry (1980), lead to operational definitions emphasizing traitlike properties of competent clinicians (responsibility, warmth, intelligence, and experience) that may be useful for screening more than for assessing training impact. Indeed, a study of psychiatric residents by Buckley *et al.* (1982) found that only 8 out of 29 competency items indicated pre- to postraining changes in supervisors' ratings. When the ratings were combined across items, training was found to have no significant effect. The authors concluded that some skills are teachable, but many qualities associated with competence are better provided via applicant screening. In addition to general sensitivity to training effects, measures must be designed to detect differential impact of various training components if we are to understand more precisely how the training process operates in order to improve it. Global competency measures employed in studies pitting one training method against another may be useful for some purposes, but the complexity of actual clinical training calls for evaluation measures that can aid in identifying "active ingredients" in training. Measures must also allow us to judge whether the final level of competence attained at the completion of training is acceptable for clinical practice. In examples provided by Ford (1979), the most successful training procedures still produced only a bare minimum of competence.

The Contents and Procedures of Competency Measures

There are several standard rubrics for classifying the content of competency measures. Knowledge, skills, and attitudes provide one useful classification scheme. Knowledge measures are used quite widely by clinical programs, though not so frequently in training clinics or internships, as the surveys described earlier in this chapter indicate. The Examination for Professional Practice in Psychology (EPPP) (Hoffman & Aderet, 1984), used by almost all states as one component in psychology for licensure examination, is an exemplar of a knowledge-oriented measure. Multiple-choice questions are used to test knowledge across a carefully defined set of content domains. Unfortunately, tests of this sort are frequently found to have little or no relationship to measures of actual performance (Albee & Kessler, 1977; Howard, 1983). Taylor, Albo, Holland, and Brandt (1985) have summarized convincing evidence that most traditional academic-style means of measuring competence are weakly or not at all related to later professional success across a wide range of professions. Knowledge may be necessary but is certainly not sufficient as a measure of clinical competence. For those attempting to develop content-valid assessments of knowledge appropriate for the practicing clinical psychologist, the EPPP serves as one model. This model, evolving in response to shifting emphases on knowledge content domains closer and farther from actual professional practice, is itself controversial. The notion of a generic, universal knowledge base for all practicing psychologists is one source of controversy (Howard, 1983). Stern (1984) raised a related issue by making a distinction between genotypic and phenotypic competence. Even when the academic underpinnings of professional practice are seen as critical, a broad range of (phenotypic) knowledge may be less useful than the (genotypic) ability to use knowledge effectively, that is, to think like a psychologist.

Technical skills, assessed by various performance-oriented measures, seem an obvious domain for measures of competence. Why study dubiously related predictors when you can sample evidence of performance directly, argued Howard (1983). Of course it does not turn out to be so easy. Defining the skills, selecting the assessment context, determining an appropriate means of judging performance, obtaining reliable judgments, and validating these judgments against some criterion remain extremely difficult tasks for the profession of clinical psychology.

A variety of means for measuring clinical skills has been devised. Most obvious, one might think, would be client outcome from treatment. This approach suffers from many problems—for example, lack of standardization of client assignment, presence of many other sources of variance in client outcome, difficulties in measuring client outcome, and logistical difficulties. For these reasons, client outcome has not been employed or even widely recommended as a direct measure of clinical competence. Several other strategies do have much to offer, although their development is just beginning to be carefully studied.

Work samples—direct evidence of behavior in clinical practice—may be evaluated in a variety of ways. Perhaps the simplest is to provide clinical supervisors with rating systems to evaluate the competence of the trainee practitioner on global or specific dimensions. These ratings are in more widespread use than other means of quantifying competence for training evaluation purposes (Norcross *et al.*, 1986) but are virtually never validated (Scofield & Yoxtheimer, 1983) and are highly suspect when used for training evaluation due to potential bias of the raters (Ford, 1979). A more demanding but promising strategy for judging competence on the basis of work samples is the panel review approach. Blanton, Swope, Armstrong, Tori, and Dienst (1984) and Bent

(1982) report two independent examples of this approach. Both call for the trainee to prepare a prestructured written presentation of a particular psychotherapy case that is discussed with a panel of independent reviewers. The panel may include representative clinical faculty, practicum supervisors, respected community practitioners, and fellow students. No panel member should be in a supervisory role with the trainee being evaluated. A standard rating form allows quantitative as well as qualitative evaluation. Interjudge reliability and predictive validity are still at issue, but Blanton *et al.* (1984) do report salutary effects of the evaluation process on the training program. Howard (1983) has reviewed strengths and weaknesses of the work sample approach and concluded that many of the objections applied to client outcome also apply here and reduce the desirability of this approach.

Simulations of practitioner tasks offer a somewhat more controlled, systematic means of assessment. Behavior frequencies in simulated live interview situations can provide directly quantified evidence (Edelstein, 1982). Actors can be used, written or videotaped problems can be presented, and the trainee's responses can be directly observed or videotaped for later evaluation (Howard, 1983). As described here, this approach allows judges to observe complex performance on a predesigned, standardized sample of tasks. Stevenson *et al.* (1984) and Nurcombe & Gallagher (1986) have employed variations of this approach in which videotaped segments of a psychotherapy session are followed by questions requiring brief written or dictated responses. It is these responses that are evaluated. The definition of competence implied by these latter strategies is a cognitive problem-solving one.

A final strategy for assessing competence is client rating of the clinician. This approach has been widely used by those investigating counseling techniques (Ford, 1979; Scofield & Yoxtheimer, 1983) but rarely used by evaluators of conventional clinical psychology training programs (Norcross *et al.*, 1986). Those who make use of client ratings as well as some who use supervisors' ratings and work samples define competence as something more than a set of demonstrable technical skills. Nonspecific personality-style factors, attitudes, and values are at least part of the content tapped by many of these measures. Admittedly constructs like empathic responsiveness can be viewed either as technical skills or as personality characteristics. For purposes of training evaluation, it is important to decide whether change in such personal qualities is a goal of training. Measurement of attitudes, values, and styles is at a more psychometrically tractable stage than the simulation and work sample strategies previously discussed. However, the lack of employment of these sorts of measures in traditional clinical psychology programs may reflect ideological differences in definitions of training goals.

Making Progress in Measuring Competence

As Howard (1983) has concluded, each of the strategies and content domains described previously represents potentially useful information. At this point, it would be most helpful if cross-site collaboration supported the development of standard, reliable, and valid instruments in each of the categories presented. Measuring competence is clearly not the only important step in evaluating clinical psychology training, but it is one where our skills as researchers seem eminently suited to meeting the challenge of the task.

ASSESSING TRAINING PROCESSES

In contrast to the attention devoted to issues surrounding the measurement of clinical competence, means for describing the component processes of training have been relatively neglected. Yet without this piece of the puzzle our picture of effective training is incomplete. Without an adequate knowledge of *what* training has been imparted, it is exceedingly difficult to evaluate *how* this training has impacted on students.

The Value of Studying Training Processes

The experiences of Stevenson *et al.* (1984), Harway and Serafica (1977), and Dickey, Vasile, and Gudeman (1982) suggest both the difficulty and the value of doing what Levy (1983) has recommended: articulating training processes with desired training objectives in order to use program evaluation to improve training quality.

Attention to training processes also has important conceptual implications. We have a very hazy idea of how training translates into competence and rarely attempt to develop a conceptual rationale for our conventional training procedures (Edelstein & Brasted, 1983). Ford (1979) and Kalafat and Neigher (1983) have reviewed evidence indicating the minimal and occasionally negative impact of traditional clinical training. By proposing a "genotypic" approach to predoctoral training, with an emphasis on learning psychological problem-solving processes rather than an encyclopedic set of facts, Stern (1984) has challenged us to conceptualize and refine the training process as the means to this end. As we are also beginning to realize in the study of psychotherapy (Greenspan & Sharfstein, 1981; Parloff, 1980; Strupp, 1984), the most promising line of questioning appears to be oriented toward understanding how the process works, rather than pitting two ill-specified approaches against each other.

Careful examination of the training process is not only useful for local direction and conceptual clarity, but it is also essential for supporting the profession in national policy struggles as well. The APA Task Force on Education, Training, and Service in Psychology (1982) has reported that one serious problem for the profession of clinical psychology is the inability of its spokespersons to describe what goes on in its training programs with any degree of specificity. For this reason, the task force has recommended nationwide study of the actual component processes of clinical training as a crucial step toward demonstrating the relationship between these processes and a set of competencies that define clinical psychology's special niche among the professions.

Approaches to Process Investigation

Several ways of conceptualizing and investigating training processes are evident in the research literature. The most common is to define a set of very concrete training tasks or training phases, typically in behavioral terms. Didactic lectures, training manuals, videotaped examples or live models, behavioral rehearsal, and concrete feedback are several examples of component processes that have been studied separately as well as in various combinations (Bernstein, 1982; Ford, 1979; Kratochwill & Van Someren, 1984). Even when the training objectives are guided by a humanistic orientation, these processes have been employed in research (Ford, 1979). The more narrowly training is focused on specified "interviewing skills" the more susceptible it is to this type of conceptualization.

A second approach to describing and evaluating training processes focuses on supervision (Ford, 1979). Because supervised clinical experience is the major skill-oriented component of training, standard clinical psychology programs' assessment of the supervision process is a logical target. Presence, amount, modes, and timing of supervision and dimensions of supervisory style (warmth, genuineness, empathy, flexibility, restrictiveness) may all play a role in the provision of clinical competence. Although these elements of the training process are clearly important, they do not capture the range of experiences in the training of a clinical psychologist that a longitudinal multicomponent program of study suggests.

An approach that does reflect the complexity of the training process is that of Howe and Neimeyer (1979). They employed a journal method to capture the detail of daily clinical activities in a graduate program. Clinical activities were defined as including clinical service, supervision, research, and academic (course-related). These activities were logged by clinical faculty and students on an hourly basis for two nonconsecutive weeks of an academic year. Changes in the training program were reported to yield predictable changes in the activity pattern. As a means of providing aggregate descriptive evidence of what goes on in clinical training, this method has promise. However, it does not address the quality of experiences, and its necessary restriction to relatively brief periods of time neglects the larger scope of training program processes.

Work carried out at the University of Rhode Island (Stevenson *et al.*, 1984; Stevenson & Norcross, 1984; Stevenson *et al.*, 1985) has provided a less well-defined but more comprehensive approach to the study of the training process in clinical psychology. A systems perspective, briefly described by Stevenson and Norcross (1984), lays the groundwork for empirical investigation. The throughput process is laid out chronologically, incorporating all of the elements of the student's training experience. (Inputs, outputs, and feedback loops are also defined.) Multiple sources of evidence are used to describe and evaluate each element. Archival and self-report data are used to build a description of the complete training process. Subjective ratings and qualitative feedback by current students, former students, faculty, practicum supervisors, and internship supervisors can provide evidence regarding social climate, decision processes, training mechanisms, and various knowledge-providing and skill-training components of the program. Ratings of student competencies by internship supervisors can be linked to descriptions and evaluations of the components of preinternship training. This approach puts heavy emphasis on the perceptions of those involved in training as a means of evaluating a program. Efforts to integrate objective and subjective sources of information are tentative and intuitive.

Linking Processes to Outcomes

In order to demonstrate how the training processes of clinical psychology generate uniquely competent clinical psychologists, we must first measure competencies and processes and then find ways to connect the two. We believe it is unfeasible to design controlled studies of the relative effectiveness of every combination and order of training process components for enhancing every dimension of clinical competence. An approach that looks more closely at how the training process works in natural settings may offer a more practical means of elucidating the connections between training and professional performance. An alternative but complementary strategy is to identify and describe clearly distinctive clinical training programs and administer the same battery of competence measures in each setting, in order to identify the differential impact of the distinctive training elements. Neither of these strategies possesses the elegance and rigor of a randomized experiment, but both come closer to addressing the practical and conceptual issues confronting the field.

FUTURE DIRECTIONS

In preceding sections we have documented current progress and issues in the evaluation of training in clinical psychology. A recurring theme has been that, despite evident benefits from and imperatives for evaluation, we are at a relatively primitive stage in both local and national efforts to describe, validate, and improve training. It is clear that our data base for building effective clinical training programs and evaluating them is sadly limited at this time (Edelstein & Brasted, 1983). Along with others, we see potentially dire consequences from inaction: decreasing federal support, diminishing professional status, attenuating legislative backing for licensure and free-choice legislation, continuing violation of APA accreditation standards, and nagging concern regarding failed professional responsibilities. However, we have also tried to examine a number of reasons for our slow progress and to suggest some promising lines of attack.

Accordingly, we conclude with eight broad recommendations for the direction of training evaluation in clinical psychology. These suggestions are grounded in our own experience, our survey findings, and the insights of others. We have tried to heed the APA Task Force's (1982) warning that

> the evaluation plan must be realistic if it is to receive professional and financial support. An evaluation plan so abstract and general as to defy implementation or so gradiose as to elicit derision will not do, but neither will an evaluation plan that invites the charge of irrelevance or triviality. (p. 41)

1. *Specify clear and measurable training objectives.* Despite the obvious need to specify objectives in order to conduct meaningful evaluation (Irby, Evans, & Larson, 1978), most clinical psychology programs do not have a specific, written set of objectives for training (Norcross & Stevenson, 1984). It is difficult to commend success or recommend change when the desired direction for outcomes is not clear. We recommend that objectives be specified for each training domain (e.g., assessment, psychotherapy, research) in each major category of learning outcome (knowledge; attitudes and values; skills—both behavioral and cognitive). The most fruitful level for specification is probably between the very concrete task (can compute WAIS-R subscale scores) and the global, unmeasurable goal (can assess adult intelligence). We believe this step is essential for both local and national progress.

2. *Organize and classify competency measures.* Our surveys have indicated that inadequate evaluation methods and measures pose one important obstacle to successful evaluation. A cataloging of existing measures, grouped by domain and category of learning objective, could provide the basis for the development of a recommended battery of evaluation measures. Waskow and Parloff (1975) and later Ciarlo (1981) have undertaken this task for psychotherapy outcome measures. Although absolute consensus on a description of the competent clinical psychologist may not be reachable, at least we can represent the major categories reflecting the range of opinion. Areas of inadequate or nonexistent measurement methods can be systematically identified. Training objectives can be keyed to appropriate measures. Newly emerging specializations can be incorporated. It would be inappropriate, we believe, to seek a single measure of generic psychotherapy skill for a field with so many rapidly developing technical domains, ranging from new assessment techniques to specialized treatment methods, to consultation, training, and research skills. And we must manage to represent the thinking, feeling, acting professional rather than an incomplete abstraction.

3. *Develop and apply descriptive methods for training processes.* The presently implemented "models" for training are not a useful level at which to describe training. We must find a means appropriate to the policy questions we wish to address, capturing major ingredients of training and alternative training methods. Diagrammatic, chronological maps of the intended and actual sequence of training experiences we provide our students can present a surprisingly useful picture. Clarifying the role of specific training methods, order effects, interactions between student characteristics and training methods, and other equally

complex issues will challenge us for many years. In the meantime it would be helpful to know what we are currently doing.

4. *Make theories explicit and use them.* Definitions of competencies, measures based on those definitions, and means of characterizing training processes all imply a conception of what professional excellence is and how to achieve it. This is even more apparent when one attempts to articulate the connections between training, competencies, and long-term career objectives. Although we may disagree on what the proper conceptual framework is, we will make more rapid progress if we make more explicit what our assumptions are and draw on them when designing and interpreting evaluations of training.

5. *Improve evaluation research designs.* We are not calling here for more rigorous experiments. Rather we are calling for designs that fit our purposes and are within our means. An important distinction is made in the literature between "formative" and "summative" evaluation. Formative evaluation is conducted as a rational means of guiding program development and improvement. Summative evaluation, typically performed by an external evaluator, is conducted to determine the overall merit of a program and may lead to program termination. Differing evaluation questions and strategies are associated with these two orientations. Local evaluation is generally conducted from a formative perspective, necessitating careful examination of the training structure, process, and results.

For some important purposes—those associated with a formative perspective—the most useful research may be an ongoing, longitudinal process embedded in the training organization. Elegant time-limited outcome studies certainly have an important role in identifying training methods and systems worth disseminating, but such studies cannot substitute for self-evaluation at the local and national level.

Respect for systematically collected qualitative as well as quantitative evidence (Cook & Reichardt, 1979; Patton, 1980) is now increasing, and there is no reason not to incorporate qualitative procedures in training evaluation. At the same time, it is important to build in quantitative measures that are more amenable to standardization, cross-site comparisons, and eventual psychometric justification. Numerical ratings of students by practicum and internship supervisors on standardized forms, for example, would require only modest additional effort beyond current impressionistic, qualitative feedback. A structured feedback questionnaire for students would also seem relatively low in cost for the gain in information. We are also likely to be increasingly concerned about measuring training costs in our effort to conduct practical and useful evaluation. No one design is going to answer the variety of questions to which we want answers; we will learn better methods as we go (APA Task Force, 1982, p. 19)—if we get started. Our recommendation is to design empirical means to achieve *utilizable* results.

6. *Get started.* The dramatic list of arguments in favor of increasing evaluation of clinical psychology training should make this activity a high priority. Waiting for the single, universally approved measure of competence or the ideal design seems an ill-advised plan. The questions are interesting scientifically and profoundly significant pragmatically, and they will be answered by policymakers with or without good empirical evidence. It is high time to build some evidence. The realistic constraints challenge our ingenuity and commitment.

7. *Collaborate.* One means for enhancing evaluation designs and generally improving the sense of support for evaluation of clinical psychology training is cross-program collaboration. This can range from joint grant proposals to simple sharing of methods and measures.

8. *Establishing a national program.* We are joined by many others in expressing an interest in a coordinated national program for clinical training evaluation. When asked whether they and their programs would be willing to cooperate in a national program if one existed, only 2% of internship directors and none of the graduate directors responded in the negative. The pronounced receptivity to such an idea and the large impact of APA's existing site visits lead us to conclude that a national program of this kind is highly desirable and long overdue.

Of special concern is the absence of precise evaluative criteria. APA (1983, p. 8) mandates "an explicit, comprehensive system for evaluation" for accredited programs. Yet, the accreditation standards fail to specify what types of data are required or what a "comprehensive system" entails. The APA accreditation procedures produce a modicum of uniformity in clinical training and program evaluation but no more than that should be assumed (APA, 1982; Levy, 1983).

The diverse and idiosyncratic approaches to evaluation identified in our studies suggest a need for greater coordination, integration, and prioritization; the APA, the Association of Psychology Internship Centers (APIC), or another organization could offer explicit criteria, provide standardized measures, and support training evaluation efforts in professional psychology. Such a program would assist interested parties in securing useful data upon which training effectivenss could be judged and program decisions could be based.

In many respects, the establishment of such a base would embody several of the preceding recommendations. The national bureau could further specify evaluation criteria, enhance evaluation design, consult on appropriate methods, classify available measures, assist in the dissemination of local results, and generally integrate the uncoordinated local efforts now underway. Such a bureau could also begin to implement the APA task force recommendations for a national-level research program.

Evaluation can play an important role in shaping training programs to more effectively meet current needs in the face of shrinking resources and in clarifying the knowledge, skills, and values that are imparted to students by a quality training experience. However, clinical training evaluation may be incorrectly perceived as a luxury in an era of fiscal retreat. In this context, we issue a call for visible support for the cherished belief that clinical psychology is a discipline in which research, training, and practice enrich one another.

REFERENCES

Albee, G. W., & Kessler, M. (1977). Evaluating individual deliverers: Private practice and professional standards review organizations. *Professional Psychology*, *8*, 502–515.

American Psychological Association (APA). (1983). *Criteria for accreditation of doctoral training programs and internships in professional psychology*. Washington, DC: Author.

American Psychological Association Task Force on Education, Training, and Service in Psychology. (1982). *Summary report*. Washington, DC: Author.

Autor, S. B., & Zide, E. D. (1974). Masters' level professional training in clinical psychology and community mental health. *Professional Psychology*, *5*, 115–121.

Ball, S., & Anderson, S. B. (1975). *Practices in program evaluation: A survey and some case studies*. Princeton, NJ: Educational and Testing Services.

Barrett-Lennard, G. T. (1962). Dimensions of therapist response as causal factors in therapeutic change. *Psychological Monographs*, *76* (Whole No. 43).

Bent, R. (1982). The quality assurance process as a management method for psychology training programs. *Professional Psychology*, *13*, 98–104.

Bernstein, G. S. (1982). Training behavior change agents: A conceptual review. *Behavior Therapy*, *13*, 1–23.

Blanton, J. S., Swope, A., Armstrong, P. M., Tori, C., & Dienst, E. R. (1984, October). *Assessing competency of clinical skills: Methodological and process issues*. Panel presented at Evaluation '84 Conference, San Francisco, CA.

Buckley, P., Conte, H. R., Plutchik, R., Karasu, T. B., & Wild, K. V. (1982). Learning dynamic psychotherapy: A longitudinal study. *American Journal of Psychiatry*, *139*, 1607–1610.

Carkhuff, R. R. (1969). *Helping and human relations*. New York: Holt, Rinehart & Winston.

Chen, H., & Rossi, P. (1983). Evaluating with sense: The theory-driven approach. *Evaluation Review*, *7*, 283–302.

Ciarlo, J. A. (1981). *Final report: The assessment of client/patient outcome techniques for use in mental health programs*. NIMH Contract. Denver: University of Denver.

Cohen, L. H. (1977). Factors affecting the utilization of mental health evaluation research findings. *Professional Psychology*, *8*, 526–534.

Cohen, L. H. (1983). Document-based peer review in a psychology training clinic. *Professional Psychology: Research and Practice, 14*, 362–367.

Cook, T., & Reichardt, C. (1979). *Qualitative and quantitative methods in evaluation research*. Beverly Hills, CA: Sage.

Dana, R. H., Gilliam, M., & Dana, J. M. (1976). Adequacy of academic-clinical preparation for internship. *Professional Psychology, 7*, 112–116.

Dickey, B., Vasile, R. G., & Gudeman, J. E. (1982). *Increasing evaluation utilization in postgraduate training progams: Developing an alliance between evaluator, faculty, and trainees*. Unpublished manuscript, Harvard Medical School and Massachusetts Mental Health Center.

Edelstein, B. A. (1982, April). *Empirical evaluation of clinical training*. Paper presented at the Working Conference on Behavioral Clinical Training, Morgantown, WV.

Edelstein, B. A., & Brasted, W. S. (1983). Clinical training. In M. Hersen, A. E. Kazdin, & A. S. Bellack (Eds.), *The clinical psychology handbook*. New York: Pergamon.

Fishman, D. B., & Neigher, W. D. (1982). American psychology in the eighties: Who will buy? *American Psychologist, 37*, 533–546.

Flaherty, E. W., & Morell, J. A. (1978). Evaluation: Manifestations of a new field. *Evaluation and Program Planning, 1*, 1–10.

Ford, J. D. (1979). Research on training counselors and clinicians. *Review of Educational Research, 49*, 87–130.

Garfield, S. L. (1977). Research on the training of professional psychotherapists. In A. S. Gurman & A. M. Razin (Eds.), *Effective psychotherapy: A handbook of research* (pp. 63–83). New York: Pergamon.

Garfield, S. L., & Kurtz, R. (1976). Clinical psychologists in the 1970s. *American Psychologist, 31*, 1–9.

Gottfredson, G. D. (1984). A theory-ridden approach to program evaluation: A method for stimulating researcher–implementer collaboration. *American Psychologist, 39*(10), 1101–1112.

Grant, D. L., & Anderson, S. B. (1977). Issues in the evaluation of training. *Professional Psychology, 8*, 659–677.

Greenspan, S. I., & Sharfstein, S. S. (1981). Efficacy of psychotherapy: Asking the right questions. *Archives of General Psychiatry, 38*, 1213–1219.

Haley, J. (1976). *Problem-solving therapy*. San Francisco: Jossey-Bass.

Harway, N. I., & Serafica, F. C. (1977). Issues in the evaluation of the psychology department clinic. *Professional Psychology, 8*, 650–658.

Henry, B. (1984). The future of clinical training: Forward into the past. *The Clinical Psychologist*, Winter, 25–26.

Hess, A. K., & Hess, K. A. (1983). Psychotherapy supervision: A survey of internship training practices. *Professional Psychology: Research and Practice, 4*, 504–513.

Hoffman, P. J., & Aderet, A. (1984). *Empirical validity of the EPPP*. A report by COGITAN to the American Association of State Psychology Boards, Palo Alto, CA.

Howard, A. (1983). Work samples and simulations in competency evaluation. *Professional Psychology: Research and Practice, 14*, 780–796.

Howe, H. E., & Neimeyer, R. A. (1979). Empirical description of clinical training: A reevaluation and validation. *Professional Psychology: Research and Practice, 10*, 168–174.

Irby, D. M., Evans, J., & Larson, L. (1978). Trends in clinical evaluation. In M. K. Morgan & D. M. Irby (Eds.), *Evaluating clinical competence in the health professions*. St. Louis: C. V. Mosby.

Kalafat, J., & Neigher, W. D. (1983). Can quality survive in public health programs? The challenge for training. *Professional Psychology, 14*, 90–104.

Khol, T., Matefy, R., & Turner, J. (1972). Evaluation of APA internship programs: A survey of clinical psychology interns. *Journal of Clinical Psychology, 28*, 562–569.

Kirchner, E. P. (1969). Graduate education in psychology: Retrospective views of advanced degrees recipients. *Journal of Clinical Psychology, 25*, 207–213.

Koocher, G. P. (1979). Credentialing in psychology: Close encounters with competence. *American Psychologist, 34*, 696–702.

Korman, M. (1973). *Resolutions of the National Conference on Levels and Patterns of Training in Professional Psychology*. Vail, CO.

Korman, M. (1974). National conference on levels and patterns of professional training in psychology: The major themes. *American Psychologist, 29*, 441–449.

Korn, J. H., Keiser, K. W., & Stevenson, J. F. (1982). Practicum and internship training in program evaluation. *Professional Psychology, 13*, 462–469.

Krasner, L. (1969). Behavior modification: Values and training. In C. M. Franks (Ed.), *Behavior therapy: Appraisal and status*. New York: McGraw-Hill.

Kratochwill, T. R., & Van Someren, K. R. (1984). Training behavioral consultants: Issues and directions. *Behavior Therapist, 7*, 19–22.

Kurz, R. B., Fuchs, M., Dabeks, R. F., Kurtz, S. M. S., & Helfrich, W. T. (1982). Characteristics of predoctoral internships in professional psychology. *American Psychologist, 37*, 1213–1220.

Lambert, M. J., & Bergin, N. E. (1983). Therapist characteristics and their contribution to psychotherapy outcome. In C. E. Walker (Ed.), *The handbook of clinical psychology* (pp. 205–241). Homewood, IL: Dow Jones-Irwin.

Levy, L. H. (1983). Evaluation of students in clinical psychology programs: A program evaluation perspective. *Professional Psychology: Research and Practice, 15*, 497–508.

Longabaugh, R., Stout, R., Kriebel, G. W., McCullough, L., & Bishop, D. (1986). DSM-III and clinically identified problems as a guide to treatment. *Archives of General Psychiatry, 43*, 1097–1103.

Malouf, J. L., Haas, L. J., & Forah, J. (1983). Issues in the preparation of interns: Views of trainers and trainees. *Professional Psychology: Research and Practice, 14*, 624–631.

Matarazzo, R. G. (1978). Research on the teaching and learning of psychotherapeutic skills. In S. L. Garfield & A. E. Bergin (Eds.), *Handbook of psychotherapy and behavior change* (2nd ed., pp. 941–966). New York: Wiley.

Norcross, J. C., & Prochaska, J. O. (1982a). A national survey of clinical psychologists: Affiliation and orientations. *The Clinical Psychologist, 35*(1), 4–6.

Norcross, J. C., & Prochaska, J. O. (1982b). A national survey of clinical psychologists: Views on training, APA, and career choice. *The Clinical Psychologist, 35*(2), 1–8.

Norcross, J. C., & Stevenson, J. F. (1984). How shall we judge ourselves? Training evaluation in clinical psychology. *Professional Psychology: Research and Practice, 15*, 497–508.

Norcross, J. C., Stevenson, J. F., & Nash, J. M. (1986). Evaluation of internship training: Practices, problems and prospects. *Professional Psychology, 17*, 280–282.

Nurcombe, B., & Gallagher, R. M., III (1986). Clinical reasoning in psychiatry: Research and education. In B. Nurcombe & R. M. Gallagher, III (Eds.), *The clinical process in psychiatry* (pp. 605–634). New York: Cambridge University Press.

Parloff, M. B. (1980). Psychotherapy and research: An anaclitic depression. *Psychiatry, 43*, 279–293.

Parloff, M. B., Waskow, I. E., & Wolfe, B. E. (1978). Research on therapist variables in relation to process and outcome. In S. L. Garfield & A. E. Bergin (Eds.), *Handbook of psychotherapy and behavior change: An empirical analysis* (2nd ed., pp. 233–282). New York: Wiley.

Patterson, C. H. (1984). Empathy, warmth, and genuineness in psychotherapy: A review of reviews. *Psychotherapy, 21*, 431–438.

Patton, M. Q. (1978). *Utilization-focused evaluation*. Beverly Hills, CA: Sage.

Patton, M. Q. (1980). *Qualitative evaluation methods*. Beverly Hills, CA: Sage.

Peterson, D. R. (1985). Twenty years of practitioner training in psychology. *American Psychologist, 40*(4), 441–451.

Peterson, D. R., & Bry, B. H. (1980). Dimensions of perceived competence in professional psychology. *Professional Psychology, 11*, 965–971.

Rice, D. G., & Gurman, A. S. (1973). Unresolved issues in the clinical psychology internship. *Professional Psychology, 4*, 403–407.

Robertson, M. (1984). Teaching psychotherapy in an academic setting. *Psychotherapy, 21*, 209–212.

Robertson, M. (1985). Training eclectic psychotherapists. In J. C. Norcross (Ed.), *Handbook of eclectic psychotherapy* (pp. 416–435). New York: Brunner/Mazel.

Rogers, C. R. (1957). The necessary and sufficient conditions of therapeutic personality change. *Journal of Consulting Psychology, 21*, 95–103.

Rosenfeld, M., Shimberg, B., & Thornton, R. F. (1984). *Job analysis of licensed psychologists in the United States and Canada*. Princeton, NJ: The Educational Testing Service.

Rosenkrantz, A. L., & Holmes, G. R. (1974). A pilot study of clinical internship at the William S. Hall Psychiatric Institute. *Journal of Clinical Psychology, 25*, 417–419.

Schacht, T. E. (1984). Toward a national clinical training system. *The Clinical Psychologist*, Winter, 26–27.

Scofield, M. E., & Yoxtheimer, L. L. (1983). Psychometric issues in the assessment of clinical competencies. *Journal of Counseling Psychology, 30*, 413–420.

Sechrest, L., & Hoffman, P. E. (1982). The philosophical underpinnings of peer review. *Professional Psychology, 13*, 14–18.

Serafica, F. C., & Harway, N. I. (1980). The psychology department clinic: Its organization and development. *Professional Psychology, 11*, 741–748.

Shadish, W. R. (1984). Policy research: Lessons from the implementation of deinstitutionalization. *American Psychologist, 39*, 725–738.

Shemberg, K. M., & Keeley, S. M. (1974). Training practices and satisfactions with preinternship preparation. *Professional Psychology, 5*, 98–105.

Shemberg, K. M., & Leventhal, D. B. (1981). Attitudes of internship directors toward preinternship training and clinical training models. *Professional Psychology, 12*, 639–646.

Steinhelber, J., & Gaynor, J. (1981). Attitudes, satisfaction, and training recommendations of former clinical psychology interns: 1968 and 1977. *Professional Psychology, 12*, 253–260.

Stern, S. (1984). Professional training and professional competence: A critique of current thinking. *Professional Psychology: Research and Practice, 15*, 230–243.

Stevenson, J. F., & Norcross, J. C. (1984, August). *Local training evaluation: Who's doing it and what works?* Paper presented at the annual convention of the American Psychological Association, Toronto, Canada.

Stevenson, J. F., & Norcross, J. C. (1985). Evaluation activity in psychology training clinics: National survey findings. *Professional Psychology: Research and Practice, 16*, 29–41.

Stevenson, J. F., Norcross, J. C., King, J. T., & Tobin, K. G. (1984). Evaluating clinical training programs: A formative effort. *Professional Psychology: Research and Practice, 15*, 218–229.

Stevenson, J. F., Norcross, J. C., Nash, J., & Grebstein, L. (1985). *University of Rhode Island Clinical Psychology Program Self-Study*. Kingston, RI: University of Rhode Island.

Stout, A. L., Holmes, G. R., & Rothstein, W. (1977). Responses by graduates to the memory of their internship in clinical psychology. *Perceptual and Motor Skills, 45*, 863–870.

Strupp, H. H. (1975). Training the complete clinician. *The Clinical Psychologist, 28*(4), 1–2.

Strupp, H. H. (1981, August). *Some implications of psychotherapy research for training*. Paper presented at American Psychological Association Annual Meeting, Los Angeles, CA.

Strupp, H. H. (1984). The Vanderbilt psychotherapy research project: Past, present, and future. In J. B. Williams & R. L. Spitzer (Eds.), *Psychotherapy research: Where are we and where should we go?* (pp. 235–246). New York: Guilford.

Strupp, H., & Schacht, T. (Eds.). (1984). The training of clinical psychologists. *The Clinical Psychologist*, Winter, 19–35.

Taylor, C. W., Albo, D., Holland, J., & Brandt, G. (1985). Attributes of excellence in various professions: Their relevance to the selection of gifted/talented persons. *Gifted Child Quarterly, 29*, 29–34.

Truax, C. B., & Carkhuff, R. R. (1967). *Toward effective counseling and psychotherapy: Training and practice*. Chicago: Aldine.

Truax, C. B., & Mitchell, K. M. (1971). Research on certain therapist interpersonal skills in relation to process and outcome. In A. E. Bergin & S. L. Garfield (Eds.), *Handbook of psychotherapy and behavior change*. New York: Wiley.

Tucker, R. (1970). Strangers in paradise. *Journal of Consulting and Clinical Psychology, 34*, 140–143.

Tyler, J. D., & Weaver, S. H. (1981). Evaluating the clinical supervisee: A survey of practices in graduate training programs. *Professional Psychology: Research and Practice, 12*, 434–437.

Walfish, S., Kaufman, K., & Kinder, B. N. (1980). Graduate training in clinical psychology: A view from the consumer. *Journal of Clinical Psychology, 36*, 1040–1045.

Waskow, I. E., & Parloff, M. B. (1975). *Psychotherapy change measures*. DHEW Publication ADM 74-120. Washington, DC: National Institutes of Mental Health.

Weiss, C. H. (1972). *Evaluation research*. Englewood Cliffs, NJ: Prentice-Hall.

Weiss, S. L. (1975). The clinical psychology intern evaluates the training experience. *Professional Psychology, 6*, 435–441.

5

Training and Evaluation in Counseling Psychology

SAMUEL H. OSIPOW and ROBIN A. REED

THE IMPORTANCE OF EVALUATION

Counseling psychology is a major professional subspecialty in psychology and the helping professions. The 1984 survey of the Council of Counseling Psychology Training Programs revealed that the council has 60 program members, each of which (in 1984) received a mean of 85 applicants and matriculated a mean of 44.5 students per program (at all year levels). That same year, approximately 290 students from these programs were awarded doctoral degrees. Clearly, the sustained and extensive production of doctorates trained in counseling psychology is significant in number and requires concerted attention with respect to the competencies and skills these graduates acquire through the course of their training.

Perhaps, because the antecedents of counseling psychology reflect such diverse issues as mental health, school guidance practices, counseling in higher education, and career development practices, to name a few, it is difficult to discern a coherent thread throughout the

SAMUEL H. OSIPOW and ROBIN A. REED • Department of Psychology, Ohio State University, Columbus, OH 43210.

evaluation of counseling psychology students' training. It is almost as if counseling psychology trainers strive to teach their students so much they cannot decide on a focus for evaluation.

In recent years, increasing attention, however, has implicitly if not explicitly been addressed to the problem of evaluating how students acquire competencies through training. Competition in the marketplace with other health care providers (e.g., clinical psychologists, social workers, and psychiatrists) has been a major impetus for counseling psychologists to address the evaluation process. The universities, as trainers, must address the issue of competitiveness in the marketplace in order to attract the kind of students to their programs that they wish to train and who have high potential for success. Factors that attract students to university programs include faculty and past graduates' reputations, placement of graduating students in appropriate and desirable positions, and the clarity of the identity of the field for which they train.

A second major impetus for examining the evaluation process is that the graduates must be able to document and demonstrate competency in their professional field in order to successfully compete for the credentials required for practice. Graduates must be licensed upon completion of their studies in nearly every jurisdiction in the United States and Canada. They must also prove themselves eligible for third-party reimbursement when they provide health services. Graduates must be eligible for professional malpractice insurance and be able to compete effectively for appropriate post- and even predoctoral internship and workshop training positions. Third parties are becoming increasingly powerful in determining the adequacy of credentials. This power is seen in the role of the National Register in designating who provides health services and which programs train psychologists, by the impact of the American Psychological Association (APA) program accreditation in making it possible for graduates of programs to obtain the appropriate credentials and, consequently, employment, and by the growing influence of the Association of Psychology Internship Centers (APIC) in determining program requirements needed to qualify for a desirable internship.

Finally, the issue of training evaluation has an equity and fairness component. Rather than rely on intuition, word of mouth, and/or "old person networks," it behooves programs to develop explicit criteria to evaluate rate of progress and competency of students during training programs so that inappropriate and irrelevant factors do not impede a student's growth and development.

EFFORTS TO EVALUATE TRAINING IN THE HELPING PROFESSIONS

Given the need to be accountable to both the parent institution and the student participants, programs need to take every possible action. Now that we have established the need to be more self-aware and active in the evaluation of the training process, the question arises of how well we have done in the past. There is a surprisingly modest literature dealing with the evaluation of training in counseling psychology. Much of that literature does not directly apply to counseling psychology but has been created by writers in counselor education and/or clinical psychology. Fortunately, there are enough similarities among the three fields to permit some generalization to counseling psychology based on those studies.

For example, a committee of the Association for Counselor Education and Supervision produced a volume to guide counselor trainers in evaluating student progress (Dameron, 1980). This volume specifically tried to address the issue of competency-based counselor education by defining which competencies are required for professional counselors to perform their tasks adequately. The resulting document includes rating scales on topics that range from professional counselors' personality characteristics to a wide variety of skills (counseling, consultation, career development services, planning and development, measurement and evaluation, research, placement and follow-up, and referral). Each of these categories is subdivided into a large number of behaviorally defined skills that relate to performance. Thus professional counselors can be rated in considerable detail on a wide range of categories of knowledge and skills that pertain to effective counseling. Such a document could be used to assess the abilities of professionals on the job as well as rate of student progress through a training program.

Although the Dameron guide is one of the more explicit and comprehensive attempts to provide a framework to use in studying progress in training, it is cumbersome to use and has not been widely applied. Specific factors may contribute to the limited utilization of this tool. The document is extraordinarily lengthy and presumably very time-consuming to complete. In addition, the data base on which to make the very detailed observations is probably not fully available to most supervisors, whether they are in a professional or a training setting. Finally, although each of these competencies has good face validity, seldom, if at all, has there been any documentation of the relationship between implementation of these competencies and desirable counseling outcomes.

The counseling psychology literature is replete with studies that assume that certain events will have a desirable outcome for clients, but a limited number of studies actually demonstrate and document these relationships.

For example, Cogan and Noble (1979) found that a fairly common set of counselor competencies could be generated by professionals in the field. According to the group of professionals queried, competency was defined in terms of the following components, from most to least important: ethical standards, personal characteristics, communication skills, adjunctive activities, counseling skills, and philosophical foundations. A number of items including case history taking, fantasy, distortion, theory, dreams, diagnosis, disapproval, and advice giving were rated as unnecessary for effective counseling. Again, although this study produces results that might be useful for evaluation and training purposes, the question remains of whether or not these competencies are related to any significant client outcomes.

Other studies have been done that deal more directly with counseling psychology and whose results suggest problems in evaluating student progress in counseling psychology. Based on an excellent review of the employment and training trends of counseling psychologists, King and Seymour (1982) suggest that external factors may refuel the identity crisis in counseling psychology. King and Seymour conclude that in the quest for professional identity, counseling psychology tends to seek new training experiences that lead to new applications of its skills. As a result, self-identity becomes more difficult to define and leads counseling psychology to focus attention on experiences outside the training setting. Therefore, external factors, such as internship site and job market opportunities, implicitly control training philosophy, course work, and priorities to a substantial degree, possibly more than we realize.

Defining clearer criteria brings us back to identity—or lack of clear identity—in counseling psychology. Myers (1982) summarized the themes and trends in counseling psychology and recommended specific steps he believed would promote a clearer identity for counseling psychology. These included: increased training emphasis on the world of work, preparing students to work in a variety of settings, the encouragement of program evaluation skills, the improved awareness of the strengths and the limits of psychotherapy as a technique, greater exposure to a variety of health care practices beyond those normally addressed by counseling psychology, the advocacy of competency-based assessment of graduate student performance, the reaffirmation of the scientist/practitioner model, and increased training in individual differences. Efforts to develop a clearer identity along these lines might significantly improve the ability of counseling psychology to specify training criteria.

Because of the similarity between clinical and counseling psychology, many of the training problems are the same for both. Thus lessons in evaluating training for counseling psychology can be learned from studies of clinical training programs.

For example, Shemberg and Leventhal (1981) conducted a survey of 282 APIC training directors to assess the perceived quality of predoctoral training in clinical psychology because these directors had expressed much dissatisfaction with the preparation of interns. Allegations were made in the survey that training in universities had not changed substantially over the past decade. These data suggest that there may be lack of congruence between training program and internship directors' perceptions of student needs and training requirements. A second article (Levy, 1983) suggested that the incongruence may result from counseling psychology's lack of a clearly defined set of criteria. Levy (1983) compared the 1973 and 1975 APA accreditation criteria and concluded that neither set of criteria significantly addressed issues of evaluation, neither discussed an assessment of the evaluation process itself for validity and reliability, and neither criterion focused on the skills to be evaluated. He concluded that the evaluation of students seems to depend on a clear set of training criteria, which is seriously lacking in counseling psychology.

The need for more equitable evaluation criteria was also addressed by Miller and Rickard (1983). These authors generated a set of specific evaluation guidelines: (a) fairly global criteria should be used for clinical judgments because the field is changing rapidly; (b) flexibility and feedback should be built into the system; (c) clear criteria should be generated; (d) evaluation should occur at least twice a year with a very extensive evaluation at the end of each year; (e) behaviorally oriented evaluation forms should be developed and; (f) evaluation should be an ongoing process, that is, evaluation should be almost an attitude as much as an event. As Miller and Rickard noted, implementing such recommendations is hindered by demands on faculty time, other department priorities and projects, and difficulties in timely monitoring of student progress and defining acceptable and clearer criteria.

Given the link between professional identity and competent practice, a retrospective look at training practices can be informative in identifying variables that define competent future professional behavior. In an examination of the variables that relate to the successful completion of a doctoral program over a 5-year period, Hirschberg and Itkin (1978) found that standard ability and admissions criteria such as Graduate Record Exams and the like predicted early graduate school success in terms of grades. Peer ratings of need for achievement, conscientiousness, and commitment predicted later success in graduate school in terms of finishing the degree. They found that factors that predicted publication included intelligence, achievement, persistence, and competency needs, whereas factors that predicted completion of the program largely included the time in the program before taking comprehensive exams. They concluded that several criteria to consider would be a multiple "hurdles" model that involves first the usual test score variables, followed by a screening by a selection committee. Later the student would be disenrolled from the program if it became clear that research productivity was not forthcoming.

This study has some interesting implications for counseling psychology training in that the interpersonal competencies to learn the skills necessary to be a good professional may be very different from those skills involved in learning to be a good scientist, something the typical PhD program is designed to teach. Because counseling psychology communicates a mixed message and has a mixed set of goals (e.g., scientist/practitioner and sometimes practitioner/scientist), many of the old models for training and selection as well may not fit counseling psychology training programs. In fact, attempts to follow inappropriate training models may create many of the problems that are seen both in the attitudes of students in counseling psychology as well as in the ability of faculties to communicate clearly the skills needed for both practice and research.

A limited number of studies have addressed evaluation of student progress during the graduate training. In a review of the clinical psychology program evaluation literature, Aronson, Akamatsu, and Page (1982) concluded that most of the previous research has assessed training quarterly, measured outcome variables over very short time periods, conducted minimal follow-up, and seemed to lack adequate controls. Aronson *et al.* designed their study to measure communication skills in two groups of graduate school students: participants and nonparticipants in a 2-year systematic skills training program. They found that groups that participated in training developed the ability to display empathic responses over time to a greater degree than did the nonparticipant groups. Participant groups with more intense experiential training showed more improvement in the ability to discriminatively perceive facilitative responses than participants with less experiential training. Experiential training and participation in training may build the adaptive interpersonal skills needed for practice.

In another clinicallly oriented study, Tyler and Weaver (1981) surveyed practices providing feedback to practicum students in clinical psychology programs assessing the frequency, the format, and the type of records that were used by the evaluating supervisor. They found that a large majority of programs maintain some kind of a training clinic (82%), that there was overall satisfaction with the nature of the evaluation, and that a very large majority of programs reported that the evaluation had a positive impact on supervisory relationships with trainees. Over 90% reported regular trainee evaluation procedures. Most of the programs (over 75%) reported the students received all the reports regarding evaluation. Ninety percent provided written records about student performance and two thirds of these programs communicated this feedback in writing to the trainee. Thus, at least among this sample, student involvement in the feedback process seemed important and to be a high priority.

In a rare study of student progress in practicum, Hill, Charles, and Reed (1981) followed graduate students longitudinally across their training program in order to study counseling skill development and attitudes toward training. The nature of the longitudinal study limited the number of individuals who could be observed to 12 male and female graduate students in the PhD program. The study assessed these trainees' process skills. The counselor trainee saw one male and one female client each fall for one visit over the 3 years of the study. Transcripts were made and judged for each session, and a final clinical interview was held at the end of the third year.

The results indicated that over time student use of minimal encouraging responses increased, that there was no significant effect of the student experience at program entry in the use of these minimal encouragers, and that there was no significant effect of time or experience on anxiety, quality, or activity measures of trainees. Self-report data indicated that the most common student experiences included changes in their expression of empathy and their overall anxiety level when working with clients. Many of them also expressed changes in their nonverbal and verbal behaviors and perceptions of supervisors and of the supervisory relationship. Most of the trainees also changed their expectations for themselves and their expectations about what they might be able to do with a client in a short session. In addition, the majority reported graduate school to be stressful in nature but also positive in the sense that they saw themselves as growing and saw counseling as a supportive enterprise. Although this study is limited because there was no control group, the sessions were short, the process variables may be questioned, and the students were all in one graduate program, it represents a methodological prototype of examining what happens to trainees during the course of a doctoral program in counseling psychology. Its results can be useful in providing insight to others in developing appropriate evaluation techniques for the training setting.

A final evaluation measure, the tried and true comprehensive examination, appears to be alive, well, and widely used, at least in counselor education programs (Thomason, Parks, & Bloom, 1980). These writers surveyed 40 counselor education departments and found that all these departments required examinations for the PhD, the majority of these departments had a fixed type of examination without much choice on the part of students, and nearly 60% used essay exams. Although some departments favored standardized or other kinds of individualized examination procedures, apparently counselor educators and probably clinical psychology and counseling psychology training programs as well generally feel more comfortable in evaluating the cognitive skills of the graduates and trainees than they do their practice skills. Again, the question must be raised as to what degree these cognitive skills in fact contribute to applied outcome. No definitive evidence exists that either cognitive skills or any one of the long lists of performance competencies clearly relate to beneficial changes in clients through counseling.

Reviewing the literature on the evaluation of training and counseling psychology, it becomes clear that, although a few schemes have been proposed for use in training evaluation, little empirical data have been collected to describe current practices in counseling psychology training evaluation. One survey dealing with the training evaluation in clinical psychology was conducted by Norcross and Stevenson (1984). Because this serves as a prototype and potential model for looking at counseling psychology training evaluation, it deserves some detailed attention. The motivations behind the Norcross and Stevenson survey were very similar to those that would suggest a similar survey is needed in counseling psychology: There is a great need for evaluation, but little of it is done. Accreditation standards require evaluation but do not specify the types of data to be used or the frequency of evaluation. There has been little documentation of what clinical training is and how its purposes can be accomplished, and, finally, those evaluation measures that are used, such as supervisor reports, are not extensive.

Norcross and Stevenson surveyed 62 APA-approved clinical psychology programs. They asked the programs to respond to questions that reflected training evaluation procedures, training evaluation practices, and training evaluation problems, that is, the obstacles to doing good training evaluation. They found that of the programs surveyed, all reported some kind of evaluation, but these ranged from informal, qualitative methods such as supervisor and faculty impressions to more formal quantitative measures such as written evaluation by supervisors and exam performance. It is clear that the results indicated that informal methods were more frequently used than formal methods, though systematic written evaluations were collected to judge effectiveness in most programs. It is not surprising that the most commonly reported obstacles to doing good training evaluation were poorly defined training objectives and criteria, poorly developed methods for evaluation, and the assignment of a low priority to training evaluation in terms of who has to do it and how many resources are allocated to its execution.

A SURVEY OF CURRENT EVALUATION PRACTICES IN COUNSELING PSYCHOLOGY

The Norcross and Stevenson study did not inspire us to conduct a similar survey of counseling psychology training programs, but it did reinforce a decision to collect data to describe what counseling psychologists are doing with respect to the evaluation of their training programs. As noted before, counseling psychology training programs have similar problems with respect to program evaluation. Programs are expected to evaluate student progress to maintain APA accreditation, but little guidance for evaluation is given by the accreditation criteria. In addition, because the evaluation of student progress through programs is so time-consuming and because faculty assign higher priorities to other tasks, student evaluation through programs is given less attention than it deserves.

In order to find out the current "state of the art" in counseling psychology in January 1985, we sent a short questionnaire to the 60 program directors listed in the Council of Counseling Psychology Training Programs. These programs represent a diverse selection because some of them are APA approved, whereas others are not. They represent the diversity of historical training emphases in counseling psychology because some of them are long-standing, well-established counseling psychology programs, whereas others have moved into counseling psychology only relatively recently, and the emphasis in training counselors has shifted from education to the mental health arena. Many of

Table 1. Frequency of Evaluation by Program

	No response	Quarterly (or semestral) only	Annual only	Annual and quarterly (or semestral)	By comprehensive exams only
Number of programs	2	11	18	4	3

the programs surveyed are in transition and are at various stages of the transition. Of the 60 surveys sent out, 38 were returned.

The questionnaire contained items related to examination procedures, research requirements and evaluation, teaching course work evaluation, evaluation with respect to professional practice skills, and elicitation of an "other" method if there was one that was used. Tables 1, 2, and 3 summarize responses of the 38 program directors.

Table 1 indicates that 18 of the 38 programs responding to the survey evaluate only on an annual basis; it is discouraging that 3 do so using only comprehensive exams. On the other hand, it is encouraging that 33 programs do some student evaluation at least annually or more frequently.

Table 2. Frequency by Program of Method of Evaluation

Method used in evaluation	Frequency	Percentage
Comprehensive exams	1	2.6
Academic performance	2	5.3
Academic performance & research comprehensive exams	1	2.6
Academic performance & agency feedback	1	2.6
Academic performance & agency feedback	6	15.8
Academic performance, research, & clinical competency	1	2.6
Academic performance, research competency, & agency feedback	2	5.3
Observations of practice, agency feedback, & clinical competency	1	2.6
Observations of practice, agency feedback, & academic performance	12	5.3
Observations of practice, clinical competency, academic performance, & agency feedback	1	2.6
Academic performance, research & clinical competency, agency feedback, & observations of practice	10	26.32

Table 3. Frequency by Program of People Involved in Evaluation

Person(s)	Number of programs
Advisor, students, professors, practicum supervisor, & others	2
Advisor, student, professors, & practicum supervisors	9
Advisor, students, & other professionals	1
Students & advisor	1
Students, advisor, & practicum supervisors	1
Advisor, other professionals, & practicum supervisors	7
Other professionals	3
Advisor, other professors, & others	1
Professors & others	1
Practicum supervisors	2
Advisor & professors	8
Professors & practicum supervisors	1
Other professionals	1

Table 2 shows the frequency of various kinds of evaluations. Most programs use a variety of events as a basis for evaluation, including observation of practice, practicum agency feedback, academic performance, and clinical and research competencies. Some, however, use only limited events as a basis for evaluation (academic performance or comprehensive exams). It would seem that programs relying on only academic criteria will pass along some number of good students but poor practitioners into the field.

Table 3 shows the range of types of participants in the evaluation process. Again, most programs involve a number of people, including various professors, the advisor, practicum supervisors, and the trainee. A few rely on only the advisor and student. It is reasonable to assume that a better description of student progress in training is gained when the cadre of evaluators represents as many spheres of professional training as possible.

Although this type of questionnaire is necessarily not as rigorous as one might perhaps like, the results and responses do lend themselves to a few tentative observations. First, a wide variety of criteria for training evaluation are used by counseling psychology programs. Second, within these, programs differ in the number, the type, and the mixture of criteria they use to evaluate student progress. Third, one third of the programs responding used the preliminary or comprehensive examination in combination with other kinds of criteria. In addition, 42% of the programs surveyed reported using a research criterion in evaluation. This research criterion seems to be primarily a progress measure across time, rather than a quality assessment of the research skills. Although there is probably some correlation between temporal progress and quality, this remains to be demonstrated. In addition, the research criteria that the programs use tend to focus on required research activities such as theses and dissertations and not on optional projects or team research. Also, more than two thirds of the programs (69%) responding required grades as a criteria reflecting progress. A few programs reported the requirement for good progress to be maintenance of a minimal passing grade point average of 3.0 or 3.5 to continue in the program, but most seemed to require some minimal grade point level in certain courses as well as specified overall grade point averages. Further, 81% of the programs responding required practice criteria to be met, defined in terms of a mixture of measures focusing on practicum evaluations, supervisor ratings, and for a very small percentage (less than 6%), direct observation of practicum skills. Finally, 58% used our "other" category and reported practices such as evaluations from supervisors on an internship site, ethical and professional behaviors, progress in the program (that is, length of time in), personal development in terms of interpersonal skills, professional development, publications, skills in supervision, report writing, consultation, and so forth. However, very little attention (8.3%) to ethics or publications was reported. Usually, once a trainee gets to the internship level, there is little feedback to the student from either program.

These results are descriptive. They do not indicate differences in levels of intensity of data collection nor the relative importance assigned to various criteria. Even so, they do provide an outline of widely used practices by almost two thirds of counseling psychology training programs.

FUTURE DIRECTIONS

The results of the Norcross and Stevenson (1984) study and the survey reported here are not cause for enthusiastic acclaim about the state of the art of evaluation of counseling and clinical psychology training. If the assumptions mentioned earlier in the chapter regarding the importance and need for professional training in counseling psychology are assumed to be valid, the two training groups are headed for potential trouble. However, there are some possible directions for improvement.

A large number of forces operating in psychology today are concerned about our limited ability to demonstrate differences in competence in professionals. These concerns range from objections to the national licensing exam and include concerns about state boards' actions and policies in implementing the licensing process. Practitioners complain of exclusion not based on competency but on credential checks of unproven validity, and students and new professionals complain of criteria for professional entry that are irrelevant to current job demands. A number of agencies are moving toward the serious examination of competency-based evaluation of professional qualifications. A competency-based model, of course, assumes that it is possible to identify the fundamental skills necessary for entry into professional practice and that the degree of presence of these skills can be measured. The American Association of the State Boards of Psychology's recent commission of the Educational Testing Service to perform a job analysis of professional psychologists is one manifestation of this concern (Rosenfield, Shimberg, & Thornton, 1983). A second manifestation is the study conducted by Fitzgerald and Osipow (1986) in which the work functions of counseling psychologists were subjected to job analysis. These efforts represent first steps in identifying a core of competencies related to professional practice that might be subject to assessment.

Granted that a core of common competencies can be identified, the next step is to develop ways to assess their presence. An example of how this procedure might work is demonstrated in a study by Fantuzzo, Sisemore, and Spradlin (1983). These investigators introduced a training model to teach skills involved in the administration of the Wechsler Intelligence Scale for Children-Revised (WISC-R). The model served both as a training device and a means to assess the attainment of a criteria of competence with respect to test administration. This kind of procedure represents one example of what might be done to assess the skills involved in a number of professional competencies. The problem with the technique proposed by Fantuzzo *et al.* is the degree to which it is highly specific in nature. If one were to assess all of the specific tests and knowledge areas that a professional psychologist in any specialty might be called upon to demonstrate at some point and try to achieve competency-modeled training and assessment for those skills, we would be encumbered with minutiae. Furthermore, frequent revisions would be needed to maintain high standards of professional performance. We would seriously risk losing the conceptual thread of professional training in exchange for training in a series of loosely related professional techniques.

Paravonian (1981) proposed a type-by-level model of learning for evaluating student performance and also for designing practica. This model identified the three major competencies: knowledge about practice; demonstrated applied skills in simulated and real settings; and finally, the integration of the self-concept to professional practice or, in other words, professional identity. According to Paravonian, these competencies develop sequentially, and their outcomes can be identified along a continuum that can be assessed by both the type and the level of performance displayed, with attention to various kinds of skills at each level. This competency-based model is at a higher level of abstraction than the Fantuzzo *et al.* model. Here, a problem in professional practice is explicated, such as needing information about a client. Then, examples of counselor behaviors are generated to represent another level of performance skill. These range from (a) selecting a test to (b) selecting a test that is based on knowledge about the test from manuals to (c) consulting with reference sources such as the *Mental Measurements Yearbook* in the selection of the test and, finally, (d) selecting a test based upon the previous steps and explaining the rationale for the selection of the particular test.

The advantage of this procedure over the Fantuzzo *et al.* procedure is its generality across situations. The procedure does not tie the evaluator to a specific skill but allows for a general format to be developed that can be applied to a specific professional situation. The disadvantage, of course, is that it relies significantly on the judgment of the evaluator to devise good examples to represent each of the four performance levels, and thus, there is some limit in the degree of interrater reliability.

With all due respect to behavioral objectives and their application to assessing counselor competency, there are so many serious limitations to the application of that model, both practical and theoretical, that its potential utility to counseling psychology evaluation is sorely limited. Even the Paravonian model is cumbersome and demands a substantial amount of "up-front" time without a sufficient assurance that it will actually work.

Some compromise between a pure behavioral competency model and the unsystematic, erratic subjective procedures that seem to be most commonly used exists, and it is that compromise that we must work toward. We have some ideas about what model might be suitable that we will propose, but fundamentally, the issue of training competencies should be addressed by a group of professional representatives of the subspecialty. This would seem to be an appropriate task for

Division 17 (Counseling Psychology) of the APA, or perhaps for the Council of Counseling Psychology Training Directors, or some subcommittee composed of the two groups. Why these groups have not addressed this task thus far is not entirely clear, although their failure to try to develop some general principles regarding the evaluation of training in counseling psychology may reflect limited resources in time and money as well as a preoccupation with immediate day-to-day matters of professional functioning and survival.

The model that we think would be useful to start with would develop cognitive and performance goals on a year-by-year basis for counseling psychology students. Year 1, for example, could start with learning the following: (a) basic principles in psychology that deal with motivation, perception, and social and group process; (b) measurement of psychological attributes; (c) research procedures and statistical techniques that may be applied to address questions of psychological significance; and (d) skills that socialize psychologists into the discipline and profession (e.g., ethics, social utility, and the role of psychology in society). On the performance side, Year 1 should require the trainee to (a) manifest skills in interviews that lead to client comfort, client talk, and client support; and (b) manifest general interpersonal skills that reflect some understanding of one's limitations as a professional as well as one's potentialities.

A similar set of cognitive and performance events could be defined for Year 2 and 3, and each of these lists should reflect the specific and idosyncratic objectives of the training program. Because we value training programs' differences, we should not want to impose competency-based information that makes everybody from every program look and act the same way, but rather we should be able to devise a general framework for how to proceed that allows individual programs the freedom to emphasize different aspects of professional skills. Thus we can still retain distinctive images so that graduates of Ohio State University generally seem to have a somewhat different flair than graduates of the University of Maryland or the University of Missouri.

Guidance for the selection and specification of cognitive and performance events year by year could be obtained from the results of job analysis studies, such as Rosenfield *et al.* (1983) and Fitzgerald and Osipow (1986). Although Rosenfield *et al.* found few professional differences among clinical, counseling, school, and even industrial/organizational psychologists, they did identify specific job-related skills. Similarly, for counseling psychologists, Fitzgerald and Osipow found variations in the performance of, identification with, and perceived importance of a variety of specific skills. These could be made even more specific and behavioral in nature to guide training and, thus, evaluation as well.

Perhaps the most overarching conclusion possible based on this literature review and survey is that training evaluation in counseling psychology cannot be done independent of awareness and explication of training philosophy, goals, and generally agreed-upon required professional competencies.

REFERENCES

Aronson, D. E., Akamatsu, T. J., & Page, H. A. (1982). An initial evaluation of a clinical psychology training program. *Professional Psychology, 13*, 610–619.

Cogan, D. B., & Noble, F. C. (1979). Ratings on a comprehensive set of counselor competencies. *Counselor Education and Supervision, 19*, 120–125.

Dameron, J. D. (Ed.). (1980). *The professional counselor: Competencies, performance, guidelines, and assessment.* Falls Church, VA: American Personnel and Guidance Association.

Fantuzzo, J. W., Sisemore, T. A., & Spradlin, W. H. (1983). A competency-based model for teaching skills in the administration of intelligence tests. *Professional Psychology: Research and Practice, 14*, 224–231.

Fitzgerald, L. R., & Osipow, S.H. (1986). An occupational analysis of counseling psychology: How special is the specialty? *American Psychologist, 41*, 535–544.

Hill, C. E., Charles, D., & Reed, K. G. (1981). A longitudinal analysis of changes in counseling skills during doctoral training in counseling psychology. *Journal of Counseling Psychology, 28*, 428–436.

Hirschberg, N., & Itkin, S. (1978). Graduate student success in psychology. *American Psychologist, 33*, 1083–1093.

King, P. T., & Seymour, W. R. (1982). Education and training in counseling psychology. *Professional Psychology, 13*, 832–842.

Levy, L. (1983). Evaluation of students in clinical psychology programs: Program evaluation perspective. *Professional Psychology: Research and Practice, 14*, 497–503.

Miller, H. L., & Rickard, H. C. (1983). Procedures and students' rights in the evaluation process. *Professional Psychology: Research and Practice, 14*, 830–836.

Myers, R. A. (1982). Education and training—the next decade. *The Counseling Psychologist, 10*(2), 39–44.

Norcross, J. C., & Stevenson, J. F. (1984). How shall we judge ourselves? Training evaluation in clinical psychology programs. *Professional Psychology: Research and Practice, 15*, 497–508.

Paravonian, S. D. (1981). Evaluating and grading pre-service counseling students. *Counselor Education and Supervision, 20*, 276–284.

Rosenfield, M., Shimberg, B., & Thornton, R. R. (1983). *Job analysis of licensed psychologists in the United States and Canada.* Princeton: Center for Occupational and Professional Assessment, Educational Testing Service.

Shemberg, K. M., & Leventhal, D. B. (1981). Attitudes of internship directors toward preinternship training and clinical training models. *Professional Psychology, 12*, 639–646.

Thomason, T. C., Parks, J. C., & Bloom, J. W. (1980). The doctoral comprehensive examination in counselor education. *Counselor Education and Supervision, 19*, 182–184.

Tyler, J. D., & Weaver, S. H. (1981). Evaluating the clinical supervisee: A survey of practices in graduate training programs. *Professional Psychology, 12*, 434–437.

6

Graduate Education and Training in Health Psychology

JOSEPH A. ISTVAN and JOSEPH D. MATARAZZO

Few fields of study in psychology have experienced as explosive a growth of interest during the past decade as health psychology. Demonstration of the interest in this emergent field can be found on a variety of fronts—in the growth of discipline-specific journals, in the award of increasing amounts of federal and private monies for health psychology research, and in the establishment of graduate programs that attempt to train students in the expanding field. It is this last area of development of this subdiscipline that is the primary focus of the present chapter.

Most scholars would probably agree that educational curricula and modes of training are the primary *internal* forces shaping a professional or scientific discipline. (Witness the extraordinary changes instituted by the faculty of medical schools in the United States that followed in the wake of the Flexner report early in this century). Concern for the education of future psychologists has resulted in the convening by the American Psychological Association (APA) over the past four decades of five major conferences whose aim was to evaluate

JOSEPH A. ISTVAN and JOSEPH D. MATARAZZO • Department of Medical Psychology, School of Medicine, Oregon Health Sciences University, Portland, OR 97201.

education and training for both scientific and professional psychology, at Boulder, Colorado, in 1949, at Stanford in 1955, at Miami Beach in 1958, at Chicago in 1965, and at Vail, Colorado, in 1973. The recommendations of these conferences have been reviewed elsewhere (Matarazzo, 1983) and need not be discussed here. In 1983, a national conference was held at the Arden House in Harriman, New York, for the primary purpose of considering training models in the specific field of *health psychology*.[1] We will discuss some of the opinions expressed at this conference as well as what might be our own views regarding education and training in health psychology. It is our contention that the nature of graduate training in *any* field of psychology—including health psychology—is and should be *generic*. However, before expanding on this point, we feel that it would be worthwhile to offer a historical perspective on the growth of training models in psychology in general.

PREDOCTORAL EDUCATION IN PSYCHOLOGY: GENERIC OR SPECIALIZED?

Since 1948–1949, psychology has enjoyed, and at times suffered, the unique hybrid role of being both a cognate scientific discipline and a profession. As discussed elsewhere (Matarazzo, 1987) and as those familiar with the modern history of American psychology might be aware, our country's need for thousands of new mental health professionals who could provide services to the emotionally disabled among the men and women being discharged following the end of World War II resulted in perhaps what was the single greatest change in American psychology in this century—the transformation of psychology into a field that was both a part-scientific discipline and a part-service-providing profession. This change did not occur overnight but evolved in stages from 1948 to the present. One of the important concomitants of this change was that beginning in 1948, in complying with the requirements of both the National Institute of Mental Health (NIMH) and the Veterans Administration (VA), psychology established the process by which the Education and Training Board of the American Psychological Association could accredit both the curricular content offered

[1]Throughout this chapter, the term *health psychology* will be used to refer to the field of *generic psychology* applied to problems and issues related to health. As discussed elsewhere (Matarazzo, 1987), we believe that the conventionally accepted delimited fields of psychology (e.g., developmental psychology, experimental psychology, social psychology) do not consist of discrete areas of knowledge or skill but are the application of the generic core of the science of psychology to a particular problem area or issue.

and the quality of doctoral programs in psychology. The accreditation was to be made available to psychology programs that wished to be publicly listed and funded as offering education and training that could lead to a subsequent career goal in the *profession* of (clinical) psychology. From 1949 until the present (1987), the curriculum for a student seeking a career in academic or scientific psychology was *not* similarly standardized by these outside national influences.

A crucial underpinning of this change that evolved since 1948 was the self-study psychology carried out of its past, present, and probable future directions during the five major national conferences on graduate education and training in psychology noted previously. What is important for the present chapter is that representatives of the national leadership in graduate education in psychology who met in Boulder asserted and then, at the four other conferences, reaffirmed that psychology was *both* an academic-scientific discipline and a profession. The effect of this decision in practical terms was twofold. First, psychology reaffirmed its decision to continue to *not* standardize the curriculum for its students heading for a scientific career. The second area of consensus was that the predoctoral student in psychology aiming for a *professional* career would need to add to this common core of courses required of all students an additional track of required (or chosen from a list of electives) advanced courses and apprenticeship experiences designed to be differentially appropriate to that particular application.

What the 1949 Boulder conference, Training in Clinical Psychology, did was to loosely codify the "extras" that had to be taken by a psychology department graduate student wishing a career of professional service or research (or both) in the then societally needed arena of *clinical psychology*. Specifically, the Boulder conferees agreed informally that henceforth such a professionally oriented student would *add* to his or her required core of generic psychology graduate courses extra work in personality theory, developmental psychology, psychopathology, clinical medicine, and clinical psychiatry as well as courses and related apprenticeship experiences in assessment and psychotherapy that dealt with the applications of such extra knowledge (Raimy, 1950, pp. 68–70). The conferees at Boulder *rejected* the suggestions that each department offering a PhD via training in clinical psychology should offer essentially the same list of standardized core courses or elective courses in the clinical track. It is interesting that, although rejecting the idea that an actual list of core courses should be mandated, the participants at Boulder did introduce a bit of standardization, even if through the back door. Specifically, the conferees agreed that "there should be a common core curriculum for all students in graduate programs leading to the doctorate in psychology" (Raimy, 1950, p. 61). Nevertheless, having stated this broad mandate they could not bring themselves to list, except in very general terms (APA, 1947, pp. 545–551; Raimy, 1950, p. 64), the actual course work or subject matter that would have introduced an element of standardization to the curriculum.

This situation began to change with the formation of the American Association of State Psychology (Licensing) Boards (AASPB) in the early 1960s. One of the key passages in licensing laws for the practice of professional psychology that had been in place in most states for at least two decades required that those seeking licensure in psychology were required to have earned a degree in psychology or its *equivalent*. This latter phrase served to recognize both the legitimate and overlapping skills of professionals in psychology-related fields—such as education, guidance counseling, and sociology—and, as such, effectively warded off court challenges of psychologist licensure laws by such individuals. However, in the 1970s it had become increasingly clear that in the absence of an agreed-upon standard for what the essential and necessary training of a licensed psychologist should include, it had become virtually impossible to determine which licensure applicants with degrees from fields allied to psychology should be eligible to sit for the licensure examinations in psychology. In addition, psychology came under increasing pressure from third-party payers of health care costs to define what distinguished the licensed psychologist qualified to provide mental health services from the licensed psychologist whose primary area of application was educational psychology, industrial psychology, or some other nonclinical area.

As a consequence of these and related concerns, the APA Council of Representatives formed a Task Force on Education and Credentialing in 1979 charged with the mission of better defining the curricular content that should be required by any unversity department or other academic entity offering a doctoral degree in psychology. The minimum core of curricular content eventually agreed upon by this task force and representatives of other interested constituencies (such as the AASPB and the Council of Graduate Departments of Psychology) was formally approved (but not implemented at that time) as official APA policy by the APA Council of Representatives in February of 1985. It was shortly thereafter independently reaffirmed as policy by both the AASPB and the Council of the National Register of Health Service Providers. A description of the content areas of this minimum core curriculum has been included in Table 1.

The first two of these requirements form the basic tools of scientific research that should be common to any program offering a doctoral degree in a scientific discipline. The third and fourth requirements are specific to psychology but provide a knowledge base that should be potentially germane to issues in any of the definable content areas of psychology. The fifth requirement—ethics—has been strongly recommended as a required course for the doctoral degree in psychology for a number of years by the APA. Requirements 6 to 9 represent a categorization of the four major content areas that define psychology as a field of scientific inquiry. Representative course work in each of these four areas might include the following:

1. *Biological bases*—physiological psychology, comparative psychology, neuropsychology
2. *Cognitive-affective bases*—learning, memory, perception, cognition
3. *Social bases*—social psychology, psychology of women, organizational psychology
4. *Individual differences*—personality theory, human development, abnormal psychology

The examples cited here should be seen as illustrative because, depending on course content, a particular curricular offering may be

Table 1. Minimum Graduate Educational Requirements That Must Be Met by a Student Seeking Credentialing as the Holder of a Doctorate from a Psychology Department or Unit That Has Been Nationally Designated as a Doctoral Program in Psychology

1. Research design and methodology
2. Statistics
3. Psychological measurement (psychometrics)
4. History and systems of psychology
5. Scientific and professional ethics and standards
6. Biological bases of behavior
7. Cognitive-affective bases of behavior
8. Social bases of behavior
9. Individual differences
10. An advanced sequence of studies appropriate to each graduate's later career "track" (e.g., an advanced research or professionally applied apprenticeship experience plus additional relevant courses in biology, neurosciences, chemistry, genetics, systems theory, computer sciences, mathematics, epidemiology, demography, anthropology, sociology, management science, linguistics, engineering)

placed in more than one category. For instance, a course offering entitled "Psychology of Women" may potentially be offered from a social psychological or individual differences perspective.

The final curricular guideline (Requirement 10 in Table 1) includes whatever sequence of coursework and/or apprenticeship experiences are deemed appropriate for the area of psychology to which a student wishes to apply the skills required in the course of his or her graduate education. These offerings, of course, would be expected to differ widely from one area of application to another. Also, no guidelines were offered by the APA task force that developed the requirements shown in Table 1 concerning relative proportions of course work and related training in these various areas.

An essentially identical earlier version of the recommendations for curriculum content outlined in Table 1 were wholly accepted by the Working Group on Predoctoral Education/Doctoral Training at the 1983 National Conference on Graduate Education and Training in Health Psychology. Working from that earlier draft of these guidelines, the conferees suggested the more specific recommenation of requiring at least three credit hours or five quarter credit hours in each of the areas described in Requirements 6 to 9. They also specified that training in the specific area of health psychology (Requirement 10) should include course work and/or practicum experience leading to some degree of expertise in the areas of

1. Biological basis of health systems and behavior
2. Social basis of health systems and behavior
3. Psychological basis of health systems and behavior
4. Knowledge and skills regarding health policy and organization

Thus, as recommended by the 1983 Arden House Conference, the incipient health psychologist should in the course of his or her graduate training be exposed to areas that form the common knowledge base of psychology as demonstrated by course work in the first nine requirements outlined in Table 1, with a somewhat greater emphasis on curricular content in the courses related to Requirements 6 to 9. Also it should be emphasized that the curriculum guidelines approved by the APA Council of Representatives in 1985, and accepted in a preliminary draft form by the Arden House conferees in 1983, are *proscriptive* rather than *descriptive*. However, they are also not meant to fix in concrete the norms for curriculum content at each and every academic institution offering the doctoral degree in psychology across the U.S. We think that it is important to emphasize this latter point because, to our knowledge, there has never been systematic research that has specifically examined the degree to which a broad spectrum of institutions offering the doctoral degree in psychology require students in their programs to take course work in the generic core of psychology.

DOCTORAL EDUCATION IN HEALTH PSYCHOLOGY

Nascent offerings of graduate training in health psychology antedated by several years the Arden House meeting. Indeed, one of the primary goals of this 1983 conference was to help identify curricular offerings that currently in-place graduate programs might strive to achieve. One of the background papers provided to these conferees was a survey of graduate programs in health psychology conducted by Belar, Wilson, and Hughes (1982). To conduct their survey, Belar *et al.* mailed a questionnaire to all departments listed as entries in the APA guide, *Graduate Study in Psychology: 1980 to 1981*. Of the respondents (slightly more than half of the total sample), some 42 individual departments or divisions reported that they offered some degree of concentration in health psychology. However, there was no specific information offered in the Belar *et al.* survey regarding the content of these curricula. In order to examine the nature of the training offered by each of these institutions in somewhat more detail, Istvan and Hatton (1987) conducted a follow-up survey on *curriculum content* in these programs. In 1983, program directors and/or department chairs at each of the institutions listed in Belar *et al.*'s paper were asked to provide specific information concerning the curricula in their health psychology training programs. In this follow-up, half of the original 42 respondents answered this follow-up questionnaire. Some one third (8) of the respondents indicated that they were unable to provide a specific curriculum for either a minor or major concentration in health psychology at their institution. Our final sample included 11 institutions, 2 with a stated specialization in health/medical psychology, 5 with a health/medical psychology track within a clinical psychology program, and 3 others with health/medical psychology tracks within social ecology, health education, and biopsychology, respectively. One institution offered a health psychology track within either a social psychology or clinical psychology program. All institutions were contacted again in 1985 for the purpose of examining changes in curricula during the succeeding 2 years. There was little, if any, change in all programs.

Using the updated 1985 survey responses, Istvan and Hatton performed a tally count of courses in each of the 10 requirements described in Table 1, as nearly as could be ascertained from inspection of course titles. (The actual 4-year curriculum offered in each of these 11 programs will be found in Istvan & Hatton, 1987). These tally counts were converted to percentages of the total sample that included one or more courses in each of these areas. Requirement 10—the specific "emphasis" of graduate training—has not been included because this will, of course, differ from program to program. These percentages are listed next. For reference, refer to the numbered content requirements in Table 1.

1	2	3	4	5	6	7	8	9
100%	100%	73%	36%	27%	73%	64%	82%	82%

Obviously, there must be substantial caution in generalizing from such a small sample of disparate programs, and the percentages listed here should be regarded as only a general reflection of the actual content of these curricula. In accord with the curriculum guidelines approved in principle by the APA Council of Representatives in 1985, students in these graduate programs generally will experience exposure to identifiable course work and/or practical experience in the areas of research design and methodology, statistics, psychological measurement, and with differing emphases on specific content areas, most curricula seem to include course work in the four "core" content areas of biological, cognitive/affective, social, and individual difference foundations of behavior.

Graduate work in scientific and professional ethics and history and systems of psychology was not as clearly identifiable in these curricula as the other areas. We suspect that in many cases such curriculum content will be embedded in other course work or will be a part of practicum experience. Regardless of the context, it is important to emphasize that all graduate students should be exposed to issues regarding the ethical and professional problems they may expect to confront later in their careers. These ethical issues are clearly *not* limited only to the health service provider, as some of the concerns of animal rights groups have made biopsychologists painfully aware.

In the field of health psychology, we believe that it is particularly important for students to have adequate exposure to the generic core of the discipline of psychology. Given the trends documented by the APA for the employment of doctoral degree recipients in psychology during the past decade, it seems likely that many of the recent PhDs with career goals in the field of health psychology will not be employed in a traditional college or university-based department of psychology upon receiving their doctoral degree. Rather, the employment settings of at least some of these graduates will more likely be community hospitals, medical schools or health science universities, or any of the broad array of institutions dedicated to research and/or service delivery in behavioral health and behavioral medicine. Psychologists employed in such settings will frequently find themselves one of a small handful of behavioral scientists in their department or institution and in exceptional cases may be the sole representative of the profession of psychology. As such, they will lack the reciprocal reinforcement of professional identity that continually occurs in a traditional department of psychology. Thus an important—and clearly not superficial—function of course work and professional experience in the content areas that define psychology as an independent scientific discipline is to foster students' identification with psychology in contrast to other scientific or professional disciplines. Indeed, how many of us have not known at least one self-identified "neuroscientist" who has been more than slightly embarassed to admit to colleagues in a basic science field that his or her doctoral degree was received in a department of psychology?

POSTDOCTORAL TRAINING IN HEALTH PSYCHOLOGY

The recommendations made at the Arden House Conference for postdoctoral training in health psychology of both service providers and research scientists were forceful and clear. For the health service provider, a 2-year postdoctoral training program was strongly recommended. Because the skills of a health psychologist are potentially generalizable to a broad variety of problems involving the relationship of behavioral and psychological factors to health and illness (e.g., somatic complaints related to on-the-job stress or classically conditioned nausea induced by chemotherapy), the setting *per se* of this postdoctoral training was not regarded as being as important as the quality of the mentorship experience (and related administrative support) provided by a professional psychologist with high-quality skills in health psychology service delivery, and most importantly, the time to supervise and nurture a recent doctoral graduate. Thus, at Arden House, universities, medical centers, and industries were all considered to potentially be appropriate sites for the training of the professional health psychologist, with the common denominator being the opportunity for supervision by a skilled senior colleague. Going hand in hand with the development of professional skills appropriate to the health care arena is the socialization experience such a supervised work experience will provide. Medical schools, hospitals, and other health care facilities are populated by, what to the novitiate, would seem to be a bewildering array of physicians and other health care professionals such as pharmacists, physical therapists, osteopaths, psychiatric social workers, and any of the broad array of specialists in the fields of nursing, medicine, and surgery. Development of the ability to acknowledge and utilize the competencies of professionals in these areas while simultaneously exercising one's own skills in an independent and professionally responsible manner is probably best acquired through appropriate modeling by a skilled and competent mentor.

Unfortunately, there are two obvious constraints on the development of training programs in health psychology for the clinical health service provider. First, because there currently is no precedent for financial support for such a 2-year postdoctoral training program, relevant funding agencies (such as NIH, NIMH, and the VA) will have to recognize that there is a demonstrable need for the skills that a health psychologist would acquire in the course of such a 2-year postdoctoral program. Second, and perhaps even more important, there is at present only a small handful of psychologists who possess the appropriate skills and qualifications to adequately supervise postdoctoral trainees (Matarazzo, 1987). As more psychologists acquire high-quality skills in health psychology service delivery, this number should dramatically increase, but it will be a matter of time.

As with the individual training for a career in clinical service, postdoctoral training is no less important for the health psychologist with career goals in the area of academic or other types of full-time research. High-quality research in health psychology demands a sound working knowledge (rather than passing familiarity) of relevant areas of clinical and basic biomedical science, in addition to the generic background in psychology that typically is acquired during predoctoral training. Although some exposure to these areas of biomedicine would ideally occur prior to postdoctoral training, the opportunities available to doctoral students at arts and sciences universities that are not contiguous to their own schools of medicine for formal training in these areas may be quite limited. Thus the medical school or health science university setting of a postdoctoral research training program offers the opportunity to acquire this background in basic and clinical science that many postdoctoral students may lack. Of course, of fundamental importance to the value of any research training experience in health psychology is access to appropriate health care settings and subject populations. The conferees at Arden House did *not* endorse any particular form of training site for postdoctoral research training. However, we feel that as with postdoctoral training for service delivery, there are undoubted advantages of postdoctoral research training sites located at or affiliated with schools of medicine or health science universities or similar types of high-quality institutions populated with specialists from many different fields, with the laboratory and computer facilities, educational opportunities, and broad array of subject populations these institutions may uniquely provide.

A case in point is the postdoctoral training in *behavioral cardiology* in our own Department of Medical Psychology at the Oregon Health Sciences University. Due to a long-standing collaborative research relationship with faculty in the Department of Medicine's Division of Cardiology examining biobehavioral issues in cardiovascular function and disease, training programs quite naturally developed a focus in this area of training and research. The initial training grant in this program was received in 1977, and we are currently completing the second 5-year cycle of this training grant. Postdoctoral students supported by this training grant have found faculty positions in departments of psychology or one of the basic biomedical sciences. The typical doctoral graduate of this program has gone on to 2 or more years of postdoctoral training in such fields as pharmacology, medicine, anatomy, or public health.

EMPLOYMENT OPPORTUNITIES FOR HEALTH PSYCHOLOGISTS

One critical concern only briefly considered at the Arden House Conference was the availability of appropriate employment opportunities for individuals who have received training in either service delivery or research-focused health psychology. Although we feel that training in health psychology today offers one of the most "marketable" backgrounds for either a clinician or researcher, the career opportunities for individuals trained in health psychology are subject to the vicissitudes of federal research funding and the economics of the health care marketplace. For instance, some speculation has centered on the possibility that as the income of physicians continues to decline in the next decade due to oversupply, some MDs may begin to offer services traditionally considered part of a psychologist's armamentarium (e.g., psychological assessment or biofeedback). Indeed, the present availability of computer-scored test "interpretation" makes the provision of such services by individuals without prior training in psychological assessment a distinct likelihood. As an area closely allied to medicine, any such changes in modes of health service delivery during the next decade will likely be felt acutely by health psychologists.

Conversely, it seems possible that much of the *growth* in employment opportunities for health psychologists in the future may come from business and private industry. Currently, there is a groundswell of interest on the part of private employers in the development of programs to promote employee health through the introduction of programs emphasizing stress reduction, smoking cessation, exercise and diet management, and the like. Indeed, some health insurance carriers have offered a reduction in rates to private employers who provide such services. The health psychologist, perhaps in collaboration with the industrial/organizational psychologist, would seem to offer an almost perfect combination of the skills that would likely be demanded for the introduction and execution of such health-enhancing programs. Although probably only the largest of companies could afford an in-house health psychologist, these programs would seem to offer substantial opportunity for the provision of services on a consultative basis.

Job opportunities in the academic marketplace for health psychologists are also difficult to predict. Because of the readily available access to both client and research populations appropriate to a health psychologist's skills and interests, we feel that the academic worksite of choice for many psychologists with expertise in health psychology will be this nation's medical schools and health science universities. Although recent years have seen an increase in the number of MDs seeking licensure or residencies in the U.S., there has actually been a slight decrease in the number of MDs graduated from American medical schools during the past 5 years. (The discrepancy is accounted for by American graduates of so-called "offshore" medical schools and foreign-born and educated MDs who have emigrated to the U.S.) As might be expected, some U.S. medical schools have found it difficult to justify increasing or sometimes even maintaining their current faculty size while there have been concurrent decreases in the size of the student body. At the present point of what is likely to be a slight trough in the inevitably cyclic pattern of academic employment, it is unclear to us what effect it will have on the growth of independent and autonomous departments of medical or health psychology and their associated new faculty positions in this nation's medical schools. That "health and behavior" constitute a salient force in today's biomedical and behavioral communities is nevertheless obvious throughout the land. We feel certain that as a general trend this interest in behavioral contributions to health will be expressed by the establishment of more such departments.

In the interim, however, the opportunities for academic employment of psychologists in *other* basic or clinical science departments in medical schools and university hospitals has only barely been exploited. At present, for instance, there are only a small handful of psychologists employed in departments of anesthesiology, surgery, and medicine in medical schools throughout the U.S. In recent years, psychologists have been at the forefront of research and clinical practice applied to both the psychological event of pain and nonpharmacologic pain control techniques (Keefe, 1982; Melzack & Wall, 1982). The utilization of both the research and clinical skills of the psychologist with expertise in this area by departments of clinical specialists concerned with problems associated with patient physical pain (and its attendant psychological stress) would seem almost inevitable.

In an analogous manner, the skills of psychologists would seem to have potentially valuable application to both research and clinical issues in the field of obstetrics and gynecology. For instance, the behavior change skills of a psychologist might be applied to a problem such as cigarette smoking or alcohol abuse during pregnancy, or the research expertise of a psychologist might be utilized in studies of the relationship of psychological stress to obstetric outcomes (Istvan, 1986). As one final example of how the skills of a psychologist might be applied to this field, one psychologist colleague of ours has been employed by a department of obstetrics and gynecology to train recent MDs in their residency program in the appropriate manner of conducting a medical history interview that might involve a substantial number of questions with sexual content. By providing these students with feedback concerning their nonverbal and paralinguistic behavior during role-played interviews, trainees develop the skills necessary to obtain open and accurate responses to questions regarding this potentially volatile area.

Also, in addition to these potential new contributions to basic and clinical science in established departments at schools of medicine, there would seem to be substantial opportunity for increases in the number of psychologists employed in schools of public health and dentistry in the U.S. The opportunities for psychologists in these areas have been discussed by Cohen (1981), Matthews and Avis (1982), and Tanabe (1982).

LICENSURE OF HEALTH PSYCHOLOGISTS

At the Arden House meetings, the conferees were generally in agreement that both the health psychology service provider *and* health psychology researcher should obtain the generic license available to all those who have received the doctoral degree in psychology. The necessity for a direct provider of health services to obtain licensure would not seem to require elaboration. However, the need for researchers to possess the same licensure would perhaps not be as obvious to many readers. At least two issues with regard to the licensure of these nonhealth service providers would seem important. First, the familiarity with ethical and legal issues involved in research that is demanded by the licensing examinations would insure that the researcher is aware of the importance these professional issues play in their work. We would emphasize that these ethical and legal issues are just as important in the work of the researcher employing animal models as they are in the efforts of a health psychologist who might primarily or wholly use human subjects in their research. For those who have forgotten, there is a section in the Ethical Principles of Psychologists governing the care and use of animals.

The second point requires slightly more elaboration, and a more complete explication of the issues we feel are involved are provided in Matarazzo (1983). In essence, we feel that health psychology, in common with the more established interest areas, is *not* at present a "specialty area," nor does it hold the prospect of being a specialty area in the near future. There has been some lack of understanding on the part of some psychologists regarding the complex legal and professional issues involved in the acknowledgment by society (both informally and by legal statutes) that a particular field of knowledge and expertise is indeed a "specialty" of a larger field. For instance, as a general issue, specialty training in any discipline involves a mandated period of intensive study of a particular subdiscipline beyond the entry-level degree. Although at the Arden House meetings, the *recommendation* was made that training beyond the entry-level PhD degree be required as a part of the education of a health psychologist, this is not yet as codified or established a procedure for acknowledgment of specialty-area status as that that exists in medicine. Indeed, although many of us who have received training in fields such as social, clinical, or developmental psychology have relabeled ourselves *health psychologists*, this is clearly a matter of self-identification and an indicator of one's professional interests and not an acknowledgment that one possesses a legally sanctioned array of competencies. (Analogously, try to imagine a family practitioner, dermatologist, or psychiatrist publicly relabeling himself or herself as an *orthopedic surgeon*.) Almost without a doubt, there will be little recognition in the worksites that will employ psychologists with training relevant to health problems that a particular psychologist is a "research health psychologist" or "service delivery health psychologist" in contrast to the application to him or her of the generic label of *psychologist*. Indeed, we have yet to encounter a physician colleague in any hospital setting who distinguishes between the "specialty areas" of psychologists. Thus these physician faculty inevitably find it difficult to understand when a "research health psychologist" admits he or she does not possess generic psychology licensure because his or her work "only" involves research. Furthermore, as research by psychologists in such settings moves from investigations involving animal models to humans, the standards and ethics of our profession as well as the relevant legal statutes will require that such psychologists be licensed in order to have the privilege of conducting biobehavioral research involving humans. Licensure is the common denominator of acknowledged competency in the health-related professions, and a psychologist who paints himself or herself with *any* professional stripe will invariably find his or her work in a health-related setting handicapped without this legal confirmation of professional status.

REFERENCES

American Psychological Association, Committee on Training in Clinical Psychology. (1947). Recommended graduate training program in clinical psychology. *American Psychologist, 2*, 539–558.

Belar, C. D., Wilson, E., & Hughes, H. (1982). Health psychology training in doctoral psychology programs. *Health Psychology, 1*, 289–299.

Cohen, L. K. (1981). Dentistry and the behavioral-social sciences: An historical overview. *Journal of Behavioral Medicine, 4*, 247–256.

Istvan, J. (1986). Stress, anxiety, and birth outcomes: A critical review of the evidence. *Psychological Bulletin, 100*, 331–348.

Istvan, J., & Hatton, D. (1987). Curriculum of graduate training programs in health psychology. In G. C. Stone, S. M. Weiss, J. D. Matarazzo, N. E. Miller, J. Rodin, C. D. Belar, M. J. Follick, & J. E. Singer (Eds.), *Health psychology: A discipline and a profession*. Chicago: University of Chicago Press.

Keefe, F. J. (1982). Behavioral assessment and treatment of chronic pain: Current status and future directions. *Journal of Consulting and Clinical Psychology, 50*, 896–911.

Matarazzo, J. D. (1983). Education and training in health psychology: Boulder or bolder. *Health Psychology, 2*, 73–113.

Matarazzo, J. D. (1987). Relationships of health psychology to other segments of psychology. In G. C. Stone, S. M. Weiss, J. D. Matarazzo, N. E. Miller, J. Rodin, C. D. Belar, M. J. Follick, & J. E. Singer (Eds.), *Health psychology: A discipline and a profession*. Chicago: University of Chicago Press.

Matthews, K. A., & Avis, N. E. (1982). Psychologists in schools of public health: Current status, future prospects and implications for other health settings. *American Psychologist, 37*, 949–954.

Melzack, R., & Wall, P. D. (1982). *The challenge of pain*. New York: Basic Books.

Raimy, V. C. (1950). *Training in clinical psychology*. New York: Prentice-Hall.

Tanabe, G. (1982). The potential for public health psychology. *American Psychologist, 37*, 942–944.

7

Evaluating School Psychologists and School Psychological Services

JONATHAN SANDOVAL and NADINE M. LAMBERT

INTRODUCTION

Without question, the practice of evaluating school psychologists is in its infancy. In spite of the fact that a number of articles have appeared on the subject (Bennett, 1980; Fairchild, 1980; Zins, 1984), there is no set methodology or approach to the evaluation of school psychologists that is widespread in the field, that has withstood the test of normal measurement standards, or that even has withstood the test of time in that it has been in use for more than a decade in a particular location. Perhaps this state of affairs exists because the practice of psychology generally is difficult to evaluate. Nevertheless, strides have been made in other fields as are reflected in the other chapters in this volume.

Perhaps the problem lies in the lack of consensus about how school psychologists should behave and what their duties consist of. Efforts are currently afoot to arrive at a job analysis of the school psychologist that may permit the planning of evaluation activities based

JONATHAN SANDOVAL • Department of Education, University of California, Davis, Davis, CA 95616. **NADINE M. LAMBERT** • School of Education, University of California, Berkeley, Berkeley, CA 94720.

on empirical data about what the school psychologist does. Until accurate data about how school psychologists spend their time are available, we must depend on speculation and theorizing.

Another reason for the lack of evaluation procedures for school psychologists may be the fact that the school psychologist serves within the school setting. In this setting, the psychologist often works in a service delivery system where the individual charged most frequently with evaluating the school psychologist is an administrator typically without a background in school psychology. Because administrators in schools are responsible for evaluating school psychologists, school psychologists may have abdicated any responsibility for peer review or other supervisory activities where they might take the initiative in being accountable to their many clients. Much of the literature on which this chapter is based comes from studies of school psychologists in training rather than of professionals in the field. As students or interns, school psychologists are evaluated by school psychologists often for the last time in their professional careers.

The American Psychological Association's (APA) specialty guidelines for the delivery of services by school psychologists (APA Committee on Professional Standards, 1981) are explicit that school psychologists have a definite responsibility to evaluate themselves and their services. Even if there is administrative review in the schools by nonpsychologists, there should be professional service evaluation by self or peers. The mandate for evaluation is multifaceted.

In this chapter, we will attempt to set forth a model for evaluating school psychologists that will have general application to particular school psychologists working in particular settings. We intend first to explicate the history of school psychology and the different models that school psychologists might identify as guiding their service delivery in the schools. We will present a three-dimensional paradigm for the evaluation of school psychological services. Next we will consider the sources of information about practice, the roles that school psychologists might assume within the school setting, and the skills the school psychologist might use to perform the various roles delineated. Although different models may apply to different theories and points of view within the discipline of psychology, all acknowledge some debt to the field of educational psychology. Finally, we hope to identify a useful sequence of strands for applying educational psychology to the practice of school psychology. Evaluation data are best used for the general purpose of improving psychological practices in the schools and increasing the lay public's awareness of the work school psychologists do. Although consumers may be educated about school psychology as a result of careful evaluation, those who will benefit most from improved evaluation practices are school psychologists themselves who will be able to finetune their skills and thus improve their delivery of psychological services in the schools. Children are the ultimate beneficiaries of high-quality school psychological services.

The Early Affiliation of Educational Psychology, School Psychology, and Clinical Psychology

Educational psychology, school psychology, and clinical psychology have common historical origins that span the history of academic and professional psychology through the 20th century. When Edward L. Thorndike joined the faculty of Teachers College as assistant professor of educational psychology early in this century, he ushered in decades of educational research and theory development pertinent to the ways individuals learn and the influence of instruction on learning and individual differences.

His first book, *Educational Psychology*, published in 1903, acknowledged assistance from 2 school superintendents and 10 school principals who had collaborated with him on chapters that included mental testing, exceptional children, and sex differences in ability. In the conclusion, Thorndike proposed that if one defined the nature of those to be educated and what forces influenced the nature of individuals, one would know how to control their education. Believing that there was no chance for any simple general theory, he proposed that each bit of knowledge, each interest, each habit, each power, each ideal, has its own best means of attainment. *Educational Psychology* in three volumes followed 20 years later. These expanded the original work into volumes on human learning, on human's original nature, and on mental work and fatigue and the antecedents of individual differences.

When educational psychology was inaugurated as an area for psychological inquiry, Lightner Witmer, like Thorndike a student of James McKeen Cattell, had already founded the first psychological clinic. He described the psychological clinic as an institution for social and public service, for original research, and for the instruction of students in psychological orthogenics, including vocational, educational, correctional, hygienic, industrial, and social guidance (Korchin, 1982). Both school psychology and clinical psychology claim Lightner Witmer as the father of their professional specialties. Until the middle of the century, around 1946 to 1956, school psychologists and clinical psychologists achieved similar graduate preparation and offered similar psychological services. These early professional psychologists worked in university clinics, school district guidance centers, and special settings for the mentally retarded and physically handicapped. Teaching clinical psychology at the University of California, Los Angeles (UCLA) in the 1930s, 1940s, and 1950s, Grace Fernald founded the psychological clinic that was devoted to developing methods for remedial reading instruction of children and adults who had failed in the regular school programs (Fernald, 1943). The development, standardization, and use of psychological tests to appraise individual differences was a major occupation of school and clinical psychologists. Few of them held doctorates, and most of them gave individual tests, later expanding their testing armamentarium to projective devices and conducting more comprehensive case studies.

The Emergence of the Specialties of Clinical Psychology and School Psychology

The change in orientation from preoccupation with mental abilities and mental testing began in the 1930s when clinical psychologists turned their attention to psychotherapy guided by the emigration of many psychiatrists and psychoanalysts from Europe. Shortly thereafter, the identity of school psychology emerged specifically in the form of state department of education credentials and certificates for educational practice. By the end of World War II, clinical psychologists had become involved primarily in mental health and the treatment of psychological disorders, whereas school psychologists continued to determine the nature of individual differences and to assist schools to cope with handicapped children, the gifted, and those with learning problems. Until the middle of this century, when each specialty identified the clients and services that were to be the center of attention, clinical psychology and school psychology shared a common research and theoretical foundation. Clinical psychology then turned its attention to mental health issues and specified the doctorate as the entry level for practice. Some school psychology programs continued the traditional affiliation with clinical psychology and emphasized clinical training at nondoctoral and doctoral levels for school psychologists who were viewed as the professionals to help schools manage the large numbers of children with behavioral problems and mental health difficulties that were not serious enough for long-term psychotherapy. Other school psychology programs explored new role models for school psychology, and gradually the clinical and school specialties became more differentiated. In addition to an older model of school psychology based on the "common ancestor" of clinical and school psychologies, other movements in psychology, social welfare, and public health began to influence the field of school psychology.

MODELS OF SCHOOL PSYCHOLOGY

At the present time, at least six models for the delivery of school psychological services may be discriminated (Sandoval, 1986). Each differs with respect to primary client, theory drawn upon, goals, and methods.

The Clinical Diagnostic Model

The clinical diagnostic model is one we equate with the "traditional" model of school psychological services. In this model, the school psychologist brings to bear psychological theories and understandings in diagnosing children's problems as they emerge in the process of schooling. Following a diagnosis, the psychologist plans a particular intervention for the child, typically in the form of special education. The major emphasis in this model is diagnosis. Intervention, although important, is secondary and follows from the diagnosis. A number of texts in school psychology implicitly incorporate this model (e.g., Fein, 1974; Gottsegen, 1960; White & Harris, 1961), and the description seems most applicable when the school psychologist is thought of as a clinical psychologist in the schools (Bardon, 1964).

For school psychologists who follow this model, the client is the child with whom they work to determine what difficulties the child is having. Many of those children are candidates for special education services. Although it is not often acknowledged, an important secondary client is the school and regular and special education teachers. The school psychologist becomes intimately involved in the operation of the special education system of the school, and in this diagnostic role he or she serves as a gatekeeper. The clinical school diagnostician works to keep the special education system functioning smoothly by finding clients for it and dismissing clients who are making progress.

The diagnostic model draws primarily on the psychology of individual differences and on psychometric theory. The diagnostician must be knowledgeable about the etiology of various psychological disturbances and be able to identify psychological processes either not operating properly or that are under- or overdeveloped for the child's age. The diagnostic psychologist must be acquainted with developmental theories, learning theory, and personality theory, but the emphasis is usually on pathology rather than on normal learning and development. Part of the theoretical package is differential psychology—notions about children differ with respect to various cognitive, affective, and psychomotor characteristics. Lately, psychologists have been turning to neuroanatomy and neuropsychology (e.g., Hynd & Obrzut, 1981) for explanations of why children have difficulty in school.

According to the clinical diagnostic model, the goals of school psychological services are to create accurate diagnoses of children and prescriptions based on those diagnoses. Following this model, a school psychologist would serve the school best if he or she is able to render a diagnosis and prescription for each child who is encountering difficulty. The diagnostic psychologist aims to respond to referrals quickly and competently and to prepare a report outlining what might be done on the basis of the difficulties in the child that have been uncovered. The principal methods used to accomplish these goals are assessment, including interviewing and observation.

The Prevention–Promotion Model

Many authors have attempted to put forward an alternative to the clinical diagnostic model, a model of the psychologist as a preventive mental health worker (Bardon, 1963; Bower, 1955; Cowen & Lorion, 1976; Lambert, 1965). They offer this model as a solution to the presumed inefficiency of assessment and remediation (Alpert, 1976; Fairchild, 1976; Meyers, 1973). The origins of the approach may be found in the pioneering work in prevention done by public health specialists, particularly the efforts by Lindemann and Caplan at Harvard (Alpert, 1976; Gilmore, 1974). As a result, adherents to this model usually adopt the strategy of mental health consultation, as outlined by Caplan (1970), although other methods are also consistent with this approach (Bower, 1955). The preventionist follows the dictate that a school psychologist is the representative of psychological theory and practice to the educational system. As the knowledgeable expert on psychology, the school psychologist is obliged to find ways to modify school programs to make them responsive to children's needs. If successful, all children will be offered individualized educational programs (primary prevention), children at risk will not fail because they will receive extra assistance (secondary prevention), and those failing will be helped to recover from their difficulties (tertiary prevention) (Bower, 1964).

The preventionist's client varies depending on the activity. In most school settings, the client is the child. Because indirect services are featured, in some sense teachers and administrators are secondary clients because the school psychologist attempts to increase their understanding and objectivity about children through the use of psychological principles. In the prevention model, all children attending school are clients, not just those experiencing difficulty.

The prevention model draws on a number of psychological theories to understand children's problems, but there is a tendency for adherents to draw often on psychodynamic principles in consultation with teachers, parents, and administrators. Theories dealing with the origin of conflicts play an integral part in consultation. In addition, consultation is particularly congruent with various developmental theories because there is an emphasis on facilitating the development of both the client and the consultee. Understanding normal development and acquisition of academic concepts helps one promote the normal acquisition of basic skills in the school setting.

The goal of school psychological services under the prevention model is to improve the functioning of the school staff and in turn, the school, in meeting the needs of all children. Efforts are made to make an entire school community more psychologically minded.

Important methods for the preventionist are consultation, early identification of children at risk, psychological education, crisis counseling, anticipatory guidance, research, and parent education (Bower, 1965). A school psychologist following this model would be evaluated based on these activities.

The Social Learning Model

Few theoretical positions have been as far-reaching in psychology as behaviorism. It was natural that behavioral notions, particularly social learning theory, would soon be taken up by school psychologists.

In this model, the child is the client, although the teacher is often the focus of intervention efforts, and as a result, becomes a secondary client. The psychological theory that is most often drawn on by the behavioral school psychologist is social learning theory particularly as outlined by Bandura. Bandura (1969), Kazdin (1982), and Kratochwill (1982) have provided comprehensive reviews of the behavioral methods and the relevant research.

The goal of the social learning theorist is first to teach teacher and parent consultees to use behavioral strategies and principles, particularly behavior modification. A second goal is to reduce pupils' behavioral problems, defined as behaviors that are deemed inappropriate by others, particularly teachers.

The special methods used by the school psychologist behavioral consultant are teaching behavior modification techniques to teachers and parents and working directly with children to change antecedents or consequences of behavior. Basic principles are reinforcement of correct responses, immediate feedback, maintenance of target behaviors, minimization of incorrect responses, enlistment of the learner's active participation, and allowance for individual differences in learning (Whitman & Whitman, 1971). Other methods used are observation (Alessi, 1980), cognitive restructuring or behavioral self-control (Mahoney & Thoresen, 1974), and interviewing in order to determine various response contingencies and reinforcers (Bersoff & Greiger, 1971; Breyer, Calchera, & Cann, 1971). Not all behavioral approaches, however, are applicable to the school setting (Woody, 1976).

The Organizational Development Model

Articles describing the organizational development model (e.g., Schmuck & Miles, 1971) are unclear as to whether proponents suggest this as a model for school psychological services generally or one particular role that a psychologist might assume in addition to others (Gallessich, 1973; Hannafin & Witt, 1983). Nevertheless, the writers are so clear in delineating important aspects of this model, it is included here separately.

Briefly stated, the organizational development model proposes that the school psychologist's work should be aimed at making the social system of the school operate efficiently in the best interest of its clients, the children. The school psychologist mediates and facilitates communication between relevant subgroups and applies organizational psychology in making the institution humanistic, effective, and democratic. Meyers, Martin, and Hyman (1977) described two types of organizational development: (a) that designed to facilitate the resolution of specific organizational problems such as racial tension, and (b) that designed to focus on general interpersonal and communication problems.

In this model, it is much more clear than in other models that the school system is the client of the school psychologist (Gallessich, 1973; Lennox, Flanagan, & Meyers, 1979). Making the organization a more relevant and effective system serves children; thus the child and parents are secondary clients.

The central psychological theories on which this model is based originate in the work of Lewin (1947) and others interested in field theory, group processes, and ecological psychology. It also draws from

Gestalt psychology as well as humanistic approaches to psychology (Argyris, 1970) that focus on human nature and the importance of relationships between individuals in a social system. Another concept from humanistic psychology is the importance of allowing a client to take an active role in problem solving that influences his or her destiny.

The goal of the organizational school psychologist is to assist the organization of the school to be more efficient in serving children and to make the school more sensitive to children's needs (Reschly, 1976). Important subgoals are to improve communication (Lennox *et al.*, 1979) and to facilitate the overall growth of the organization (Gallessich, 1973). Schmuck (1976) includes the establishment of collective goals, the uncovering of conflict, the importance of group processes, solving organizational problems, making collective decisions, and assessing change.

The methods used in organizational development include interviewing and observation as well as the use of surveys in assessing the functioning of an organization, consultation with key personnel in helping them open up the organization to democratic decision making, and feedback sessions aimed at increasing communication between important members of the organization. Group meetings and training are additional important methods used by organizational school psychologists.

The Prescriptive Intervention Model

This model of school psychological services is one that brings the psychologist's duties closest to those of the educator (Gilmore, 1974). Unlike the diagnostic model, the focus of this model is on gathering information of educational and classroom relevance (Forness, 1970) and delivering this information to multidisciplinary teams creating prescriptions and individual educational plans. Reger (1965) used the term *educational programmer* in an early description of this model.

The difference between the prescriptive intervention model and the diagnostic model is that criterion-referenced assessment is preferred over norm-referenced assessment, and the stress is on responsibility for remediation, even to the extent of directly supervising tutorial personnel (Osguthorpe, 1979).

In this model, the client is primarily the child who benefits from accurate prescriptions in educational settings and secondarily the teacher, although the teacher is the main focus of the prescriptive interventions. This model primarily draws upon the learning theories, particularly classroom learning theories like those of Gagne (1977) that allow the prescriptive educator to specify a learning hierarchy. Other proposals that have come from the notion of learning modalities and perceptual deficits have occasionally been used (Valett, 1969).

The goal of the prescriptive interventionist is to prevent problems from becoming worse in the school setting by the accurate educational assessment of the child's educational needs and the design of educational programs to improve academic and social functioning. The special methods used by the prescriptive interventionist are those within the area of assessment. A prescriptive interventionist relies much more heavily on criterion-referenced tests and measures, makes observations, examines work samples, and orients most of the assessment toward the child's achievement of curriculum goals (Dickinson, 1980). A recently revived method used most by psychologists following this model is trial teaching as a means of assessment (Forness, 1970). The contemporary proponent of this technique is Feuerstein (1979) with his system of instrumental enrichment.

The Child Advocacy Model

The child advocacy model places the school psychologist in the position of working on behalf of the child in a system that is seen as essentially antagonistic to children's needs and best interests. Child advocacy takes two forms (Mearig, 1974). The first is social advocacy or working for children's rights in the public arena and attempting to establish programs that are focused on primary prevention. In addition to social advocacy, child advocate school psychologists are interested in individual advocacy. They see this second form as the psychologist standing up for children and children's rights against all comers—teachers, parents, administrators, or others.

Another distinction in the literature on this model is between (a) change agent or activist, (b) ombudsman or mediator, and (c) child advocate (Catterall & Hinds, 1972; Chesler, Bryant, & Crowfoot, 1976). The first does social advocacy, the second protects the child from the school but also represents the institution (Trachtman, 1971), and the third actively fights for the child specifically.

For the child advocate, the child is the only client. Others in the child's world are seen as potential antagonists and the subject of the school psychologist's advocacy, including parents (Catterall & Hinds, 1972). In the ombudsman role, however, Trachtman (1971) suggests that parents may be the client.

The psychological theories that the child advocate draws upon are those that prescribe the optimal environment in which a child functions. As a result, a child advocate must be familiar with both developmental theory and learning theory. Some special theoretical points of view may come from the notions of how environments can be destructive to children so that theories of learned helplessness and others centering on the ecology of the child's world are of great interest to the child advocate and would be the focus of this kind of school psychologist.

The goals of the child advocate school psychologist are to create a situation in which children may flourish by opposing forces that stifle their development and working to create environments that are healthy for them.

The special methods used by child advocates are those focused on representing the child. Lobbying, using the courts, and the legal system are all part of social advocacy. Individual advocacy draws on methods for being persuasive in fighting for children's rights, including conflict resolution techniques. Learning how to argue, how to use the system on the child's behalf, and fighting for children's rights are all special skills that must be developed by the child advocate.

MODELS OF SCHOOL PSYCHOLOGY SERVICES AND EVALUATION

The first step in the evaluation of a school psychologist or a school psychology delivery system is to specify the model the individual or system is following. Identifying a model results in more explicit goals, duties, and methods and allows priorities to be assigned to their evaluation. If a school psychologist cannot identify a model that describes how he or she functions (and the previously mentioned models are not exhaustive of the field, only the ones that have most frequently appeared in the literature), it is imperative that one carefully describe a coherent set of goals, duties, functions, methods, and theories drawn upon. Next, one would proceed to plan ways of collecting data to determine how well one is complying with the model.

A THREE-DIMENSIONAL PARADIGM FOR EVALUATION

Once a model has been selected to guide the evaluation, attention shifts to a consideration of data collection. We have found the following paradigms useful to guide the construction of data collection devices and procedures. The paradigm, presented in Figure 1, is intended to

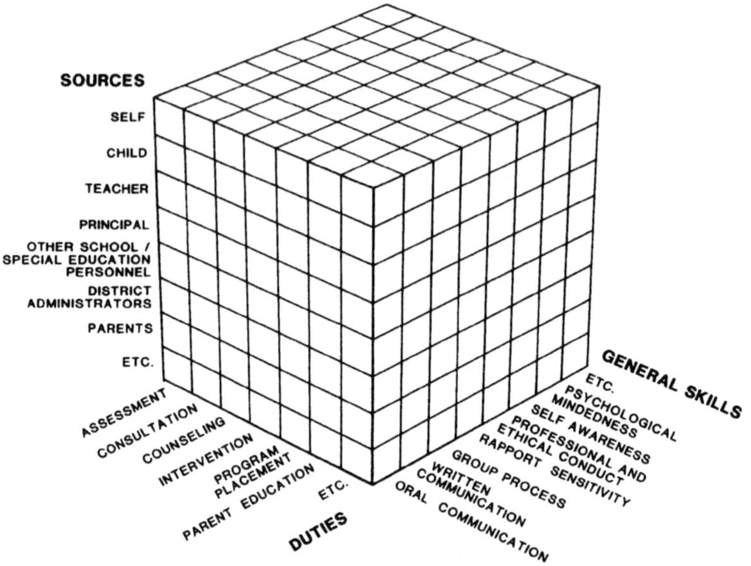

Figure 1. A three-dimensional paradigm for evaluation considering sources, skills, and duties.

represent the universe of decisions to be made about how one might learn about a particular school psychologist's services.

Figure 1 consists of a three-dimensional cube. The three dimensions are sources of evaluation information, duties or roles of school psychologists, and general skills necessary for effective work as a school psychologist. The intersection of the sources, duties, and skills represents one or more items on a data collection device or a basic data point in an evaluation.

The sources of information about the psychologist's performance include the psychologist himself or herself and people with whom the psychologist has worked. The others are children, teachers (both regular and special education), principals, other special education personnel, district administrators, and parents. The list of sources can be expanded or contracted, depending on those with whom the psychologist comes in contact.

The duties that the psychologist performs depend on the model to which he or she subscribes and also may vary from employment setting to employment setting. We have listed in the evaluative paradigm typical duties that school psychologists assume. Duties include assessment, consultation, counseling, intervention with children, program placement, and parent education. Needless to say, the list of duties could be lengthened, or the categories could be differentiated into finer subcategories. The assessment category, for example, might be broken down into screening, group assessment, and individual assessment, and each of these assessment areas might take on different aspects depending on services being evaluated. The skills listed on the skills dimension also are subject to interpretation, refinement, and expansion. The ones listed in the figure are individual oral communication, written communication, group facilitation, rapport sensitivity, professional-ethical judgment, self-awareness and openness to supervision, and psychological mindedness. Regardless of the duty performed, the school psychologist must have good interpersonal working relationships as well as knowledge translated into professional skills.

If one wished to use the top slice of the cube in an evaluation, one would develop an instrument to collect information from the psychologists themselves, that is, a self-assessment. Topics on the self-assessment device would focus on assessment that would include the oral communication skills, the written communication skills, the group communication skills, the rapport building, the ethical behavior, the self-awareness, and the ability to apply psychological theory that is involved in the assessment process. Continuing across would lead one to consider topics examining individual communications in consultation, written records of consultation, group consultation skills, sensitivity to consultees as well as professional, ethical, and other skills involved in consultation. One would continue on across the slice of the cube. Having a complete model causes one to consider a universe of possible items for data collection devices. One may reject a cell as not producing a topic relevant to a particular model or employment setting, however. For example, some school psychologists may not be involved in group screening or group assessment experiences, either not viewing these activities as important or not having sanction from the school district to do them.

The Source Dimension

Sources of information about a school psychologist's functioning may be either direct or indirect. Direct sources include those who are in a position to witness the school psychologist's behaviors on the job. Indirect sources are those who receive the benefits of the school psychologist's activities but who are relatively naive about the profession.

Direct Sources. The major direct sources are the psychologist, the psychologist's peers, supervisors, or others who are knowledgable about the field and who can observe the psychologist's functioning. Sources may gather information about the psychologist in both artificial and naturalistic settings.

Miller and Engin (1974) described an imagined evaluation center to which district school psychologists might report in order to be evaluated by experts. Braden (1985) recently produced an expanded version of this idea in a proposal for a school psychologist's assessment center. Unfortunately, such centers are not widely available, and no data are available to evaluate the effectiveness of such a regional center. In the proposed center, a school psychologist would undertake simulations produced by computer and videocassette that would test theory application and decision making. The subject would also engage in role playing and writing so that by the end of the day, the evaluation team would have a record of responses, videotaped observations, and other work products generated by responses to artificially generated everyday referrals.

Obviously such a center for psychologists would be expensive to establish and finance. Nevertheless, the technology does exist, and the methods of simulation have been shown to have utility in other settings (see Chapter 9 in this volume).

Collecting direct sources of information in naturalistic settings creates a number of problems, the greatest of which are ethical in nature. Observing psychologists working with clients or consultees creates great risks of influencing negatively the process under observation. Even if the psychologist is not anxious about being scrutinized, the client may well be or may not have entered into the relationship expecting to be observed. Protecting confidentiality of information becomes quite important.

If there are problems observing psychologists doing testing, counseling, and consultation, it is less of a problem observing the school psychologist in other roles. Observation during parent or inservice education or during special education interdisciplinary team meetings would not be intrusive. Also, the written products of the psychologist's work can be reviewed.

One example of such a review exists in the literature. Rosenfeld and Blanco (1974) reported a case in which a team of expert school psychologists in Pennsylvania reviewed the work of Dr. Gestalt, a school psychologist charged with incompetence. Among other data, the evaluators reviewed the raw data and reports written on 181 children during the 9 months prior to the evaluation. Although in this instance the evaluation team made relatively subjective judgments about the psychologist's behaviors against what they held to be best practice, other methods could be used to objectify the process. It is clear, however, that such a review is exceedingly time consuming and expensive; it is most likely to occur when an important or difficult decision must be made such as to terminate a professional in the face of stringent tenure laws.

Another method of collecting data in situ is using logs of the daily activities of school psychologists. Fairchild (1974, 1975) has written on this procedure and detailed a system for recording activities related to assessment, intervention, evaluation, consultation, and administration. The problem with such logs is that although it is possible to establish what it is the psychologist does with his or her time, one does not get an idea of the quality of the services delivered. Nevertheless, the use of logs might well supplement other sources of information in a comprehensive evaluation plan.

Peer review has become well established in a number of fields of professional psychology (Stricker, Claiborn, & Bent, 1982) but has not yet been developed for school psychologists. The imperative of review for third-party payment is one factor absent in school psychology that is present for other mental health workers. It is time for the field of school psychology to look to other areas of professional psychology for guidance in this direction. We might do well to imitate their successes and avoid their failures.

A much less expensive solution to the collection of direct data in naturalistic settings is to use self-study. The two professional organizations, the National Association of School Psychologists and the Division of School Psychology of APA, have worked hard at producing materials for continuing professional education. One option for implementing professional development is through the use of self-evaluation and study (Rosenfeld, 1981). The effective use of self-study materials in an evaluation demands that the materials have content validity and be designed to elicit accurate appraisals but also that the psychologist respond without defensiveness. A popular feature of a number of magazines is the self-quiz of the ten-questions-to-test-you-on-your-effectiveness-as-a-parent sort. If self-study can be done in a relatively unthreatening environment and coupled with an opportunity to remedy any deficiencies discovered, it has great potential as an evaluative tool.

Indirect Sources. School administrators, teachers, children, and parents all have evidence of a school psychologist's effectiveness or demonstrate through change in their behaviors that a school psychologist has done his or her work with skill. They may not realize that changes in their own attitudes and behavior have occurred, and these changes may be only remotely linked to the school psychologist; nevertheless they are important sources of evaluative data.

A number of authorities have suggested the use of the perceptions of indirect sources (Clair & Kiraly, 1971; Conti & Bardon, 1974; Fairchild, 1974, 1975; Sandoval & Lambert, 1977). Administrators, teachers, parents, and children are more objective than the school psychologist or a supervisor in many cases and are the primary and secondary clients whom the school psychologist serves. Customer satisfaction has always been an important means of evaluating any service or product.

One important group of consumers are teachers. Bennett (1980) believed that teachers are not particularly good sources of information about school psychologists because their perceptions are inconsistent with judgments made by school psychologists and supervisors and therefore may lack concurrent validity. He believes that teacher judgments are affected more by personality characteristics of the psychologists than by their ability to deliver effective services.

In spite of these problems, teachers do have information about how school psychologists perform. The challenge is to develop ways to circumvent the measurement difficulties. We have created a number of approaches to collecting teacher data (Sandoval & Lambert, 1977), but they have not been cross-validated in other studies. Conti and Bardon (1974), Fairchild (1975), Martin, Duffey, and Fischman (1973), and Waters (1973) also have generated teacher questionnaires, but these efforts also have not been used in settings other than the original studies.

Those suggesting the use of administrators as sources of information (e.g., Clair & Kiraly, 1971) do so because they believe that administrators are both fair and accustomed to evaluation. In addition, administrators' perceptions seem to correspond to school psychologists' perceptions (Hughes, 1979). Examples of data collection from administrators are relatively scarce in the literature, however.

Other potentially rich sources that have not often been tapped in school psychology evaluations are parents and children. It would not be difficult to devise questionnaires for use with both. Conti and Bardon (1974) have given some suggestions for the content and format of such questionnaires.

It seems logical to consider that changes in the behavior of children and, in the evaluation of consultation, of teachers would be the most rigorous test of a school psychologist's effectiveness. Although a number of authors recommend this criterion (Fairchild, 1975; Tomlinson, 1973, 1974), Reilly, Barclay, and Culbertson (1977) dismiss this focus as impractical because of costs and the time needed and because so many factors beside the school psychologist's intervention may be influencing change or lack of change. In addition, Bennett (1980) argues that there are parallels between holding psychologists responsible for client change and holding teachers accountable for changes in pupil test scores, a practice long deplored.

Tomlinson's (1973, 1974) approach to accountability based on client change involved specifying for each case one or more target behaviors. In a follow-up, he determined from teachers whether or not interventions were implemented and whether or not behavior subsequently changed. Although this system is subject to a number of criticisms, it was an effort to collect data in a relatively innovative manner for our field, although this methodology is more common in applied behavior analysis.

The Roles Dimension

Each of the roles broadly listed in the roles dimension have been discussed in some length in the school psychology literature. The roles listed are similar to the ones outlined by Clair and Kiraly (1971), Catterall (1973) and Fairchild (1974), and are related to the roles mentioned in the Specialty Guidelines for the Delivery of Services by School Psychologists (APA Committee on Professional Standards, 1981). Once again this list is not exhaustive of all of the roles a school psychologist might play but rather stands as a representative set. Roles or functions are very much determined by the model followed as well as local sanctions.

Assessment. A lot has been written about the evaluation of school psychologists' functioning in assessment. Because this role is by far the most prominent one, it seems reasonable that attention has been given to the establishment of competencies in testing, particularly in administering individual intelligence tests. Both Warren and Brown (1973) and Boehm, Duker, Haesloop, and White (1974) have developed checklists for evaluating a number of errors in test administration that could be determined from an examination of a completed protocol. Errors in administration procedures, recording responses, application of scoring criteria, transferring data, calculation of totals, and converting scores can all be evaluated. Other investigators have established the typical mechanical scoring errors made by Wechsler Intelligence Scale for Children-Revised (WISC-R) examiners (Miller & Chansky, 1972; Miller, Chansky, & Gredler, 1970).

Fantuzzo, Sisemore, and Spradlin (1983) have reported on a checklist for the WISC-R be used by observers through a one-way mirror, a procedure that permits an assessment of such factors as the establishment of rapport and proper questioning of a child's responses. Conti and Bardon (1974) and Zins (1984) have described checklists for judging the quality of test reports.

Special problems occur when the subject of assessment is not competent in the English language. Figueroa, Sandoval, and Merino (1984) have developed a set of competencies for school psychologists working with children with limited English proficiency focusing on various aspects of the assessment process. These may be used in an evaluation of psychologists working with this population.

Consultation. The most extensive work in the evaluation of the consultation role has been done by those following a behavioral model. Kratochwill and Bergan (1978) have written about the competencies needed by school psychologists doing behavioral consultation. Some support for this set of competencies comes from the studies of Bergan and Tombari (1975, 1976) who evaluated the consultation skills of 11 school psychologists through the examination of service efficiency, flexibility in applying psychological principles, and sensitivity in interviewing. Their research is the most extensive data base on the process of behavioral consultation.

Other researchers have reported evaluations based on other models of consultation. We have reported on teacher perceptions of consultants using a mental health consultation approach (Lambert, Sandoval, & Corder, 1975) as has Gutkin, Singer, and Brown (1980). Stewart and Medway (1978) have discussed approaches to accountability for those following this model. Most recently, Zins (1984) has produced a consultation services questionnaire but has not reported on its use in an evaluation.

Counseling. Although counseling is a role that is usually mentioned in connection with school psychology, very little has been written explicitly on this topic for school psychologists. The chapter in this volume on counseling provides a source of information on the evaluation of counseling that might be relevant for school psychologists.

Specific counseling roles for school psychologists include vocational counseling for exceptional children (Hohenshil & Warden, 1978) and group counseling using structured psychoeducational materials such as the Magic Circle (Bessell & Palomares, 1967). Competencies and objectives from the literature on these topics might be used to guide evaluations of these functions.

One counseling function of school psychologists is crisis counseling and intervention for elementary and secondary schoolchildren

(Sandoval, 1985a). Evaluations aimed at this role might focus on some of the generic crisis counseling skills described by Sandoval (1985b).

Intervention. Studies of the school psychologist's function of planning changes in pupils' educational programs have typically focused on the efficiency of the decision-making process. Fairchild (1974, 1975) recommended keeping a record of the amount of time between referral and the completion of a report containing recommended interventions. McDermott (1977) measured the amount of time taken by psychologists in reaching a diagnostic decision based on case study data. These are intriguing efforts, but the correlation between speed and accuracy or quality is not always high.

Zins (1984) produced a 10-item questionnaire on referral services that was used in an effort to provide data to psychologists and administrators on the usefulness of psychological interventions. In a similar effort, Maher (1980a) produced a checklist for determining the completeness of a program developed by a special service team.

Program Placement and Evaluation. The individual who has written the most about the school psychologist as program evaluator is Charles Maher (1980b). His writings contain lists of competencies on this topic. Maher and Kratochwill (1980) provided an overview of this topic that may be used for the basis of an evaluation.

Research. Several types of research may be conducted by school psychologists. Reynolds, Gutkin, Elliott, and Witt (1984) discussed 8 broad categories and 16 finer categories based on research published in the leading journals for school psychologists. But not all research done by school psychologists finds its way into press. Often requests are made by school district administrators for research on the effectiveness of a new curriculum package, on the achievement gains made by children from different groups, on the effectiveness of special education programs, and on a variety of other questions. Research of this type might be reviewed by other psychologists in the school district or could be submitted to external evaluators for their comments. If the research products are not to remain within the school district for the use of district personnel but are instead to be distributed widely, such as at regional or national conferences or through publication in a book or journal, there can be direct evaluation of the research efforts by those who attend the conference or by the comments of reviewers when the manuscripts are submitted for publication. As many school psychologists do not do research in their school district jobs, perhaps a direct and unobtrusive measurement device is the simple count of the research efforts made by a school psychologist over a designated period of time.

The Skills Dimension

It is difficult to discuss skills out of context. Nevertheless, there are skills possessed by school psychologists that are used in a variety of roles; we will review them here briefly in an attempt to encourage a comprehensive approach to evaluation.

Written Communication. All professionals must write. They must communicate to other professionals, leave a record of their work, or explain their practice to a lay audience. The normal standards of good English usage can be applied to their work, but additional effort is necessary to learn if they have communicated clearly and accurately to their intended audience. We have observed that the largest problem school psychologists have in their writing is an excessive use of jargon.

Conti and Bardon (1974) suggested the use of a Likert questionnaire to evaluate school psychologists' test reports, the most common writing they do. Unfortunately, their measure contains some rather vague items such as "dwelt upon the obvious," and one would anticipate the questionnaire may not have good interrater reliability. The evaluation of school psychologists' writing will need to be content-specific in that test reports will need to be looked at differently from letters to parents or reports to school boards. The ultimate test is clarity of communication, which can only be obtained by asking questions to the recipients of the writings.

Oral Communication. The effectiveness of the school psychologist's spoken communication needs also to be examined. Conti and Bardon (1974) have observed the importance of looking at how pupils hear and understand the psychologist's communications. School psychologists speak to groups as well as individuals and to other professionals as well as laymen. Although there will be some relationship, the effectiveness of oral communication to a group of parents and teachers is based on different factors than a communication to a child before testing. Most of the considerations present in the evaluation of writing will apply to the evaluation of speaking.

Professional Behavior. Most evaluations of workers include an examination of the mundane traits of punctuality, dependability, and appearance. These, along with ethical behavior, make up the category of professional behavior. The two are grouped together because such behaviors contribute to the psychologist being perceived as trustworthy by clients and by the community at large. Professional organizations have expressed their concern about gaining public trust by creating and adopting codes of ethics. Stressed in the codes are responsibility, competence, attention to legal and moral standards, public statements, confidentiality, and other issues where professionals in the past, by their actions, have caused harm to their clients and to the profession. These codes of ethics describe behaviors that may form the core of an evaluation of professional behavior. Davis and Sandoval (1982) explicated a number of special ethical considerations for school-based consultants.

Although not in codes of ethics, punctuality, tendency to follow up on committments, appearance, and openness (as appropriate) all contribute to establish that a professional can be trusted and is competent. As a result, they should not be cavalierly discarded for evaluations.

Self-Awareness. By self-awareness we do not mean some deep philosophical predisposition but rather the ability to note accurately what the effects of one's behavior are on others. Such a self-monitoring skill is what enables a professional to grow and change and what facilitates effective supervision. The inclination to review what has occurred and to consider alternatives does not always come naturally, nor is the exploration of professional weaknesses a very pleasant activity. Another term for this skill might be *openness to supervision*, but self-awareness was chosen as being more general. It may be, however, that this skill can only be assessed by supervisors during the process of supervision.

Group Process. One of the changes wrought by the Education for All Handicapped Children Act (PL 94-142) has been that the school psychologist now functions frequently as a member of an interdisciplinary team where group decisions are made. Skill in making this group function smoothly and efficiently is essential, as are skills associated with promoting the goals of counseling and consultation groups, parent and teacher instructional groups, and other groups with which the school psychologist comes in contact. Group process skills include summarizing, structuring, releasing tension, and a host of others found in texts on that topic.

Interpersonal Skills. Obviously, interpersonal skills are important when working with an individual. Usually these skills are captured in the word *rapport* when it is applied to testing, counseling, and consultation. Carkhuff and his colleagues have been researching the Rogerian concepts of nonpossessive warmth and have developed a set of behaviors to facilitate the experience of being understood and appreciated by a client (Egan, 1986). Behaviors such as active listening and physical attention can be evaluated, as Carkhuff has shown.

Psychological Mindedness. Psychological mindedness refers to the propensity to perceive situations and solve problems using psychological principles and theories. Rather than learning a set of tricks of the trade or a set of techniques to be applied blindly, an effective applied psychologist works at applying the discipline to the tasks at hand. Individuals rely on psychology to a different extent in their practice, and we assume that effective professionals are more adept at drawing on theory than are hacks. Very little has been written on this topic in the school psychological literature. In the next section, we will speculate on how psychological mindedness develops and changes over time in professionals.

DEVELOPMENTAL STRANDS FOR EVALUATING CHANGES IN SCHOOL PSYCHOLOGISTS OVER TIME

The usual evaluation focus on roles and skills of school psychologists based on direct and indirect sources of information often has no scale of measurement representing a continuum of development of competence for the individual being evaluated. Implicit in the notion that school psychologists are grounded in a scientific knowledge base that they apply to various service delivery roles and skills is that one ought to be able to assess the extent to which psychological science or psychological theories are evident in the school psychologist's work and the degree to which the application of these theories has been acquired. School psychologists and other professional psychologists must first learn the theoretical material, next learn the types of behaviors or situations to which a particular theoretical and competing theoretical explanations are applicable, and then show through their professional behavior that their services reflect increasingly more sophisticated application of psychological knowledge. This developmental sequence of the application of psychological knowledge to professional practice has not been delineated in the literature, but any professor who has guided students in acquiring a knowledge of theory and learning to apply it to research and practice has at hand a number of observations that are relevant to the evaluation of the psychologist's development over time.

We believe that it is time to set forth some possibilities for evaluating the growth of competence in the application of psychological science to school psychological practice. Bardon (1982) proposed that school psychologists should become applied educational psychologists. From its inception in 1965, the school psychology program at Berkeley was designed to prepare students to apply behavioral science theory to assessment, intervention, consultation, and research on children in the school setting. From our observations over 20 years, we are now able to set forth some examples of observable developmental changes of school psychologists in training (and we assume that these developmental changes continue as students enter practice in the field). We provide here three examples of developmental sequences that are related to assessment and educational planning, teacher or parent education, and school-based research.

Developmental Strand for Applying Psychological Theories to Assessment

Keeping in mind that the following hierarchy of skills is presented as an observable but not necessarily fully refined continuum, we propose that school psychologists who become competent in applications of psychological theory to assessment will develop sequentially as follows:

1. Uses a psychological or individual difference perspective to explain observations and reports of functioning of individuals in the school setting
2. Uses the appropriate diagnostic psychological procedure in professional practice
3. Reports the results of an appropriate use of psychological procedures in an objective manner so that others can replicate the application
4. The following items seem to be interchangeable types of evidence of the ability to analyze the relationship between specific behavior and general theory:
   a. Identifies relevant theoretical explanations for behavior and suggests ways to determine what theory or theories are most applicable to the behavior in question
   b. Given a referral by a teacher or observations in the classroom, can explain behavior from a theoretical perspective
   c. Given a theoretical perspective, can identify behavior of children or teachers that are illustrative of aspects of that theory
5. Using a theoretical perspective, can make an objective interpretation of strengths and weaknesses in an individual's performance on a battery of test results and/or systematic observations to diagnose individual educational problems

These skills in applying theory to assessment may be evaluated prior to becoming a school psychologist as well as during one's professional career. Each model of school psychologist service delivery assumes skill in applying one or more theories to practice. In addition to evaluation designs that center on specific roles and skills, it can be hypothesized that the individual school psychologist's skills with respect to the development of an ability to use and apply theory to practice will be reflected in the evaluation outcomes. In other words, one can hypothesize that the more "developed" the psychologist, the more positive the evaluation outcomes will be.

Developmental Strand for Teaching the Relevant Psychological Theories in Parent and Teacher Education

The goal of most parent and teacher education programs is to inform the learner about what psychology has to say about the selected topic behavior to be discussed in the program. Many parents as well as teachers are informed somewhat about contemporary psychological theories and research through newspapers, magazines, and other popular sources. The school psychologist's task often is to identify the relevant psychological perspective, to discuss the scientific evidence supporting that perspective, and to show how it might apply in several circumstances. Often the school psychologist may find himself or herself debunking popular notions such as that left-handed children have learning disabilities, poor large motor coordination suggests that a child is brain-damaged, or that a pure phonics method is the best instructional approach for all children to learn to read. It takes well-developed professional skills to assess the entry-level understanding of the parent or teacher group in order to know what knowledge they bring to the program; nevertheless, the extent to which the school psychologist can succeed in assessing entry knowledge of participants and in educating parents or teachers about those psychological theories that are applicable as well as the research evidence supporting the relevant theories is a critical test of parent and teacher education competence.

Some of the observable steps in the development of the psychologist as an educator who is able to organize material for presentation might be the following:

1. Defines operationally the phenomena of interest to the group so that a search can be made of the relevant literature
2. Identifies and summarizes the most salient research findings on a particular educational topic
3. Identifies the major factors that account for individual differences of sources of variation in the phenomenon (or variable of interest) based on an analysis of the research literature

4. Given a theoretical perspective that provides a robust explanation of the topic, can identify supporting evidence from a variety of research findings as well as from the everyday experience of the members of the parent or teacher education class
5. Given two or more competing theoretical perspectives, evaluates research articles and the experiences and observations of the class to select the theory with the best empirical evidence for the issue in question
6. Given research that is designed to test a particular theoretical perspective, presents a critical review of the research in terms of the strength of its support for the theory and proposes follow-up activities that the psychologist and/or the class members may perform that would illuminate the appropriateness of a particular perspective
7. Knowledgeably critiques the relationship between relevant theoretical constructs and the variables designed to measure them
8. Given two or more competing or complimentary theoretical perspectives, organizes the research literature to propose a merger of the two theories or a modification of one or the other that provides a better explanation of the phenomenon in question
9. Based on comprehensive examination of the literature, proposes a new theoretical perspective to explain educational phenomena that has the potential for robust explanatory power

Teachers and parents participating in educational programs offered by school psychologists may be able to master understanding of Steps 1 through 4 or 5 assuming that the school psychologist has control over the material that is being presented and is able to make suitable translations of the material for the level of understanding of the class members. A school psychologist who assumes a position of supervisor of school psychological services or a post as a college professor in a school psychology program might be able to show evidence of mastery of all of the proposed levels. Certainly, one would expect that a journeyman school psychologist's understanding of the theoretical and research literature appropriate to a particular issue regarding children or their classroom programs would demonstrate competence in Steps 1 through 5. One suspects, however, that programs that emphasize only the development of professional skills, not the development of the theoretical and empirical knowledge base for psychology, would graduate students into practice who might be competent at disseminating their knowledge at only Steps 1 through 2 or 3. This proposed competence hierarchy can be used to test the assumption that school psychology graduates of scientist professional doctoral programs use psychological knowledge in different ways than those with master's-level or specialist-level preparation. Further, it is assumed with respect to evaluating school psychologist service delivery that services of the more highly developed school psychologists would be reflected in the outcomes of the evaluation process.

Developmental Strand for Acquiring Competence in Conducting Research on Educational Topics

Practicing school psychologists often complain that there is little time in their weekly schedule of responsibilities for any type of research effort. Other school psychologists, seemingly with similar workloads, manage to prepare papers for delivery at conferences and occasionally are successful in having these papers published in newsletter or journal outlets. It seems reasonable to assume that the extent of research by practicing school psychologists is jointly a function of the ways research is perceived by educators in the school system as well as of the school psychologist's own development abilities to conduct research on educational problems. Moreover, for those school psychologists who are students in graduate programs or those who are university professors, attainment of research competence is a necessity. The following developmental continuum identifies some of the observable steps through which psychologists move as they acquire independent skills in conducting research on educational topics:

1. Describes educational phenomena in objective, reliable ways
2. Uses appropriate psychological methods for measuring phenomena related to education
3. Accurately describes the relationship between two educational phenomena
4. Contrasts the powers of two independent variables to explain an educational phenomenon
5. Contrasts the explanatory power of two independent variables and can identify the underlying constructs that are responsible for, or the theories that explain, the findings
6. Designs a study to test a theoretical statement about an educational phenomenon, carries out the study, and expands or modifies the theory as a result of the research
7. Given two competing theoretical explanations of an educational phenomenon, designs a study to test the application of the theories; expands, modifies, eliminates, or combines one or more theoretical perspectives on the basis of the results

8. Based on innovative research work, proposes a theory to explain an educational phenomenon, and provides supportive evidence from original research on the topic

The articles submitted to journal editorial boards reflect this continuum very well. Often there are reports of correlations between two variables without satisfactory explanation of the underlying construct (Step 3) that are usually rejected for publication. An article that could be recommended for publication, for example, reports the merits of two competing theoretical perspectives such as a developmental or learning perspective in research on learning to do simple subtraction (Step 6).

In this competence continuum as well as with the others proposed before, the assumption is that school psychologists develop throughout their careers, beginning with their undergraduate work in psychology, continuing through study, research, and practice in school psychology programs at the graduate level, and in their professional careers. Evaluation of school psychologists and school psychological service delivery systems usually center attention on evaluating services and do not inquire as to the nature of the developed abilities of the school psychologists who offer the services. If we are to give serious consideration to continuing education for school psychologists, evaluation systems might center attention on both psychological services offered as well as the characteristics of the scientific and professional knowledge base of school psychologists and the ways they apply it to practice.

DESIGNING CUSTOM EVALUATIONS

Once the evaluator has selected a model of school psychological services, has considered the matrix of roles and skills for competencies, and has decided on what sources to use, the design of the evaluation should be fairly straightforward. The usual data collection device is a questionnaire, although, as mentioned, other sources of information are possible. Supervisors, for example, may wish to conduct structured interviews based on the items chosen. A large variety of models for constructing questionnaires ranging from traditional Likert scales through semantic differentials (Sandoval & Lambert, 1977) may be found in the literature. The model, the source, the role, and the skill all delineate a series of item contents. We must also remember that the professional school psychologist is in the process of continuing to develop and take this factor into account in the design.

A good data collection plan gathers data from more than one source yet attempts to cover as many roles and skills as are possible and appropriate. There may be an advantage to include in the data collection questions about roles that the psychologist may not be currently assigned. In this way, the respondent learns about possible activities the psychologist may undertake in the future.

CONCLUSION

We have sought in this chapter to present some dimensions on which choices may be made in the planning of the evaluation of school psychologists and school psychological services. We have intended to cover the probable universe of evaluation decisions but recognize that each dimension is overly finite. Surely there are other models of school psychological service. We may have omitted important sources of information. No doubt there are additional roles and functions school psychologists perform and unidentified general skills we have not included. Not all of the developmental strands have been identified, and the stages within a strand have not been subjected to empirical verification. Nevertheless, we believe the system we have proposed will lead to the collection of important data about school psychologists. Data are important to stimulate personal change in the profession, to test different models of service, and to make decisions that will identify best practices and that will provide the public with information about the cost-effectiveness of psychological services in the schools. We hope the system presented will stimulate others to do more evaluative research and to face the challenges confronting the profession for accountability.

REFERENCES

Alessi, G. J. (1980). Behavioral observation for the school psychologist: Responsive-discrepancy model. *School Psychology Review, 9*, 31–45.

Alpert, J. L. (1976). Conceptual bases of mental health consultation in the schools. *Professional Psychology, 7*, 619–625.

American Psychological Association Committee on Professional Standards. (1981). Specialty guidelines for the delivery of services by school psychologists. *American Psychologist, 36*, 620–681.

Argyris, C. (1970). *Intervention theory and method: A behavioral science view*. Reading, MA: Addison-Wesley.

Bandura, A. (1969). *Principles of behavior modification*. New York: Holt, Rinehart & Winston.

Bardon, J. I. (1963). Mental health education: A framework for psychological services in the schools. *Journal of School Psychology, 1*(1), 20–27.

Bardon, J. I. (1964). Summary of views presented to the conference. *Journal of School Psychology, 3*(2), 6–14.

Bardon, J. I. (1982). School psychology's dilemma: A proposal for its resolution. *Professional Psychology, 13*, 955–968.

Bennett, R. (1980). Methods for evaluating the performance of school psychologists. *School Psychology Monograph, 4*, 45–59.

Bergan, J. R., & Tombari, M. L. (1975). The analysis of verbal interactions occurring during consultation. *Journal of School Psychology, 13*, 209–226.

Bergan, J. R., & Tombari, M. L. (1976). Consultant skill and efficiency and the implementation and outcomes of consultation. *Journal of School Psychology, 14*, 3–14.

Bersoff, D. N., & Greiger, R. M. (1971). An interview model for the psychosituational assessment of children's behavior. *American Journal of Orthopsychiatry, 41*, 483–493.

Bessell, H., & Palomares, U. (1967). *Methods in human development*. San Diego, CA: Human Development Training Institute.

Boehm, A. E., Duker, J., Haesloop, M. D., & White, M. A. (1974). Behavioral objectives in training for competence in the administration of individual intelligence tests. *Journal of School Psychology, 12*, 150–157.

Bower, E. M. (1955). The school psychologist. *Bulletin of the California State Department of Education, 24*(12).

Bower, E. M. (1964). Psychology in the schools: Conceptions, processes and territories. *Psychology in the Schools, 1*, 3–11.

Bower, E. M. (1965). Primary prevention of mental and emotional disorders: A frame of reference. In N. M. Lambert (Ed.), *The protection and promotion of mental health in schools* (pp. 1–9). Mental Health Monograph 5. Bethesda, MD: U.S. Department of Health, Education and Welfare.

Braden, J. P. (1985, April). *Using assessment center methodology for assessing school psychologists*. Paper presented at the meeting of the National Association of School Psychology, Las Vegas, Nevada.

Breyer, N. L., Calchera, D. J., & Cann, C. (1971). Behavioral consulting from a distance. *Psychology in the Schools, 8*, 172–176.

Caplan, G. (1970). *Theory and practice of mental health consultation*. New York: Basic Books.

Catterall, C. D. (1973). A competency based school psychology internship. *Journal of School Psychology, 11*, 269–275.

Catterall, C. D., & Hinds, R. (1972). Child advocate-emerging role for the school psychologist. *The School Psychology Digest, 1*, 14–22.

Chesler, M. A., Bryant, B. I., & Crowfoot, J. E. (1976). Consultation in schools: Inevitable conflict, partisanship, and advocacy. *Professional Psychology, 7*, 637–645.

Clair, T., & Kiraly, J. (1971). Accountability for the school psychologist. *Psychology in the Schools, 8*, 318–321.

Conti, A., & Bardon, J. I. (1974). A proposal for evaluating the effectiveness of psychologists in the schools. *Psychology in the Schools, 11*, 32–37.

Cowen, E. L., & Lorion, R. P. (1976). Changing roles for the school mental health professional. *Journal of School Psychology, 14*, 131–138.

Davis, J. M., & Sandoval, J. (1982). Applied ethics for school-based consultants. *Professional Psychology, 13*, 543–551.

Dickinson, (1980). The direct assessment: An alternative to psychometric testing. *Journal of Learning Disabilities, 13*, 472–476.

Egan, G. (1986). *The skilled helper* (3rd ed.). Monterey, CA: Brooks/Cole.

Fairchild, T. W. (1974). An analysis of the services performed by a school psychologist in an urban area: Implications for training programs. *Psychology in the Schools, 11*, 275–281.

Fairchild, T. W. (1975). Accountability: Practical suggestions for school psychologists. *Journal of School Psychology, 13*, 149–159.

Fairchild, T. W. (1976). School psychological services: An empirical comparison of two models. *Psychology in the Schools, 13*, 156–162.

Fairchild, T. W. (1980). STEPPS: A model for the evaluation of school psychological services. *School Psychology Review, 9*, 252–258.

Fantuzzo, J. W., Sisemore, T. A., & Spradlin (1983). A competency-based model for teaching skills in the administration of intelligence tests. *Professional Psychology: Research and Practice, 14*, 224–231.

Fein, L. G. (1974). *The changing school scene: Challenge to psychology.* New York: Wiley.

Fernald, G. (1943). *Remedial techniques in basic school subjects.* New York and London: McGraw-Hill.

Feuerstein, R. (1979). *The dynamic assessment of retarded performers.* Baltimore: University Park Press.

Figueroa, R., Sandoval, J., & Merino, B. (1984). School psychologists and limited English-proficient (LEP) children: New competencies. *Journal of School Psychology, 22*, 131–143.

Forness, S. R. (1970). Educational prescription for the school psychologist. *Journal of School Psychology, 8*, 96–98.

Gagne, R. M. (1977). *The conditions of learning* (3rd. ed.). New York: Holt, Rinehart & Winston.

Gallessich, J. (1973). Organizational factors influencing consultation in schools. *Journal of School Psychology, 11*, 57–65.

Gilmore, G. E. (1974). Models for school psychology: Dimensions, barriers and implications. *Journal of School Psychology, 12*, 95–101.

Gottsegen, M. G. (1960). The role of the school psychologist. In M. G. Gottsegen & G. B. Gottsegen (Eds.), *Professional school psychology* (pp. 2–17). New York: Grune & Stratton.

Gutkin, T., Singer, J. H., & Brown, R. (1980). Teacher reactions to school-based consultation services: A multivariate analysis. *Journal of School Psychology, 18*, 126–134.

Hannafin, M. J., & Witt, J. C. (1983). System intervention and the school psychologist: Maximizing interplay among roles and functions. *Professional Psychology, 14*, 128–136.

Hohenshil, T. H., & Warden, P. (1978). The emerging vocational school psychologist: Implications for special needs youth. *The School Psychology Digest, 7*(1), 5–17.

Hughes, J. N. (1979). Consistency of administrators' and psychologists' actual and ideal perceptions of school psychologists' activities. *Psychology in the Schools, 16*, 234–239.

Hynd, G. W., & Obrzut, J. E. (1981). *Neuropsychological assessment and the school-age child: Issues and procedures.* New York: Grune & Stratton.

Kazdin, A. E. (1982). Applying behavioral principles in the schools. In C. R. Reynolds & T. B. Gutkin (Eds.), *The handbook of school psychology* (pp. 501–529). New York: Wiley.

Korchin, S. J. (1982). The history of clinical psychology: A personal view. In M. Hersen, A. E. Kazdin, & A. S. Bellack (Eds.), *The clinical psychology handbook* (pp. 32–54). New York: Pergamon Press.

Kratochwill, T. (1982). Advances in behavioral assessment. In C. R. Reynolds & T. B. Gutkin (Eds.), *The handbook of school psychology* (pp. 314–350). New York: Wiley.

Kratochwill, T. R., & Bergan, J. R. (1978). Training school psychologists: Some perspectives on a competency based behavioral consultation model. *Professional Psychology, 9*, 71–82.

Lambert, N. M. (1965). Applications of the taxonomy of "Strens" in specific school situations. In N. M. Lambert (Ed.), *The protection and promotion of mental health in schools*. Mental Health Monograph 5. Bethesda, MD: U.S. Department of Health, Education and Welfare.

Lambert, N. M., Sandoval, J., & Corder, R. (1975). Teacher perceptions of school-based consultants. *Professional Psychology, 6*, 204–216.

Lennox, N., Flanagan, D., & Meyers, J. (1979). Organizational consultation to facilitate communication within a school staff. *Psychology in the Schools, 16*, 520–526.

Lewin, K. (1947). Group decision and social change. In T. Newcomb & E. Hartley (Eds.), *Readings in social psychology* (pp. 330–344). New York: Holt, Rinehart & Winston.

Maher, C. A. (1980a). Training special services teams to develop I.E.P.S. *Exceptional Children, 47*, 206–210.

Maher, C. A. (1980b). Program evaluation and school psychology: Perspectives, principles, procedures. In T. R. Kratochwill (Ed.), *Advances in school psychology* (Vol. 1, pp. 402–458). Hillsdale, NJ: Lawrence Earlbaum Associates.

Maher, C. A., & Kratochwill, T. R. (1980). Principles and procedures of program evaluation: An overview. *School Psychology Monograph, 4*, 1–24.

Mahoney, M. J., & Thoresen, C. E. (1974). *Self control: Power to the person*. Monterey, CA: Brooks/Cole.

Martin, R. P., Duffey, J., & Fischman, R. (1973). A time analysis and evaluation of an experimental internship program in school psychology. *Journal of School Psychology, 11*, 263–268.

McDermott, P. A. (1977). Measures of diagnostic data usage as discriminants among training and experience levels in school psychology. *Psychology in the Schools, 14*, 323–331.

Mearig, J. S. (1974). On becoming a child advocate in school psychology. *Journal of School Psychology, 12*, 121–129.

Meyers, J. (1973). A consultation model for school psychological services. *Journal of School Psychology, 11*, 5–15.

Meyers, J., Martin, R., & Hyman, J. (Eds.). (1977). *School consultation*. Springfield, IL: Charles C Thomas.

Miller, C. K., & Chansky, N. M. (1972). Psychologists' scoring of WISC protocols. *Psychology in the Schools, 9*, 144–152.

Miller, J. N., & Engin, A. W. (1974). Performance based school psychology certification: Situational response testing. *Psychology in the Schools, 11*, 422–424.

Miller, C. K., Chansky, N. M., & Gredler, G. R. (1970). Rater agreement on WISC protocols. *Psychology in the Schools, 1*, 190–193.

Osguthorpe, R. T. (1979). The school psychologist as a tutorial systems supervisor. *Psychology in the Schools, 16*, 88–92.

Reger, R. (1965). *School psychology*. Springfield, IL: Charles C Thomas.

Reilly, D. H., Barclay, J., & Culbertson, R. (1977). The current status of competency-based training, Part 1: Validity, reliability, and ethical issues. *Journal of School Psychology, 15*, 68–74.

Reschly, D. J. (1976). School psychology consultation: "Frenzied, faddish, or fundamental?" *Journal of School Psychology, 14*, 105–113.

Reynolds, C. R., Gutkin, T. B., Elliott, S. N., & Witt, J. C. (1984). *School psychology: Essentials of theory and practice*. New York: Wiley.

Rosenfeld, J. G., & Blanco, R. F. (1974). Incompetence in school psychology: The case of "Dr. Gestalt." *Psychology in the Schools, 11*, 263–269.

Rosenfield, S. (1981). Self managed professional development. *School Psychology Review, 10*, 487–493.

Sandoval, J. (1985a). Crisis counseling in the schools. *School Psychology Review, 14*, 255–256.

Sandoval, J. (1985b). Crisis counseling: Conceptualizations and general principles. *School Psychology Review, 14*, 257–265.

Sandoval, J. (1986). Models of school psychological service delivery. In S. N. Elliott & J. C. Witt (Eds.), *The delivery of psychological services in schools: Concepts, processes, and issues* (pp. 139–169). Hillsdale, NJ: Lawrence Erlbaum.

Sandoval, J., & Lambert, N. (1977). Instruments for evaluating school psychologists' functioning. *Psychology in the Schools, 14*, 172–179.

Schmuck, R. (1976). Process consultation and organizational development. *Professional Psychology, 7*, 626–631.

Schmuck, R., & Miles, M. (1971). *Organizational development in schools*. Palo Alto, CA: National Press Books.

Stewart, K. J., & Medway, F. J. (1978). School psychologists as consultants: Issues in training, practice, and accountability. *Professional Psychology, 9*, 711–718.

Stricker, G., Claiborn, W. L., & Bent, R. J. (1982). Peer review: An overview. *Professional Psychology, 13*, 5–8.

Tomlinson, J. R. (1973). Accountability procedures for psychological services. *Psychology in the Schools, 10*, 42–47.

Tomlinson, J. R. (1974). Functional analysis and accountability of psychological services. *Psychology in the Schools, 11*, 291–294.

Trachtman, G. M. (1971). From the editor. *Journal of School Psychology, 9*, 98.

Valett, R. E. (1969). *Programming learning disabilities*. Palo Alto, CA: Fearon.

Warren, S., & Brown, W. (1973). Examiner scoring errors on individual intelligence tests. *Psychology in the Schools, 10*, 118–122.

Waters, L. G. (1973). School psychologists as perceived by school personnel: Support for a consultant model. *Journal of School Psychology, 11*, 40–45.

White, M. A., & Harris, M. W. (1961). *The school psychologist*. New York: Harper & Brothers.

Whitman, M., & Whitman, J. (1971). Behavior modification in the classroom. *Psychology in the Schools, 8*, 176–186.

Woody, R. H. (1976). The school psychologist as a behavior therapist: Past and future. *Psychology in the Schools, 13*, 266–268.

Zins, J. E. (1984). Scientific problem-solving approach to developing accountability procedures for school psychologists. *Professional Psychology: Research and Practice, 15*, 56–66.

8

Clinical Evaluation of Medical Students in U.S. Medical Schools

XENIA TONESK

INTRODUCTION

The purpose of this chapter is twofold. First, the current status of the evaluation of medical students during their clinical training is described. Second, an alternative definition of the evaluation task is presented that may facilitate the development of improved evaluation systems.

The structure of clinical education is depicted along the continuum, starting with the clinical courses offered in the first 2 years of medical school and ending in graduate medical education (residency). This description provides the context within which the evaluation process is explored.

Current evaluation practices focus primarily on the methods of evaluation. Problems arising from the constraints of such a narrow perspective and the directions of research on methods are addressed.

Finally, a systems approach to evaluation is suggested as a means of identifying and addressing appropriately all of the components important for effective evaluation.

XENIA TONESK • President, Xenia Tonesk, Inc., Suite 1006, 3101 New Mexico Avenue, NW, Washington, DC 20016.

STRUCTURE OF CLINICAL EDUCATION IN U.S. MEDICAL SCHOOLS

In 1985, there were 125 MD-degree-granting accredited medical schools in the United States (U.S.). In addition, one school had provisional accreditation; another offered only the first 2 years of medical education and was organized as an affiliate of an MD-granting school (Liaison Committee on Medical Education, 1985). Enrollment of students in the 127 schools for the 1984–1985 academic year was 67,016. Approximately 32% of the students were women (Association of American Medical Colleges [AAMC], 1985).

All programs for obtaining the MD degree are 4 years in duration. Twelve schools offer an option of completing the 4-year program in 3 calendar years (AAMC, 1984). Generally, the first 2 years of medical school are referred to as the basic science years, and the last 2 as the clinical science, clinical education, or clerkship years. Some clinically oriented courses are offered during the first 2 years with the goal of teaching students basic clinical skills and techniques required upon entry into clinical education.

Clinical Courses in the First 2 Years of Medical School

Prior to entry into clinical education, at the latest by the third semester or the fifth quarter of medical school, students are required to take courses designed to expose them to basic clinical skills. These skills include taking a history from a patient and performing a physical examination. They may also include basic technical and laboratory procedures. Students are most frequently assigned to small groups. The course director selects patients with whom the students interact and thereby gain experience in the basic skills.

The courses differ from school to school as to title, duration, and time of inclusion in the curriculum. Table 1 shows the type and duration of courses offered.

Clinical Clerkships

With few exceptions, medical students embark on the clinical portion of their education in the last four semesters (or six quarters) of medical school. It is during this time that in their encounters with patients they act as student-physicians, mostly on hospital wards and in emergency rooms; less frequently in ambulatory care settings, such as clinics and private physicians' offices.

Table 1. Range of Hours of Instruction in Preclinical Curricula Devoted to Clinical Preparatory Courses in 127 U.S. Medical Schools, 1984–1985

Course	Hours	Number of schools offering course	
		First year	Second year
Introduction to clinical medicine (ICM)	5–600[a]	50	89
Physical diagnosis	16–348	10	36
Interviewing	15–68	6	3
Introduction to clinical psychiatry	17–72	4	10
Clinical problem-solving	9–294	2	5
Clinical judgment/decision-making	28–180	0	2
Clinical rounds/preceptorship/basic clerkship	14–240	9	13
Laboratory medicine	25–359	1	10
Emergency medicine	8–48	15	0
CPR/life support	4–33	9	7

Note. The data are from *1984–1985 AAMC Curriculum Directory*.
[a]Two schools, which register an unusually high hour count, are excluded. One school offers an ICM course within the context of a 6-year BA–MD program; the second integrates other specialty content into the ICM course.

The clinical years are divided into blocks of time, called clerkships, in the major clinical disciplines. Clerkships can be required, elective, or selective, that is, a particular clerkship chosen by the student from a required category. A list of the required clerkships and their duration appears in Table 2. Students are encouraged to take the required clerkships, that is, medicine, surgery, pediatrics, obstetrics-gynecology, and psychiatry during their third year. A few schools also require students to take basic, or introductory, clerkships in the third year, prior to the other required clerkships and in addition to clinical courses in the first 2 years (AAMC, 1984a). These clerkships range from 2 to 8 weeks and allow the student to acquire and test the knowledge and skills necessary for functioning in the clinical setting.

For many students, the fourth year thus becomes a year for electives during which the students play a major role in defining their own curricula. Some elect clerkships in areas they plan to pursue during their graduate medical education (residency). By contrast, others choose subjects they will not encounter during their residency years. For example, a student who is planning a residency in internal medicine might elect additional surgery clerkships. Correction of deficiencies and general broadening of clinical experience are two major reasons for choosing particular electives.

Table 2. Content and Duration of Required Clerkships in 124 U.S. Medical Schools, 1984–1985

Discipline	Number of schools[a]	Number of weeks	
		Mode	Range
Medicine	124	12	8–26
Surgery	124	12	4–22
Pediatrics	124	8	5–16
Obstetrics/gynecology	124	6	4–12
Psychiatry	124	6	4–12
Neurology	64	4	2–6
Family medicine	51	6	2–14
Internship/preceptorship	34	4	4–12.5
Surgical specialties/surgical selectives	26	4	2–10
Primary care	20	6	2–8
Anesthesiology	19	2	1–4
Radiology	12	2/4	36hr–4wk
Ophthalmology	11	1	0.8–4
Emergency medicine	10	4	1–4
Ambulatory care	9	8	2–8
Otolaryngology/otorhinolaryngology	7	1	1–2
Dermatology	6	1/2	19hr–3wk
Cardiac/CPR	6	1/2	20hr–3wk
Physical medicine and rehabilitation	5	2	0.2–4
Orthopedics	5	2	1–4
Urology	5	2	2
Preventive medicine	2	2	2
Geriatrics	1	4	4

Note. The data are from *1984–1985 AAMC Curriculum Directory*.
[a]Data are not available for 3 of 127 schools.

Elective clerkships are generally taken at the home medical school or at affiliated hospitals or clinical sites. These clerkships may also be arranged at other medical schools in the U.S. or even abroad. Students wishing to pursue special interests are accommodated through clerkships arranged individually under the sponsorship of a faculty member.

Table 3 shows the range of weeks available for elective clerkships during the third and fourth years. Table 4 lists the most frequently chosen electives as reported by senior medical students in 1984.

The choice of electives is also heavily influenced and sometimes restricted by competition for residency placement. In all medical specialties, there are now fewer residency positions than MD graduates seeking such positions. Thus, in order to increase their chances of competing successfully, some students feel constrained to take senior clerkship electives at hospitals in which they wish to secure residencies (Swanson, 1985).

Table 3. Weeks Reserved for Electives during the Third and Fourth Years in 116 U.S. Medical Schools, 1984–1985

Weeks	Number of schools[a]
1–4	2
5–8	3
9–12	9
13–16	14
17–20	17
21–24	20
25–28	12
29–32	17
33–36	12
37–40	3
41–44	2
⩾ 45	5

Note. The data are from *1984–1985 AAMC Curriculum Directory.*
[a]Data are not available for 11 of 127 schools.

The clerkship experience of students in U.S. medical schools is anything but uniform. In 1984, medical student and resident education was conducted in 1,736 separate clinical facilities (Crowley, Etzel, & Petersen, 1984). Clerkships in the various disciplines were offered at numerous sites; medicine used 609 facilities; surgery, 566; pediatrics, 430; obstetrics-gynecology, 458; psychiatry, 471; family medicine, 313; and other clerkships, 336. The educational environment of the many facilities varies widely. In some settings, students are expected to assume a passive role and do little more than observe. In other settings, much direct patient experience is permitted and encouraged. Within each facility, commitment to student education on the part of the clinical faculty also varies greatly. Teaching responsibilities tend to conflict with other pressures on the clinical faculty: to generate practice income; to reduce the length of hospital stay for patients; to deal with an older, more severely ill patient population; and to stay abreast of the rapidly increasing knowledge base as well as the expanding array of technological advances (Rabkin, 1985).

In part, because of class size that ranges from 24 to 331 and averages 129 students, not all students of a given class are able to take a given clerkship at the same clinical site and at the same time (AAMC, 1985). The result is a recommended but often unenforceable sequence of required clerkships. For example, a required clerkship in medicine

Table 4. The 10 Clinical Electives Most Frequently Chosen by 10,421 Students Graduating from U.S. Medical Schools, 1983–1984

Clinical electives	Students taking elective[a]	
	Number	Percentage
Cardiology	6,411	61.5
Radiology	5,981	57.4
Emergency medicine	4,337	41.6
General internal medicine	3,577	34.3
Infectious diseases	3,282	31.5
Anesthesiology	3,194	30.6
Dermatology	3,061	29.4
Intensive care medicine	2,797	26.8
Nephrology	2,593	24.9
Family medicine	2,545	24.4

Note. The data are from AAMC Graduation Questionnaire (1984b). Adapted by permission.
[a]Number and percentage are based on students who indicated at least one elective; 126 additional students reported taking no elective.

may be taken at any time during the third, sometimes even the fourth, year. Also, a 12-week clerkship may consist of a number of separate "rotations," for example, 6 weeks at the university hospital and the remaining 6 weeks divided between two affiliated hospitals.

Other factors combine to make clinical education an individual learning experience (Ways & Engel, 1982). Expectations on the part of the faculty vary and are sometimes contradictory; for example, some expect introductory knowledge of a range of subjects pertaining to patient care; others favor intensive preparation in their respective specialty areas. Patient populations to which students are exposed also differ widely. Some students see only severely ill patients with a limited range of medical problems; others are exposed to a broader range and intensity of disease. The faculty also vary greatly in the amount of preparation before assuming the teaching role. Last, the residents (persons with the MD degree pursuing graduate medical education) play a major role in the teaching of students, but often have little, if any, training for this responsibility (Tonesk, 1979).

Graduate Medical Education

Graduate medical education, or residency, is the period that begins with the receipt of the MD degree and ends with the completion of educational requirements for one of 23 specialty certifying boards. Over the years, graduate medical education has evolved from a short apprenticeship during which practical hospital experience was acquired by the resident into a formal, structured educational system ("Graduate," 1981). Depending on the specialty, residency can last from 3 to 7 years.

In 1984, there were 4,691 accredited residency programs in the United States (American Medical Association [AMA], 1985). Forty specialty areas are comprised in this count. Internal medicine has the greatest number of programs, followed by family practice, general surgery, obstetrics-gynecology, and pathology. There were a total of 74,495 residents in training in 1984, 25% of them women (AMA, 1985). Approximately 54% of the residents were in programs of internal medicine, general surgery, family practice, and pediatrics.

EVALUATION OF MEDICAL STUDENTS DURING CLINICAL EDUCATION

In 1981, the AAMC appointed an 18-member panel, chaired by Steven Muller, PhD, president of The Johns Hopkins University, to review and examine the general professional education of the physician, that is, the period of education from entry into medical school to receipt of the MD degree. The study also addressed the issue of proper college preparation for medicine. The purpose of the project was to evoke a national discussion that would result in a broad consensus on certain fundamental principles necessary to guide the general preparation of physicians in the future (Cooper, 1984). The report of the study, "Physicians for the Twenty-First Century," was distributed in 1984 ("Physicians," 1984).

Content and Method of Evaluation

Some of the work of the panel was conducted through three working groups convened to address the content areas of (a) knowledge, (b) fundamental skills, and (c) personal qualities, values, and attitudes. Evaluation practices with respect to each of these areas were addressed in this report.

One of the conclusions of the panel was that faculty rely too heavily on multiple-choice examinations. Such examinations are popular because they are easily administered and graded and yield numerical scores. The fund of knowledge within a specific content area may indeed be measured satisfactorily in this way. However, it was agreed that new evaluation approaches are needed to assess the extent to which students are prepared to function as critical thinkers, problem solvers, and lifelong learners.

A case in point is the use by the medical schools of examinations prepared and administered by the National Board of Medical Examiners (NBME). It has been said that evaluation drives the curriculum. In this respect, the NBME sequence of examinations is a major evaluation force in U.S. medical schools.

The original purpose of the NBME was to develop tests of quality for use by state jurisdictions for the licensing of physicians. However, medical schools have used the examinations for two other purposes: evaluation of students and evaluation of the curriculum. In 1984–1985, 46.5% of U.S. medical schools required students to achieve a passing total score on Part I of the NBME (knowledge of basic medical sciences) for promotion and/or graduation; 37.8% required a passing grade on Part II (knowledge of clinical sciences). Approximately 12% of medical schools use scores from Part I and II in the determination of final course grades (AAMC, 1984a).

The NBME examinations, cast in the multiple-choice format, address primarily the ability to recall information. The working group on knowledge expressed a grave concern that such an approach focuses only on a narrow range of cognitive abilities to the exclusion of other important competencies and that the reliance on simple numerical scores discourages the development of broader-based and, by necessity, more complex approaches to evaluation.

The group on fundamental skills identified the following as the content to be acquired during medical education: (a) clinical skills, including data gathering through history, physical examination, and diagnostic tests, diagnostic formulation, patient management, communicating clinical data, and life support skills; (b) learning skills; (c) critical appraisal skills; (d) medical information skills; (e) teamwork skills; and (f) personal management skills.

The group on personal qualities, values, and attitudes summarized the expectations by listing a set of personal qualities and dispositions:

> [Medical students] should possess stamina, moral sensitivity and integrity, curiosity and creativity, the ability to cope with intellectual and emotional demands, and a commitment to help and work with others. They should value intellectual growth, science and the scientific method, social responsibility, and altruism. They should be respectful, modest, compassionate toward their patients and toward other health professionals. ("Report of the Working Group on Personal Qualities," 1984, p. 177)

In a separate effort to define "humanism" in internal medicine, the American Board of Internal Medicine (ABIM) has focused on

(a) integrity, (b) respect for the patient, and (c) compassion (ABIM, 1985).

Unlike the prescribed fund of knowledge, this content of medical education—application of knowledge, problem solving, clinical skills, and personal qualities, values and attitudes fostered in medical school—does not lend itself to traditional academic examination methods and is conducted chiefly through the observation of students by faculty and residents in the course of clinical training. To record their observations, faculty and residents use a series of rating scales and/or provide a narrative summary of their impressions of the student. This is typically done at the end of each "rotation" of a clerkship, and the information is then passed on to the course (or clerkship) director.

The contact of faculty and residents with the students, on which these assessments are based, varies greatly both in duration and intensity. Direct observation of the student may range from a total of an hour or two to many hours over a period of several months and occurs in a variety of contexts: interaction with a patient at the bedside during medical rounds; performance of the physical examination and of specific technical procedures; participation in conferences and lectures; presentation of the case of a patient to faculty and peers; and performance during oral examinations. In addition, faculty and residents typically review the write-ups (written records) the student has prepared for each of the patients for whom he or she has been assigned responsibility. Also, evaluators may contact their colleagues, the nursing staff, and other professionals to obtain additional information about the student or to validate their impressions.

Individual evaluations are collated, information from different assessment techniques weighted, and the final grade is assigned by the clerkship director in a process that is structured to varying degrees at various institutions. The director may study the evaluations submitted, consult with individual evaluators if discrepancies surface, and arrive at a composite set of ratings and/or prepare a narrative summary. During this process, he or she may decide how to weight the information from other assessment techniques, for example, scores on the written examination, performance on an oral examination, quality of patient write-ups, and performance during patient case presentations to arrive at the final grade. In this scenario, the final grade reflects the ultimate judgment of the clerkship director.

Alternatively, the director may hold regularly scheduled meetings with the faculty and the residents and arrive at a final grade through a group decision process. Some clinical departments have defined explicitly the process for compiling a composite rating and the weights to be assigned to information yielded by each assessment technique for the determination of the final grade. The most common practice is to weight the composite rating at least 50% and accord the score on the written examination the remainder.

The final grade, along with narrative summaries, is then forwarded to the dean's office. In 11% of the schools, the final grade is recorded as pass/fail; 48% use a system of honors/pass/fail; and 41% assign letter or numerical grades (AAMC, 1984a).

Problems with Current Evaluation Practices

With the exception of a few institutions and clinical departments at which some innovative approaches are being explored, the evaluation practices that have been described characterize most medical education settings. The level of satisfaction with these practices, however, is low. Most clinical faculty are concerned that they are not effectively meeting their evaluative responsibilities (Tonesk, 1983a). In a recent AAMC survey, faculty from 46 U.S. medical schools indicated that they viewed their respective evaluation systems as requiring a major overhaul (Tonesk & Buchanan, 1985).

There are several reasons for this widespread dissatisfaction:

1. The set of desirable end-goal characteristics in a physician is not a uniform domain and presents different assessment challenges (AAMC, 1981; Tonesk, 1983b). *Cumulative* characteristics, such as fund of knowledge and technical skills, are developed and improved by students during each successive phase of their medical education. These characteristics lend themselves most readily to assessment by objective instruments but require explicit definition of what is to be assessed at a particular stage of development in the educational process and the rate of growth and improvement that is expected. *Enduring* characteristics, such as sensitivity, diligence, and ethical behavior, affect clinical performance but are not acquired in the same sense as the fund of knowledge and certain clinical skills. Some of these characteristics cannot be readily observed upon limited contact. Assessment situations for eliciting relevant behaviors are very difficult to arrange, and some of the dimensions can only be meaningfully documented in the converse, for example, irresponsibility, or unethical behavior, or over a period much longer than a clerkship of several weeks' duration. There are also meaningful end point characteristics, such as supervisory ability, teaching ability, and independent decision making, that are *latent* in the student and can only be inferred on the basis of other related behavior. When a single method, such as global rating scales, is used

to assess these varied characteristics, the quality of assessment inevitably varies also, leading to disaffection with the method itself.

2. Uniformity and standardization of evaluation across all categories of students result in the lack of sufficient or relevant information on some students and a burdensome amount of noncontributive information on most. In the recent AAMC survey, faculty from 98 medical schools indicated that their current evaluation systems are adequate for the majority of students but do not handle the situations arising with problem students well (Tonesk & Buchanan, 1985). These situations are the most difficult and time-consuming to resolve and are those for which an effective and efficient evaluation system is most necessary. Also instruments designed to be applicable to every student tend to provide little distinction between superior students and those who are merely doing well. Similarly, "adequate" students comprise very different categories of students: those who are indeed average and unremarkable; those whom no one knows well enough to rate otherwise; and those who have serious shortcomings balanced by compensating strengths (Tonesk, 1983b). The sheer volume of ratings provided on large numbers of students periodically in a uniform way limits the comprehensiveness and detracts from the usefulness of any general instrument.

3. Because over the course of clinical education a typical medical student encounters literally scores of mentors and supervisors who also serve as the evaluators, evaluation methods are at the mercy of variation in the motivation, diligence, sophistication, and training of the evaluators. Some evaluators, themselves specialists, have unreasonable expectations of novices in their field. Some are not sufficiently acquainted with individual students to make valid assessments, and therefore the "halo" effect tends to determine assessments on specifics.

4. The two purposes of evaluation, guidance and screening are rarely made explicit and are distinguished even more rarely. The result is that faculty often waver between their role as student advocates and their role as gatekeepers, making evaluations useless for one purpose if they happen to be completed with the other in mind.

5. There is a general reluctance on the part of faculty to record negative evaluations despite the fact that in most instances the courts have upheld faculty judgments about students (Kapp, 1981). Faculty maintain that the time and anxiety spent in involvement in legal actions or even the threat of such actions are too costly personally and professionally, and, therefore, record negative evaluations only in the most extreme cases.

The reasons enumerated for dissatisfaction on the part of the faculty also apply to the evaluation of graduate medical students (residents), with one important difference. Having already chosen a specialty, residents have entered particular career tracks and, therefore, tend to be accepted as "part of the family," rather than as simply passing through. This intensifies the investment in the student on the part of the faculty. In a recent survey conducted by the AAMC for the American Board of Medical Specialties (ABMS), members of 11 specialty boards cited seven reservations they have about the ratings of residents provided by their program directors. These ratings are submitted by program directors as part of the documentation required of the residents before they qualify to sit for certifying examinations. The reservations include subjectivity of the evaluation; the investment that program directors have in the resident by having accepted him or her into the program; the supportive role of the program directors in residents' education as protectors, facilitators, and mentors; variabilty in the quality of programs; the lack of articulation as to what global ratings encompass; the fact that failure of a resident is unlikely in some programs due to the difficulty of attracting residents to those programs; and the threat of legal challenge as it influences the objectivity of the ratings (Tonesk, 1985).

Research on Methods of Evaluating Clinical Competence

Dissatisfaction with the current status of the evaluation of students in medical education settings has spurred considerable activity in the exploration of selected methods for assessing clinical competence. A recent collection of essays, *Assessing Clinical Competence* (Neufeld & Norman, 1985), details the research conducted on particular measurement techniques: direct observation, oral examinations, written examinations, global rating scales, medical record review, patient management problems, computer simulations, and the use of simulated patients. The history of each technique, its use, the evidence for its validity, and its strengths and limitations are reviewed.

Current interest in the evaluation of clinical performance is also evinced by two recent international conferences devoted entirely to the topic. The International Workshop on the Assessment of Clinical Skills was held in Cambridge, England, in June 1984; Newer Developments in Assessing Clinical Competence took place in Ottawa, Canada, in July 1985 (Hart, Harden, & Walton, 1986; Wakeford, Bashook, Jolly, & Rothman, 1985).

In general, investigators tend to find that particular techniques may work well as measures of very circumscribed aspects of clinical behavior and skills but do not yield a satisfactory assessment of overall clinical competence. For example, a study of direct observation by faculty of student encounters with simulated patients found that evaluation of clinical actions (interviewing, problem orientation, and physical examination) by this method does not tap those diagnostic or management skills in which understanding of the case plays a major role (Harper, Roy, Norman, Rand, & Feightner, 1983). Similarly, exercises in patient management problems, which require the student to make decisions upon being prompted with information about a patient, may reasonably assess whether a student knows what additional information to collect or what intervention to undertake. However, these exercises reveal nothing about the student's ability to execute the intervention. Furthermore, some recent research showed that problem-solving ability, presumably tapped by such techniques, tends to be content-specific, that is, performance on one case predicts the performance on another poorly (Norman, Tugwell, Jacoby, & Muzzin, 1983).

Recognizing the limitations of any one evaluation method, some institutions or clinical departments have consciously developed evaluation systems that combine several available techniques. Anderson and Botticelli (1981) have combined an objective test for knowledge, simulations to assess problem-solving skills, a clinical skills examination with a checklist of standards, and a criterion-referenced rating scale to assess professional habits and attitudes. Littlefield, Harrington, Anthracite, and Garman (1981) used a combination of a multiple-choice examination, an oral examination, and ward ratings.

An approach that has captured considerable current interest is an evaluation format called the Objective Structured Clinical Examination (OSCE; Harden & Gleeson, 1979). Originated in Scotland but now used in several medical schools in Canada, Australia, and the United States, the examination format requires students to rotate through a series of stations, spending an appropriate time (from 4–5 minutes to half an hour or more) at each station to execute a prescribed task or procedure, for example, perform a physical examination, take a medical history, interpret laboratory findings, or demonstrate a particular technical skill. The approach may accommodate any assessment technique, that is, simulated patients, direct observation, computer-driven patient management problems, and even brief written examinations of the multiple-choice or essay variety. Some evidence has been adduced for the predictive and concurrent validity of this approach (Harden, Stevenson, Downie, & Wilson, 1975; Hart, 1983; Newble, Hoare, & Elmslie, 1981). Compared to faculty ratings of clinical competence on the basis of general knowledge of the student's performance, the OSCE has the attraction of being a public, structured procedure, demanding well-defined criteria and explicit standards and minimizing examiner and patient variation. The limitations of the approach have to do mainly with issues of practicality. The method seems to work well as an exercise in standardizing a multimethod examination. Even as such, it requires considerable faculty effort in development, in administration, and in the resolution of problems with scheduling, space, patient availability, patient fatigue, and confidentiality. Furthermore, in order to ensure an acceptable level of reliability of the entire examination and an adequate sampling of skills and behaviors, the method might require numerous sessions, with the consequent severalfold increase in costs.

DEVELOPING AN EFFECTIVE SYSTEM OF EVALUATION

In 1978, the AAMC inaugurated a nationwide program to study the problems of evaluation of medical students during their clinical education and to assist clinical faculties in improving their practices of evaluation. The program was established on the assumption that improvement in evaluation cannot be achieved by concentrating exclusively, or even primarily, on methods of assessment. As previously discussed, particular methods of assessment of clinical competence and of related professional qualities are limited in their reliability, validity, and practicality. But even improved methods of assessment do not guarantee effective evaluation. Reliable and valid methods do not yield reliable and valid results if inappropriately used. Furthermore, reliable and valid information obtained from one source is useless and may be misleading if adulterated and pooled with questionable information from a biased source. Even if painstakingly assembled and verified, information is rendered useless if it is not timely. Information also becomes useless if it fails to be integrated in the student's record in such a way that faculty's actions regarding subsequent steps in the student's educational program are appropriately affected.

The Clinical Evaluation Program set out to identify the problems of current evaluation systems through (a) site visits to approximately 30 medical schools; (b) a survey of clerkship directors in the six major specialties (medicine, surgery, obstetrics-gynecology, pediatrics, psychiatry, and family medicine); and (c) interviews with several hundred clinical faculty, department chairs, residents, and medical students regarding evaluation policies, practices, and problems (Tonesk, 1983a, b). Following this information-gathering phase, the program has undertaken to develop materials for self-study of clinical evaluation systems that have now been piloted at 10 medical schools (Tonesk, 1986a).

The findings from studies conducted as part of this program and the experience of working with many different medical schools have clearly shown that there is no one optimal system for effective evaluation of clinical competence (Tonesk, 1986b). What works in a relatively small, compactly organized medical school with two or three affiliated teaching hospitals does not work in a large school with affiliated clinical facilities spread over several states. Issues of coordination of information, quality control of information, heterogeneity or homogeneity of the student population, institutional philosophy, and administrative leadership style are not transferable from one institution to another and are rarely transferable across various clinical departments within the same school. Yet these issues determine to a large extent the requirements of an effective system.

Nevertheless, certain concerns are common, in principle, to all institutions and clinical departments:

1. Although efforts to improve evaluation almost invariably center on methods and techniques, more immediate and substantial improvement may be realized by focusing on the evaluators themselves. The quality of evaluation depends to a very important degree on *who* conducts the assessment: who supplies the information, who synthesizes or interprets it, who transmits it to whom, and who acts on it. It is often the case that persons who are given the responsibility to evaluate do not have the necessary information; conversely, those who have first-hand knowledge of the student and the student's performance may not even be asked to contribute to the evaluation. In the selection of evaluators, authority to judge often takes precedence over opportunity to know. In an effective system, evaluators (a) must be willing to take the time not only to produce discrete assessments but to follow through with the consequences of those assessments; (b) must either possess, acquire, or be supplied with information for each aspect of the performance to be evaluated; and (c) must understand and believe in the purposes of evaluation and be interested in learning to act effectively in the role of evaluators.

2. For the evaluators to be willing, able, and interested to do the task, the purposes of evaluation must be clearly articulated and, even more important, visibly implemented in the overall educational program. For example, what appears to be widespread reluctance of evaluators to record negative judgments may be attributed largely to the fact that very few medical students, once admitted, fail to graduate if

they persist. Moreover, even when used as signals for guidance rather than screening, negative evaluations tend to be ineffective because of the rapid rotation of students through the separate clerkships. One of the most common complaints of the clinical faculty is that the system fails to provide "early warning" about problems that students bring with them to their rotation (Tonesk, 1986b).

The dual function of evaluation, to teach and to judge, is problematic in itself. On the one hand, as an educator, the evaluator is invested and involved in a positive way in the development of competence; on the other, he or she is required to act as a judge, with the negative mandate of detecting disqualifying flaws or deficiencies. The problem is compounded if the uses to which particular evaluations are put are mixed, inconsistent, or unknown to the evaluator.

3. An effective evaluation system also requires that every student be evaluated fairly, but that need not mean that all students are to be evaluated uniformly. Uniform procedures are wasteful, cumbersome, and through sheer weight may frustrate their own purposes. Due to their generality, they are poorly matched to the needs of individual students. To be useful, evaluative documentation in the case of a consistently good student must be of a different kind than in the case of a marginal, or problem, student. Starting each of the many stages and steps of evaluation from scratch is neither fair nor efficient. The fact is that most clinical faculty, just as they do in clinical practice with their patients, are able to categorize students on the basis of their experiential data base as evaluators. This "gut-level" categorization is inevitably reflected in the evaluations. If explicitly recognized and viewed as a legitimate step in the evaluation process, such initial categorization of students can be harnessed not only to make the system more efficient but to improve the quality of evaluation in each case. Figure 1 summarizes suggested evaluative actions with various categories of students.

4. It is increasingly recognized that the choice or development of methods and techniques of evaluation is inextricably linked with the content of evaluation. Because of the modular structure of undergraduate medical education and because clinical training takes place in many varied settings with constantly changing mentors, institutions and clinical departments rely on multiple "snapshot" assessments of students at discrete points in time from many separate sources. Concentration on the technical improvement of these separate snapshots, that is, attempts to improve their reliability and validity, has only a negligible effect on their usefulness in the aggregate. Resorting to common formats or techniques, such as rating scales, in order to facilitate the pooling of information unfortunately tends to be counterproductive

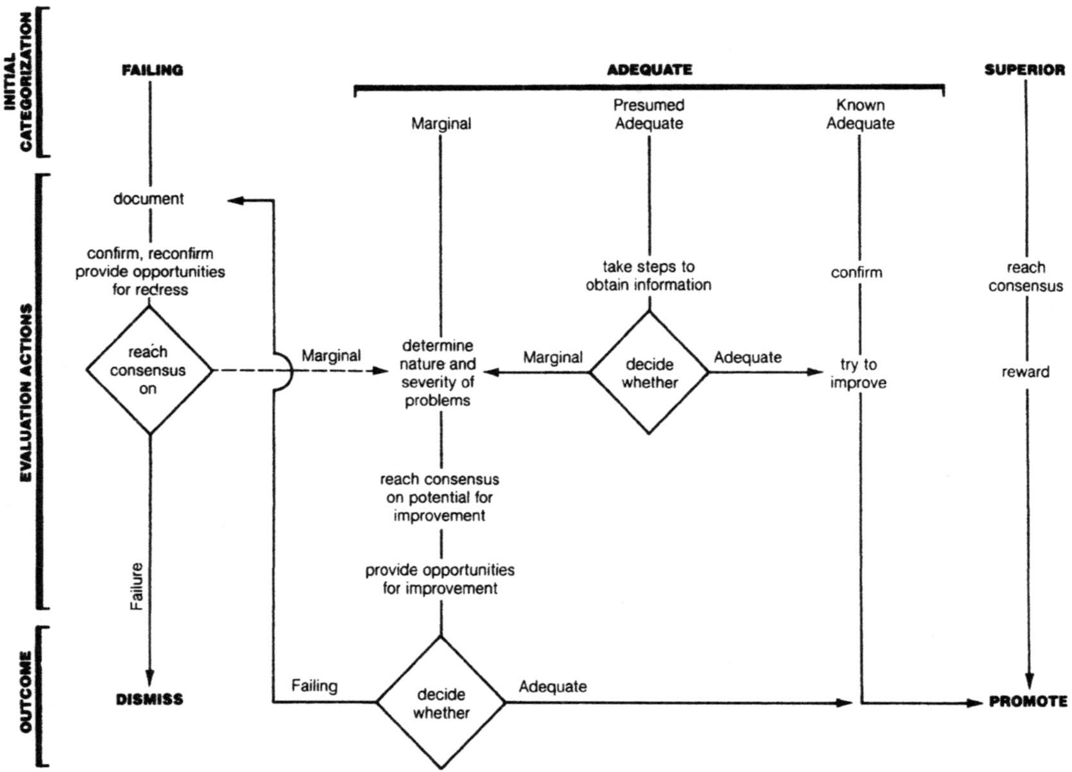

FIGURE 1. Initial categorization of students and subsequent evaluation actions. From *The Evaluation of Clerks: Perceptions of Clinical Faculty* (p. 6) by X. Tonesk, 1983, Washington, DC: Association of American Medical Colleges. Copyright 1983 by the Association of American Medical Colleges. Reprinted by permission.

in many instances. This occurs, for example, when well-documented information on well-defined content is mixed with inferences, speculations, or surface impressions on qualities that are complex or not easily observable. Inevitably, useful and valid information is attenuated by information that is ill-founded, questionable, or contradictory.

What is especially needed are effective procedures for integrating the accumulating information on the student into an ongoing longitudinal record of student performance, so that each new snapshot is interpreted, that is, highlighted, discounted, or adjusted in light of the total picture to date. Many important dimensions of professional competence and fitness can only be tapped over a period of time within such a longitudinal perspective.

Acknowledgments

I gratefully acknowledge the assistance of Robin G. Buchanan, research assistant for the Clinical Evaluation Program, for data and reference compilation and general editorial comments on the chapter and of Leigh Ann Kemp, program secretary, for technical preparation and production of the manuscript.

REFERENCES

American Board of Internal Medicine. (1985, June). *A guide to awareness and evaluation of humanistic qualities in the internist.* Philadelphia: Author.

American Medical Association. (1985). *Directory of residency training programs* (71st ed.). Chicago: Author.

Anderson, A. S., & Botticelli, M. G. (1981). Evaluating M.D.-level competence in internal medicine. *Journal of Medical Education, 56,* 587–592.

Association of American Medical Colleges. (1981). External examinations for the evaluation of medical education achievement and for licensure. *Journal of Medical Education, 56,* 933–962.

Association of American Medical Colleges. (1984a). *AAMC curriculum directory* (13th ed.). Washington, DC: Author.

Association of American Medical Colleges. (1984b). *Medical student graduation questionnaire summary report for all schools.* Washington, DC: Author.

Association of American Medical Colleges. (1985). *Medical school admission requirements* (36th ed.). Washington, DC: Author.

Cooper, J. A. D. (1984). Afterword. *Journal of Medical Education, 59*(11, Pt. 2), 29–31.

Crowley, A. E., Etzel, S. I., & Petersen, E. S. (1984). Undergraduate medical education. *Journal of the American Medical Association, 252,* 1525–1532.

Graduate medical education: Proposals for the eighties. (1981). *Journal of Medical Education, 56*(9, Pt. 2).

Harden, R. M., & Gleeson, F. A. (1979). Assessment of clinical competence using an objective structured clinical examination (OSCE). *Medical Education, 13*, 41–54.

Harden, R. M., Stevenson, M., Downie, W. W., & Wilson, G. M. (1975). Assessment of clinical competence using an objective structured clinical examination. *British Medical Journal, 1*, 447–451.

Harper, A. C., Roy, W. B., Norman, G. R., Rand, C. A., & Feightner, J. W. (1983). Difficulties in clinical skills evaluation. *Medical Education, 17*, 24–27.

Hart, I. R. (1983). Correlation of performance in the OSCE with later clinical performance. *Annals of the Royal College of Physicians and Surgeons* (Canada), *16*, 356.

Hart, I. R., Harden, R. M., & Walton, H. J. (Eds.). (1986). Newer developments in assessing clinical competence. *Proceedings of the World Federation for Medical Education International Conference*. Montreal, Quebec, Canada: Heal Publications Ltd.

Kapp, M. B. (1981). Legal issues in faculty evaluation of student clinical performance. *Journal of Medical Education, 56*, 559–564.

Liaison Committee on Medical Education. (1985, April). *Medical schools of the U.S.A. and Canada: Status of accreditation* (Internal Memorandum). Washington, DC: Author.

Littlefield, J. H., Harrington, J. T., Anthracite, N. E., & Garman, R. E. (1981). A description and four-year analysis of a clinical clerkship evaluation system. *Journal of Medical Education, 56*, 334–340.

Neufeld, V. R., & Norman, G. R. (Eds.). (1985). *Assessing clinical competence*. New York: Springer.

Newble, D. I., Hoare, J., & Elmslie, R. G. (1981). The validity and reliability of a new examination of the clinical competence of medical students. *Medical Education, 15*, 46–52.

Norman, G. R., Tugwell, P., Jacoby, L. L., & Muzzin, L. J. (1983). The generalizability of measures of clinical problem solving. *Proceedings of the 22nd Annual Conference on Research in Medical Education* (pp. 110–114). Washington, DC: Association of American Medical Colleges.

Physicians for the twenty-first century: Report of the project panel on the general professional education of the physician and college preparation for medicine. (1984). *Journal of Medical Education, 59*(11, Pt. 2).

Rabkin, M. T. (1985). The teaching hospital and medical education: One-room schoolhouse, multiversity, dinosaur? *Journal of Medical Education, 60*, 92–97.

Report of the working group on personal qualities, values, and attitudes. (1984). *Journal of Medical Education, 59*(11, Pt. 2), 177–189.

Swanson, A. G. (1985). The 'preresidency syndrome': An incipient epidemic of educational disruption. *Journal of Medical Education, 60*, 201–202.

Tonesk, X. (1979). The house officer as a teacher: What schools expect and measure. *Journal of Medical Education, 54*, 613–616.

Tonesk, X. (1983a). Clinical judgment of faculties in the evaluation of clerks. *Journal of Medical Education, 58*, 213–214.

Tonesk, X. (1983b, March). *The evaluation of clerks: Perceptions of clinical faculty*. Washington, DC: Association of American Medical Colleges.

Tonesk, X. (1985). How specialty boards use residency directors' ratings. In J. S. Lloyd (Ed.), *Residency director's role in specialty certification* (pp. 11–16). Chicago: American Board of Medical Specialties.

Tonesk, X. (1986a). Draft *Guide for the self-study of clinical evaluation systems*. Washington, DC: Association of American Medical Colleges.

Tonesk, X. (1986b). AAMC program to promote improved evaluation of students during clinical education. *Journal of Medical Education, 61*(Pt. 2), 83–88.

Tonesk, X., & Buchanan, R. G. (1985). Faculty perceptions of current clinical evaluation systems. *Journal of Medical Education, 60*, 573–576.

Wakeford, R., Bashook, P., Jolly, B. & Rothman, A. (Eds.). (1985). *Directions in clinical assessment* (Report of the first Cambridge Conference). Cambridge, England: Office of the Regius Professor of Physic, Cambridge University School of Clinical Medicine.

Ways, P. O., & Engel, J. D. (1982, September). *A socio-cultural view of clerkship education*. Paper commissioned by the Association of American Medical Colleges for the panel on The General Professional Education of the Physician and College Preparation for Medicine, Washington, DC.

9

Improving Evaluation in Counselor Training and Credentialing through Standardized Simulations

NORMAN L. BERVEN

INTRODUCTION

Professional competence may be conceptualized in terms of three broad domains (Klemp, 1979; Loganbill, Hardy, & Delworth, 1982). The knowledge domain is comprised of "what one knows," whereas the skill domain is comprised of "what one *can* do." Finally, the affective domain is comprised of a variety of personal characteristics, including attitudes, values, beliefs, self-schema, and motives that influence professional behavior (Klemp, 1979; Scofield, Terzella, Berven, & Thomas, 1983). The three domains interact in complex ways, along with situational variables, to determine the actual performance of professionals in clinical situations.

Clinical training and credentialing mechanisms are established within professions to promote and provide formal recognition of the

NORMAN L. BERVEN • Department of Rehabilitation Psychology and Special Education, University of Wisconsin–Madison, Madison, WI 53706.

attainment of competence (Pottinger, Weisfeld, Tochen, Cohen, & Schaalman, 1980). In fact, clinical training may be viewed as one important credentialing mechanism in that degrees awarded are themselves credentials, assumed to be indicative of competence attained; however, this basic assumption has frequently been questioned (e.g., Hogan, 1979a, b; Pottinger *et al.*, 1980; Scofield, Berven, & Harrison, 1981). In addition to being credentials in their own right, academic degrees are often prerequisites to obtaining other credentials, such as certificates and licenses. Together, clinical training and credentialing mechanisms perform a gatekeeping function in controlling entry to the practice of a profession.

Evaluation of professional competence is basic to clinical training and credentialing. In clinical training programs, competence is evaluated repeatedly, in individual courses and course modules, in practica and internships, and through comprehensive examinations required for graduate degrees. In certification and licensure, competence is typically evaluated through review of academic credentials, ratings or letters of reference from clinical supervisors and colleagues, and examinations.

Traditional Evaluation Methods

A standard method of evaluating competence has been the written examination, often in multiple-choice format. Written examinations are widely used in clinical training and credentialing. Typically, the focus of written examinations is on the knowledge domain of professional competence. If examinations are well constructed with adequate attention to content validity and psychometric characteristics, they can provide objective, reliable, and valid indicators of knowledge. In addition, it is possible to design written examinations to evaluate some aspects of the skill domain, particularly cognitive skills (Klemp, 1977). However, written examinations are typically restricted to evaluating knowledge or, more specifically, the recall of facts (Pottinger, 1979; Pottinger *et al.*, 1980).

In addition to their objectivity, written examinations are efficient in providing quick, easy, and inexpensive evaluations of large numbers of persons simultaneously. Given their advantages, written examinations may be relied upon as the primary evaluation method in clinical training and credentialing. However, their restricted focus on knowledge, to the exclusion of the skill and affective domains of competence, can severely limit their ability, when used alone, to predict clinical performance (Berven & Scofield, 1980b; Pottinger, 1979; Pottinger *et al.*, 1980).

Traditional evaluation methods focusing on the skill domain of professional competence tend to be much less objective, reliable, and systematic. Common procedures include selection interviews for graduate study, ratings or letters of reference commenting on clinical skills, and oral examinations or interviews conducted by examining boards for licensure or certification. Such methods tend to be highly subjective and, typically, psychometric characteristics have not even been investigated.

In clinical training, evaluation of the skill domain is concentrated in the practicum and internship components of training. One common procedure is the evaluation of clinical skills through case conferences in which students describe their clinical activities, including diagnostic impressions and intervention plans. Another common procedure is the observation of clinical performance through audio or video recordings or live observation of clinical encounters. Often, evaluation is based on the qualitative, subjective impressions of the observer. Rating scales may also be used, which may or may not be well constructed with adequate attention to psychometric characteristics. Also performance in clinical situations is subject to multiple sources of variation. In addition to professional competence, clinical performance is also influenced by other factors, including unique characteristics of the client and of the clinical situation. Consequently, it is often difficult to separate the different influences on performance in order to draw conclusions about the professional competence possessed by a student or clinician.

There would appear to be a need for innovative approaches to the evaluation of the skill domain of professional competence to supplement those focusing on knowledge. The Next Decade Project, sponsored by Division 17 (Counseling Psychology) of the American Psychological Association (APA), noted a high priority need to develop and refine methods of evaluating professional competence (Myers, 1982). In the words of Pottinger (1979), we need to move beyond assessing what people know to assessing what they can do.

Standardized Simulations as an Evaluation Method

Standardized simulations provide an alternative method of evaluation focusing on the skill domain of professional competence (Berven & Scofield, 1980b). Standardized simulations are reproductions or mockups of actual clinical practice situations. Individuals being evaluated are confronted with a simulated clinical practice situation and are asked to behave as they would in actual practice. The rationale underlying the use of standardized simulations is intuitively appealing—to evaluate particular skills, individuals are placed in situations approximating real-life situations that require those skills, and their performance is observed and evaluated.

Standardized simulations permit the evaluation of professional competence without any inconvenience or threat to actual clients. *Standardization* implies that clinical situations and the conditions under which evaluations are conducted are carefully specified and remain constant for all individuals being evaluated. Thus simulations can be designed so that particular skills of interest will be required, permitting their observation and evaluation. In addition, because the clinical situations are standardized, parameters of successful performance can be prespecified, facilitating objectivity and reliability in evaluation. Further, because characteristics of the client and the clinical situation are controlled as sources of influence on subject performance, a larger proportion of the variation among subjects can be attributed to differences in skills possessed.

Applications of Standardized Simulations in Medicine

Particularly innovative applications of standardized simulations have occurred in medicine. One type is the "simulated" or "programmed patient" (Barrows, 1971; Barrows & Abrahamson, 1964). An actor is given several hours of training and practice with feedback in order to play a standard patient role with a particular medical condition. Medical students or physicians being evaluated then interact with the simulated patient to achieve a diagnosis, compliance with a treatment program, or some other clinical objective. The encounter occurs in a standardized clinical situation where performance can be observed and target skills evaluated.

A second type of simulation in medicine has been termed the *patient management problem* (McGuire & Babbott, 1967; Rimoldi, 1961; Williamson, 1965). A medical student or physician being evaluated is given a brief description of a patient and the chief medical complaint in a written or audiovisual format. A long list of potential actions is also presented, including diagnostic procedures (e.g., history-taking questions, physical examination procedures, and laboratory tests) and patient management interventions (e.g., physical treatment, medications, and hospitalization). The subject selects an action from those available, and the results are provided. Another action is selected, with results provided, and the procedure is repeated until no further action is seen as indicated.

Patient management problems have often been prepared in written formats with latent image response forms that provide written results or direct the subject to a visual display, for example, of an X ray or blood smear (McGuire & Babbott, 1967; McGuire & Solomon, 1971; Williamson, 1965). Card decks have also been used with a diagnostic or treatment procedure printed on one side of each card and the results on the reverse (Barrows & Tamblyn, 1977; Rimoldi, 1961). In addition, patient management problems have been prepared in computer-based formats (e.g., Diserens, Schwartz, Guenin, & Taylor, 1986; Distlehorst & Barrows, 1982; Friedman, Korst, Schultz, Beatty, & Entine, 1978; Harless, Drennon, Marxer, Root, & Miller, 1971; Johnson, Moller, & Bass, 1975; Pickell, Medal, Mann, & Staebler, 1986; Schumacher, Burg, & Taylor, 1975).

Standardized simulations, including live simulated patients and patient management problems, have been frequently used in medical training (e.g., Newble, Elmslie, & Baxter, 1978; Sajid, Lipson, & Telder, 1975). Both types of simulations have also been applied in the credentialing of physicians (e.g., Hubbard, 1978; Lamont & Hennen, 1972; Norcini, Swanson, Grosso, & Webster, 1985; Taylor, Grace, Taylor, Fincham, & Skakun, 1976). These applications of standardized simulations in medicine can serve as models for similar applications in clinical training and credentialing in other professions, including counseling. As evaluation procedures, they complement traditional methods, providing more comprehensive evaluations of both the knowledge and skill domains of professional competence.

TYPES OF STANDARDIZED SIMULATIONS IN COUNSELING

Two general categories of standardized simulations in counseling have been developed. One is comprised of interview simulations, focusing on basic communication and counseling skills in direct client interaction. Live simulations similar to those in medicine are included along with a variety of other types of interview simulations. A second category is comprised of case management simulations, focusing on case management and clinical problem-solving skills. Case management simulations are similar to patient management problems in medicine.

Simulations reported in the counseling literature have been developed primarily for use in research. One common research application is in documenting the effects of training methods on target skills. Subjects will be provided training in interviewing or other clinical skills using one or more methods. Effects of training will then be evaluated by observing the subject performance in standardized simulations requiring the target skills. Applications of simulations in counselor training and credentialing have been reported much less frequently. However, simulations developed for research purposes would also be available for use in training and credentialing.

In examining different types of simulations, it is helpful to consider separately the stimulus and response characteristics, including fidelity (Berven & Scofield, 1980b; Fitzpatrick & Morrison, 1971). Stimulus characteristics include instructions, display (specific stimuli presented), and surround (the environment in which the simulation is completed). Response characteristics refer to the responses made by subjects while engaging in the simulation. Fidelity concerns the degree to which reality is approximated.

It is generally assumed that higher simulation fidelity is associated with more valid assessment of subject skills, although there is probably insufficient evidence to support this assumption (Fitzpatrick & Morrison, 1971). On the other hand, as simulation fidelity increases, control of extraneous sources of variation in subject performance decreases. Also, evaluation of performance may become more subjective, and difficulty and cost of administration may increase substantially. As will be seen in the following review of simulation types, there is considerable variability in both stimulus and response fidelities.

Interview Simulations

Interview simulations have been reported frequently in the counseling literature. A variety of simulation types have been developed, with stimulus and response characteristics varying in fidelity from very low to high.

Responses to Brief Interview Interchanges. Several types of interview simulations require responses to brief interchanges taken from counseling interviews. The stimuli are the interchanges that may be as brief as a single client response, usually along with the preceding counselor statement, or they may involve a sequence of several counselor–client responses. A simulation will typically be comprised of a number of such interchanges, with subject responses scored and summed to produce a total score.

The interchanges may be presented in written, audio, or video formats, with stimulus fidelity progressing from very low to moderate. Written interview interchanges present only verbal cues—the actual words communicated. In contrast, video interchanges provide paralinguistic and kinesic cues in addition to the verbal, with the audio format providing some but not all of these additional cues. Thus, of the three formats, video interchanges provide stimulus complexity closest to that available in an actual interview. Within each of the three stimulus formats, different types of subject responses may be required, characterized by varying response fidelities.

One type presents a series of interview interchanges, each ending with one or more counselor responses. The subject may be asked to rate or classify the counselor responses according to some criteria or to select the preferred counselor response from the alternatives presented. This type of simulation can be used to evaluate skills in discriminating the "helpfulness" or "appropriateness" of the counselor responses. The response fidelity is very low, as subjects need only to recognize certain attributes in a response rather than actually producing the response; consequently, the response demands differ considerably from the actual conduct of an interview. Examples of this type of simulation are the Index of Discrimination (Carkhuff, 1969) and the Microcounseling Skill Discrimination Scale (Lee, Zingle, Patterson, Ivey, & Haase, 1976).

Another type also presents brief interchanes in a written, audio, or video format, each ending with a client response. Rather than simply evaluating or selecting from responses provided, subjects are asked to provide written counselor responses, as if they were actually conducting the interview. The response fidelity is higher than the previously discussed type, but still low, as the demands of composing written interview responses are still quite different than the demands of conducting actual interviews. This type of simulation has been reported frequently in the counseling literature. One example is provided by the Index of Communication (Carkhuff, 1969). In addition, this general type of simulation has been used to assess counselor skills in confrontation (Rosenthal, 1977), formulating questions (Robinson, Kurpius, & Froehle, 1981), and communication of empathy (Crabb, Moracco, & Bender, 1983).

A third type typically uses video interchanges as the stimulus and requires subjects to make oral responses. The response fidelity is higher than written responses but should probably be considered only moderate. Talking to an image on a television screen is quite artificial, and formulating single responses is qualitatively different from carrying on an extended interaction. This type of simulation has been used to assess basic counseling skills in formulating questions (Robinson, Froehle, & Kurpius, 1979; Robinson *et al.*, 1981), reflection of feeling (Froehle,

Robinson, & Kurpius, 1983), and communication of empathy (Hodge, Payne, & Wheeler, 1978; Payne, Weiss, & Kapp, 1972; Payne, Winter, & Bell, 1972; Ronnestad, 1977; Strohmer, Biggs, Haase, & Purcell, 1983); a battery of interchanges has also been developed to assess eight different counseling skills (Fong & Borders, 1985). In addition, simulations of this type have been used to assess skills in consultation interviews (Errek & Randolph, 1982).

Several different methods have been used to quantify and evaluate interview responses in the various types of simulations. Ratings of empathy and related therapeutic conditions have frequently been used, such as the Empathic Understanding Scale (Carkhuff, 1969) and the Accurate Empathy Scale (Truax & Carkhuff, 1967). Another approach records frequencies of target responses, either frequencies of single response types or the mix of multiple response types, using comprehensive taxonomy systems (e.g., Hill, 1978). Some researchers have emphasized the importance of evaluating responses not only in terms of quantity or frequency but also in terms of quality, such as ratings of content, type appropriateness, and delivery (Froehle *et al.*, 1983; Robinson *et al.*, 1979; Robinson *et al.*, 1981). Another approach uses more objective behavioral measures, such as number of topic changes, response latency, and the number of words in responses (e.g., Errek & Randolph, 1982; Ivey & Authier, 1978).

Computer Simulations. One computer simulation of an initial interview, CLIENT 1, has been reported in the counseling literature (Hummel, Lichtenberg, & Shaffer, 1975; Lichtenberg, Hummel, & Shaffer, 1984). An extended counselor–client interaction is conducted via an interactive computer terminal, and the subject's task is to move the client toward problem identification. Counselor responses are constructed by referring to menus of alternative leads, affect, content areas, person references, qualifying phrases, and connecting prepositions, and then entering corresponding code numbers. Client statements and movement toward verbalizing a problem depend on factors such as threat, strength of relationship, and counselor competence that are reflected in the sequence of subject (counselor) responses.

Both stimulus and response fidelities associated with a computer simulation such as CLIENT 1 may be characterized as low to moderate. Stimulus characteristics are similar to those of the written interview interchanges discussed previously. Only the words communicated by the subject are provided, without paralinguistic and kinesic cues. Response fidelity is affected by the complex and laborious method of constructing counselor responses, reducing subject spontaneity. In contrast to the brief interview interchanges, however, extended interaction is provided, with responses influenced by previous response sequences, enhancing fidelity.

Quantification and evaluation of subject performance can focus both on subject interview behavior (process) and the effects produced in problem identification (outcome). Many of the same methods applied to brief interchanges could also be applied to evaluating subject responses in a computer simulation, such as ratings of therapeutic conditions, frequencies of target response types, and some of the objective, behavioral measures. In addition, the subject's success in moving the client toward recognition and definition of the problem being brought to the counselor can also be evaluated.

Live Simulations. Live interview simulations are similar to the simulated or programmed patient method developed in medicine. A subject carries on a live, extended interaction to accomplish some counseling objective with a person portraying a client. All aspects of a clinical practice situation are approximated as closely as possible, and the person portraying the client is trained to provide a standardized stimulus situation for all subjects. Different applications of live simulations vary in the amount and nature of training provided to the simulated client and, consequently, in the degree of standardization achieved. The simulated client is not expected to behave in exactly the same way with all individuals conducting the interview but, rather, to adopt the role of the client and always behave as he or she would likely behave. Because the demands placed on a simulated client are similar to those placed on actors, individuals with experience in drama may be used. Given the close approximations to actual clinical practice situations that can be achieved with live interview simulations, both the stimulus and response fidelities are high.

Applications of live interview simulations have been reported frequently in the counseling literature. They have been applied in evaluating basic interviewing skills, such as use of questions, reflections of feeling, and interpretations (e.g., Hirsch & Stone, 1982; Thompson & Blocher, 1979). Other applications have focused on skills in responding to negative affect (Davis, Hector, Meara, King, Tracy, & Wycoff, 1985; Hector, Davis, Denton, Hayes, & Hector, 1979), setting counseling goals (Peters, Cormier, & Cormier, 1978), interpreting testing information (Baker, Johnson, Kopala, & Strout, 1985), facilitating client decisions (Baker, Scofield, Clayton, & Munson, 1984), and conducting initial interviews in rehabilitation settings (Pape & Berven, 1983). Rosenthal (1977) provides an example of a highly standardized live simulation to evaluate skills in confrontation. Simulated clients were trained to provide three content/content and three content/affect discrepancies in their communication during 15-minute interviews, so that subject skills could be evaluated in recognizing and responding to the conflicting messages.

A variety of methods is available for quantifying and evaluating performance in live interview simulations. Virtually all of the methods described for evaluating performance in responding to brief interview interchanges can also be applied to live simulations, including ratings of basic therapeutic conditions, frequencies and quality of response types used, and objective measures of interview behaviors. In addition, several other rating scales are available that can be used in live simulations, to be completed either by the simulated client or observers, such as the Counselor Effectiveness Scale (Ivey & Authier, 1978). The most widely used of these scales is the Counselor Rating Form (Barak & LaCrosse, 1975), which evaluates counselor expertness, attractiveness, and trustworthiness. Scales may also be developed specifically for use in evaluating skill in implementation and/or quality of implementation of each of a sequence of steps in an intervention strategy. As an example of another type of measure, Pape and Berven (1983) evaluated assessment skills in the accurate identification of client assets, limitations, and preferences following a simulated initial interview.

Case Management Simulations

Case management simulations are similar to patient management problems developed in medicine. As with patient management problems, case management simulations begin with some client information provided, such as a referral letter, a client application for service, or a summary of an initial interview. A subject is then given a list of alternative case service actions from which to choose and moves through a sequence of taking actions and receiving corresponding reports until no further actions are seen as indicated. Thus subjects make the clinical judgments and decisions necessary to move through the sequence of case service actions, which might require months or even years in actual practice, and their performance may be presumed to reflect their clinical problem-solving skills.

Case management simulations can be prepared in written format, with reports stored in envelopes or sealed booklets, with latent image response forms directing the subject to reports from actions taken. Computer-based formats can also be used, facilitating administration, scoring, and record keeping. Stimulus fidelities are low, as information is typically provided in a written or printed format; however, advances in interactive video offer future possibilities with computer-based versions to expand the methods of presenting information, thus enhancing stimulus fidelity (Baron & Hutchinson, 1984). Response fidelity may be considered moderate. The sequential nature of the tasks required in a simulation is similar to actual case service situations, but there are many differences in demands from those in actual clinical practice.

Relative to interview simulations, case management simulations have not been reported as frequently in the counseling literature, but a few have been described. Six case management simulations in rehabilitation counseling have been developed in a written format (Coker, Currie, Menz, Andrew, & Dunn, 1976; Currie, 1977). The simulations were set in a state vocational rehabilitation agency, providing 15 alternative case service actions and up to six interviews. Each simulation proceeded from the point of referral to the determination of eligibility for state agency services. Berven and Scofield (1980a) adapted one of the six simulations in a computer-based format, providing automated administration and scoring of subject performance. Chan, Parker, Lam, Mecaskey and Malphurs (in press) prepared a microcomputer version of the Berven and Scofield computer program that, in comparison to the original mainframe version, made the simulation usable in many more locations. Berven (1985b) developed another set of three case management simulations in rehabilitation counseling, adding a number of features to the Berven and Scofield method. Each simulation provided 78 alternative actions and proceeded through the entire rehabilitation case service process from intake to completion of service. In addition to automating administration and record keeping, the simulations also allowed multiple actions to be taken simultaneously, monitored time in case service weeks, and provided reports from some actions, such as counseling and training interventions, in a series of progress reports. Finally, a set of two simulations in community mental health practice, one inpatient and one outpatient, has been developed (Butcher & Scofield, 1984; Butcher, Scofield, & Baker, 1984, 1985; Scofield, 1981). Each simulation provided 28 alternative actions in diagnosis and assessment and concluded with the subject writing a treatment plan on the basis of information obtained.

Performance on case management simulations has been quantified and evaluated relative to the performance of criterion groups of experienced professionals (Berven & Scofield, 1980a). Proficiency scores have been derived indicating the extent to which all important actions were taken. Efficiency scores have also been derived indicating the extent to which important actions were taken *and* unimportant actions were avoided. These scoring procedures have been based on methods developed for patient management problems in medicine. In addition, Butcher *et al.* (1984) used a competency index, based on a combination of the proficiency and efficiency indexes.

APPLICATIONS OF STANDARDIZED SIMULATIONS

The majority of applications of standardized simulations reported in the counseling literature have been in research. However, there are also many potential applications in counselor training and credentialing that could supplement traditional methods in evaluating the skill domain of professional competence. Again, models are available in medicine for such expanded applications.

Evaluation in Counselor Training

Standardized simulations can provide useful evaluation procedures in any course or module in counselor training that focuses, at least in part, on the acquisition of skills. In fact, even those courses focusing primarily on the knowledge domain of professional competence might profitably use simulations to provide evaluation situations requiring the application of that knowledge in clinical practice. The use of standardized simulations is particularly consistent with competency-based models of counselor training. Competency-based models begin with specific areas of competence that will provide the focus of training. Instructional objectives are specified in each area, and courses or course modules are designed to accomplish each objective (Horan, 1972; Winborn, Hinds, & Stewart, 1971). In each case, evaluation procedures are also designed that are appropriate to the target areas of competence for that objective.

Miller (1972) provides a model for counselor training comprised of four levels of instructional objectives. At each successive level, methods of instruction and evaluation are used that are progressively higher in fidelity. The first level, "reading and listening" objectives, focuses on knowledge basic to counseling using didactic instruction and traditional written evaluation methods. "Modeling" objectives provide demonstrations of specific counseling skills; evaluation is conducted through interview simulations requiring *the discrimination of* appropriate responses in brief interview interchanges. "Practice responses and role-playing" objectives provide practice and simulated experience in the development and application of counseling skills. Two phases are included at this level, each using interview simulations of different fidelities for evaluation. The first phase uses low-to-moderate fidelity simulations requiring *written or oral responses to* brief interchanges presented in written, audio, or video formats; the second phase uses high-fidelity live interview simulations. Finally, the fourth level, "supervised experience," requires the application of skills with clients in actual clinical settings.

Interview simulations appear to be, by far, the most prevalent type of simulation used in counselor training (e.g., Anthony, Slowkowski, & Bendix, 1976; Carkhuff, 1969; Horan, Stone, & Herold, 1976; Ivey & Authier, 1978). The use of case management and other types of simulations in counselor training has seldom been reported in the literature. Live simulations are the most frequently used type of interview simulation, but they may often differ in important ways from the live simulations discussed here. Often, fellow students in a class may serve as simulated clients that can reduce simulation fidelity. Where paid or volunteer "clients" are used, only limited training will sometimes be given to the client, reducing standardization of the evaluation situation.

An example of standardized simulations in both interviewing and case management used in counselor training is provided by a graduate course in counseling techniques taught by the author. Early in the course, low-to-moderate fidelity interview simulations are used, requiring written responses to either written or video interchanges, to evaluate basic counseling and communication skills. Later in the course, live interview simulations are used with a client portrayed by an individual with experience in drama. The client role is based on an actual client served in a local rehabilitation agency. Prior to beginning the interviews, the simulated client is given several hours of training using written case materials, videotapes, and practice interviews with video feedback, in order to develop a consistent client role. Students then conduct a series of several interviews with the client during the remainder of the semester. The interviews are observed and evaluated, and videotapes of the interviews are made available to students for self-evaluation. Between interviews, students have access to a computer-based case management simulation where they can take actions in assessment and intervention using outside resources. The interview and case management simulations together simulate service to a client in a rehabilitation setting. Because the focus of the course is on counseling and problem-solving skills, the simulations serve as "examinations," with course grades based on performance.

Variations on interview and case management simulations could be developed to evaluate skills in courses and modules in various content areas. For example, in assessment course work, variations of computer-based case management simulations, perhaps combined with interactive video, could be developed to evaluate skill in administering and scoring individual intelligence tests; in selecting assessment methods and instruments as assessment data accumulates; or in integrating assessment data in formulating diagnoses and treatment plans. Also, simulations with video displays depicting client behavior in various situations could be used to evaluate skills in behavior observation and analysis.

Evaluation batteries, including simulations of various types, could also be developed, similar to assessment centers that have been used in business to evaluate candidates for management and sales positions (Bray & Campbell, 1968; Bray & Grant, 1966). Such evaluation batteries could be used to evaluate readiness for supervised clinical experience or as part of comprehensive examinations required for graduate degrees. Again, models are available in medicine where problem-based examinations of clinical competence have been developed for evaluating medical students in their final year of training (Harden, Stevenson, Downie, & Wilson, 1975; Newble *et al.*, 1978). The examinations have included written sections, comprised of traditional objective and free-response items, and practical sections. The practical sections have utilized a variety of different simulations, each at a different work station. Students being evaluated move from station to station in completing the examination. The use of similar evaluation batteries in counselor training could make examinations more comprehensive in reflecting the skill domain as well as the knowledge domain of professional competence.

Evaluation in Counselor Credentialing

A number of credentialing mechanisms have been implemented for practitioners in counseling (Fretz & Mills, 1980; Hedgeman, 1985; Messina, 1985; Stone, 1985). Licensing mechanisms are provided in nearly every state for the practice of psychology, through which many counseling psychologists are licensed, and a growing number of states have developed licensing mechanisms specifically for counselors. Certification mechanisms are provided in counseling psychology by the American Board of Professional Psychology (ABPP), in counseling by the National Board for Certified Counselors (NBCC), in rehabilitation counseling by the Commission on Rehabilitation Counselor Certification

(CRCC), and in mental health counseling by the National Academy of Certified Clinical Mental Health Counselors (NACCMHC). In addition, counselors may obtain credentials in other specialties or related fields, such as marriage and family therapy or sex education, counseling, and therapy.

In general, the various credentialing mechanisms for counselors rely upon traditional methods for evaluating and documenting professional competence, including academic degrees, supervised experience in professional practice, letters of references or ratings of competence by supervisors or peers, and oral examinations or interviews by an examining board. In addition, traditional written examinations are also commonly used. Often, items that attempt to evaluate application of knowledge and clinical judgment and problem-solving skills are included; for example, items may present a clinical situation in writing and present several alternative diagnostic determinations, case service actions, or interventions in a multiple-choice format. Such items may be conceptualized as variations on simulations with low-fidelity stimulus and response characteristics.

Some innovation is currently in progress that may lead to expanded use of standardized simulations in credentialing mechanisms related to counseling. Some research is currently in progress that may lead to the use of case management simulations in the licensing examination for psychologists (Hall, Chapter 11 in this volume; Smith, 1983). In addition, the NACCMHC has also studied the use of case management simulations in the certification of mental health counselors (Butcher *et al.*, 1984; Scofield, 1981). Finally, a particularly innovative approach is being explored by ABPP in testing the assessment center model on actual candidates for certification (Mayfield, Chapter 12 in this volume). For some time, ABPP has included review and observation of candidate work samples in its examination procedures.

Models for the application of interview simulations in the credentialing of counselors are again available in medicine. The American Board of Orthopedic Surgery has included live simulations in its certification procedures, with candidates required to carry on 7- to 10-minute interactions with examiners playing prespecified roles of patients, physicians, and other health professionals (Levine & McGuire, 1970). In addition, the College of Family Physicians of Canada has also included live simulations in its examination procedures, using three simulated office visits with actors trained to portray standard patient roles with specified medical conditions (Lamont & Hennen, 1972). The cost and logistical problems associated with live simulations would limit their utility in many credentialing applications for counselors.

However, low-to-moderate fidelity interview simulations, requiring written responses to written or video interchanges, could be much more feasible to implement, and live simulations might be possible in certain applications.

Models for the use of case management simulations in credentialing are more widely available in medicine. Patient management problems in a written, latent-image format have been included for a number of years in the licensing examinations for physicians, prepared by the National Board of Medical examiners (NBME) (Hubbard, 1978). In addition, patient management problems have been used in the certification examinations for at least eight medical specialties (Smith, 1983). It would seem quite feasible to develop case management simulations in a written format for use in credentialing examinations for counselors. In addition, with the increasing availability of microcomputer-equipped classrooms where certification examinations might be administered, the use of computer-based case management simulations might be feasible, providing automated administration and scoring, further enhancing feasibility.

Evaluation of Counselor Training Programs

Evaluation of training programs may occur at both informal and formal levels. Informal evaluations may be conducted by counselor training programs themselves in an attempt to identify their strengths and limitations and to develop recommendations for improvement. Formal evaluations may be conducted for purposes of program accreditation. Accreditation mechanisms attempt to ensure minimum standards of training program quality. They are an important part of overall credentialing systems, as graduation from an accredited training program is often required for certification or licensure. Several accrediting mechanisms have been developed for training programs in counseling (see Hollis & Wantz, 1986). Mechanisms are administered by APA for doctoral programs in counseling psychology, by the Council on Rehabilitation Education (CORE) for master's degree programs in rehabilitation counseling, and by the Council for Accreditation of Counseling and Related Educational Programs (CACREP) for doctoral programs in counselor education and master's degree programs in school counseling, community and agency counseling, and student personnel services in higher education.

Evaluation of training programs must go beyond evaluation of process to also consider product—the competence attained by program graduates (Berven & Wright, 1978; Pottinger *et al.*, 1980; Rimmer, 1981).

Process is generally evaluated through a review of curriculum, faculty qualifications, admission procedures, administrative support, resources for supervised clinical experience, and other aspects of the training program itself and procedures followed. Product evaluation is typically accomplished through a review of employment and professional accomplishments of graduates and subjective impressions of competence achieved through interviews with students, graduates, and faculty, and, perhaps, a review of selected student products such as theses and dissertations. Another aspect of program product is the success of graduates in obtaining appropriate certification and licensure.

It would seem clear that any evaluation procedures used in counselor training or credentialing to provide comprehensive evaluation of professional competence would reflect on the product of training programs and, thus, could contribute to training program evaluation. Consequently, applications of standardized simulations in evaluating the skill domain of professional competence can serve as product evaluation data for accreditation as well as informal program evaluation.

EXPANDING APPLICATIONS OF STANDARDIZED SIMULATIONS

Standardized simulations have been used on a limited basis for evaluation in counselor training and credentialing. However, they could be applied much more extensively than is currently the case. Expanded applications could lead to more comprehensive evaluations of the skill domain of professional competence. A number of issues and needs should be addressed in order to facilitate expanded applications.

Definitions of Competence

If standardized simulations and other procedures are to be developed for evaluation in counselor training and credentialing, the concept of competence must be comprehensively defined as it relates to the professional practice of counseling. Methods that have commonly been used to define competence have included expert opinion regarding competence required or comprehensive models for conceptualizing competence (e.g., Palmo & Seary, 1983). Research to define competence has generally focused on the functions or tasks performed in professional practice (e.g., Rubin, Matkin, Ashley, Beardsley, May, Onstott, & Puckett, 1984; Wright & Fraser, 1975). Thus traditional approaches in defining professional competence have focused on the functions or tasks performed.

An alternative approach to defining competence focuses on the performer, rather than the tasks performed, in attempting to *explain* rather than describe competent behavior. In other words, an attempt is made to determine the knowledge, skill, and affective characteristics that distinguish competent performers rather than focusing on competent behavior itself. Behavioral event analysis, developed by McClelland and colleague (e.g., McClelland & Boyatzis, 1980), characterizes this approach. The first step in this analysis is the identification of a group of superior performers in the profession and a group of average performers, through supervisor and peer nominations. Then "behavioral-event interviews" are conducted with individuals in each group, discussing specific events that have occurred in practice and how individuals behaved in relation to those events, including their covert thoughts and feelings. Through the interviews, hypotheses are formulated regarding the behaviors, both overt and covert, that distinguish the superior from average performers. Finally, the distinctions between superior and average performers are reconceptualized in terms of knowledge, skills, and personal characteristics in order to define critical competencies.

As an example, McClelland and Boyatzis (1980) applied behavioral event analysis to defining competence for Navy alcoholism counselors. As a result, five critical areas of competence were identified: (a) sense of personal efficacy; (b) skill in conceptualizing patterns of causation in client behavior; (c) empathy or sensitivity to verbal and nonverbal client behaviors; (d) genuineness or awareness of one's own personal feelings while engaged in counseling; and (e) desire for personal growth. As another example, Klemp (1977) identified three cognitive skills that distinguish superior performers in a broad array of professions and occupations: (a) skills in organizing complex information to identify predominant themes and issues; (b) skill in understanding different points of view when confronted with a controversy; and (c) skill in learning from experience. Such listings of areas of competence go well beyond those that would be defined through studies of tasks performed.

Measurement Characteristics of Standardized Simulations

As areas of competence are defined, standardized simulations or other types of evaluation procedures must be either developed or selected from those already available. As with any evaluation procedure, the reliability and validity of standardized simulations must be determined.

Reliability and validity of measurement may be influenced both by aspects of the simulation itself (e.g., simulation type, characteristics of a specific live simulated client) and the instrument used to quantify performance as well as a variety of other characteristics of the individuals conducting the evaluation, the individuals being evaluated, and the situational context. Consequently, it is important to assess the reliability and validity of specific applications of standardized simulations and instruments (Scofield & Yoxtheimer, 1983). However, it is also important to know whether acceptable reliabilities and validities can be achieved with specific applications of particular types of simulations to determine whether further research and applications might be warranted.

In reviewing applications of interview simulations, it appears possible to achieve acceptable interobserver reliabilities in evaluating performance. With various combinations of interview simulation types and measurement devices and procedures, multiple observers have achieved more than 90% agreement in categorizing interview responses and have attained interrater reliabilities in the .80s and .90s in rating performance (e.g., Baker *et al.*, 1985; Crabb *et al.*, 1983; Davis *et al.*, 1985; Errek & Randolph, 1982; Fong & Borders, 1985; Froehle *et al.*, 1983; Robinson *et al.*, 1981; Strohmer *et al.*, 1983). Interobserver reliabilities reflect observer error in measurement, which is one of the most significant reliability considerations in the use of interview simulations. However, alternate forms reliability estimates, focusing on content-sampling error, and test–retest reliability estimates, focusing on time-sampling error, are also important and have seldom been investigated (Scofield & Yoxtheimer, 1983).

Validity of interview simulations is specific to the purpose for which a simulation is used; thus an interview simulation may be valid for one purpose but not for another. However, one validity question that is important for many applications concerns the extent to which performance in a simulation is consistent with other indicators of counseling skill, such as training and experience. Another important validity question concerns the extent to which performance in a simulation corresponds with interview performance in actual clinical practice. Such validity questions have generally not been even addressed with interview simulations (Scofield & Yoxtheimer, 1983). Ponterotto and Furlong (1985) have provided a recent review on the reliability and validity of the most common rating scales used to evaluate performance in counseling.

Some limited research has been conducted on reliabilities and validities associated with case management simulations. According to McGuire, Solomon, and Bashook (1976), the most important reliability consideration with such simulations is content-sampling error, the extent to which estimates of skill are consistent across different cases or problems. All research to date has focused on this source of error and suggests that alternate forms reliabilities in the .50s can be achieved (Berven, 1985b; Butcher *et al.*, 1984), which are somewhat higher than those achieved with patient management problems in medicine (Elstein, Shulman, & Sprafka, 1978; McGuire *et al.*, 1976). Further, reliability estimates in the .70s have been obtained for composite scores across three case management simulations (Berven, 1985b).

Regarding validity, there is some evidence that performance differences on case management simulations may be consistent with differences in training and experience (Berven, 1985b; Butcher *et al.*, 1984). Research on performance consistencies between case management simulations and actual clinical practice has not yet been pursued, but comparable research has been conducted on patient management problems in medicine. In general, the research has suggested that a one-to-one correspondence does not exist (Goran, Williamson, & Gonnella, 1973; Newble, Hoare, & Baxter, 1982; Norman & Feightner, 1981). In other words, it would not be safe to conclude that an individual taking a particular action in a patient management problem would take that same action in serving that same patient in an actual clinical situation. (See Berven [1985b] for a more extensive review of research on reliability and validity relevant to case management simulations.)

One additional validity question that relates to both interview and case management simulations is content validity. Content validity concerns the adequacy with which a simulation samples the content domain of a particular area of competence. Content validity depends on defining the content domains from which to sample in constructing simulations. It also depends on the representativeness of situational and client characteristics simulated. Content validity is achieved through careful construction of simulations, basing them on actual representative client situations and, perhaps, involving practitioners who are familiar with day-to-day clinical practice.

Obviously, much additional research is needed to document the reliabilities and validities that can be achieved with standardized simulations in counseling, particularly with case management simulations. In addition, differences in reliabilities and validities associated with varying simulation fidelity should be examined. Practical advantages in terms of cost and ease of implementation are generally associated with lower fidelity. If comparable reliabilities and validities can be achieved with lower fidelity simulations, many applications will become more feasible.

Defining Performance Criteria

A continuing problem in the development and application of standardized simulations is the definition of suitable performance criteria. "Competent behavior" in a clinical situation, and a corresponding simulation, should be defined on the basis of empirical evidence that it is, in fact, related to the accomplishment of desired clinical objectives. Unfortunately, such evidence is often not available. Further, there is seldom one "correct" response to make in a particular interview situation or one "correct" action to take in a particular case management situation. However, it may be possible to identify responses or actions that are more desirable than others.

Often performance criteria are based on theory or on expert opinion. With case management simulations, performance criteria are often defined in terms of the performance of a sample of experienced practitioners on the same simulation (Berven, 1985b; Berven & Scofield, 1980a; Butcher *et al.*, 1984). The assumption underlying this approach is that the performance of an "expert" criterion group should approximate effective clinical practice. This assumption has been questioned by research on the diagnostic skills of physicians, where more experienced physicians have sometimes been found less effective because of more frequent diagnostic shortcuts (McGuire *et al.*, 1976).

Alternative methods for defining performance criteria should be sought, including alternative methods of defining "expertness" of potential criterion groups of practitioners. In particular, care must be taken that performance criteria do not merely reflect traditional practices, stiffling innovation and creativity (Berven, 1985b).

CONCLUSION

A number of standardized simulations in counseling have been developed, and interview simulations have been frequently applied in research. Applications in counselor training and credentialing have been much less frequent, but simulations developed for research are available for such applications. Models are provided in medicine for expanding applications in training and credentialing. Advancing technology and increased availability of microcomputers will continue to make applications of computer-based simulations more feasible (Berven, 1985a). Research is needed to comprehensively define professional competence in counseling and counseling specialties; to continue the development of additional simulations and the documentation of their measurement characteristics; and to resolve issues in defining performance criteria. In addition, applications of standardized simulations should be attempted in course and comprehensive examinations in counselor training and in credentialing examinations to determine their effectiveness and feasibility.

REFERENCES

Anthony, W. A., Slowkowski, P., & Bendix, L. (1976). Developing the specific skills and knowledge of the rehabilitation counselor. *Rehabilitation Counseling Bulletin, 19,* 456–462.

Baker, S. B., Scofield, M. E., Clayton, L. T., & Munson, W. W. (1984). Microskills practice versus mental practice training for competence in decision-making counseling. *Journal of Counseling Psychology, 31,* 104–107.

Baker, S. B., Johnson, E., Kopala, M., & Strout, N. J. (1985). Test interpretation competence: A comparison of microskills and mental practice training. *Counselor Education and Supervision, 25,* 31–43.

Barak, A., & LaCrosse, M. B. (1975). Multidimensional perception of counselor behavior. *Journal of Counseling Psychology, 22,* 471–476.

Baron, A., & Hutchinson, J. (1984). Interactive video: A promising technology for counseling services. *Journal of Counseling and Development, 63,* 244–247.

Barrows, H. S. (1971). *Simulated patients (programmed patients). The development and use of a new technique in medical education.* Springfield, IL: Charles C Thomas.

Barrows, H. S., & Abrahamson, S. (1964). The programmed patient: A technique for appraising student performance in clinical neurology. *Journal of Medical Education, 39,* 802–805.

Barrows, H. S., & Tamblyn, R. M. (1977). The Portable Patient Problem Pack: A problem-based learning unit. *Journal of Medical Education, 52,* 1002–1004.

Berven, N. L. (1985a). Computer technology in professional education. *Rehabilitation Counseling Bulletin, 29,* 26–41.

Berven, N. L. (1985b). Reliability and validity of standardized case management simulations. *Journal of Counseling Psychology, 32,* 397–409.

Berven, N. L., & Scofield, M. E. (1980a). Evaluation of clinical problem solving skills through standardized case management simulations. *Journal of Counseling Psychology, 27,* 199–208.

Berven, N. L., & Scofield, M. E. (1980b). Evaluation of professional competence through standardized simulations: A review. *Rehabilitation Counseling Bulletin, 24,* 178–202.

Berven, N. L., & Wright, G. N. (1978). An evaluation model for accreditation. *Counselor Education and Supervision, 17,* 188–194.

Bray, D. W., & Campbell, R. J. (1968). Selection of salesmen by means of an assessment center. *Journal of Applied Psychology, 52,* 36–41.

Bray, D. W., & Grant, D. L. (1966). The assessment center in the measurement of potential for business management. *Psychological Monographs, 80*(17, Whole No. 625).

Butcher, E., & Scofield, M. E. (1984). Use of a standardized simulation and process tracing for studying clinical problem solving competence. *Counselor Education and Supervision, 24*, 70–84.

Butcher, E., Scofield, M. E., & Baker, S. B. (1984). Validation of a standardized simulation for the assessment of competence in mental health counseling. *American Mental Health Counselors Association Journal, 6*, 162–172.

Butcher, E., Scofield, M. E., & Baker, S. B. (1985). Clinical judgment in planning mental health treatment: An empirical investigation. *American Mental Health Counselors Association Journal, 7*, 116–126.

Carkhuff, R. R. (1969). *Helping and human relations.* New York: Holt, Rinehart & Winston.

Chan, F., Parker, H. J., Lam, C. S., Mecaskey, C., & Malphurs, L. (in press). Computer case management simulations: Applications in rehabilitation education. *Rehabilitation Counseling Bulletin.*

Coker, C. C., Currie, L., Menz, F., Andrew, J., & Dunn, D. (1976). *Rehabilitation facilities referrals: Step I—Determining client eligibility.* Menomonie: University of Wisconsin-Stout, Rehabilitation Research & Training Center.

Crabb, W. T., Moracco, J. C., & Bender, R. C. (1983). A comparative study of empathy training with programmed instruction for lay helpers. *Journal of Counseling Psychology, 30*, 221–226.

Currie, L. E. (1977). Simulated casework: Some training and research aspects. *Rehabilitation Counseling Bulletin, 20*, 254–259.

Davis, K. L., Hector, M. A., Meara, N. M., King, J. W., Tracy, D. C., & Wycoff, J. P. (1985). Teaching counselor trainees to respond consistently to different aspects of anger. *Journal of Counseling Psychology, 32*, 580–588.

Diserens, D., Schwartz, M. W., Guenin, M., & Taylor, L. A. (1986). Measuring the problem-solving ability of students and residents by microcomputer. *Journal of Medical Education, 61*, 461–466.

Distlehorst, L. H., & Barrows, H. S. (1982). A new tool for problem-based, self-directed learning. *Journal of Medical Education, 57*, 486–488.

Elstein, A. S., Shulman, L. S., & Sprafka, S. A. (1978). *Medical problem solving: An analysis of clinical reasoning.* Cambridge: Harvard University Press.

Errek, H. K., & Randolph, D. L. (1982). Effects of discussion and role-play activities in the acquisition of consultant interview skills. *Journal of Counseling Psychology, 29*, 304–308.

Fitzpatrick, R., & Morrison, E. J. (1971). Performance and product evaluation. In R. L. Thorndike (Ed.), *Educational measurement* (pp. 237–270). Washington, DC: American Council on Education.

Fong, M. L., & Borders, L. D. (1985). Effect of sex role orientation and gender on counseling skills training. *Journal of Counseling Psychology, 32*, 104–110.

Fretz, B. R., & Mills, D. H. (1980). *Licensing and certification of psychologists and counselors.* San Francisco: Jossey-Bass.

Friedman, R. B., Korst, D. R., Schultz, J. V., Beatty, E., & Entine, S. (1978). Experience with the simulated patient-physician encounter. *Journal of Medical Education, 53*, 825–830.

Froehle, T. C., Robinson, S. E., & Kurpius, D. J. (1983). Enhancing the effects of modeling through role-play practice. *Counselor Education and Supervision, 22*, 197–206.

Goran, M. J., Williamson, J. W., & Gonnella, J. S. (1973). The validity of patient management problems. *Journal of Medical Education, 48*, 171–177.

Harden, R., Stevenson, M., Downie, W. W., & Wilson, G. M. (1975). Assessment of clinical competence using an objective structured examination. *British Medical Journal, 1*(5955), 447–451.

Harless, W. G., Drennon, G. G., Marxer, J. J., Root, J. A., & Miller, G. E. (1971). CASE: A computer-aided simulation of the clinical encounter. *Journal of Medical Education, 46*, 443–448.

Hector, M. A., Davis, K. L., Denton, E. A., Hayes, T. W., & Hector, J. H. (1979). Teaching counselor trainees how to respond consistently to client negative affect. *Journal of Counseling Psychology, 26*, 146–151.

Hedgeman, B. S. (1985). Rehabilitation counselor certification. *Journal of Counseling and Development, 63*, 609–610.

Hill, C. E. (1978). Development of a counselor verbal response category system. *Journal of Counseling Psychology, 25*, 461–468.

Hirsch, P. A., & Stone, G. L. (1982). Attitudes and behavior in counseling skill development. *Journal of Counseling Psychology, 29*, 516–522.

Hodge, E. A., Payne, P. A., & Wheeler, D. D. (1978). Approaches to empathy training: Programmed methods versus individual supervision and professional versus peer supervisors. *Journal of Counseling Psychology, 25*, 449–453.

Hogan, D. B. (1979a). Is licensing public protection or professional protectionism? In P. Pottinger & J. Goldsmith (Eds.), *New directions for experimental learning: No. 3. Defining and measuring competence* (pp. 13–24). San Francisco: Jossey-Bass.

Hogan, D. B. (1979b). *The regulation of psychotherapists.* Cambridge, MA: Ballinger.

Hollis, J. W., & Wantz, R. A. (1986). *Counselor preparation. 1986–89. Programs, personnel, trends* (6th ed.). Muncie, IN: Accelerated Development.

Horan, J. J. (1972). Behavioral goals in systematic counselor education. *Counselor Education and Supervision, 11*, 162–170.

Horan, J. J., Stone, C. I., & Herold, P. L. (1976). Systematic desensitization as an instructional module. *Counselor Education and Supervision, 15*, 286–291.

Hubbard, J. P. (1978). *Measuring medical education. The tests and experience of the National Board of Medical Examiners* (2nd ed.). Philadelphia: Lea & Febiger.

Hummel, T. J., Lichtenberg, J. W., & Shaffer, W. F. (1975). CLIENT 1: A computer program which simulates client behavior in an initial interview. *Journal of Counseling Psychology, 22*, 164–169.

Ivey, A. E., & Authier, J. (1978). *Microcounseling: Innovations in interviewing, counseling, psychotherapy, and psychoeducation* (2nd ed.). Springfield, IL: Charles C Thomas.

Johnson, P. E., Moller, J. H., & Bass, G. M. (1975). Analysis of expert diagnosis of a computer simulation of congenital heart disease. *Journal of Medical Education, 50*, 466–470.

Klemp, G. O. (1977). Three factors of success. In D. W. Vermilye (Ed.), *Relating work and education. Current issues in higher education 1977* (pp. 102–109). San Francisco: Jossey-Bass.

Klemp, G. O. (1979). Identifying, measuring, and integrating competence. In P. S. Pottinger & J. Goldsmith (Eds.), *New directions for experiential learning: No. 3. Defining and measuring competence* (pp. 41–52). San Francisco: Jossey-Bass.

Lamont, C. T., & Hennen, B. K. E. (1972). The use of simulated patients in a certification examination in family medicine. *Journal of Medical Education, 47*, 789–795.

Lee, D. Y., Zingle, H. W., Patterson, J. G., Ivey, A. E., & Haase, R. F. (1976). Development and validation of a microcounseling skill discrimination scale. *Journal of Counseling Psychology, 23*, 468–472.

Levine, H. G., & McGuire, C. H. (1970). The use of role-playing to evaluate affective skills in medicine. *Journal of Medical Education, 45*, 700–705.

Lichtenberg, J. W., Hummel, T. J., & Shaffer, W. F. (1984). CLIENT 1: A computer simulation for use in counselor education and research. *Counselor Education and Supervision, 24*, 155–167.

Loganbill, C., Hardy, E., & Delworth, U. (1982). Supervision: A conceptual model. *Counseling Psychologist, 10*(1), 3–42.

McClelland, D. C., & Boyatzis, R. E. (1980). Opportunities for counselors from the competency assessment movement. *Personnel and Guidance Journal, 58*, 368–372.

McGuire, C. H., & Babbott, D. (1967). Simulation technique in the measurement of problem solving skills. *Journal of Educational Measurement, 4*, 1–10.

McGuire, C. H., & Solomon, L. M. (1971). *Clinical simulations: Selected problems in patient management*. New York: Appleton-Century-Crofts.

McGuire, C. H., Solomon, L. M., & Bashook, P. G. (1976). *Construction and use of written simulations*. New York: Psychological Corporation.

Messina, J. J. (1985). The National Academy of Certified Clinical Mental Health Counselors: Creating a new professional identity. *Journal of Counseling and Development, 63*, 607–608.

Miller, T. V. (1972). Simulation and instructional objectives in counselor education. *Counselor Education and Supervision, 12*, 83–87.

Myers, R. A. (1982). Education and training—The next decade. *Counseling Psychologist, 10*(2), 39–44.

Newble, D. I., Elmslie, R. R., & Baxter, A. (1978). A problem-based criterion-referenced examination of clinical competence. *Journal of Medical Education, 53*, 720–726.

Newble, D. I., Hoare, J., & Baxter, A. (1982). Patient management problems. Issues of validity. *Medical Education, 16*, 137–142.

Norcini, J. J., Swanson, D. B., Grosso, L. J., & Webster, G. D. (1985). Reliability, validity and efficiency of multiple choice question and patient management problem item formats in assessment of clinical competence. *Medical Education, 19*, 238–247.

Norman, G. R., & Feightner, J. W. (1981). A comparison of behavior on simulated patients and patient management problems. *Medical Education, 15*, 26–32.

Palmo, A. J., & Seary, T. A. (1983). A comprehensive model for multidimensional competencies in the training of secondary school counselors. *Counselor Education and Supervision, 23*, 83–89.

Pape, D. A., & Berven, N. L. (1983). Effects of training on intake interviewing skills in rehabilitation counseling. *Rehabilitation Counseling Bulletin, 26*, 164–173.

Payne, P. A., Weiss, S. D., & Kapp, R. A. (1972). Didactic, experiential, and modeling factors in the learning of empathy. *Journal of Counseling Psychology, 19*, 425–429.

Payne, P. A., Winter, D. E., & Bell, G. E. (1972). Effects of supervisor style on the learning of empathy in a supervision analogue. *Counselor Education and Supervision, 11*, 262–269.

Peters, G. A., Cormier, L. S., & Cormier, W. H. (1978). Effects of modeling, rehearsal, feedback, and remediation on acquisition of a counseling strategy. *Journal of Counseling Psychology, 25*, 231–237.

Pickell, G. C., Medal, D., Mann, W. S., & Staebler, R. J. (1986). Computerizing clinical patient problems: An evolving tool for medical education. *Medical Education, 20*, 201–203.

Ponterotto, J. G., & Furlong, M. J. (1985). Evaluating counselor effectiveness: A critical review of rating scale instruments. *Journal of Counseling Psychology, 32*, 597–616.

Pottinger, P. S. (1979). Competence assessment: Comments on current practices. In P. S. Pottinger & J. Goldsmith (Eds.), *New directions for experiential learning: No. 3. Defining and measuring competence* (pp. 25–39). San Francisco: Jossey-Bass.

Pottinger, P. S., Weisfeld, N. E., Tochen, D. K., Cohen, P. D., & Schaalman, M. L. (1980). *The assessment of occupational competence* (Contract NIE 400-78-0028). Boston: McBer.

Rimmer, S. M. (1981). A systems approach model for counselor education program development and redefinition. *Counselor Education and Supervision, 21*, 7–15.

Rimoldi, H. J. A. (1961). The Test of Diagnostic Skills. *Journal of Medical Education, 36*, 73–79.

Robinson, S. E., Froehle, T. C., & Kurpius, D. J. (1979). Self-instructional modules: Comparison of modeling and feedback media. *Counselor Education and Supervision, 18*, 251–259.

Robinson, S. E., Kurpius, D. J., & Froehle, T. C. (1981). A two-study comparison of written and video modeling and of written and oral assessment. *Counselor Education and Supervision, 21*, 45–56.

Ronnestad, M. H. (1977). The effects of modeling, feedback, and experiential methods on counselor empathy. *Counselor Education and Supervision, 16*, 194–201.

Rosenthal, N. R. (1977). A prescriptive approach for counselor training. *Journal of Counseling Psychology, 24*, 231–237.

Rubin, S. E., Matkin, R. E., Ashley, J., Beardsley, M. M., May, V. R., Onstott, K., & Puckett, F. D. (1984). Roles and functions of certified rehabilitation counselors. *Rehabilitation Counseling Bulletin, 27*, 199–224.

Sajid, A., Lipson, L. F., & Telder, T. V. (1975). A simulation laboratory for medical education. *Journal of Medical Education, 50*, 970–975.

Schumacher, C. G., Burg, F. D., & Taylor, W. C. (1975). Computerization of a patient management problems examination to prevent "retracing." *British Journal of Medical Education, 9*, 281–285.

Scofield, M. E. (1981). *Written treatment planning simulation in mental health*. University Park, PA: Pennsylvania State University.

Scofield, M. E., & Yoxtheimer, L. L. (1983). Psychometric issues in the assessment of clinical competence. *Journal of Counseling Psychology, 30*, 413–420.

Scofield, M. E., Berven, N. L., & Harrison, R. P. (1981). Competence, credentialing, and the future of rehabilitation. *Journal of Rehabilitation, 47*(1), 31–35.

Scofield, M. E., Terzella, J. M., Berven, N. L., & Thomas, K. R. (1983). Personal constructs in rehabilitation counseling: Empirically derived dimensions for competence assessment. *Rehabilitation Counseling Bulletin, 27*, 68–80.

Smith, I. L. (1983). Use of written simulations in credentialing programs. *Professional Practice of Psychology, 4*, 21–50.

Stone, L. A. (1985). National Board for Certified Counselors: History, relationships, and projections. *Journal of Counseling and Development, 63*, 605–606.

Strohmer, D. C., Biggs, D. A., Haase, R. F., & Purcell, M. J. (1983). Training counselors to work with disabled clients: Cognitive and affective components. *Counselor Education and Supervision, 23*, 132–141.

Taylor, W. C., Grace, M., Taylor, T. R., Fincham, S. M., & Skakun, E. N. (1976). The use of computerized patient management problems in a certifying examination. *Medical Education, 10*, 179–182.

Thompson, A. J. M., & Blocher, D. H. (1979). Co-counseling supervision in microcounseling. *Journal of Counseling Psychology, 26*, 413–418.

Truax, C. B., & Carkhuff, R. R. (1967). *Toward effective counseling and psychotherapy*. Chicago: Aldine.

Williamson, J. W. (1965). Assessing clinical judgment. *Journal of Medical Education, 40*, 180–186.

Winborn, B. B., Hinds, W. C., & Stewart, N. R. (1971). Instructional objectives for the professional preparation of counselors. *Counselor Education and Supervision, 10*, 133–137.

Wright, G. N., & Fraser, R. T. (1975). Task analysis for the evaluation, preparation, classification and utilization of rehabilitation counselor-track personnel. *Wisconsin Studies in Vocational Rehabilitation* (Series 3, Monograph 22). Madison: University of Wisconsin, Regional Rehabilitation Research Institute.

10

Accreditation

A Link between Training and Practice

PAUL D. NELSON and PATRICIA J. ALETKY

THE NATURE OF ACCREDITATION: VALUES, OBJECTIVES, AND METHODS

Accreditation implies quality in education, training, and professional service. It is both a process and a status by which institutions or programs are publicly recognized as having met certain criteria or standards of performance. The Council on Postsecondary Accreditation, whose function is to promulgate principles of practice in accreditation and facilitate high-quality of service among postsecondary education accrediting agencies, refers in its definition of accreditation to a recognition of institutions and programs for the level of performance, integrity, and quality that entitles them to the confidence invested in them by the educational community and the public they serve (Council on Postsecondary Accreditation, 1985). Thus public accountability is at the heart of accreditation. Although it is a voluntary, nongovernmental process as practiced in the United States, accreditation has assumed a quasi-public nature in the evaluation of education and training as well

PAUL D. NELSON and PATRICIA J. ALETKY • American Psychological Association, Washington, DC 20036.

as professional service functions. It is a process founded on institutional or program self-study, peer evaluation, and adherence to valid published standards.

Although most persons agree on the goals of accreditation, namely quality assessment and enhancement in education, training, or professional service for benefit of the public, there is less agreement on how to best achieve these goals. The history of accreditation indeed is one of conflict and confluence among philosophies of method and procedure. In a prologue to a comprehensive history and prospectus on accreditation, Young (1983) suggested four themes or contrasting approaches that have characterized the evolution of accreditation practices over the past 70 years. These might be described as (a) an emphasis on quantitative versus qualitative assessment, reflected in methods by which institutional or program quality is verified against specific quantifiable standards in contrast to more general criteria or guidelines; (b) an emphasis on standardization versus individuality of structure and function among institutions and programs, the result of which is varying degrees of equivalence in process and outcome between institutions or programs of the same general type; (c) an emphasis on external versus internal review and regulation, the former depending on assessment by parties external to the institution or program being evaluated and the latter placing more emphasis on self-evaluation and self-regulation; and (d) an emphasis on judgmental versus facilitative objectives, a difference between accreditation as an evaluative process that works toward classification and certification, and accreditation as a consultative process focused on development and enhancement of quality in institutions or programs.

Millard (1983a) also described the evolution of accreditation practices in a manner of contrasting emphases. During the earlier years, as among some accrediting agencies today, the emphasis was upon what Millard called the "definitional-prescriptive" approach to institutional or program review, often based on quantifiable verification of how well an institution or program compared with the profile of what is defined as a "good" institution or program. In contrast, Millard referred to the alternative, "mission-objective" approach, in which there is emphasis placed on evaluating institutions and programs in terms of the clarity and appropriateness of their mission and goals as well as their demonstrated effectiveness in achieving the same. The same variations in philosophy and practice might be depicted, as Kissick and Grubb (1984) have done, in terms of an "accounting or standards approach" to accreditation in contrast to a "criteria-based approach." The methods and procedures of the former are based chiefly on externally imposed standards, compliance with which is frequently quantifiable, and the outcome of which is a rather high level of homogeneity or standardization among accredited institutions and programs. By contrast, the "criteria-based approach" employs guidelines, perhaps normative expectations, more often qualitative than quantitative in nature, that afford the institution or program parameters against which to evaluate their objectives, processes, and outcomes. The latter requires much greater dependence upon methods of self-study and self-regulation, augmented by outside peer consultation and evaluation.

All of these emphases of method and purpose are present to some extent in accrediting practices today, often within the same accrediting agency. One might argue, in fact, that a salient feature of the way in which accreditation has evolved is its increased complexity, not only in procedure but in objective as well. This complexity is reflected in variations of practice among recognized accrediting agencies, all of which adhere nonetheless to a common set of accreditation principles. In illustration of this point, Petersen (1979) profiles the accreditation standards and guidelines among accrediting agencies, whereas Kells (1983) analyzes the opinions and practice of those who make accreditation decisions. Regardless of differences in philosophy and practice, however, there are four basic elements in the accreditation process. These are (a) the public statement of standards or criteria by an accrediting body; (b) voluntary institutional or program self-study; (c) peer consultation and evaluation invited by the institution or program; and (d) review, decision, and public acknowledgment of accreditation status by a recognized accrediting body. For the professions, these elements of self-governance are not new. Indeed, they reflect the very processes by which professionals should establish their standards of training and practice; monitor and evaluate their performance in meeting those standards; invite outside peers to consult, critique, or otherwise review their performance; and volunteer review of their performance against accepted standards by an outside body of professional and public representatives. It is a practice of professional quality assurance.

Although accreditation is a voluntary, nongovernmental process, its significance to the public has placed it in the middle of competing political forces, all of which have rights and responsibilities in higher education. In companion articles, Millard (1983b) and Scott (1983) summarized a few of those forces and discussed some of the criticisms of accreditation in higher education. Millard, serving as president of the

Council on Postsecondary Accreditation, described accreditation in higher education as "an unusual blend of self-regulation and academic conscience." He posed the question: "What steps must be taken to preserve its integrity?" Scott, speaking from experience with a state commission for higher education, asked: "Who controls the accreditation process? And a more fundamental question: Just what accreditation is needed by higher education institutions and programs?" Such judgments and questions of the accreditation process imply a multiplicity of perspectives about the purposes of accreditation and about whose interests are to be served best by accreditation. It is questions such as these, reflecting upon values, objectives, and methods of accreditation, that must be borne in mind as one reviews the history and looks to the future of accreditation practices specific to the profession of psychology. Such questions are not entirely of recent vintage, of course. Even in psychology, the historical experience of the accreditors and those accredited bears resemblance to the different perspectives of contemporary times. Note that in 1949, after the first 2 years of accreditation experience in professional psychology, the committee responsible for such accreditation activity had this to say:

> The Committee is naturally concerned with policies relating to accreditation and the implications and broad ramifications of such a program. We are involved and concerned both through membership on the Committee and through connection with graduate departments which are themselves subject to evaluation. During our visits to universities, we have found attitudes toward the Committee's work which varied all the way from those of hearty acceptance, confidence, and appreciation, to those of honest conviction that the Committee is a usurper of power and authority and that by the use of its power and its methods does damage to the work of graduate departments. (APA Committee on Training in Clinical Psychology, 1949, p. 340)

ACCREDITATION OF EDUCATION AND TRAINING PROGRAMS IN PROFESSIONAL PSYCHOLOGY

Sanford (1951), in his appraisal of psychology as a young profession following World War II, noted among the criteria of a "good profession" the imperative sense of social responsibility. Avoiding guild functions, a "good profession," Sanford argued, is one that continually seeks its unique pattern of competencies and renders a unique service on the basis of those competencies. Similarly, in speaking to the responsibilities of professional associations, Merton (1969) charged professions with an obligation to serve the public welfare by setting and enforcing rigorous standards of education, training, and practice for their disciplines. These writers thus speak to issues of professional self-regulation and public accountability, issues that are central to accreditation.

It was indeed through a sense of public accountability that the American Psychological Association (APA) established standards for graduate education and training in clinical psychology and thus initiated a system of accreditation in professional psychology in the late 1940s. Those standards, developed by the APA's Committee on Training in Clinical Psychology (1947), were responsive to a request for assistance by two public agencies, the Veterans Administration and the U.S. Public Health Service (Sears, 1947). Under the leadership of David Shakow, the Committee on Training in Clinical Psychology established goals and principles of doctoral education and training in professional psychology rather than a blueprint thereof. It is also clear, from the text of its initial recommendations in 1947, that the committee was keenly aware of the need for professional training to have a functional and valid relationship with what constitutes good practice in the profession. That emphasis on validity of education and training for professional psychology was signaled even more clearly 2 years later by the APA Committee on Training in Clinical Psychology (1949) in a progress report on the earliest accreditation reviews of programs in clinical psychology. Concluding that report, the committee wrote that

> we are convinced of the importance of setting standards and evaluating performance in clinical training—in fact we see this process as inevitable if clinical psychology is to establish itself soundly and be a credit to psychology as a whole. We have set up criteria and administered procedures in ways that seemed best; we are neither satisfied that they are perfect nor persuaded that they are dangerous or ineffective. It is natural that there should be differences of opinion in the Association regarding the goals and the techniques we have accepted. Both these differences and our own convictions are still matters of opinion rather than demonstrated fact. The real answer to the question "Shall we evaluate?" lies somewhere in the future—a future which must include among other considerations, a systematic appraisal of the effects of the committee's work, not only on the clinical psychological products which the universities turn out, but on other psychological products and university staffs and administrations as a whole. (APA Committee on Training in Clinical Psychology, 1949, pp. 340–341)

The committee's expressed concern with program outcomes is significant for two reasons, the first of which is that it speaks to the quality of program graduates and what that means for the practice of psychology. Thus it addresses the validity of training and of the status afforded an accredited program. The second account on which the committee's statement assumes significance is that it asks what effect the accreditation process might have on university staffs and administrations as a whole. In other words, how might the process of accreditation facilitate staff and program development?

By the mid-1960s, Goodstein and Ross (1966) reflected on the first two decades of progress in the accreditation of graduate programs in psychology. They concluded that accreditation had made a difference in promoting improvements in graduate education for professional psychology and provided a useful public service to prospective students as well. In more recent years, however, accreditation has been equally the target of critics, some of whom would argue that accreditation has "lost its teeth," no longer being sufficiently rigorous to protect the public; others, in contrast, maintain that the accreditors have become too narrow and rigid in setting forth and enforcing standards. Have the goals or standards of education and training in professional psychology changed? Are there different philosophies even among psychologists about the purpose of accreditation? Or is there no longer sensed to be a functional relationship between education and training and practice in professional psychology?

In perhaps the broadest sense, the goals of doctoral education and training have not changed appreciably over the past three decades. Although certainly there is a greater number and diversity of doctoral programs in professional psychology today than there was in the late 1940s, the earliest guidelines by which accreditation of doctoral education and training was practiced in psychology (APA Committee on Training in Clinical Psychology, 1947) embraced certain principles that remain today as basic to the preparation of professional psychologists. These are (a) that breadth first, then depth, of training should be emphasized; (b) that the student's preparation should be directed toward broad professional, nor narrow technical, goals; (c) that theory, research, and practice should be integrated throughout the student's training; (d) that emphasis should be given to the socialization of students into the profession; and (e) that students should develop a sense of professional responsibility at the community and societal level as well as at the level of the individual patient or client.

The culmination of learning experiences throughout the doctoral program of study, from the accumulation of knowledge or mastery of skills to the integration of those with attitudes, values, and ethics of professional practice, has always been the requirement for demonstrated competence of students, whether in the classroom, the laboratory, the clinic, or elsewhere in the field. In the current criteria by which doctoral programs in psychology are accredited, indeed, the ultimate test of student competence is the requirement that students demonstrate their readiness to practice, to wit: "In order to assess students' competence to practice, programs must develop an explicit, comprehensive system for evaluation" (American Psychological Association, 1979, p. 8). Accredited programs are expected to demonstrate how such a requirement is met, how comprehensively students are evaluated, and by what means such is accomplished. Indeed, there is an emphasis throughout the criteria for accreditation of doctoral progams and predoctoral internships that outcomes of learning be assessed through student performance. The latter is linked conceptually, at least, to standards of professional practice.

Accreditation introduces yet another link between training and practice, that of the values and attitudes, interpersonal behaviors, and administrative experiences that students develop through the socialization process. The criteria for accreditation of professional psychology training programs suggest in several instances the importance of interaction between faculty or staff and students as well as within each of those peer groups. Some of the references pertain to role modeling in general, some to attitudes and behaviors of critical inquiry among colleagues in research or practice, some to the development of observational skills useful in evaluating one's performance or that of one's colleagues, and some to simply the informal exchange of ideas among peers. These interpersonal behaviors are ideally the grist of everyday practice in a profession—the modus operandi. Furthermore, the values and attitudes that evolve in relation to these behaviors are central to being professional. Indeed, Shakow and his colleagues, when first developing guidelines for evaluating the quality of doctoral programs in clinical psychology, encouraged students to value and participate in a team approach to professional practice as in research, given the complexities of most problems addressed by psychologists (APA Committee on Training in Clinical Psychology, 1947). Such exhortation is quite consistent with the requirements and standards of practice in a wide array of public and private settings in which professional psychologists serve today. Indeed, this emphasis on interactions among colleagues and upon the process of having one's performance evaluated by peers as well as superiors is a special characteristic of professions. It is an emphasis on self-regulation, peer consultation, and evaluation against professionally acceptable standards for purposes of public accountability. Thus student participation in the accreditation process itself is an important part of the socialization process, for it introduces the young professional aspirant to a formal system of self-study, peer review, and evaluation against national standards of practice.

The issue of self-governance in professions, serving the interests of public accountability, is one that brings us to yet another link between training and practice and the accreditation of programs or institutional units in each. It is the issue of how programs or institutional units of training or practice in a profession adhere to national standards or criteria of quality while, at the same time, they are sufficiently innovative, flexible, and experimenting in attitude and procedures to seek constantly a more effective way to practice. This issue is especially important for those professions within which practice is based on the application of technologies and bodies of knowledge derived from scientific inquiry. Psychology is such a profession.

In the accreditation criteria for doctoral programs of professional psychology, the construct that best represents this issue is that of the program's "training model." It embodies (a) the program's underlying philosophy of education, training, and professional practice; (b) the program's goals and objectives; (c) the operational means by which the program intends to achieve its goals and objectives; and (d) the relevance of the program goals to local, regional, and national needs. Variation in training models may reflect differences between institutional contexts in which progams reside or different philosophical positions regarding the practice of a profession and the preparation of students for the same. Within the same profession, however, all program training models are expected to incorporate a common set of goals and objectives, if not always standard methods of achieving them, for entry into the profession. Once more, Shakow and his colleagues expressed the importance of this concept nearly 40 years ago in stating that

> our aims are . . . to achieve general agreement on the goals of training and encourage experimentation on methods of achieving those goals and to suggest ways of establishing high standards in a setting of flexibility and reasonable freedom. (APA Committee on Training in Clinical Psychology, 1947, p. 543)

It is a principle of accreditation that professional programs be evaluated in terms of their compliance with national standards or criteria but also in the context of their particular training models and unique institutional objectives. More than being an emphasis for the accreditors, this principle encourages a professional program to be engaged continuously in the process of self-study, ensuring that its goals and objectives are clear, that it has the means to achieve the same, that it carefully plans the allocation of resources to program achievements, and that it develops a set of systematic procedures by which to evaluate how effectively it is achieving its goals and objectives. Consequently, to the extent that students as well as faculty and staff are encouraged through the accreditation process to participate in program self-study and evaluation, another vital link is fostered between training and practice in the profession. For such participation, as an element in the professional socialization process, affords the student an opportunity to learn firsthand about the importance of goal setting, resource definition and allocation, and evaluation in any program, whether it is for education and training or providing professional services to the public. It places emphasis on program outcomes but only in the context of appropriate goals and objectives. It also places emphasis on public accountability and in so doing is a process of quality assurance.

The standards for practice in a profession and for quality assurance in professional service settings or units provide the raison d'être for the profession's education and training standards. They are the criteria, in a sense, against which the education and training standards should be validated. Issues of practice in a profession, of course, are complex. They involve political, economic, social, and legal considerations in addition to those of a professional or scientific nature. The practice of psychology has been no exception to that during the past few decades. The following section of this chapter summarizes some of the more salient issues of professional practice during that period and suggests some possible changes for the future, among those, the accreditation of psychological service delivery settings.

STANDARDS FOR PRACTICE IN PROFESSIONAL PSYCHOLOGY

For the past three decades, the APA has been involved in the development, promulgation, dissemination, and continual revision of standards for the practice of psychology. The objective of these standards has been to promote quality assurance of psychological services for providers, consumers, and third-party sanctioners of such services.

The first version of the "Standards for Providers of Psychological Services," produced by the Task Force on Standards for Service Facilities, was adopted as APA policy on September 4, 1974. In 1975, the APA Council of Representatives established a standing committee charged with updating and revising the standards. The second version was adopted in 1977. There were many changes in content as well as conceptualization of the document. Two notable changes are as follows: (a) the revised standards were to represent minimally accepted levels of performance and (b) they were seen as applying only to psychological services representing " 'human services' with the goal of facilitating more effective human functioning" (APA, 1977, p. 1).

Thus the 1977 "Standards for Providers of Psychological Services," the extant policy, is generally viewed as referring to clinical, counseling, school, and industrial/organizational psychologists. Functions such as teaching psychology and conducting scientific research in psychology were excluded from consideration. The 1977 "Standards" addressed issues of quality assurance related to providers, programs, accountability, and general environment in which services are provided. In addition, the "Standards" formalized APA's definition of a "professional psychologist": An individual possessing a doctoral degree from a regionally accredited university or professional school in a program that is primarily psychological in nature and having appropriate training and experience in the area of service offered. Along with the "Ethical Principles of Psychologists" (APA, 1981a), the "Standards for Providers of Psychological Services" (APA, 1977) represents the major policy statement of the APA, with relevance for state regulatory bodies as well as for federal agencies that look to the APA for general policy regarding the practice of psychology.

Although "Standards" is viewed as the generic policy defining the practice of psychology, the "Specialty Guidelines for the Delivery of Services" (APA, 1981b) was developed to explicate the various issues in the specific contexts of clinical, counseling, school, and industrial/organizational psychology, respectively. The four specialty guidelines were adopted by the council of representatives in 1980, after more than 3 years of committee work, with consultation from the relevant divisions. "Specialty Guidelines" offers more specific detail regarding practice issues such as the composition and organization of a psychological services unit as well as definitional issues for each of the four specialties, such as grandparenting rules. "Specialty Guidelines" is thought to be descriptive rather than prescriptive, in recognition of the fact that there is much overlap between the specialties in actual practice.

"Standards" and "Specialty Guidelines" are seen as being "living documents"; that is, revision is an ongoing process, currently overseen by the Committee on Professional Standards of APA's Board of Professional Affairs. Moreover, the revisions are conducted as alternating projects, with a cycle of work on the generic standards followed by explication in the specialty guidelines, followed by an updating of the generic standards. Currently, the committee sees itself as being in the final stages of revision of the generic standards and plans to turn its attention soon to reviewing and revising the specialty guidelines. Such revisions are made with input from hundreds of individual APA members who represent a variety of constituencies and interest groups.

Recently, the general interest in and intensity of involvement in the content of APA standards have increased significantly. Possible explanations of this phenomenon would include a changing legal climate and increasingly competitive marketplace for psychological services. The attempt to balance such practical realities with the need for quality assurance is a continual source of tension in the field. Perhaps because of such complexities, the most recent revision of the "Standards," originally planned for approval and publication by early 1985, is as of this writing many months away from being submitted for approval by the council of representatives.

Two major legal issues of great concern to psychologists are antitrust and malpractice litigation, both of which have sensitized practitioners to APA's policies. In simple terms, alleged violations of the Sherman Act (U.S. Code Ann., 1986, 15 U.S.C. § 1 *et seq.*) involve accusations of conspiracy to hinder someone's ability to operate in the free marketplace, and if such an allegation is proved, treble damages can be awarded to the plaintiff. To the extent that APA policy affects state legislation or reimbursement rules of third-party payers, there is a potential for lawsuits against the association or individual members or subgroups. Because standards for practice are inherently exclusive in their definitions of practitioners or the practice of psychology, the issue of anticompetitive practice remains. Nevertheless, professional associations acting in good faith for the benefit of consumers of its services have a valid role in setting such standards. To this end, organized psychology's relationship with its consuming public has become of increasing significance as it becomes crucial that professional standards are not simply self-serving. Thus as the marketplace becomes more competitive and more psychologists enter the private practice arena, it will become increasingly important to be able to demonstrate that standards and definitions for psychologists indeed contribute to higher quality services.

Malpractice actions have received much attention in the media and have been the subject of great concern to all the practicing professions, for example, to medicine and law as well as psychology. The cost of professional liability or malpractice insurance has increased significantly in the past few years. Within the field of psychology, the recent efforts to revise the generic standards have been met with strong opposition from some who feel that professional standards that are taken as being mandatory can be used against a practitioner in a malpractice action, possibly resulting in millions of dollars lost. An effort is now underway in response to such concerns to draft a preamble for the revised standards that presents them as aspirational; that is, standards define the highest quality of psychological service delivery, which may not always be feasible or possible. Controversy also exists regarding just how specific a formal policy document should be; some people believe in the necessity for elaborate explication and interpretive statements, and some prefer a more skeletal document that defines only the core of minimum standards for service delivery. In the end, of course, there is no guarantee that an individual or group will not be sued, but there is agreement that such situations must be avoided because the cost is exorbitant even when the end result is a successful defense.

APA policy reflects and affects both APA's internal relationships with members and its external relationships with other professions, governments, and the general public. Policy regarding specialties can be viewed as relating to internal relationships, whereas generic standards and policies relating to the regulation of practice are directly relevant to external relationships. Both types of relationships involve areas of common concern and, at times, bitter conflict. Furthermore, it is predictable that, as APA moves from theoretical discussion to projects such as promulgation of a model licensing law, the intensity of involvement and concern on the part of practitioners is increased. Such dynamics are well illustrated by the evolution and definition of new specialty areas within psychology.

Clinical, counseling, school, and industrial/organizational psychology have been viewed as being "de facto" specialties; that is, they are described in the "Specialty Guidelines" (APA, 1981b), which implies some kind of official recognition of their existence. In recent years, however, several new specialties such as health psychology, forensic psychology, and neuropsychology have evolved to a degree of organization such that official description and recognition of training and practice are sought. Since 1981, while a special subcommittee of the Board of Professional Affairs has been working on determining what defines a specialty, there has been an official moratorium on the recognition of new specialties. Currently, after determining that the APA as not ready to approve a formal document outlining either principles or procedures for designating specialties within psychology, the board decided to plan a conference for 1986 where interested constituent groups would have a new opportunity to provide input to the project. In the meantime, of course, there is nothing to prevent organizations other than APA, including well-established bodies such as the American Board of Professional Psychology (ABPP) and an unknown number of newly formed and perhaps loosely organized accrediting units, to develop mechanisms for recognizing new specialties. There is always the issue, however, of looking beyond psychologists' views of themselves to the outside world, which, incidentally, remains generally unclear about the more basic question, "What's a psychologist?" Thus it seems appropriate that the national organization would be in the best position to have a broad perspective that includes APA's relationship with the population at large—with other providers, governments, and the general public.

It is out of that broader perspective that APA has chosen to promote generic rather than specialty licensing or recognition in the public sector. The general belief is that psychologists' specialties are not sufficiently evolved or defined such that they can be translated into regulation or law. Given the many practical and political realities, the APA has defined "professional psychologist" and leaves it to the individual practitioner to practice ethically within his or her areas of competence (APA, 1981a). State governments, which ultimately define the legal practice of psychology, vary in their concurrence with this policy. The APA, certainly representing the largest number of psychologists of any organization in the world, develops and disseminates policy; however, in practice, it must be remembered that APA's policies (other than ethical principles, which can be enforced by expelling a member from the association) carry no force of law or formal sanction. The effect of APA standards on the actual regulation of practice is, therefore, indirect, and its impact rather slow to occur. APA's external relationships are many, and there is much confusion among the general public that must dissipate before APA can expect outsiders to appreciate its diversity as well as its common core. It is, of course, the responsibility of the profession to do just that; that is, psychologists should decide first who they are and what they do.

The effects of dissent within the psychological community cannot be underestimated. For example, the exclusion of psychologists as independent providers in Medicare could perhaps have been avoided if organized psychology had presented a more meaningful and timely response to the original legislative proposal (U.S. Code Ann., 1986, 42 U.S.C. § 1395x [r]). Psychology's exclusion from Medicare has cost practitioners millions of dollars in the aggregate and has deprived the consumer of the benefit of psychological services. Since the enactment of this legislation in 1965, the federal government and many states have adopted the Medicare definition of "physician," that is, an independent provider of health services, which includes physicians, osteopaths, dentists, podiatrists, and optometrists but *not* psychologists.

This leaves psychologists with the many battles they fight today for recognition in hospitals and other health care settings. Psychologists cannot expect to be recognized or respected in the public sector unless they can clearly define in comprehensive terms their standards for education and training as well as the delivery of services. Obviously, competition in the marketplace exists also for other deliverers of services such as social workers, psychiatrists, and counselors of various backgrounds. Although psychologists have much in common with other mental health practitioners, they also have much that is unique, perhaps even superior, such as an expertise in evaluating what they do. To the extent that this uniqueness is lost, the place of psychologists in the open market will be jeopardized. For example, psychological services are nowhere defined as unique and different from the services of social work in the Joint Commission on Accreditation of Hospitals (JCAH) accreditation standards for hospitals (JCAH, 1984) or for psychiatric facilities (JCAH, 1985). Psychological services will remain undefined until their uniqueness relative to disciplines can be demonstrated. This has been difficult for APA because of lack of agreement within psychology regarding the proper role of psychologists in the health care arena and because of the APA's interest in maintaining nonpsychologist allies such as social workers.

In promoting generic licensing, APA's relationship with the states is consultative rather than directive. For the most part, APA has supported organizational development rather than being involved in the specific content of state-level political battles. This relationship is changing, however, as states are asking for more direct support, and the policies disseminated by the APA, such as those in the "Ethical Principles" (APA, 1981a), have been adopted directly into statute or regulation. In dealing with state legislatures, as in dealing with the U.S. Congress, there is a need for timely and concerted response. Other professions have been able to organize such responses, but psychology has at times been immobilized by its commitment to democracy in a less than uniform group. Thus, for example, APA has been involved in developing a model state psychology licensing law since the late 1960s (APA Committee on Legislation, 1967) but has developed no usable product to date. Again, the inability of psychologists to make a public statement about who they are and what they do has taken its toll on psychologists' relationships with outside groups.

In the evolution of standards for practice, several factors emerge as significant:

1. There must be a consensually validated *generic core* from which all psychological specialties are founded; otherwise, practitioners will find themselves painted into a corner; that is,

perhaps they will only be allowed to practice in a highly delimited area.

2. There must be a balance between *purist theories and political realities*—when viewed as a cost benefit issue, the need for compromise becomes obvious as the cost of alienating one's colleagues may be too high to bear.
3. *Motivational issues* must be considered; that is, why should a psychologist abide by specific standards of training or practice? Are the rewards greater for noncompliance?
4. The need for *consciousness raising* within the profession is great—psychologists are their own worst enemies.
5. *Consumers have the right to know* and understand who psychologists are and what kinds of services they can expect; psychology has been sorely absent in the mass media.

Ultimately, a balance must be struck between the similarities and differences, within and outside of psychology. It would, of course, serve psychology well to accomplish such a balance in a proactive way, changing the current pattern of response ranging from inaction to blatant "me too-ism." It is essential that psychology define itself before others do so. As the trend toward new health care financing arrangements and increased public accountability continues, the need for clear standards and definitions increases tremendously.

ACCREDITATION OF PSYCHOLOGICAL SERVICE DELIVERY SETTINGS

While debate continues within psychology with regard to standards for practice, specialties, and the proper role of APA policy, tens of thousands of psychologists, in growing numbers, practice psychology in applied settings. Some are employees, some are employers; some work with other health disciplines, whereas others work exclusively with other psychologists. Nevertheless, all psychological practitioners experience firsthand the gap between ideal standards they have learned and the practical reality in which they function. In this arena, the years of work on development of standards seem wasted in the absence of a formal accreditation mechanism with which implementation of standards can be sanctioned. Even with the best of intentions, there are many impediments to offering high-quality services. As psychology struggles with so many barriers, external, rather than internal, relationships and the problems therein become most obvious. Ultimately, it will be the relationships of psychologists and the rest of the world—the general public—that will determine their fate in the health care marketplace.

For the past decade or so, increasing numbers of psychologists have gone to work in nonacademic settings and have entered independent practice (Stapp, Fulcher, & Wicherski, 1984). Currently, approximately 36,000 psychologists, greater than half of the APA's membership, are individuals providing psychological services—in private practice, organized health care settings, counseling centers, school systems, and other applied settings (VandenBos & Stapp, 1983). Recently, state psychological associations and state psychology licensing boards were surveyed by the APA's Committee on Professional Standards (COPS) about their utilization of APA policy documents. Of 39 state psychological associations responding, 30 reported some routine use of the "Standards for Providers" (APA, 1977), and 23 reported routine use of the "Specialty Guidelines" (APA, 1981b), particularly in studying complaints against members or in formulating charges. In addition, three associations reported having formally adopted APA standards. Use of the "Ethical Principles" (APA, 1981a) was even greater. Of state or provincial licensing boards or other regulatory bodies, 24 reported using the "Standards," and 19 reported using the "Specialty Guidelines" in reviewing complaints against psychologists. Sixteen boards have formally adopted APA standards, and 8 have formally adopted the "Specialty Guidelines" into their statute or regulation. Thus APA standards and guidelines are in fact taken rather seriously by the states in their efforts to regulate the practice of psychology on behalf of the consumer. Whatever APA governance may view as the proper role or function of policy statements, the APA's constituents have a need for such structure and look to the national organization to provide it.

Among the several organizations that accredit service delivery settings, psychology's role has varied from little if any to very active participation in shaping standards. Perhaps the best known of such organizations is the JCAH. The JCAH accredits general hospitals as well as psychiatric facilities, rehabilitation facilities, hospice care programs, and long-term care settings. Although they are based on an interdisciplinary health care model, the policies and procedures have been clearly medical and medically dominated. Although organized psychology has had an official voice on a JCAH technical advisory committee since 1979, it has only been since 1984 that JCAH standards have included psychologists as professionals eligible for medical staff privileges (JCAH, 1984). The fact that the JCAH is well known and respected is a significant matter because the effect of its reputation has been automatic approval of JCAH-accredited facilities for reimbursement by federal agencies and many private third-party payers. The APA now has a representative on the JCAH advisory committee for the psychiatric facilities and hospice accreditation programs but none on the Board of Commissioners, the governing body of the organization. In JCAH as well as in other interdisciplinary programs, the degree to which psychological standards are incorporated is highly related to involvement of organized psychology.

Two other interdisciplinary accreditation bodies in which psychologists are more actively involved are the ACMRDD, the Accreditation Council for Services for Mentally Retarded and other Developmentally Disabled Persons, and more recently CARF, the Commission on Accreditation of Rehabilitation Facilities. The APA has two representatives to ACMRDD, is a sponsoring member of the organization, and has a psychologist representative on the board of directors. Psychologists have thus had stronger influence in the implementation of standards in settings for the developmentally disabled. Although recently invited to apply for membership in CARF, the APA to date has had no formal relationship with this accrediting body. CARF has been in existence for almost 20 years and accredits a wide variety of rehabilitation facilities for persons with mental or physical disabilities. Although accreditation by these and other such organizations is strictly voluntary, one can easily see how funding contingencies have a dramatic effect on a facility's decision to seek accreditation.

Other efforts to develop quality assurance programs have been made in prison settings and counseling centers. The American Association of Correctional Psychologists (1980) published standards for adult jails and prisons several years ago, but this organization is a special interest group that does not have the sponsorship of APA. In addition, the American Medical Association has been working on an accreditation program for health care delivery in prisons but did not invite APA to be involved. Although APA invited itself upon hearing of this effort, it was excluded from the list of sponsoring organizations. To date, organized psychology's involvement in correctional settings has been minimal, in spite of the fact that many psychologists are employed in such facilities.

Many psychologists, however, have had an active role in the accreditation of college counseling centers. Since 1970, there have been guidelines for the accreditation of university and college counseling centers (Garni *et al.*, 1982), which were promulgated by the International Association of Counseling Services (IACS). IACS is affiliated with AACD (American Association for Counseling and Development) but not with the APA.

The APA, in summary, has not had much of a voice to date in the business of accrediting psychological services. This lack of impact may be a cause as well as consequence of a lack of recognition by the public as well as third-party sanctioners and payers of psychological services. Although APA has had a well-established and highly respected system of accrediting graduate and internship training in psychology, the issue of accrediting service delivery settings has remained in the discussion stages for at least a decade. Despite many philosophical and practical problems that must be overcome, it seems that the current health care environment calls for action on the part of organized psychology.

Many of the lessons that APA has learned from accrediting training sites could be applied to similar efforts in the service delivery arena. For example, APA has learned to work cooperatively with other organizations in multidisciplinary efforts, and it has well-developed operational systems such as budgeting, site visiting, and survey procedures. The APA has dealt extensively with the more philosophical issues relating to respect for individual program differences and needs for consistency across programs. There is, however, a very significant difference between the educational arena and that of health care delivery; that is, psychology has a well-respected place in academia but has been grossly overshadowed by medicine in the health care setting. Medicine, in fact, has dominated in terms of official sanction by third-party payers as well as acceptance by the general public, even in areas such as psychotherapy that have little to do with medicine. Thus, for example, countless employed psychologists, in violation of their own standards, must have their clinical work approved by physicians, who often have no psychiatric training.

The current health care climate is in a dramatic state of flux, presenting psychology with an opportunity as well as a need to make a mark in this area. There is a growing trend toward developing formal quality assurance mechanisms in response to a growing demand for public accountability as well as toward increasing awareness of the economics of health care. Other professional groups, such as medicine and, specifically, psychiatry, have been at the forefront of efforts to affect public and government opinion. In the absence of a strong voice of organized psychology, other groups will define what psychologists do. This has already occurred in several contexts, in Medicare regulations and in the policies of third-party payers who require approval or supervision by a physician for psychological services. Beyond being professionally demeaning, such policies do a great disservice to consumers in placing professional accountability out of the hands of the professional performing a given service. Such procedures offer a typical illustration of how APA's own professional standards are continually violated, often placing psychologists in the position of choosing between their own standards and requirements of law or their employer's policy. As various groups vie for recognition as providers of health services or as organizations that accredit service delivery settings, psychologists have a choice—they can be silent observers, followers, or trend-setting leaders.

If psychologists are to enter the health care accreditation arena successfully, there are many practical issues to be addressed. To be able to practice independently, without being supervised by physicians or other nonpsychologists, psychologists must first educate themselves and each other about who they are and what they do. Only then can psychologists begin a full-blown consumer education and marketing program that will be necessary to compete with the professionally executed marketing efforts such as those conducted by the medical fields. There are also technical issues to be addressed; for example, cooperative interorganizational linkages or an umbrella organization, such as exists for educational accreditation through the Council of Postsecondary Accreditation, must be developed. The APA bureaucracy will also have to address this by differentiating the policymaking from implementing mechanisms and providing support for the needed resources. Furthermore, a conceptual model must be developed that will be appropriate to the wide variety of institutions in which psychological services are provided such as schools, hospitals, and prisons. In principle, such a model should flow from the generic "Standards for Providers of Psychological Services" (APA, 1977).

In order to ensure quality psychological services to the consumer and a place in the emerging health care arena for psychology, organized psychology must escalate its efforts to promote psychological accreditation of psychological service settings. Initial discussions have occurred, and the following steps should be considered in the near future to assure psychology's self-determination as a profession:

1. *Networking.* The APA's central office can serve as a clearinghouse of information and resource people with knowledge and interest in the area and can disseminate such information to the mass media, government bodies, and researchers.
2. *Marketing.* Psychologists themselves must start by defining their unique skills and areas of expertise and must disseminate this information to other professions and the consuming public.
3. *Developing a concrete proposal.* The following must be specified: Who would write such a proposal (e.g., a funded task force), what resources would be needed, how funding possibilities would be explored, and how an umbrella organization to operate the system should be conceptualized.

4. *Upgrading involvement with other groups.* The APA should increase its involvement, both individual and organizational, in the work of other accrediting organizations and government agencies involved in similar efforts, such as the Health Care Financing Administration (HCFA).
5. *Developing a workable model of quality care.* In order to promote facility accreditation, there must be a set of qualitative and quantitative criteria for evaluating services. Successful accreditation programs have come to recognize the continuous and educational relationship between facilities and accrediting bodies. In the interdisciplinary setting, this will require delineation of the relationship of psychologists to other health care professionals such as psychiatrists. Thus professional standards must be translated into operational terms at the level of service delivery.

To serve the public better, psychology as a profession must move from its current pattern of being reactive and imitative to being proactive and innovative. In taking such action, however, there is a need for a shared, long-term conceptualization of professional service in psychology to be used as a guide.

CONCLUDING REMARKS

Indeed, this may result in questions about professional identity, especially when other professions are involved in the same or related services. It is a continual search for what Sanford (1951) referred to as a profession's unique pattern of competencies and unique service based on those competencies. A profession, in its continued effort to serve the public better, must continuously address issues of its practice standards and procedures. These are issues that must be addressed ultimately in the accreditation of psychological service delivery units and, therefore, as well, in the review of education and training standards for the profession of psychology. That link between standards of training and practice in professional psychology, albeit more conceptual than empirical in its validity, is borne out historically in the criteria for accreditation of doctoral education and training programs in professional psychology, within which there has been from the earliest years a commitment to the development of knowledge, skills, attitudes, interpersonal behaviors, and a sense of ethics consistent with the prevailing standards and guidelines of practice.

REFERENCES

American Association of Correctional Psychologists. (1980). Standards for psychology services in adult jails and in prisons. *Criminal Justice and Behavior*. 7(1), 81–127.

American Psychological Association. (1977). Standards for providers of psychological services. *American Psychologist*, *32*(6), 495–505.

American Psychological Association (1979). *Criteria for accreditation of doctoral training programs and internships in professional psychology*. Washington, DC: Author.

American Psychological Association. (1981a). Ethical principles of psychologists. *American Psychologist*, *36*(6), 633–638.

American Psychological Association. (1981b). Specialty guidelines for the delivery of services. *American Psychologist*, *36*(6), 640–681.

APA Committee on Legislation. (1967). A model for state legislation affecting for practice of psychology 1967. *American Psychologist*, *22*(12), 1095–1104.

APA Committee on Training in Clinical Psychology. (1947). Recommended graduate training programs in clinical psychology. *American Psychologist*, *2*, 539–558.

APA Committee on Training in Clinical Psychology. (1949). Doctoral training programs in clinical psychology. *American Psychologist*, *4*, 331–341.

Council on Postsecondary Accreditation. (1985). *The balance wheel for accreditation*. Washington, DC: Author.

Garni, K., Gelwick, B., Lamb, D., McKinley, D., Schoenberg, B., Simono, R., Smith, J. E., Wierson, P., & Wrenn, R. (1982). Accreditation guidelines for university and college counseling services. *The Personnel and Guidance Journal*, 1–6.

Goodstein, L. D., & Ross, S. (1966). Accreditation of graduate programs in psychology: An analysis. *American Psychologist*, *21*, 218–223.

Joint Commission on Accreditation of Hospitals. (1984). *Accreditation manual for hospitals*. Chicago: Author.

Joint Commission on Accreditation of Hospitals. (1985). *Consolidated standards manual for child, adolescent, and adult psychiatric, alcoholism, and drug abuse facilities*. Chicago: Author.

Kells, H. R. (1983). *The accreditors*. Washington, DC: Council on Postsecondary Accreditation.

Kissick, W. L., & Grubb, C. T. (1984). Perspectives on specialized accreditation in health services administration. *The Journal of Health Administration Education*, *2*(4), 419–429.

Merton, R. K. (1969). The functions of the professional association. *American Journal of Hospital Pharmacy*, *26*, 636–641.

Millard, R. M. (1983a). Evolution of accrediting standards. *Accreditation, Council on Postsecondary Accreditation Newsletters*, *8*, 2.

Millard, R. M. (1983b). The accrediting association: Ensuring the quality of programs and institutions. *Change*, May/June, 33–36.

Petersen, D. G. (1979). *Accrediting standards and guidelines: A current profile*. Washington, DC: Council on Postsecondary Accreditation.

Sanford, F. H. (1951). Annual report of the executive secretary: 1951. *American Psychologist*, *6*, 664–670.

Scott, R. A. (1983). The state commission: Who controls the process? *Change*, May/June, 33–37.

Sears, R. R. (1947). Clinical training facilities: 1947. A report from the Committee on Graduate and Professional Training. *American Psychologist*, *2*, 199–205.

Stapp, J., Fulcher, R., & Wicherski, M. (1984). The employment of 1981 and 1982 doctorate recipients in psychology. *American Psychologist 39*(12), 1408–1423.

U.S. Code Ann. (1986) 15 U.S.C. § 1 *et seq.*

U.S. Code Ann. (1986) 42 U.S.C. § 1395x (r).

VandenBos, G., & Stapp, J. (1983). Service providers in psychology: Results of the 1982 APA human resources survey. *American Psychologist, 38*(12), 1330–1352.

Young, K. E. (1983). Prologue: The changing scope of accreditation. In K. E. Young, C. M. Chambers, H. R. Kells, and Associates (Eds.), *Understanding accreditation*. San Francisco: Jossey-Bass.

11

Licensure and Certification of Psychologists

JUDY E. HALL

INTRODUCTION

This chapter summarizes the elements of the licensure process that relate to the determination of competence and delineate the impact of these criteria on clinical training programs, faculty, and students and on those responsible for administering the licensure procedures. Hopefully, this provides an orientation for those involved.

Critics (Hogan, 1983) and supporters (Theaman, 1982) of the licensure process often debate whether licensure measures the competence of practitioners. The word *competence* has several definitions. Competence in a narrow sense means reaching a specific behavioral objective of a specific skill; in a broad sense, being competent means possessing all the needed knowledge, skills, and abilities (Menne, 1981). The narrow interpretation, such as in the term *competency-based training*, is closely comparable to Webster's (1976) second definition of competence: having an ability or capacity. That notion of competence then focuses on differentiating by some performance measure those who are qualified (or competent) from those who are not. The primary definition

JUDY E. HALL • New York State Education Department, Cultural Education Center, Albany, NY 12230.

provided by Webster defines competent people as those who answer all requirements. Assessing competence in the 60 jurisdictions in the United States and Canada fits the primary definition of competence, separating those who have met all statutorily specified requirements from those who have not.

State and provincial licensure boards employ a number of evaluation and accountability procedures to ensure that minimal standards have been met by potential practitioners prior to independent, unsupervised practice. This process is termed the *demonstration of minimal competence*, which is variably defined but usually includes good moral character, a doctoral degree in psychology (or the equivalent), 1 to 2 years of supervised and appropriate experience, culminated by satisfactory written and/or oral examination performance. Having met those requirements, the psychologist is presumed qualified for independent practice.

Boards assure the continuing competence of practitioners by (a) establishing safe practice standards; (b) then disciplining errant or incompetent practitioners deviating from those standards; and in some states (c) requiring practitioners to continue their education and training and thus maintain their competence. Psychology as a licensed profession has had 40 years of experience in defining and measuring minimal competence. Because continuing competence has only recently received attention (Shimberg, 1982; Wiens & Dorken, 1986), this chapter will focus on the determination of minimal competence.

Terms must be defined and abbreviations noted. The term *state* will refer to the 50 United States, the District of Columbia, the U.S. territory of Puerto Rico, and the eight Canadian provinces, all of which regulate either the title or the practice of psychology. (Although Guam has also passed legislation governing the practice of psychology, I have not secured a copy of that legislation.) Therefore, 60 jurisdictions will be considered. The data presented are based upon an in-depth review of those 60 statutes and regulations available as of October, 1985, correlated with earlier published material (American Association of State Psychology Boards [AASPB], 1985a; American Psychological Association [APA], 1983; Stigall, 1983) and clarified by phone conversations with board members or staff.

To represent oneself and/or to independently practice as a psychologist, one must be *licensed* or *certified* as a psychologist by the state. *Licensure* is defined

> as a process by which an agency of government grants permission to an individual to engage in a given occupation upon finding that the applicant has attained the minimal degree of competency required to ensure that the

> public health, safety, and welfare will be reasonably well protected. (United States Department of Health, Education & Welfare, 1977, p. 4)

Licensure laws (L) define the scope of practice in order to limit the practice only to those qualified. *Certification* (C) is another form of public protection but one that limits only the title to those individuals who have met specified educational, experiential, and examination standards. With certification, there is no definition nor restriction of practice, although a few states have a definition in regulation (e.g., Illinois and New York). Certification allows other individuals to perform the same or similar functions as long as they do not refer to themselves by the protected title. In a state with a certification law, even though other individuals may "practice psychology," they do not violate the law unless they refer to themselves as psychologists or to their services as psychological. Following the analysis by state of the criteria for demonstration of minimal competence, the term *licensure* will be used to refer to either form of statutory recognition.

SUMMARY OF MINIMAL COMPETENCE BY STATE

Periodically, authors (Stigall, 1983) and organizations (APA, 1983) attempt to summarize the differential characteristics of the different state licensure laws. Often, by the time of publication, legislation or regulations have been modified. The reader should recognize that the information to follow may be influenced by the fluid nature of the licensure laws and regulations, but the information to be summarized in Tables 1 and 2 is current as of October, 1985.

Type of Governmental Regulation

In the United States, 25 states have true licensure laws (L): A person must be licensed if he or she uses either the title of psychologist or practices psychology (even without the title). An additional 15 states have "permissive" licensure laws (PL) that require the person to be licensed if he or she uses the title and practices psychology.

Eighteen states, including all eight Canadian provinces, have certification laws (C). Two jurisdictions have a "permissive" certification law (PC), requiring an individual to be licensed if he or she uses the title while engaged in the *private* practice of psychology (separately defined).

Definition of the Psychologist

Sixteen states require a doctoral degree in psychology (DD) in order to meet the educational requirement for licensure, but the majority of states allow individuals with degrees in fields other than psychology to be licensed as a psychologist. Nineteen states specify a doctoral degree that is primarily psychological or the equivalent (PP). Twelve states require either a doctoral degree in psychology or the substantial equivalent (SE,) whereas 11 jurisdictions permit those with a doctoral degree in psychology or in a closely allied field (CA) to meet the educational requirement. Although some U.S. jurisdictions regulate at both the master's and doctoral levels, only two Canadian jurisdictions make no distinction between the doctoral and master's levels (MA).

Beginning in the middle 1970s, representatives of many different constituent groups developed 10 criteria defining a "doctoral program in psychology" (Wellner, 1978). Those criteria were ratified by the National Register of Health Providers in Psychology in 1977 and became effective January 1, 1978 (Wellner, 1985, personal communication) by the AASPB in August 1977 (Wiens, 1977) and in February 1985 by the APA (APA Council of Representatives, 1985). In some states, the criteria defining a core program in psychology have been used to define *the substantial equivalent* in SE and PP.

Experiential Requirements

An important check on the education and training of a psychologist is how well that person performs on the job. Although predictive validity estimates are impossible to provide on the employment of psychologists because of the many professional activities and because those not licensed can never be directly evaluated as practicing psychologists, one critical element in assuring minimal competence is how well the person performs under supervision prior to licensure. As a result, state boards place great reliance on the feedback from supervisors and on the assurance provided by doctoral programs that graduates have satisfied all requirements before being allowed to graduate. In spite of the importance of this feedback, the profession of psychology has yet to determine empirically the proper amount and timing of experience necessary for licensure (APA Task Force on the Evaluation of Education, Training, and Service in Psychology, 1983).

Of course, the standards and guidelines of the APA (APA, 1979, 1981a, 1981b) do refer to competence as a sequence of education, training, and experience and do require an internship for graduation from an APA-approved professional psychology program. Partly as a result of those standards, the majority of states (53) do require supervised experience before admission to licensure. Eleven states require 2 years of postdoctoral experience (2p); 20 states require 2 years of experience, only 1 of which must be postdoctoral (2,1p). Nine states require 1 year of experience after the doctoral degree (1p); 4 states specify 2 years experience either pre- or postdoctoral (2); 9 states dictate 1 year of experience for licensure (1). Seven states do not require any experience for licensure (0).

Examinations

Although some professional psychologists assume that all state boards use only one exam for licensure (Fox, Kovacs, & Graham, 1985), actually only 15 states use one examination measure (1M). The examination process in 7 states consists of three examination components (3M), and in 37 states two examinations are given (2M).

Pass Point on the EPPP

All but two jurisdictions, Michigan and New Brunswick, use as part of their examination process the national examination entitled the Examination for Professional Practice in Psychology (EPPP). Table 1 lists for each state the pass-point criterion and the score needed to pass the April 1985 EPPP. Based upon that criterion, Table 2 provides a rating for each state from high (1) to low (6) that was determined by dividing the range of the pass points set on that form of the EPPP into approximately equal frequency intervals.

Restrictiveness

By adding the restrictiveness scores on each of the preceding five criteria, a total score (R) can be given to each state as indicated in Table 2. The term *restrictiveness* here refers to the use of the most stringent criteria.

RELATIONSHIPS AMONG THE CRITERIA OF MINIMAL COMPETENCE

The question often asked of state licensure board members is why were certain requirements chosen: Why are 2 years of experience required for licensure? Why was a high pass point set for the exam? Often,

Table 1. Pass-Point Criteria and Score on April 1985 Examination for Professional Practice in Psychology (EPPP)

State	Criterion	Score
Alabama	Mean of doctoral	143
Alaska	70% items	140
Arizona	Mean of doctoral	143
Arkansas	64.5% items	129
California	Criterion referenced	146
Colorado	70% items	140
Connecticut	Mean of doctoral	143
Delaware	65% items	130
District of Columbia	Mean of candidates minus .5*SD*	130
Florida	Mean of first-time doctorates (FTD)	147
Georgia	Lower of mean of doctorates or 75%	143
Hawaii	Mean of FTD	147
Idaho	70% items	140
Illinois	70% items	140
Indiana	Mean of doctoral[a]	143
Iowa	70% items	140
Kansas	75% items	150
Kentucky	Mean of candidates minus .75 *SD*	125
Louisiana	25th percentile of candidates	132
Maine	70% items	140
Maryland	Mean of PhD minus .75 *SD*	136
Massachusetts	Mean of doctoral minus .5 *SD*	134
Michigan	No applicable	
Minnesota	60% items	120
Mississippi	75%	150
Missouri	Mean of candidates	139
Montana	72% items	144
Nebraska	Mean of doctoral minus .75 *SD*	130
Nevada	75% items	150
New Hampshire	Mean of doctoral	143
New Jersey	Mean of doctoral minus 1 *SD*	126
New Mexico	75% items	150
New York	Set by review of exam and NY performance	125
North Carolina	Mean of FTD minus 1 *SD*	131
North Dakota	Mean of FTD minus .5 *SD*	139
Ohio	Mean of FTD minus .5 *SD*	139
Oklahoma	70% items	140
Oregon	Mean of FTD	147
Pennsylvania	72% items	144
Puerto Rico	Not testing yet	
Rhode Island	70% items	140
South Carolina	Lower of mean of FTD minus .5 *SD* or 70% items	139
South Dakota	Mean of FTD minus 1 *SD*	131
Tennessee	Mean of candidates minus .75 *SD*	125
Texas	70% items	140

Table 1. *(Continued)*

State	Criterion	Score
Utah	70% items	140
Vermont	Mean of candidates minus .5 *SD*	130
Virginia	Mean of candidates minus .5 *SD*	130
Washington	Lower of mean of FTD or 75% items	147
West Virginia	Mean of FTD minus .5 *SD*	139
Wisconsin	Mean of doctoral	143
Wyoming	Mean of candidates	139
	Canadian provinces	
Alberta	55% items	110
British Columbia	65% items	130
Manitoba	No information	
New Brunswick	Not applicable	
Nova Scotia	65% items	130
Ontario	65% items	130
Quebec	70% items	140
Saskatchewan	Mean of doctoral minus 1 *SD*	126

[a]For 1985 only, the pass point is mean of candidates minus .5 *SD*. As a result, the figure for the April 1985 passing score should read 130.

individuals question whether the procedures used to assess competence bear any relationship to the type of regulation. In other words, do state boards attempt to "make up for" the lack of a licensure law that restricts the practice of psychology only to those licensed by instituting more restrictive procedures for a certification law? To determine such relationships among the various criteria used to define minimal competence, each jurisdiction was categorized on the restrictiveness of each criterion (type of law, education, experience, number of examinations, pass-point criterion).

A chi-square test for independent means was performed, combining adjacent categories to increase expected frequencies, (Siegel, 1956) to answer the following questions:

1. Is there a relationship between the type of law (L, PL, C, or PC) and the restrictiveness of the definition of a psychologist (DD, PP, CA or SE)?
2. Is there a relationship between the type of law and the number of examination parts administered to candidates (1M, 2M, or 3M)?
3. Is there a relationship between the definition of psychologist and the pass point (6 intervals)?

Table 2. Minimal Competence Criteria by United States and Canadian Jurisdictions[a]

State	Law	Degree	Experience	Exams	PP	Lim	ABPP	R
Alabama	L	DD	0	2m	2nd	X	X	12
Alaska	L	PP	1p	2m	3rd	X	X	11
Arizona	C	PP	0	1m	2nd		X	16
Arkansas	L	CA	1	2m	6th	X		17
California	L	SE	2,1p	2m	2nd		X	11
Colorado	L	SE	2p	3m	3rd		X	10
Connecticut	PL	PP	1p	1m	2nd		X	12
Delaware	L	PP	2p	2m	5th	X	X	11
District of Columbia	L	CA	2p	2m	5th	X	X	12
Florida	C	DD	2,1p	2m	1st			9
Georgia	PL	CA	1	2m	2nd	X		14
Hawaii	L	DD	2,1p	3m	1st		X	6
Idaho	L	CA	2p	1m	3rd	X		11
Illinois	C	DD	2,1p	1m	3rd			12
Indiana	C	SE	2,1p	3m	2nd	X	X	12
Iowa	L	SE	1p	1m	3rd	X	X	14
Kansas	C	PP	2p	1m	1st			10
Kentucky	L	SE	1	3m	6th	X		17
Louisiana	PL	DD	2,1p	2m	4th	X	X	11
Maine	L	DD	2	3m	3rd	X		10
Maryland	L	PP	2,1p	2m	4th		X	11
Massachusetts	L	CA	2,1p	1m	4th		X	13
Michigan	PC	CA	2p	1m		X		—
Minnesota	L	DD	1p	2m	6th		X	11
Mississippi	PL	DD	1p	2m	1st	X	X	9
Missouri	L	PP	1	1m	4th	X		15
Montana	PL	PP	2,1p	2m	2nd	X	X	10
Nebraska	PL	DD	1p	2m	5th			13
Nevada	PL	DD	1p	2m	1st	X		9
New Hampshire	PL	PP	2,1p	1m	2nd	X	X	11
New Jersey	PC	CA	2,1p	2m	6th	X	X	17
New Mexico	C	PP	2p	2m	1st			9
New York	C	DD	2	2m	6th			16
North Carolina	L	PP	2p	1m	5th		X	12
North Dakota	PL	PP	1	2m	4th		X	15
Ohio	PL	SE	2,1p	2m	4th	X	X	14
Oklahoma	L	PP	2,1p	2m	3rd		X	10
Oregon	PL	SE	2,1p	2m	1st	X	X	11
Pennsylvania	PL	CA	2p	2m	2nd		X	10
Puerto Rico	L	DD	0	—	—			—

Table 2. (*Continued*)

State	Law	Degree	Exper-ience	Exams	PP	Lim	ABPP	R
Rhode Island	C	CA	2,1p	2m	3rd	X	X	13
South Carolina	L	CA	2,1p	2m	4th		X	12
South Dakota	L	DD	2,1p	2m	5th		X	11
Tennessee	L	CA	1	2m	6th		X	17
Texas	L	PP	2,1p	2m	3rd	X	X	10
Utah	L	PP	2,1p	3m	3rd	X		9
Vermont	C	SE	2p	1m	5th		X	16
Virginia	PL	DD	2p	3m	5th	X	X	10
Washington	C	DD	2,1p	2m	1st	X	X	9
West Virginia	L	DD	1p	2m	4th	X	X	11
Wisconsin	PL	SE	1	2m	2nd		X	15
Wyoming	PL	PP	0	1m	4th	X	X	17
Canadian provinces								
Alberta	C	MA	0	2m	6th			22
British Columbia	C	SE	1	2m	5th	X		19
Manitoba	C	PP	2,1p	2m	n/a			—
New Brunswick	C	SE	1p	1m	—			—
Nova Scotia	C	SE	2,1p	2m	5th	X	X	16
Ontario	C	PP	1p	2m	5th	X	X	15
Quebec	C	MA	0	1m	3rd	X		20
Saskatchewan	C	PP	0	2m	5th			19

[a]*Scale of Restrictiveness* (1 = most restrictive). *Law*: 1 = licensure (L); 2 = permissive licensure (PL); 3 = certification (C); 4 = permissive certification (PC). *Degree*: 1 = doctoral degree in psychology (DD); 2 = doctoral degree primarily psychological or equivalent (PP); 3 = doctoral degree in psychology and closely allied field (CA); 4 = doctoral degree in psychology or substantial equivalent (SE); 5 = master's level (MA). *Experience*: 1 = 2 years postdoctoral (2p); 2 = 2 years, one of which must be postdoctoral (2,1p); 3 = 1 year postdoctoral (1p); 4 = 2 years experience (2); 5 = 1 years experience (1); 6 = 0 experience (0). *Exams*: 1 = 3 measures (3m); 2 = 2 measures (2m); 3 = 1 measure (1m). *Passpoint* (PP): 1 = score of 147–150 (1st); 2 = score of 143–146 (2nd); 3 = score of 140 (3rd); 4 = score of 132–139 (4th); 5 = score of 130–131 (5th); 6 = score of 110–129 (6th). *Limitation* (Lim): X = restriction on access to examination. *ABPP*: X = diploma of ABPP may substitute for the EPPP. *R*: number indicates score on first five criteria.

4. Is there a relationship between the amount and timing of the experience required for licensure (6 categories) and the placement of the pass point on the national exam?
5. Is there a relationship between the number of examination components and the pass point established on the national exam?

Table 2 presents those parameters by jurisdiction and explains in the legend the number used in the chi-square analysis. None of the chi-square tests performed proved to be significant.

Another approach is to examine the total restrictiveness score by jurisdiction that is also provided in Table 2 and ranges from 6 to 22. The lowest total score (5) would be earned by a state with a licensure law that requires a doctoral degree in psychology, 2 years postdoctoral experience, a score of 75% of the items (or a score at the mean of first-time PhD candidates), and a passing score on another exam. Hawaii comes closest to fitting that description, with a score of 6. Within the United States, those with the highest score (17), indicating easy access to licensure, were Arkansas, Kentucky, New Jersey, Tennessee, and Wyoming. The Canadian jurisdiction with the highest score (22) was Alberta.

Summary

To simplify, the type of regulation and the definition of the education, experience, and examination requirements vary across jurisdictions. The procedures used to assess competence begin with the unassembled examination (review of moral character, education, and/or experience) and follow with an assembled examination using differing and multiple technologies (multiple-choice, essay, oral, work sample, and jurisprudence examinations). The authority for these examinations typically stems from statutory language specifying that an applicant must demonstrate that he or she "is competent in psychology as shown by passing such examinations, written or oral, or both, as the Board will prescribe" (e.g., Alabama, Arkansas, Delaware, Louisiana, Mississippi, Tennessee). Therefore, for psychologists, the education, experience, and examination lead to licensure.

THE NATIONAL LICENSURE EXAMINATION

The profession of medicine passed its first licensure law in 1639 (Derbyshire, 1969); the first licensure law for psychology did not come into existence until 1945 in Connecticut. Soon after, a number of states had passed statutory legislation; a small group of licensure board representatives founded the American Association of State Psychology Boards (AASPB) in 1961 and proposed that AASPB develop an examination that could be used by all states to facilitate interstate mobility (Carlson, 1978). Still today, each form of this multiple-choice examination is developed by the AASPB Examination Committee for use by state boards. The first examination was administered in 1965. Since then, an additional 23 forms have been given to 50,000 candidates for licensure.

Today, the EPPP consists of a representative sample of the core knowledge basic to and necessary for the practice of psychology. Also assessed is the ability to integrate and to apply knowledge of scientific, professional, and ethical standards to the problems confronted by professional psychologists. The EPPP provides a common yardstick because it is intended for all candidates regardless of specialty. Except for Wisconsin, the EPPP is administered to all candidates for licensure.

Proper Use of the EPPP

The EPPP is designed to measure doctoral degree graduates in psychology from regionally accredited institutions who secured 1 or 2 years of postdoctoral experience satisfactory to the licensing board (AASPB, 1985b). However, AASPB expects that "the EPPP will be supplemented by other assessment techniques to determine candidates' competence to practice psychology as a profession" (AASPB, 1985b, p. 2). In spite of this recommendation regarding the proper use of the EPPP, seven jurisdictions (Arizona, Connecticut, Idaho, Illinois, Iowa, Missouri and Wyoming) use only the EPPP. (Michigan constructs its own written examination, and New Brunswick uses an oral examination).

Therefore, even though the EPPP assesses generic psychological knowledge and some skills, this measure is necessary but not sufficient for practice. The licensure process assumes that the accreditation of educational institutions and the APA-approval of certain programs ensure that graduates have met the specific objectives set by those programs and that these objectives include both performance and affective domains (Katzell, 1979). As pointed out by Katzell,

> faculty members in those institutions are in an ideal situation to observe students' performance in clinical and other work settings, to judge their affective skills and their attainment of other performance objectives. The institutions are then expected to award their credentials . . . only to those who have attained the required educational objectives in all domains. (p. 54)

Because the EPPP focuses on knowledge, there is usually a specialty emphasis in the oral and essay examinations that complement the EPPP. This combination of generic knowledge and specialty skill assessment speaks directly to a long tradition in the measurement of competence for practice. It also speaks to the official position taken by the APA in model state legislation guidelines published in 1955 and 1967 and in a 1978 draft revision that was not adopted. These guidelines conceptualized licensure as assessing the generic foundation followed by a specialty focus ("Joint Report of the APA and the CSPA, 1955; APA Committee on State Legislation," 1967, 1978). This is the second generalization in the examination for licensure: The examination procedure consists of a generic knowledge examination complemented by a specialty examination component.

Establishment of a Pass Point on the EPPP

To determine the minimum level of performance to be considered a passing score on the EPPP, a state board has two major sources of information: (a) national and state candidates' performance on the exam and (b) characteristics of the exam. To set a pass point, the boards can use information from (a) to set a normative pass point, from (b) using experts to review the items on the exam to set an absolute pass point, or from (a) and (b) to set a pass point.

If a normative pass-point procedure is used, the percentage of candidates in that particular state passing the EPPP will depend upon the national normative data (one of the seven sets of norms), the distribution of scores in that state, and the rounding procedure employed. Choosing a normative pass point means that the acceptable score on the 200-item EPPP may fluctuate due to changes in the difficulty level on each form of the exam or due to the sample of candidates taking the examination or both. Using a normative pass point also means that there will always be a portion of the national candidates to fail.

For these and other reasons, the AASPB, the Professional Examination Service (PES), and others have encouraged state boards to adopt an absolute (also called a criterion-referenced or content-referenced) pass-point procedure using expert panels to review the exam items and set the pass point (Richman, 1984; Smith, 1985; Werner, 1978). In 1980, when 2-item judgmental methods were reviewed with the state board delegates, only 11 states were using a pass-point procedure other than normative (Smith, 1980). Currently, 27 states set an absolute cutoff, expressed in terms of the number of items that must be answered correctly. However, it is not known how many of these absolute cutoffs are simply legislatively determined, that is, arbitrarily reached without reference to reviewing the content of the examination because the end result of both procedures is expressed in the number or percentage of items that must be answered correctly in order to pass. Many states set the pass point using a modified Angoff procedure (Smith, 1980), estimating the percentage of minimally competent psychologists who would know the answer to each of the questions. Another procedure (modified Nedelsky) takes into account the distractors in the judgmental process (Gross, 1985). Because either method does not require use of normative data, using such a pass-point methodology also allows the state to specify in advance the criterion for passing the EPPP, as is required in Connecticut, Michigan, Ohio, and Texas. But in spite of the arguments for either criterion-referenced approach, 26 boards still retain a normative pass-point procedure, and 3 specify the lesser of the absolute and the normative pass point.

The end result of the current approaches to determination of pass/fail is approximately 25 different pass points with a range of 40 points on the 200-item EPPP. As a result of the variation in pass points, there has been discussion of adopting a national criterion on each form of the examination, which would, in turn, facilitate interstate mobility for psychologists. Today, a successful applicant in one jurisdiction may not be eligible for licensure in another without taking the EPPP again. For instance, Table 1 displays the pass points set on the April 1985 exam (AASPB, 1985a). Any candidate moving to Kansas, Mississippi, Nevada, or New Mexico would have to score at 150 (75%) of the items in order to be eligible for licensure. Similarly, any candidate moving to Florida, Hawaii, Oregon, or Washington would have to score at the mean for first-time doctoral candidates (FTD). The highest pass point adopted by any jurisdiction on any form of the EPPP fluctuates between those two standards. These and the data in Table 2 suggest another important consideration for the way competence is evaluated in the licensing process: Minimal competence is not measured the same in each of the 60 jurisdictions in the United States and Canada.

To assist them in that decision, given that states vary as to the definition of a psychologist, seven sets of national norms are provided to boards on each administration of the EPPP. One of the consistent indicators of the content validity of the EPPP is evident in the ordering of the mean scores of the different reference groups. In the national sets of norms provided to all boards, the average percentage score achieved by doctoral first-timers is approximately 10 points higher than that of master's first-timers. In descending order of average score, the candidate groups rank as follows: (a) all first-time PhD candidates; (b) all first-time doctoral candidates; (c) all first-time candidates; (d) all doctoral candidates; (e) all candidates; (f) all master's degree first-time candidates; and (g) all master's degree candidates.

In addition, Table 2 indicates the 30 jurisdictions that restrict failed candidates from taking the examination again, until they have met certain additional criteria (time, education, or experience). In the other states, there are no limitations on access to further examination for a failed candidate.

To facilitate licensure in at least 38 states, the EPPP may be waived for candidates holding a diplomate by examination from the American Board of Professional Psychology (ABPP); in 24 of those states, boards may waive all examination components for ABPP diplomates (Hall, 1987).

Equating Procedure

The difficulty level of the EPPP has fluctuated somewhat over the past nine administrations, with an average percentage score range of 68.59 to 75.97. Although the items on the April and the October forms of the EPPP do not overlap, 40% to 50% of the items on the April administration appear on the subsequent April administration and likewise for October. Because the state boards using an absolute cutoff need an examination that has a predictable difficulty level, PES will institute an equating procedure based on item response theory (latent trait theory) to provide boards with a raw score equivalent of later forms to Forms 22 and 23 (April and October 1985, respectively). This equating procedure, which will be based upon 20% of the items with a difficulty level equal to the overall form of the examination, will enable boards to determine whether the candidate population or the examination difficulty has changed and to set the pass point accordingly.

CONTENT VALIDATION OF THE EPPP

Most of the $400,000 spent by the AASPB in recent years on examination research has addressed the issue of the content validation of the EPPP. To define the domain of professional practice, Loveland (1977) indicated that the use of experts is both traditional and acceptable, but the use of such opinion should be supplemented by empirical methods such as diaries kept by practitioners, use of critical incident methodology, and task analysis. The AASPB has used content experts not only to construct the items, to review the items, and to determine which items should constitute the examination but to define the domain of practice (Richman, 1981), to conduct a job analysis (Rosenfeld, Shimberg, & Thornton, 1983), and to conduct a recent content validation study of the item bank (Smith, 1985). A review of those three projects follows.

Role Delineation Study

The role delineation study was initiated in 1978 through a contract between AASPB and PES. The intent was to determine the most appropriate content for an entry-level examination and then to determine how closely the EPPP fits those specifications. Ten distinguished (blue ribbon) academic and professional psychologists determined the domains in which professional psychologists worked, the roles performed by those working in the various domains, and ascertained which knowledge areas were needed to perform those roles. Then, 80 additional psychologists rated each domain, role, and knowledge on importance to entry-level practice and indicated the percentage of the EPPP that should be devoted to each. Subsequently, 90 APA fellows were asked to revise and refine the domains, roles, and knowledge statements.

Following this refinement of the role delineation provided by another "blue ribbon" panel, 1,000 psychologists were asked to rate the domains, roles, and knowledges on six scales. The scales were as follows: (a) importance to generic, entry-level practice; (b) importance to their own practice; (c) frequency of use by generic, entry-level psychologists; (d) frequency of use in their own practice; (e) percentage of EPPP that should be devoted to each domain and role; and (f) most appropriate assessment technique for each role and knowledge statement.

Of the 1,000 psychologists who agreed to participate, 600 returned rating packages, with 432 of those submitting complete data. The characteristics of the respondent sample of 432 psychologists were "closely representative of the focus, primary affiliation and highest degree of the candidate population" (Richman, 1981, p. 9). The result of the role delineation study was the identification of five domains of psychological practice under which six roles were placed. The percentage of items determined appropriate for each of the roles and the names of the domains follow:

Domain I. Techniques for appraising and assessing	*Percentage*
Role 1: Select, modify, and use psychological assessment techniques/instruments	20

Role 2: Interpret and report results of assessment	17
Domain II. Design, implementation, and assessment of interventions	
Role 3: Design, implement, and evaluate an intervention plan, based on interpretation of assessment results and including ongoing monitoring and final evaluation	20
Domain III. Uses of psychological literature	
Role 4: Interpret general psychological literature and apply it to practice	14
Domain IV. Techniques of Research	
Role 5: Design and implement research	12
Domain V. Professional and ethical issues	
Role 6: Evaluate activities within the limitations of professional, ethical, and legal statutes	15

The recommendations from that study placed a greater emphasis on items assessing knowledge of two performance domains (I and II) and a lesser emphasis on two other domains (III and IV). This information necessitated the development and inclusion of new items and the adherence to the new test specifications beginning with Form 14 (April, 1981). In order to meet the demand for new items, writing workshops sponsored by the state boards are held across the United States and Canada. After an item is generated, either at such a workshop or by direct solicitation, the quality assurance process involves the review by approximately 40 different psychologists who are experts in their area of specialization. If the item is placed on a draft form of the examination, it is reviewed by the members of 15 to 20 licensure boards before the AASPB Examination Committee decides on inclusion in a final form of the examination. This is another example of the content validation process. Content experts create the items; many experts review and edit the items; exam experts select the items, using the weightings established before; and then the draft form is reviewed by another set of experts, the state boards, before referring the exam back to the AASPB Examination Committee for a final decision.

Empirical Verification: The Scottsdale Conference

Even though the role delineation study (Richman, 1981) constitutes an empirical test of the content validation of the EPPP, the AASPB Executive Committee decided to consider funding another approach to validation—a job analysis. After great discussion and some opposition to the idea that professional practice could be properly analyzed (Menne,

1981; Wiens, personal communication, 1980), the special advisory committee consisting of three members of the AASPB Examination Committee, two outside test experts, and the AASPB Executive Officer assisted the AASPB Executive Committee in the formulation of a request for proposals (RFP). This RFP was sent to over 20 testing agencies with experience in conducting a job analysis, with four of the proposals received given final consideration. After several modifications were made in one of the proposals, both parties found the terms and the changes agreeable. The decision to go ahead with a job analysis and the choice of the testing contractor occurred in Scottsdale, Arizona.

The opposition to funding such a project focused on (a) the question of whether the complex role of a psychologist could be defined properly with due consideration to judgment, attitudes, critical thinking, and the like and (b) the frequently cited implication of competency-based assessment that once the task is minutely defined, an applicant need only pass the exam testing these competencies in order to be licensed—professional education and experience and identification with the profession are inconsequential. However, the purpose of the job analysis was not to produce competency-based assessment tools that would test all the minute tasks of a psychologist. That would be impossible, given the myriad activities performed by psychologists. The intent was to define those generic or entry-level knowledge areas, skills, and abilities necessary for minimal competence in the profession and to sample from them on any examination component. In contrast, competency-based assessment procedures attempt to assess all the skills necessary in a narrow area of practice of the ability to use a technique (such as biofeedback or intelligence testing) or to practice an occupation (as distinguished from a profession) that involves a routine, repetitive job (e.g., hairdresser, vocational counselor, etc.)(Berven & Scofield, 1980). Such an approach is not feasible nor appropriate with a complex profession such as psychology.

Therefore, in 1981 the AASPB contracted with the Center for Occupational and Professional Assessment of Educational Testing Service (ETS) to identify major responsibilities of licensed psychologists and the knowledge areas, skills, and abilities (KSAs) considered important by licensed psychologists in the United States and Canada. Except for the AASPB Executive Officer, the authors (Rosenfeld *et al.*, 1983), the National Advisory Committee (seven nationally recognized experts in their field), and the Project Steering Committee (four AASPB officers, two outside testing experts, and AASPB Examination Committee Chairperson) were psychologists.

Following the field testing of the instrument, the Advisory and

Project Steering Committees reviewed and approved the inventory and other measures. The inventory contained 59 responsibilities in three broad areas: defining the problem and making decisions, dealing with the problem defined, and research and development activities. There were 62 procedures, techniques, and resources as well as 49 knowledge areas presumed relevant to psychologists. The responsibilities were to be rated on the time spent and the importance of each as well as the degree to which competence was necessary at the time of initial licensure.

For the United States sample, all psychologists licensed in at least one jurisdiction who held membership in the American Psychological Association Divisions 3 (Experimental), 14 (Industrial/Organizational), 15 (Educational), 16 (School), or 17 (Counseling) and a random, stratified sample of 1,717 licensees (35 from each state) with membership in Division 12 (Clinical) were sent a card inviting them to participate. When overlap in division membership was eliminated, 5,975 were actually contacted. Fifty-one percent responded (2,994), and 1,886 returned the inventory. With attrition, the final number of usable returns came to 1,585.

The ratings of the responsibilities by that sample indicated that all 59 responsibilities on the inventory were judged to be "moderately important" or greater and some degree of competence was required in each at the time of licensure. This provided a check on the comprehensiveness of the inventory. Then, using psychologists who had identified themselves as practicing clinical, counseling, school, or industrial-organizational psychology, a factor analysis was performed, producing four factors that appeared to be similar for the four groups. The four job factors were labeled as follows: (I) Research and Measurement, (II) Intervention, (III) Organizational Applications, and (IV) Assessment. To estimate similarity of the factor structure for the four groups, two additional analyses were conducted. With both, the results were the same: The clinical, counseling, and school psychology job factor structures appeared very similar to one another and somewhat less similar to the practice of industrial-organizational psychology. Second, the first factor (Research and Measurement) appears to be very similar for all four groups. Factor III (Organizational Applications) is the job factor that is different for industrial-organizational psychology. The remaining two factors appeared moderately related for all four groups.

The next step was to ascertain which of the 111 knowledge areas and techniques were judged important. Using the decision rules of (a) used by 50% or more of the respondents in each of the practice areas and (b) rated as moderately important or higher by a majority of practitioners in each practice area, 49 of the 111 knowledges and techniques were identified. By correlating importance ratings with each job dimension (a) separately by specialization and also (b) for the combined four practice areas and by using only statistically significant correlations of .20 or higher, the job analysis provides a description of the structure of each of the four practice areas and a statistical linkage from 38 of the 49 knowledge and techniques areas to one or more of the four subfactors.

Therefore, by using the results of the job analysis, educators can identify the 12 techniques that are important for an entry-level licensed psychologist to possess: interviewing techniques, group tests of mental ability, tests of social maturity, stress management techniques, decision-making strategies, standardized test procedures, observational techniques, diagnostic tests, measures of self-concept, conflict management techniques, consultation techniques, and data collection techniques.

The 26 knowledge areas important for a minimally competent psychologist are as follows: human growth and development, personality, motivation, cognition, test construction, validity concepts, strengths and limitations of assessment procedures, factors affecting test performance, test fairness, research and experimental design, basic statistics, sampling theory, organizational morale, learning, individual differences, perception, intelligence, test scores and norms, reliability concepts, coaching and practice, advanced statistics, criterion measures, ethical guidelines, test standards, specialty guidelines, and ethics for research.

Summary

Recent criticisms of this job analysis focus on the author's collection of general data that enhance the similarities and lessen the differences between the four specialty areas and the use of a criterion that required respondents from all four specialty areas to indicate use of the technique or knowledge, thus dropping from analysis 24 areas used by 50% of clinical, counseling, and school psychologists because a similar percentage of industrial/organizational (I/O) psychologists did not use those techniques or knowledge. The same was true for activities of I/O psychologists that were not chosen by clinical, counseling, and school psychologists. However, this same author "did not dispute the presence of a common core of knowledge, involving largely research and measurement skills" (Sackett, 1985, p. 4). Because the major purpose of the two studies was to determine the feasibility of a common licensure examination, questions tapping the 38 KSAs from the job analysis could form the basis for a generic licensing examination for psychologists as well as for defining components of the oral, essay, and jurisprudence examinations administered to licensure candidates. By comparing the results of the two validation studies, it is clear that three of the domains (I, II, and IV) in the job analysis are parallel to three of the domains in the role delineation study. Currently, the results from the job analysis are being used to refine the test specifications for the EPPP, under another contract to the PES (Richman, 1984). The target date for making the new test specifications available to the AASPB Examination Committee is January, 1986.

Content Validation of the Item Bank

Another study recently addressed the content validation of the EPPP item bank by assessing the cognitive complexity of 900 items currently in the item bank, the occupational relevance of the items, and the degree to which the items contribute to the public protection function of the EPPP (Smith, 1985). The results of the ratings by the three expert panels in this latest study were as follows: (a) because only 20% of the items were judged to emphasize professional problem solving and evaluation rather than recall or recognition and given the cognitive level determined for each of the knowledge areas in the Job Analysis, AASPB could increase the cognitive complexity of many of the items in the bank and still produce a licensure examination that is no more difficult than required and as suggested by the *Uniform Guidelines* (Equal Employment Opportunity Commission, 1978); (b) the panels judged 59% of the items as generic items; (c) the experts evaluated 50% of the items as making a substantial and/or critical contribution to the public protection function of the EPPP; and (d) 57% of the items met both the generic standard (affirmed by 50% that rated it) and the public protection criterion (received an average panel rating of 1.5 indicating a small or modest contribution to public protection); this was especially true for Roles 5 (design and implement research) and 6 (evaluate activities within the limitations of professional, ethical, and legal statutes).

One additional question in this study was the degree to which items could be correctly classified by both role and associated knowledge statements as described in the current test outline. Slightly over 70% of the panel members were able to make the correct role classification, defined as identifying the role under which the item is currently classified. There was a higher level of agreement among items representing Roles 4, 5, and 6 than Roles 1 to 3, which may be a function of the definitional clarity of those roles. With regard to the classification of the knowledge statements, there was less agreement, indicating the necessity for further refinement of the knowledge statements or the possibility of test questions being associated with multiple knowledge statements.

NEW AND OTHER EXAMINATION METHODS

The content validation studies summarized herein contribute significantly to the EPPP meeting professional standards for the proper construction of a licensure examination (Kane, 1982; Loveland, 1977; Shimberg, 1982, 1985). The studies have supported and refined the content validation by using the most current and appropriate methods available. Recognizing that several different sources of information are necessary to make the minimal competence distinction, AASPB has decided to evaluate and validate other methods, both current and future.

Oral Examination

The state boards use other examinations to supplement the EPPP. In frequency of use, these exams are an oral examination, an essay examination, and an objective examination on the state laws and regulations and national standards and ethics. Because the board (or the department administering the board) is authorized to determine the components of the examination process, most states have the latitude to use any examination. In fact, only Alaska and Arizona are restricted by law to written examinations. In spite of the authority to do so in 58 states, an oral examination is administered to all candidates in only 36 states, whereas 6 other states use the oral on a discretionary basis. The statutes/regulations specify in 16 of those 36 states (Hawaii, Kentucky, Maine, Mississippi, Montana, Nebraska, New Jesey, Nevada, New Mexico, Ohio, Oregon, South Carolina, South Dakota, Alberta, British Columbia, Manitoba) that the oral focus be on the applicant's intended area of practice, sometimes by also requiring a work sample or direct observation by the examiners and that it determine the applicant's familiarity with state statutes governing practice. The various oral examinations differ tremendously in structure, use of outside examiners, content, pass rate, and degree of interaction with and feedback to the candidates. The approaches used by the jurisdictions of California, Colorado, Maine, and Ontario have been summarized by board members Crawford (1984), Watson (1984), Hymoff (1984), and Edwards (1984). Only 2 of the states provide data on the agreement or reliability of scoring on a recent administration. All except Colorado emphasize the flexibility inherent in the oral examination.

As pointed out by Loveland (1977), sufficient literature exists to point to the perils as well as the presumed value of the oral examination. McGuire (1966) found that oral examinations for medical specialty boards measured predominantly recall, not interpretive skill or problem solving, and that the candidates rarely cited evidence for their answers. In general, that study questioned that particular oral examination as a measure of "how well a candidate thinks."

No systematic studies have been reported on the oral examinations conducted by state licensure boards, except for the data reported by Watson (1984) and Edwards (1984). As long as the failure rate is low (5%–10%), as it is in the majority of the states using the oral, these examinations may not be challenged. However, recently Colorado and California reported a failure rate of 30% to 40% (Crawford, personal communication, August, 1985; Watson, personal communication, August, 1984). It will be incumbent upon those and other states with a significant failure rate to maintain reliability estimates and make data available to the public that would demonstrate the relationship between the oral examination to the requirements of the job of psychologist, assisted by the results of the role delineation study and the job analysis.

The number of states using an oral examination has encouraged the ASSPB to examine carefully the oral examination procedures, to develop a handbook for the oral examination (Wand & Hess, 1982), and to propose the development of a manual on oral examinations, similar to the one developed by the Colorado Department of Personnel (1983). Such an oral examination protocol and scoring system developed by AAPSB for use by state board examiners will assist those state boards members who prefer an oral examination to one of the other methods available.

Jurisprudence and Essay Examinations

A complementary examination strategy is the jurisprudence examination given by Alabama, Colorado, the District of Columbia, Florida, Hawaii, Maine, Nevada, North Dakota, Pennsylvania, Texas, Utah, Virginia, and Wisconsin. This exam assesses knowledge of laws and regulations directly related to the practice of psychology in that jurisdiction as well as knowledge of professional ethics and standards. These exams typically have a high pass rate, and boards have not evaluated them in any systematic way.

Essay examinations are given to all candidates in Alaska, Colorado, Indiana, Kentucky, Maryland, New Hampshire, New York, Saskatchewan, and Virginia. No published information is available on these examinations, with the exception of that provided by members or staff of the New York state board, which has had the longest experience with this type of examination (Cohen, 1984; Ricks, 1973) and where an essay examination has been administered to all candidates since 1957. Ricks provided a summary of the New York examination procedure with reliability estimates in 1973. Since then, the exam has been modified to make the organization more generic and the questions more directly related to practice, while retaining its uniqueness in assessing research skills.

In New York, each candidate is required to pass this three-question essay examination, even if previously licensed in another jurisdiction. The essays are developed and scored by current and former members of the board and cover the following areas of psychology: clinical, counseling, developmental, educational, school, industrial, organizational, statistics, measurement, general experimental, social, and personality. The correlation between the EPPP and the essay examination final score (composed of three essay scores added together) is always around .5. Because the essay is intended to measure abilities that are different from those measured by the EPPP, such a correlation is desired. Each essay is scored on a 20-point scale, with 15 indicating a passing score. There are two scores per question provided by independent raters that must fall within 3 points of each other. If not, the raters must discuss their scoring criteria and adjust their scores within that range, or a third rater is asked to score. This forced reliability is partly responsible for the high estimate of reliability. The co-rater reliability over all essays and across all board examiners was estimated at .81 on the 1981 examination (R. Hansen, personal communication, December 1981). Co-scores are then averaged, and the three averages combined to determine the final score. The pass point is set in the interval between 45 and 42, that is, between the total score for three passing and three failing papers.

As Cohen (1984) pointed out, the component of the essay examination that requires candidates to demonstrate competence in designing research is a necessary skill for "incorporating state-of-the-art advances into professional practice." Supporting that opinion are the results of both the role delineation study and the job analysis, both of which emphasize research skills. New York appears to be the only state requiring candidates to demonstrate these skills, independent of the knowledge of research methodology assessed on the EPPP. Because both the role delineation study and the job analysis pointed to Techniques of Research (Domain IV) and Research and Measurement (Domain I) as domains of practice, it is unfortunate that more attention is not paid to assessing research skills in the complementary examination strategies used by other states.

The common weakness of essay examinations stems from the subjectivity of scoring. As a result, Colorado and Virginia, which reuse questions on their essay examination, develop scoring criteria to aid in reliability. The development of scoring criteria and the scoring of essay examinations is a lengthy process and the major disadvantage of an essay examination. A criticism of this type of examination is that it also measures writing skills, but as long as that skill is part of the job of a psychologist, an essay examination is an appropriate method to use. The advantage of the essay, like the oral, is the ease with which items can be constructed, unlike the construction of the EPPP.

Written Simulation

At the same time ETS was conducting the job analysis, PES was educating the state boards on the potential use of another technology in the licensure examination process. Building on the component of the role delineation study that asked psychologists how best to measure the various roles (Smith, 1983), it became apparent that Role 5 was best measured by a multiple-choice format examination and Roles 1 and 6, although measurable by multiple-choice questions, could also be measured effectively by a structured work sample and task simulation. Because many of the problem-solving skills necessary for practice may be tested best through simulation (Howard, 1983), the AASPB provided funding to PES to develop a series of written simulation problems.

This methodology provides the following advantages: (a) actual performance can be judged in terms of the reasoning process employed in decision making; (b) when large groups of individuals are tested even at different locations, it is cost-effective and efficient; (c) the simulation process imitates lifelike situations without the involvement of real clients; (d) candidates enjoy the exercises and support their face validity; (e) correlations between the simulation exercises and multiple-choice tests of knowledge are in the low-to-moderate range (cf. Smith, 1983); (f) content validity may be easier to establish for these tests than for multiple-choice questions; (g) the individual problems can be reused because the scoring criteria are not easily determined by the candidate; (h) this assessment is less subject to memorization of the items and thus violation of the security of the examination; and (i) simulation problems can be adapted to a computerized format.

The disadvantages of the written simulation are attributes of its complicated development and choices in scoring. Both linear and branching response options are available; the first is the easiest to score because it presents a standard situation and set of choices to each candidate. The linear approach is more suitable to the licensure process; the branching approach is appropriate for self-assessment exercises. After development of a series of problems using the linear model, the issue becomes one of weighting the various responses and combining the weights into a score. The strategies used typically involve a combination of proficiency (percentage agreement with experts and avoidance of undesirable choices), efficiency (percentage of selected options leading to a desired conclusion), and overall competence (combination of proficiency and efficiency). In addition, expert judges can determine which options should have been avoided at all costs and which should have been selected no matter what. These can be combined to determine an acceptable level of performance (Smith, 1983, 1985).

Although it is too soon to evaluate the simulation problems developed by the content experts hired by PES, this technology provides an exciting prospect for the future of the evaluation of licensure candidates on a national scale. The first set of problems will be pilot tested with first-time candidates on a voluntary basis in a number of states in October 1985 and April 1986. The earliest date for introduction of the simulation problems for use in licensure decisions will be October 1986.

IMPLICATIONS FOR GRADUATE FACULTY

Given the expansion into alternate examination strategies, it is obvious that applicants for licensure will not only have to demonstrate they are knowledgeable of the core areas in scientific and professional psychology but will have to demonstrate that knowledge and skill through multiple and different measures. This fact has implications for the curriculum design and evaluation provided by graduate schools. This concept of a core component to graduate education has influenced graduate education, at the same time producing anger and resistance from some graduate faculty. For instance, reaching a consensus on the definition of a core program in psychology has been a hotly debated issue, as is evidenced by the 8 years that passed between the 1977 education and credentialing conference (Wellner, 1978) and the adoption of similar standards by the American Psychological Association

(APA, 1985). For the academic sector, this common core has seemed an intrusion into academic freedom, in this instance more appropriately termed *curriculum freedom*. For the state boards, the specification of this core has been a way of ensuring that there is a common body of knowledge that any psychologist can be expected to master so that consumers know what to expect. In turn, this requirement states clearly to graduate students what they are expected to learn, either through formal course work or through comprehensive examinations. It is important to note that part of the clash between educators and state board members, who are often educators themselves, is a result of ensuring due process for applicants. The clear and detailed delineation of requirements that must be met for licensure causes a somewhat inflexible system of credential review. Add the failure on the part of state boards to discipline after licensure, and it becomes apparent why boards have been characterized as "toothless tigers" (Shimberg, 1985).

More recently, educators are responding in a proactive manner rather than adopting a defensive posture. Faculty members are making themselves available for board service and as examiners. Representatives of new areas of practice such as health, forensic, clinical neuropsychology, and the like are defining training standards that can then be used by state boards to assist in the evaluation of candidates. Those who are affected most are realizing that an effective system to protect the public must be a cooperative venture among educators, trainers, supervisors, practitioners, employers, and consumers.

Some specific suggestions for these educators are as follows:

1. Faculty must be completely familiar with licensure requirements and informed about the knowledge areas and skills considered necessary for independent practice so that they can assure that their graduates will meet these standards. For instance, graduates who do not comply with program requirements or are excused from these requirements on the basis of employment or a master's-level internship will be at a disadvantage when they apply for licensing because these requirements often cannot be waived. Also, because those educational and experiential requirements are considered part of doctoral education, they cannot be remedied after graduation. A shortcut in graduate school may eliminate the candidate from eligibility for licensure or from meeting the internship requirements for listing in the *National Register for Health Service Providers in Psychology*.

2. Graduate students should be given frequent opportunity to learn of the licensure requirements directly from the state board or the state board staff. Invite those individuals to give a colloquium each year, perhaps as a part of the ethics course.

3. Data on the performance of graduates on the licensure examinations should be reviewed by training program directors. This may provide valuable information on strengths and weaknesses in the educational curriculum. If such information is not provided to your training program, request that data from the state board office.

4. Assessment of knowledge, skills, and abilities in graduate school should be accomplished with a variety of methods, should require oral and written communication skills similar to those tested in the licensure process, and should include critical thinking tasks like those encountered in written simulation or patient management problems. Understanding how multiple choice questions are constructed may help graduate students perform on such objective examinations.

5. Determine whether there is a faculty member who is interested in serving on the state board. If so, assist that person to make his or her willingness to serve known to those individuals responsible for appointing state board members.

6. Recognize that whistle blowing on psychologists in the community may be necessary in order to protect the public. The steady increase in malpractice actions against psychologists is partly a function of an ineffective disciplinary system. Support legislative efforts to improve financial support for such a system.

REFERENCES

American Association of State Psychology Boards. (1985a). *Handbook of licensing and certification: Requirements for psychologists in North America*. (Available from AASPB, PO Box 4389, Montgomery, AL 36103.

American Association of State Psychology Boards. (1985b). *Information for candidates: The Examination for Professional Practice in Psychology*. (Available from AASPB, PO Box 4389, Montgomery, AL 36103)

American Psychological Association Committee on State Legislation. (1967). A model for state legislation affecting the practice of psychology. *American Psychologist, 22*, 1095–1103.

American Psychological Association Committee on State Legislation. (1978). *Revision of the APA model guidelines for state legislation affecting the practice of psychology*. (Available from APA, 1200 Seventeenth St., NW, Washington, DC 20036.

American Psychological Association. (1979). *Criteria for accreditation of doctoral training programs and internships in professional psychology*. Washington, DC: Author.

American Psychological Association. (1981a). *Ethical principles of psychologists* (revised). Washington, DC: Author.

American Psychological Association. (1981b). *Specialty guidelines for the delivery of services*. Washington, DC: Author.

American Psychological Association Task Force on the Evaluation of Education, Training and Service in Psychology. (1983). *Final Report*. Washington, DC: Author.

American Psychological Association. (1983). *A summary of state laws regulating psychological practice through licensure (L) or certification (C).* (Available from APA, 1200 Seventeenth St. NW, Washington, DC 20036)

American Psychological Association Council of Representatives. (February, 1985). *Minutes.* Washington, DC.

Berven, N. L., & Scofield, M. E. (1980). Evaluation of professional competence through standardized simulations: A review. *Rehabilitation Counseling Bulletin, 24,* 178–202.

Carlson, H. S. (1978). The AASPB story: The beginnings and first 16 years of the AASPB, 1961–1977. *American Psychologist, 33,* 486–495.

Cohen, E. (1984). Screening candidates for a lifetime license in a changing profession: Testing for competencies for today's practice is not enough. *Professional Practice of Psychology, 5,* 123–125.

Colorado Department of Personnel (1983). *Oral exams manual.* (Available from Colorado Dept. of Personnel, First floor, State Centennial Building, 1313 Sherman Street, Denver, CO 80203)

Crawford, W. (1984). The California model: A semi-structured oral examination. *Professional Practice of Psychology, 5,* 86–93.

Derbyshire, R. (1969). *Medical licensure and discipline in the United States.* Baltimore: Johns Hopkins.

Edwards, H. P. (1984). The Ontario model: The oral examination with invited examiners. *Professional Practice of Psychology, 5,* 94–102.

Equal Employment Opportunity Commission. (1978). *Uniform guidelines on employee selection procedures.* Washington, DC: U.S. Government Printing Office.

Fox, R. E., Kovacs, A. L., & Graham, S. R. (1985). Proposals for a revolution in the preparation and regulation of professional psychologists. *American Psychologist, 40,* 1042–1050.

Gross, L. J. (1985, December). *How to set a defensible passing point.* Workshop at the annual convention of the National Commission for Health Certifying Agencies, New York, NY.

Hall, J. E. (1987). The ABPP diploma privilege: Does it really exist? *Professional Practice of Psychology, 6,* 251–265.

Hogan, D. B. (1983). The effectiveness of licensing: History, evidence and recommendations. *Law and Human Behavior, 7,* 117–138.

Howard, A. (1983). Work samples and simulations in competency evaluation. *Professional Psychology: Research and Practice, 14,* 780–796.

Hymoff, I. (1984). The Maine model: The oral examination utilizing work samples. *Professional Practice of Psychology, 5,* 103–112.

Joint Report of the APA and the CSPA. (1955). *American Psychologist, 10,* 727–756.

Kane, M. T. (1982). The validity of licensure examinations. *American Psychologist, 37,* 911–918.

Katzell, M. E. (1979). Credentialing. *New Directions for Testing and Measurement,* (3), 49–60.

Loveland, E. (1977). Alternatives and innovations. *Proceedings of a national conference for evaluating competence in the health professions.* New York: Professional Examination Service.

McGuire, C. H. (1966). The oral examination as a measure of professional competence. *Journal of Medical Education, 41,* 267–272.

Menne, J. W. (1981). Competency based assessment and the profession of psychology. *Professional Practice of Psychology, 2,* 17–28.

Richman, S. (1981). *Final report to the American Association of State Psychology Boards on the role delineation study for the Examination for Professional Practice of Psychology.* (Available from AASPB, PO Box 4389, Montgomery, AL 36101)

Richman, S. (1984). Setting passing points on the EPPP: A discussion of normative and absolute methodologies. *Professional Practice of Psychology, 5,* 21–30.

Ricks, J. H., Jr. (1973, August). *Certifying psychologists in New York State.* Paper presented at the convention of the American Psychological Association, Montreal, Quebec.

Rosenfeld, M., Shimberg, B. & Thornton, R. F. (1983). *Job analysis of licensed psychologists in the United States and Canada: A study of responsibilities and requirements.* (Available from Educational Testing Service, Princeton, NJ 08541)

Sackett, P. R. (1985, August). *I/O psychology: The state of the practice.* Paper presented at the convention of the American Psychological Association, Los Angeles, CA.

Shimberg, B. (1982). *Occupational licensing: A public perspective.* Princeton, NJ: Educational Testing Service.

Shimberg, B. (1985). Overview of professional and occupational licensing. In J. C. Fortune & Associates (Eds.) *Understanding testing in occupational licensing* (pp. 1–14). San Francisco: Jossey-Bass.

Siegel, S. (1956). *Nonparametric statistics for the behavioral sciences.* New York: McGraw-Hill.

Smith, I. L. (1980). *Issues related to passing point strategies on the EPPP.* Paper presented at the American Association of State Psychology Boards annual meeting, Montreal, Quebec.

Smith, I. L. (1983). Use of written simulations in credentialing programs. *Professional Practice of Psychology, 4,* 21–50.

Smith, I. L. (1985). *Content validity study of the AASPB item bank.* (Available from AASPB, PO Box 4389, Montgomery, AL 36103)

Smith, I. L. (1985). Issues in the development and scoring of written simulations for credentialing applications. *Professional Practice of Psychology, 6,* 156–193.

Stigall, T. T. (1983). Licensing and certification. In B. D. Sales (Ed.), *The professional psychologist's handbook* (pp. 285–337). New York: Plenum Press.

Theaman, M. (1982). A critical appraisal of Daniel Hogan's position on licensure. *Professional Practice of Psychology, 3,* 1–18.

United States Department of Health, Education & Welfare (1977). *Credentialing health manpower* (DHEW Publication No. [05] 77-50057). Washington DC: Author.

Wand, B. & Hess, A. (1982). *Guidelines for conducting oral examinations: A draft for discussion.* (Available from AASPB, PO Box 4389, Montgomery, Al 36103)

Watson, M. A. (1984). The Colorado model: A structured oral examination. *Professional Practice of Psychology, 5,* 79–85.

Webster's new twentieth century dictionary of the English language, unabridged (2nd ed.). (1976). United States: World.

Wellner, A. M. (Ed.). (1978). *Education and Credentialing in Psychology.* Washington, DC: Steering Committee of APA, AASPB and the National Register.

Werner, E. (1978). *Cutting scores for occupational licensing tests: Manual of considerations and methods.* (Available from Central Testing Unit, California Department of Consumer Affairs, Sacramento, CA 95814)

Wiens, A. N. (1977). *Toward a definition of training.* (Available from AASPB, PO Box 4389, Montgomery, AL 36103)

Wiens, A. N. & Dorken, H. (1986). Establishing and enforcing standards to assure professional competency. In H. Dorken & Associates (Eds.), *Professional psychology in transition: Meeting today's challenges* (pp. 174–199). San Francisco: Jossey-Bass.

12

Certification of Psychologists by the American Board of Professional Psychology

PETER NELSON MAYFIELD

INTRODUCTION

We psychologists are human—human first and psychologists only secondarily. As such, we have undertaken to sublimate and control such powerful human emotions as greed, lust, and envy in the service of becoming professional psychologists. Yet professional training in psychology is not likely to strengthen emotional controls over primitive instincts, nor is such training designed to correct significant flaws in character development. Newly created psychologists vary widely in the degree to which they have acquired emotional maturity and strength of character. Moreover, the skills acquired during professional training are learned to varying levels of proficiency. Some psychology students have more aptitude than others, some work harder at learning to be psychologists than others, some go through better training programs

PETER NELSON MAYFIELD • Private Practice of Clinical Psychology, Suite 1211, Lenox Towers, 3400 Peachtree Road, NE, Atlanta, GA 30326.

and have better role models, and some work harder at maintaining their professional skills once formal training is completed.

From the foregoing, an inference may be drawn that graduates of professional training programs in psychology vary on important dimensions—emotional maturity, character development, and level of competence in actual practice. The profession has implicitly recognized this problem by having established ethical standards for psychologists and by having encouraged the development of objective examinations for the licensing of professional psychologists. In addition, the *National Register for Health Service Providers in Psychology* has set certain criteria of training and experience for listing in its directory. These efforts serve to promote some quality standards for the generic "professional psychologist" but none offer any means of certifying specialists in even the most broadly agreed-upon areas of practice. Similarly, none scrutinize the "whole" psychologist in any depth. The American Board of Professional Psychology (ABPP), established in 1947 by the American Psychological Association (APA), uniquely serves the profession by offering examinations and certification in now six areas of professional practice: clinical psychology, clinical neuropsychology, counseling psychology, forensic psychology, industrial and organizational psychology, and school psychology. Moreover, these 3-hour oral examinations offer a comprehensive, in-depth look at the way in which each candidate integrates emotional maturity, character development, and professional competence in working with a "live" client. The balance of this chapter will focus on the maintenance of standards of excellence within the profession by the ABPP and on the implication for training programs of the certification procedures and criteria established by the Board.

History

Prior to 1946, there were no APA-approved training programs in professional psychology, no APA-approved internships, and few state licensing laws for psychologists. Yet applied psychology was in increasing demand following World War II. Individuals with widely varying levels of training (if any) were calling themselves psychologists, and there were few quality assurance mechanisms for the profession or the public. Professional psychology needed an immediate means of identifying itself and of establishing credibility. Licensing laws were beginning to be written but in a slow and piecemeal fashion. The APA responded to this dilemma by establishing a committee to consider ways of professionalizing psychology and of gaining a place as an independent profession. In 1946, this committee recommended that an independent examining board award specialty diplomas to qualified psychologists, and in April 1947, the American Board of Examiners in Professional Psychology (ABEPP) was incorporated (Hess, 1984). It was designed as a body independent from the APA. (The name was later changed to the American Board of Professional Psychology, or ABPP.) The APA indicated it would support the right of ABPP-diplomated psychologists to practice independently because they had been judged by their peers to be of an advanced level of competence.

The first board reviewed the applications of 1,557 psychologists under the "grandfather" provision and awarded diplomas to 1,097 (70%) of the applicants. Standards for training and experience were set, and procedures for written and oral exams were developed. (Written exams were dropped in 1967 as they did not seem to add to the discriminatory power of the total examination process.) Examinations were offered at that time in the broad specialties of clinical, counseling, and industrial psychology. Oral examinations were initially separated into three parts: (a) diagnosis (appraisal, evaluation); (b) therapy (counseling, constructive action); and (c) ethical and professional attitudes and knowledge. A "professional field situation" or live observation of the candidate examining and interviewing a patient or client was and has been an integral part of every ABPP examination.

Over the years, as the profession grew and experience was gained in examining candidates, the board has made modifications in the examinations (see Marrow, 1969) and has added examinations in three additional areas of professional practice (formerly called specialties): school psychology (1967), clinical neuropsychology (1983), and forensic psychology (1985). Other practice areas are being studied and will probably come under the ABPP umbrella in the next few years.

The American Board of Professional Psychology Today: Structure and Function

Structurally, the ABPP consists of a national board of trustees and six regional boards. In addition, contractual relationships exist between the ABPP and the American Board of Clinical Neuropsychology (ABCN) and between ABPP and the American Board of Forensic Psychology (ABFP). The board of trustees consists of 11 diplomates, 6 of whom are appointed by the 6 regional boards and one each appointed by the ABCN and the ABFP. The remaining trustees are at-large members, and at present, are elected by the board itself. Each area of professional practice is represented on the board. Members serve a term of 4 years with the possibility of one additional consecutive term. The board meets twice each year, currently maintains a central office in Columbia, Missouri, and is served by a full-time executive officer, the only salaried individual in the ABPP structure. All board members, regional board members, and examiners serve without pay. Financial support for the ABPP comes from examination fees ($300 for the application fee and $400 for the examination fee) and from annual dues of diploma holders who join an ABPP membership organization (mandatory for new diplomates after 1984). Sixty-five percent of the budget goes to central office operations, with the balance being allocated to expenses of board meetings and to regional board expenses. The regional boards are charged with the actual conduct of the examinations. Each state has one or more representatives on its regional board, and these representatives appoint the individual examination committees. At present, approximately 4,000 psychologists hold the ABPP diploma.

REQUIREMENTS FOR CERTIFICATION BY ABPP

The ABPP diploma represents a standard of excellence and the highest recognition of competence in professional psychology. The steps toward attainment of this diploma are described next.

Training and Supervised Experience Requirements

Applicants must detail their academic training and professional experience. The basic training requirement as outlined in the ABPP policies and procedures manual is "a doctoral degree in psychology from a college or university which, at the time the degree was awarded, met the existing standards of the American Psychological Association for doctoral training in the specialty of the applicant" (ABPP, 1984a, p. 1). Exceptions may be made for applicants whose doctoral degree is not from an APA-approved program. In such cases, the following requirements must be met:

a. The institution awarding the doctoral degree must be accredited by one of the regional accrediting associations or be a recognized candidate for accreditation within three years of the time the degree was conferred.
b. The doctoral degree must be awarded by a department of psychology. The locus of that department may be in a college or school of Education, Theology, Business, etc., but the department must be clearly identified as a department of psychology in the official catalogue of the institution and must be so identified in written statements by the Chief Administrative Officers of the institution. For Clinical, Counseling, and School

> Psychology the department must clearly indicate that it is offering education and training in the specialty for which the applicant applies.
> c. The doctoral program in psychology must be an integrated, organized program in psychology as opposed to an accumulation of credits or courses.
> d. Over half of the courses must be psychology courses, psychological in content, and taught by psychologists.
> e. The basic core of psychology courses must be comparable to those required for APA accreditation.
> f. For Clinical, Counseling, and School Psychology, the program must have appropriate practicum and internship (supervised field experiences) in applied, professional areas. (ABPP, 1984a, p. 4)

Applicants in clinical, counseling, and school psychology are required to take their examination in the specialty in which they received their doctoral degree. For the other practice areas, specific training requirements exist in addition to a generic doctorate in psychology. Provision is made for individuals who have been formally retrained in a specialty area other than that in which they received their doctorate.

For applicants in clinical, counseling, and school psychology, an APA-approved internship is required. Again, provision is made for applicants whose internship was not in an APA-approved program; they must document a minimum of 1,800 hours of training experience within a 2-year period in an organized psychological service setting. Supervision must be direct and face-to-face and must include substantial supervision by psychologists. Again, parallel supervised field training experience is required in the other practice areas.

As its final experience requirement, the ABPP is unique among credentialing groups by requiring a full 5 years of acceptable qualifying experience. In the clinical, counseling, and school areas, a predoctoral internship is credited as one of these 5 years. Part-time professional experience (e.g., as in the case of university-based psychologists) is acceptable provided the candidate devotes a "significant" amount of time to professional practice in his or her area (ABPP, 1984a). Also private practice experience is acceptable if preceded by 3 years of experience under professional supervision, in a setting where systematic, direct supervision is provided by a qualified person and in which the applicant's total work is subject to review.

Other Requirements

The ABPP requires that an applicant be licensed in the state in which he or she engages in professional psychology, be a member of the APA, provide three acceptable endorsements, provide evidence of continuing education in the profession of psychology, and agree to be bound by the professional ethics of psychology. Again the entire thrust of these comprehensive requirements for candidacy is to screen out individuals who are only partially trained or self-supervised or who are only partially identified with the profession of psychology. The standards set by the ABPP even for candidacy are all-inclusive and go beyond those set by any other credentialing body, yet are within reach of the majority of experienced psychologists who have been well trained, adequately supervised, and who have fully identified with the profession from the outset of their professional career.

Professional Work Sample

Once an applicant has met the foregoing requirements, he or she is admitted into candidacy. The next step is preparation of a professional work sample. Detailed guidelines are provided by the ABPP, but basically the work sample should reflect a typical professional activity of the candidate. Usually, it consists of a verbatim transcript of interaction with a client. In the areas of clinical and counseling psychology, the work sample might consist of a therapy transcript with additional information to provide a contextual background, a report of a psychological evaluation with supporting test data, and/or a transcript of a therapy supervision session with a student with supporting background information. In the other practice areas, the work sample will vary in accord with what constitutes a typical work activity. The work sample is submitted in advance to the examining committee and should reflect the fact "that the psychologist possesses an explicit and coherent rationale for what he/she does" (ABPP, 1983, p. 1). The work sample should reflect a realistic assessment of a client problem and an approach toward a solution of that problem for purposes of constructive change.

Oral Examination

The oral examination is conducted by a carefully chosen committee of three diplomates who reflect to the extent possible the candidate's practice area and theoretical orientation. The chair is always a highly experienced examiner. The exam usually lasts 3 to 4 hours, including an initial hour of observation of the candidate in an "on-the-job" situation with an actual client. The client is obtained by the committee in advance and is unknown to the candidate. The candidate is asked to assess the client in whatever manner he or she believes to be appropriate and be prepared to discuss impressions and recommendations for any future work with the client. The remainder of the oral examination is an effort on the part of the examiners to judge competence "at the diplomate level" in the broad practice area of the candidate. The work sample and "on-the-job" observation serve as springboards for discussion. The candidate will have been asked to describe his or her theoretical orientation and then show how he or she is working within that orientation. The committee seeks to establish if the candidate does in practice what the candidate says he or she does and if the candidate knows why he or she is doing it. "The board recognizes that professional psychologists use a variety of approaches, techniques, and theoretical orientations. The examiners will seek to establish the candidate's level of competence within his or her own frame of reference" (ABPP, 1984a, p. 7).

Dimensions of Competency Covered by the Oral Examination

Each member of the examining committee is provided with rating scales covering the three basic dimensions of competency that have been developed by the ABPP over the years. These dimensions are:

1. The effectiveness of the candidates efforts toward constructive intervention based on realistic assessment of the problem presented
2. Awareness of the relevance of research and theory
3. Sensitivity to the ethical implications of professional practice (ABPP, 1984a, p. 6)

These areas are interrelated and are examined within the context of the candidate's actual work with clients. It is assumed that a professional psychologist at the diplomate level maintains an awareness of the ethical issues involved in his or her daily work and is conversant with the APA ethical standards. Similarly, it is assumed that the diplomate-level professional psychologist stays abreast of current psychological knowledge and theory in his or her practice area and can discuss critically the relevance of this information to his or her actual work. Finally, diplomate-level psychologists are felt to have an ethical obligation to the profession to identify with it through appropriate memberships and activities and to be able to discuss current issues and problems within the profession of psychology. Examiners are instructed on these dimensions and make independent ratings immediately after the examination is concluded. If there is significant variance among the ratings, discussion is held and another rating made. A final vote is taken on the single dimension of pass/fail.

Award of the Diploma

Diplomas are conferred on successful candidates at a convocation held during the annual convention of the American Psychological Association. Historically, approximately 70% of candidates pass the examination on the first attempt. For those who do not pass, the right of reexamination is offered. An explanation of the reasons for failure is supplied to each unsuccessful candidate to assist in further professional development. If an unsuccessful candidate feels he or she was not examined in an appropriate and fair way, a review may be requested in which case the examination may be nullified and a reexamination held with a new committee at no cost to the candidate.

FUTURE TRENDS IN CREDENTIALING BY ABPP

The ABPP Board of Trustees continuously studies and modifies its examination procedures and approach to credentialing. It has consistently resisted pressures to dilute the requirements. In fact, the educational requirements have been tightened in the past few years, requiring now that the applicant take the examination in the specialty in which he or she received the doctoral degree or else submit detailed evidence of retraining in a new specialty. Beyond this, however, the board has spent a number of years developing an alternative examination procedure to make the oral examination as reliable and as valid as possible. Also the present method requires over 4 hours of donated time on the part of three examiners for one candidate, and thus a more efficient examination method is being sought. The following section describes the board's current efforts toward an alternative examination model.

Alternative Examination Procedures Based on "Assessment Centers" Model

Douglas Bray, member of the ABPP Board of Trustees in the late 1970s and early 1980s and its president before his retirement, was a pioneer in the development of the "assessment centers" concept in his role as research psychologist with AT&T. He brought this expertise to the ABPP examination and has helped develop an alternative model in which four examiners examine four candidates in the space of a day. This experimental format still calls for the prior submission of a work sample and focuses on the same basic dimensions of competence described previously. However, a simulated rather than actual client is presented, along with a set of videotaped case vignettes. The candidate responds to a series of questions, such as "what should the therapist say or do at this point?" Each of four assessment centers is manned by an examiner who sees each candidate in rotation. Each examiner is assigned one of four areas in which to examine each candidate: personal interview, knowledge and understanding of professional practice and ethics, fact-finding and client analysis exercise (using the videotape), and work sample review. Thus at any one point in the process, each candidate is with one of the four examiners and at certain predesignated times rotates to another examiner for another area. At the end of the day, the examiners discuss their ratings and come to a consensus regarding each candidate. The videotaped vignettes and simulated case study would seem to offer more reliability to the examination than is provided by the uncertainties of a live client, but some loss of validity may be suffered by not being able to observe the candidate in a face-to-face client interaction. On the other hand, being examined by only one examiner at a time may reduce the usual candidate anxiety that at times raises validity problems. In December 1984, this experimental format was used with actual (volunteer) candidates for the first time. The examiners were enthusiastic about the approach but made a number of suggestions for further refinement, including, unfortunately, that two examiners man each assessment center area, thereby doubling the number of examiners needed for what was designed to be a more efficient approach. The approach has limited applicability in the short range because only a limited series of videotaped vignettes have been produced and only for clinical candidates with a psychoanalytic approach. The long-range outlook depends on funding by the board for further development to broaden the applicability of the approach. For now, it remains strictly experimental for use with informed, volunteer candidates.

New Areas of Professional Practice

As stated earlier, the ABPP Board of Trustees has recently added two new professional practice areas (clinical neuropsychology and forensic psychology), this marking the first time in over 15 years that new areas have been added. This move on the part of the ABPP comes in response to the proliferation of "specialty" and "subspecialty" boards within psychology during the past 10 years. The APA has been wrestling with the issue of specialization for years, attempting to define a "specialty"; in 1981 it published the "Specialty Guidelines for the Delivery of Services" (APA Committee on Standards for Providers of Psychological Services, 1981), covering the basic four areas of clinical, counseling, school, and industrial/organizational. The APA continues to work on developing criteria for the definition of a specialty (APA Board of Professional Affairs Subcommittee on Specialization, 1984) but may be several years away from "officially" designating any new specialties, subspecialties, or special proficiencies. After several years of waiting for the APA to come to some resolution of the issue, the ABPP trustees decided to develop their own guidelines for adding new areas for certification and dropped the use of the term *specialty* in favor of *areas of professional practice* or *practice areas*. Thus some practice areas could be more broad in scope than others. At this time, the ABPP was being approached by some of the newly emerging "boards" about a formal affiliation. Each board was carefully evaluated to ensure that its educational, training, and experience requirements met those of ABPP diploma holders. Finally, in 1983 a contractual agreement was made with the American Board of Clinical Neuropsychology under which those ABCN diplomates who also held the ABPP diploma would serve as an initial pool of examiners for other ABCN diploma holders. Now applications are reviewed by the ABPP for general requirements and by the ABCN for more specific neuropsychology requirements. A special examination format has been developed, modeled after the basic ABPP procedures, and utilizing a modification of the assessment center approach described previously. Diplomate status will be conferred jointly by the ABPP and ABCN through the ABPP Board of Trustees on which the ABCN now has representation. Clinical neuropsychology is proving to be a popular practice area, with several hundred applications being received in the first year since coming under the ABPP umbrella (ABPP, 1984b).

In 1985, the ABPP trustees voted a formal affiliation with the American Board of Forensic Psychology (ABFP). Details of the affiliation are being worked out, but the ABFP examination procedures are noted to be quite rigorous, and 40% of current ABFP diplomates also hold an ABPP diploma. The ABFP was also chosen because it has never "grandfathered" anyone, and candidates are examined both on their forensic skills as well as on the knowledge in the underlying science and professional practice area of their identification (ABPP, 1985). Other practice areas are being evaluated by the ABPP trustees, for example psychoanalysis, and several additional areas are likely to be added in the next few years.

CERTIFICATION PROCEDURES AND CRITERIA ESTABLISHED BY THE ABPP: IMPLICATIONS FOR TRAINING IN PROFESSIONAL PSYCHOLOGY

The ABPP was originally established through an action of the APA, and though independent of the APA, the ABPP for most of its history has maintained liaison with the APA. In retrospect, this liaison has not been as close as it should have been and especially with such bodies within the APA as the Council of University Directors of Clinical Psychology, Council of Counseling Psychology Training Programs, Council of Directors of School Psychology Training Programs, Association of Directors of Psychology Training Centers, and the Association of Psychology Internship Centers. The present section will attempt to describe a model for linking training programs in professional psychology to ultimate ABPP requirements and examinations. First, however, some background is needed regarding the present situation.

Incentives to Seek the ABPP Diploma

The decision to seek certification by the American Board of Professional Psychology is at present one based largely on the intrinsic rewards offered the applicant. In an unpublished pilot study of ABPP eligible psychologists that I conducted, the majority of respondents marked that they would consider seeking the ABPP diploma because "it would be a learning experience for me—having to prepare and update myself for the examination" and "it would represent a challenge which I would like to meet, for a feeling of personal satisfaction." Far down the list were reasons related to departmental promotions or more referrals. At present, there are only scattered extrinsic incentives for seeking the ABPP diploma. Promotion and tenure in academic departments sometimes require ABPP certification. The APA strongly recommends that directors of professional psychology training programs hold the ABPP diploma. Some states, for example, Missouri, offer merit system incentives to ABPP diplomates. The federal government has taken steps toward incentive pay for Veterans Administration psychologists, and there are similar moves within the Department of Defense. APA accreditation committees take cognizance of the number of diplomates on the faculty or training staff of an institution or internship being evaluated. Finally, a number of states offer some form of reciprocity in licensing for ABPP diploma holders. These extrinsic incentives often come after the fact, however; after a psychologist finds himself or herself in a situation that encourages applying for candidacy. At that point, it may be too late to qualify to take the examination if the psychologist has not taken care to meet the ABPP standards for training and supervised experience starting back in his or her graduate school days.

"Cradle-to-Grave" Concept

Explicit linkages between professional psychology training programs and the ABPP could promote a higher quality of professional practice by developing a "cradle to grave" concept in the minds of entering graduate students. Students would be guided toward credentialing steps that would begin with licensing and end with specialty or professional practice area "boards." Such would promote a longer period of specialized postdoctoral supervised experience or training (comparable to a medical residency) prior to private practice; the ABPP requires 3 years of supervised experience (including internship) before private practice. Board exams would be anticipated and planned for as the last step in becoming a fully credentialed professional psychologist. Such planning would especially be needed in graduate and professional school programs lacking APA approval. Students who cannot enter an APA-approved internship would be encouraged to heed the ABPP requirements. As a part of this "cradle to grave" concept, the ABPP would each fall seek the names of all entering graduate students in professional psychology training programs, enter these in a computer, and send out periodic informational materials about ABPP and credentialing. A career-monitoring process by the ABPP would begin in the early days of a student's training and continue well past the award of the doctoral degree. The student could consult the ABPP on any question he or she might have about his or her graduate program or internship in time to make corrections. In a similar way, the newly created psychologist could consult the ABPP about the appropriateness of his or her supervised experience during the early years, to ensure that such will meet ABPP requirements a few years hence. The psychologist from an APA-approved training program and an APA-approved internship might be granted early "candidacy" to take the board exams.

Formal channels of communication could be established between training directors (both individually and as associations) and ABPP so that information exchange could take place. The ABPP could offer feedback to training directors regarding the performance of their graduates on the exams, to help training programs better evaluate their long-range strengths and weaknesses. As new trends in training develop, the ABPP could stay abreast of these and modify the examination to make it more relevant. Already, plans are underway for a new "Boulder" conference; and there are strong voices urging that the "Boulder model" be abandoned (Sechrest, 1985a). The ABPP should be intimately involved in such basic changes in professional training.

Through such formal linkages, the ABPP and training directors could together develop more and better retraining programs for psychologists wishing to change their specialty or add a new practice area. The ABPP requires formal retraining before an individual may take an exam in a field other than that in which he or she received the doctorate. Such retraining must meet explicit ABPP requirements, and "it must be stressed . . . that merely taking an internship or acquiring experience in a practicum setting is not, for example, considered adequate preparation for becoming a clinical, counseling, or school psychologist when prior training had not been in the relevant area" (ABPP, 1984a, p. 10). The ABPP has strongly encouraged psychology departments to develop programs for retraining doctoral-level psychologists who wish to change their specialty, but this "encouragement" is buried on the last page of its policies and procedures manual, and to the author's knowledge, it has never been pursued by the ABPP in the systematic manner that formal linkages would permit. Finally, through joint cooperation, training directors and the ABPP could develop programs to meet the continuing education needs of ABPP candidates. The ABPP is an APA-approved sponsor of individualized continuing education programs and offers continuing education credit for preparation leading up to the oral examination. Training programs might develop post-graduate review courses for diplomate candidates in such areas as ethics, current research trends, assessment, and intervention.

CREDENTIALING: TURF GUARDING OR OPPORTUNITY FOR COOPERATION?

As a final note, the whole area of credentialing and especially specialty credentialing is undergoing significant evolutionary movement. Even what have been considered "traditional" specialties are being reexamined; clinical psychology may now be too broad a field to be considered a "specialty," and counseling psychology could be considered a subfield within clinical (see Sales [1985] and Sechrest [1985b] for excellent discussions of this topic). As specialties, subspecialties, practice areas, and areas of special proficiency evolve, credentialing must of necessity also change. With the various credentialing bodies in existence today and other ad hoc bodies forming, there is every possibility of competition and turf guarding but also the opportunity for cooperation. In 1982, the ABPP took the initiative in holding a conference on the evaluation of professional competence as a preliminary discussion of issues. Representatives from various training program associations, APA divisions, the Board of Professional Affairs (BPA), and certain credentialing boards attended, making this a precedent-setting conference. The APA's Board of Professional Affairs Subcommitee on Specialization continues its work in defining specialties and proficiencies (APA, 1984), and the BPA Committee on Professional Standards is now revising its "Specialty Guidelines for the Delivery of Services," published in 1981 (APA). Communication and an attitude of working toward what is best for the profession is essential as these efforts proceed. Competency-based training and evaluation is the common denominator (see Howard, 1983), and at present, the American Board of Professional Psychology would seem the logical umbrella board for competency-based evaluation in the emerging areas of professional practice. The ABPP has recognized the need for growth and change, and its recent addition of two new practice areas is only the beginning. Hans Strupp, 10 years ago, warned of the "erosion of excellence" in clinical psychology training, research, and practice (Strupp, 1975); perhaps the focus today on competency-based training and evaluation will be reassuring to him, and, incidentally, to the rest of us who were disquieted by his remarks.

REFERENCES

American Board of Professional Psychology. (1983). *Guidelines for the work sample submitted prior to the ABPP examination*. Columbia, MO: Author.

American Board of Professional Psychology. (1984a). *Policies and procedures for the creation of diplomates in professional psychology*. Columbia, MO: Author.

American Board of Professional Psychology. (1984b). Clinical neuropsychology board joins ABPP. *The Diplomate, 4*, 1.

American Board of Professional Psychology. (1985). Board votes ABFP affiliation. *The Diplomate, 5*, 1.

American Psychological Association Committee on Standards for Providers of Psychological Services. (1981). Specialty guidelines for the delivery of services. *American Psychologist, 36*, 639–681.

American Psychological Association Board of Professional Affairs Subcommittee on Specialization. (1984). *Specialization in psychology: principles. November, 1984 draft*. Washington, DC: Author.

Hess, A. K. (1984). American Board of Professional Psychology. In R. J. Corsini (Ed.), *Encyclopedia of Psychology* (Vol. 1, p. 54) New York: Wiley.

Howard, A. (1983). Work samples and simulations in competency evaluation. *Professional Psychology, 14*, 780–796.

Marrow, A. J. (1969). American Board of Professional Psychology; new directions and approaches; 1968 annual report. *American Psychologist, 24*, 151–154.

Sales, B. (1985). Specialization: Past history and future alternatives. *The Clinical Psychologist, 38*, 48–52.

Sechrest, L. B. (1985a). Specialization? Who needs it? *The Clinical Psychologist, 38*(1), 3.

Sechrest, L. B. (1985b). The lithotripter and the monolith. *The Clinical Psychologist, 38*(45), 47.

Strupp, H. H. (1975). The erosion of excellence. *The Clinical Psychologist, 28*, 1.

13

Criterion-Referenced, Competency-Based Training in Behavior Modification

RICHARD H. HIRSCHENBERGER,
PATRICIA S. McGUIRE, and DON R. THOMAS

OVERVIEW

The field of behavior modification relies on the use of both professionals and paraprofessionals for the delivery of treatment. The competence of the people involved in the delivery of treatment is an essential element in ensuring high-quality and effective services. The need for both initial training and ongoing in-service training is and will continue to be a critical factor in assuring that the services provided in a behavioral program are of the highest quality.

The purpose of this chapter is to describe the development of a competency-based, criterion-referenced assessment and training program. The assessment and training materials were developed to meet

RICHARD H. HIRSCHENBERGER, PATRICIA S. McGUIRE, and DON R. THOMAS • Brainerd Regional Human Services Center, Brainerd, MN 56401. Initial support of the competency surveys was provided by a special allocation of funds by Wesley Restad from the Minnesota Department of Human Services. Later a grant from the National Institute of Mental Health (L-T24MH16059) provided support for 3 years while tests and some training materials were developed.

the needs of practicing professionals and paraprofessionals. An overview of the competency-based, criterion-referenced training system will be provided. The process that was used in identifying, verifying, and operationalizing specific behavioral competencies as well as information regarding the methods of assessment and training will be presented. Problems and issues in verifying the effectiveness of training will be discussed, and future directions for continued development will be outlined.

Definitions

Since the popularization of "behavior modification," problems have arisen with both the use of the term and the misuse of techniques. Behavior modification has been used to refer to many concepts including psychosurgery and the use of drugs to "modify" behavior. Although these procedures do, in fact, "modify" behavior, it is inaccurate to equate them with behavior modification. *Behavior modification,* as it is used in this chapter, refers to

> procedures based on the explicit and systematic application of principles and technology derived from research in experimental psychology, procedures that involve some change in the social or environmental context of a person's behavior. (Stolz, Wienckowski, & Brown, 1975, p. 1029)

Competency, in this chapter, refers to specific skills/knowledge that professionals in the field view as being essential to the delivery of effective and ethical treatments. These include both verbal and performance skills. These skills and knowledge become the content of a competency-based training program. Criterion statements are the operational definitions of the competencies. Criterion statements include the specific behaviors that the trainee is to exhibit, the minimum level of performance required, and the conditions under which the performance is to be measured.

A criterion-referenced, competency-based training program differs from traditional programs. Traditional training models emphasize participation in targeted training processes. Training can be completed even though the trainee may not acquire all of the skills targeted as training objectives for the course of training. For example, a student taking a class in statistics may receive a passing grade even though he or she has never mastered the ability to differentiate between parametric and nonparametric statistics. Competency-based, criterion-referenced training, on the other hand, focuses on the outcome of training. In this type of training program, the learner cannot complete the training without demonstrating each of the targeted competencies at the criterion level.

NEED FOR COMPETENCY-BASED TRAINING

The impetus for the development of training programs that ensure acquisition of specific competencies came from several sources. Pressure has been partly created by publicity about abusive and excessively intrusive behavior modification procedures. Advocates and civil rights lawyers acted on behalf of a variety of clients to clarify relationships between the constitutional rights of clients and the responsibilities of therapists and other care givers. Judicial decrees made explicit the increased likelihood of clients becoming successful in suing state and local governments as well as program administrators and the therapists they hired to provide care and treatment. In an attempt to reduce the legal risks of working in a litigation-filled environment, administrators in human service systems developed laws, rules, regulations, policies, or guidelines (Griffith, 1980). The courts of the 1970s poured out a flood of lawsuits demanding appropriate, effective and well-documented, individualized treatment (Parry *et. al.*, 1984). School districts, residential treatment programs, state hospitals, and statewide departments of human services across the country developed systems to control elements of the treatment environment.

Within the community of behavior analysts, concern was generated that societal controls would be imposed in the form of licensure or certification procedures that would restrict or limit future development of the field.

Resistance to the identification and assessment of practitioner competencies has at least four issues as a foundation. First, there is a realistic concern that information on competencies could be used for further development of regulatory mechanisms that would restrict the professional's freedom to treat clients or conduct research with procedures with which the professional had not already demonstrated competence. This issue is already addressed by many state licensing boards that permit the addition of competencies to the professional's license. However, this is done via testimonials from other licensed individuals. Second, there is the fear that competencies used for regulatory purposes may "freeze" existing treatment knowledge and technology and prevent the development of new and more effective treatment procedures. Third, there is the frequently presented argument that skill in implementing treatment programs should be entirely identified by the extent to which the procedure ultimately provides a solution to the client's presenting problem. This focus on treatment outcome fails to recognize that there may be several procedures that can achieve identical treatment outcomes. In those cases where multiple procedures are available, the primary question is not simply whether the selected procedure is effective but rather which of the effective procedures intrudes least on the clients' individual freedoms and constitutional rights. The fourth issue concerns the method by which competencies are to be identified. Two alternatives that have been proposed are to survey practitioner opinions regarding skills deemed necessary in the delivery of treatment or to actually analyze the skills demonstrated by outstanding therapists. Both alternatives have readily identifiable deficiencies, and it will be necessary to refine the issue with extensive research.

Guideline Development

While behavior analysts were wrestling with processes to ensure high-quality ethical treatment, others in the human services field were responding to the issues of abuse and misuse by imposing guidelines on the use of behavioral procedures. These guidelines shared common characteristics, namely an emphasis on individualization and use of treatment procedures that protect clients' privacy, autonomy, and freedom of speech (Naumann, Maus, & Thomas, 1982; Pollack, 1981; Thomas, McAllister, & Thompson, 1976).

In Minnesota, the development of guidelines controlling the use of behavior modification procedures has undergone considerable evolution. These guidelines were initially drafted in 1969 by the Minnesota Department of Public Welfare's medical director, Dr. David Vail. They were so restrictive that the practice of behavior therapy was virtually impossible within the state institutions. However, this situation created a condition of potential neglect—a condition made obvious when subsequent litigation (*Welch v. Likins* [1974], *Welch v. Noot* [1980]) forced the issue of the client right to treatment. The Department of Public Welfare, in consultation with the Minnesota Association for Behavior Analysis (MNABA), began a long series of revisions of the guidelines.

In December 1975, a public hearing was conducted on the proposed guidelines. Analysis of the responses from human service agencies, consumer groups, professional societies, and individuals testifying at the hearing indicated that there was strong consensus on the specific improvements needed in the draft rule. An often-cited problem was lack of specification of the competencies of those who would plan, supervise, implement, and/or review the procedures controlled by the rule. There was no data base for specifying the skills required of practitioners at the various levels of treatment intensity. The Minnesota Department of Human Services provided funds to survey professionals working with targeted treatment procedures in order to solicit their opinions about essential skills.

IDENTIFICATION OF COMPETENCIES AND ASSESSMENT CRITERIA

First Survey

The effort to identify relevant competencies and associated screening criteria began with a survey of professionals active in the field. Forty-four proposed competency statements, each with associated criteria, comprised the content of the survey. They were developed using the State of Minnesota Behavior Analysis Career Ladder competencies (Jackson & Thomas, 1974) and the competencies and criteria proposed by Sulzer-Azaroff, Thaw, and Thomas (1975). The items were organized into the following general categories:

1. Measurement, which included items relating to knowledge of measurement apparatus, reliability, and observational recording systems
2. Behavioral observation, which included items relating to objective specification of target behaviors as well as relevant antecedent and consequent events
3. Behavior modification model, which included items relating to specifying the essential steps in carrying out a behavior change program as well as writing a proposal for such a program and a report of a completed program
4. Communication, which included items relating to written proposals and reports, audiovisual presentation of information, and oral communications to individuals and groups
5. Administration, which included items relating to knowledge of agency policies and staff organization patterns as well as supervisory skills
6. Ethics, law, and philosophy, which included items relating to professional ethical standards, federal and state laws as they affect treatment practices, and frequently discussed ethical issues

7. Design, which included items relating to the selection of appropriate experimental designs, identification of possible confounding variables, and use of single-subject designs
8. Assessment, which included items relating to the specification of appropriate and realistic program goals
9. Research, which included items relating to reading current research, writing research proposals, and conducting experimental research
10. Techniques, which included items relating to knowledge of a set of behavior change procedures and demonstrated use of at least some of those procedures
11. Training, which included items relating to the conduct of in-service training and workshop sessions

The sample for the survey was drawn from two sources. Surveys were sent to 218 professionals nationwide who had done research and published articles on the use of aversive and deprivation techniques. An additional 93 were sent to members of the MNABA. The membership of this group is composed of professionals, primarily practitioners, from a variety of occupations, including psychologists, teachers, social workers, physicians, psychiatrists, nurses, speech therapists, and rehabilitation therapists.

The survey respondents were asked to rate the relevancy of proposed competency items to users of aversive and deprivation procedures on a scale from 1 ("irrelevant") to 5 ("highly relevant"). Respondents were also asked to rate the adequacy of screening criterion items in measuring these competencies on a scale from 1 ("inadequate") to 5 ("highly adequate"). In addition, comments were solicited. Respondents were urged to suggest improvements or alternatives to the proposed competencies and criteria.

The overall return rate of the distributed surveys was 27% (84 surveys). The national return rate was 25% as compared to 32% for the MNABA sample. Analyses of these data included (a) ratings for competency items and categories; (b) ratings for criterion items and categories; (c) ratings for criterion items by item type; and (d) item comments, general comments, and suggested additional competency and criterion items.

The overall mean relevancy rating for competency items was 3.78 of a possible 5 (range 2.20–4.58). The criterion items had a mean adequacy rating of 3.75 of a possible 5 (range 3.28–4.15).

The mean rating and rank for competency and criterion items analyzed by category are given in Table 1. As can be seen in the table,

Table 1. Mean Rating of Competency and Criterion Items by Category

Category	Competency		Criterion	
	$\bar{X}$ rating	Rank	$\bar{X}$ rating	Rank
Measurement	4.12	4	3.88	3
Behavioral observation	4.23	3	4.02	1
Behavior modification model	4.07	5	3.77	8
Communication	3.66	8	3.80	6
Administration	4.00	6	3.62	10
Ethics, law, and philosophy	4.26	2	3.78	7
Design	3.64	9	3.80	5
Assessment, goal formulation, and targeting	4.50	1	4.00	2
Research	2.61	11	3.46	11
Techniques	3.94	7	3.80	4
Training	3.10	10	3.76	9

there is some disparity between the ratings for competencies and criterion items. The greater disparity between rankings of the competence and criteria items occurred in the category of ethics, law and philosophy. The competency items were ranked second, but criterion items were ranked seventh. The research category was ranked eleventh (last) for both competencies and criteria. The Spearman Rank Correlation between competency ratings and criterion ratings for the 11 categories is $rs = .609$ ($p < .05$). The correlation between competency ratings and criterion items for the individual survey items was $rs = .575$ ($p < .001$).

Comparisons of ratings by the MNABA sample and the national sample showed that respondents in the national sample rated items in every competency category lower than did respondents in the MNABA sample. However, the Spearman Rank Correlation between MNABA and national mean ratings for the 11 categories is $rs = .954$ ($p < .001$). A separate analysis was performed for all comtetency items. For these 44 items, the correlation between MNABA and national mean ratings is $rs = .929$ ($p < .001$). These analyses suggest that although the MNABA sample rated the relevancy of the competencies higher, there was a strong tendency for both samples to rate items in the same relative order.

The mean ratings by the two samples for criterion items in each of the 11 categories show that respondents in the national sample rated items in 8 out of the 11 criterion categories lower than did respondents in the MNABA sample. The Spearman Rank Correlation between MNABA and national mean ratings for the 11 categories is $rs = .545$

($p < .10$). A separate analysis for the 44 individual criterion items results in a correlation between MNABA and national mean ratings of $rs = .689$ ($p < .001$). In interpreting this correlation, it should be noted that the range of mean ratings for criterion items was much narrower than the range of mean ratings for competency items.

The criterion items were also rated by type of assessment procedure proposed. The eight categories representing major types of criteria, the number of items in each category, the mean ratings of items in each category, and the mean ranks of items in each category are presented in Table 2. The types of criteria considered the least adequate by respondents were the "paper, project or discussion with references to published literature," "supervisor certification," and "project report or graphs to APA specifications."

In addition to the ratings, comments were solicited for each of the competency and criterion items. A total of 716 separate item comments were received. The comments were scored in one of three possible categories: (a) comments suggesting possible changes in a competency; (b) comments suggesting possible changes in a criterion; and (c) general comments.

Comments that made specific suggestions for item changes or suggested a direction that changes might take were counted in the first two groups. Comments that were redundant with the respondents' numbered ratings and comments relating to specific job categories were included in the general comments category. This scoring procedure resulted in 58 (8.1%) competency-related comments, 312 (43.6%) criterion-related comments, and 346 (48.3%) general comments.

Table 2. Mean Ratings and Ranks of Criterion Items by Type of Criterion

Type of criterion	Number of items	$\bar{X}$ rating	$\bar{X}$ rank
Written proposal or portion of proposal	4	4.00	5.1
Trainee and/or audience data	5	3.89	13.4
Objective or short answer test	6	3.88	14.9
Listing, explanation, or illustration	9	3.83	19.3
Reliability data	3	3.81	21.3
Project report or graphs to APA specifications	2	3.73	26.5
Supervisor certification	6	3.62	30.7
Papers, project, or discussion with references to published literature	9	3.49	37.6

Of the completed surveys, 82% had specific-item-related comments; 34% contained more general comments; and 23% suggested additional competencies and criteria.

The results of the first survey suggested some modifications of the proposed competencies and criteria. As a consequence of the low ratings for items in the research category, this area was deleted. The high ranking for the competency items in the ethics, law, and philosophy category and the low ranking of the corresponding criterion items resulted in the decision to separate ethics and law into two categories and revise the criteria for evaluating the competency.

Certain types of criteria were rated lower than others, specifically those requiring references to publish literature, certification by a supervisor and the utilization of American Psychological Association (APA) specifications for reports and graphs. In general, criterion items of these types were eliminated.

Although the results of this survey were roughly analogous to those found in the Sulzer-Azaroff, Thaw, and Thomas survey, a number of competency areas that were considered necessary for behavior analysts in the Sulzer-Azaroff *et al.* survey were rated as less than relevant in the present survey. These included items dealing with identifying current research trends, formulating new research questions, writing a research paper, writing a research proposal, conducting research, and conducting a workshop. These descrepancies may be related to the differences in purpose of the surveys. The Sulzer-Azaroff *et al.* survey attempted to define competencies for behavior analysts in general, whereas the present survey's purpose was to define specific competencies for users of aversive and deprivation treatment procedures.

Second Survey

Following the analysis of the initial survey, a panel was convened to begin the task of revising the listed competencies and to recommend a screening process. Because the vast majority of comments received on the initial survey were directed at the criteria statements, the work of this group focused on refining and elaborating the criteria associated with the identified competencies. As a result, the criteria were revised so greatly that it was determined that an additional survey needed to be conducted to ensure that the results of the first survey were iterpreted accurately.

The second survey contained 32 items. The items consisted of those rated "relevant" (i.e., a mean score of above 4.0) in the first survey results. Each survey item consisted of a competency statement and a proposed screening criterion. Twenty-two of the items specified skills that the panel considered to be necessary to obtain initial certification as an "expert" in the use of restrictive procedures. Ten additional items were competency demonstrations required to retain certification.

The items were grouped into six general content categories. Items from each of these general content areas were included for both initial and continuing certification. These categories were:

1. Measurement, which included items relating to knowledge of observational recording systems and variables that confound evaluation of treatment effects and to demonstrations of skills in target identification, observational data collection, and attainment of reliability
2. Ethics, which included knowledge of professional ethical standards and major ethical issues and demonstration of skills in incorporating ethical standards in treatment programs
3. Law, which included items relating to knowledge of federal and state laws as they pertain to treatment practices
4. Programming, which included items relating to knowledge of and/or demonstration of skills in the essential steps in program design, writing treatment programs, reporting treatment results, identifying variables that may contraindicate specific treatment procedures, selecting appropriate and realistic program goals, and knowledge of the primary literature on behavior change procedures
5. Supervision, which included items related to the knowledge of procedures for altering staff behavior with regard to program implementation and demonstration of skills in staff and parent training
6. Communication, which included items relating to demonstration of report writing skills, data analysis, and presentation of written reports

The criteria associated with each of these competencies were classified according to the testing circumstance and the type of behavioral product required for demonstration of the competency. Two of the criteria required oral responses to an interview, 11 required essay, short-answer, or multiple-choice responses to written examination materials. Nine of the criteria required the individual to respond to simulated situations such as videotapes or narrative reports. Ten involved the rating of on-the-job performance by a review panel.

Directions for survey respondents were identical to those used for criterion items in the first survey. Again, space was provided for the rater's comments on both the competency statement and the corresponding criteria.

A total of 202 surveys were distributed. Fifty of these were sent to members of the national sample referenced in the preceding survey who had returned the original survey. One hundred fifty-two were distributed to the membership of the MNABA.

Forty percent of the 202 surveys distributed were returned. The national return rate of 54% was slightly higher than the MNABA return rate of 34.9%.

The average criterion statement generated a mean rating of 3.99 on the 5-point scale. Mean ratings for individual criterion items ranged from 3.59 to 4.33 with the range being 0.74. The overall mean ratings for the MNABA and the national sample were identical (i.e., 3.99). Mean ratings for individual criterion items ranged from 3.52 to 4.40 for the MNABA sample and from 3.58 to 4.54 for the national sample.

In view of the fact that there were neither systematic nor major differences between the samples, the data were combined for all other analyses.

Analysis of the criteria ratings for each of the major content areas is summarized in Table 3. Mean ratings across categories did not differ significantly. The range in mean scores was 0.44.

Responses to the proposed criteria were also analyzed as to the type of testing circumstances and the behavioral product required. The mean ratings for the items in each of the five criterion groups is presented in Table 4. Simulation criterion items were rated as the most adequate type of criterion. The range across the type of criterion was 0.75.

Fifty-seven percent of the returned surveys contained at least one comment from the rater. There were a total of 361 separate comments

Table 3. Mean Rating of Criterion Items by Content Category

Category	Number of items	Mean rating
Measurement	6	4.10
Ethics	4	3.94
Law	5	4.09
Programming	13	4.00
Supervision	2	3.66
Communication	2	3.85

Table 4. Mean Rating of Criterion Items by Types of Criterion

Category	Number of items	Mean rating
Simulation	8	4.14
Written examination/simulation	1	4.13
Written examination	11	4.02
Review committee certification	10	3.39
Oral examination	2	3.72

received. Each of the comments was scored as being competency related, criterion related, or general in nature. The same scoring criterion was used as that identified in the first survey. This scoring procedure resulted in 27 (7.5%) competency-related comments, 222 (64.5%) criterion-related comments, and 112 (31%) general comments.

In that this survey focused primarily on criterion statements, an analysis of the content of these comments was undertaken. In this analysis, 75 representative comments (i.e., 20.8% of all comments) were independently classified by two scorers. The formula for computing interscorer agreement was 100 × number of agreements ÷ (number of agreements + number of disagreements). Interscorer agreement was 90.67%.

Results are presented in Table 5. Over half fall in the "be-more-specific category." This category includes comments relating to checklists that had not yet been developed, exam items that had not yet been written, and cutoff scores that had not yet been developed. All of these comments were considered to be legitimate indicators of additional work to be completed before individuals could be assessed. A "larger sample of behavior" included comments such as those suggesting a simulation exercise be used in place of a written examination. "More or less accurate behavior" refers to respondents' opinions that the cutoff scores were too stringent or not high enough. There were no consistent

Table 5. Analysis of the Content of Criterion-Related Comments

Content of criterion comment	Number	Percentage
Be more specific	118	53.15
Larger sample of behavior	30	13.51
Alternate sample of behavior	29	13.06
More or less accurate behavior	8	3.61
Minor wording or sequence change	37	16.67
TOTAL	222	100.00

trends in the categories, and none of the criterion comments outside of the "be-more-specific" category were viewed as having serious implications for the revision of the criteria statements. There were no significant correlations between the criteria ratings and the frequency of criteria comments, general comments, or total comments.

Comparison of First and Second Surveys

The first survey resulted in the deletion of several competencies and a reduction in content categories. The surviving competencies were relatively unaltered. The first survey also resulted in the decision to extensively revise the screening criteria. The second survey, dealing primarily with these criteria, generated responses that were uniformly more positive than those of the first survey. The final list of competencies and criteria are presented in the Appendix.

DEVELOPING TESTS FOR TARGET COMPETENCIES

The product of the survey process was a set of competencies and associated assessment criteria. The next step required the development of specific test items that matched the assessment criteria. A grant from the National Institute of Mental Health (NIMH) was obtained to develop an assessment and training program. The project was called ASSET, Adjusting the Service System to Evolving Therapies, and was to serve as a continuing education model to allow for the upgrading of the skills of staff within existing systems.

Initially the competencies were sorted into three levels. In determining which competency was to be included at each level, several factors were weighed. The proposed Minnesota guidelines included the concept that behavioral procedures could be divided into levels of intrusiveness and had established four levels. The Minnesota Civil Service system had identified a four-step career ladder for behavior analysts. The process of establishing the ASSET levels became one of matching the competency to the programmatic responsibilities of the staff to be trained. Recognizing that prior to implementing restrictive procedures, it is necessary to demonstrate competence in the use of positive procedures, another more basic level was added. Although not identified in the formal survey process, these competencies focused on ensuring that basic skills in measurement and the delivery of positive procedures were mastered before proceeding to the more complex skills. The second level of competencies consisted of those that appeared to be necessary for an individual to design and supervise the implementation of what was considered to be only mildly intrusive in the guidelines. The third level was designed to parallel those skills needed for the design and supervision of moderately intrusive procedures and the fourth for the most intrusive procedures.

Because competency-based instruction focuses by definition on the target competencies as training objectives, the initial effort emphasized developing instruments to assess whether a competency was present or needed to be trained. The initial steps in developing assessment items consisted of reviewing published material relevant to each competency. Questions were written to cover the topic area. Finally, the question formats were adjusted to match the criterion statement. A variety of testing formats were used. Specific types of assessmenet included true/false, multiple-choice, fill-in-the-blank, and essay tests. Simulations were developed for data recording, data reduction and analysis, program writing, and report writing. Upon completion of the assessments, training materials for each of the competencies were assembled. The training materials consisted of readings pertinent to the specific competency. Where the competency covered material not readily available from another source, project staff developed materials.

Testing materials were subjected to external reviews. Two reviews were conducted by professionals selected by MNABA to determine the adequacy of the match between the test items and the criteria statements for each competency. Revisions were made, and the group again met to review the product.

As the federal grant project came to its end, a third review of the assessment materials was conducted. This final review required each of the participants to make judgments about the extent to which the assessment items matched the assessment criteria established by the survey process. Overall agreement that the tests continued to meet the criterion was 92%.

Following the development of the testing and training materials and the formal reviews, efforts were made to assess their effectiveness. A total of 342 individuals participated in the assessment and training process. Included were staff and interns at the Minnesota Learning Center, students at St. Cloud State University, and staff from Brainerd and Cambridge State Hospitals. They generally fell into seven categories related to their prior contact with applied behavior analysis:

1. *Graduate behavior therapists* consisted of individuals responsible for the design and supervision of behavioral programming that covered all procedures. All had advanced training in behavior analysis.

2. *Paraprofessional* consisted of individuals who provided primarily direct care services to mentally retarded clients.
3. *Human services specialists/behavior modification (HSS/BM)* consisted of direct-line staff whose positions specifically required the implementation of behavioral procedures.
4. *Special teachers/recreation therapists* consisted of teachers specifically trained in special education and professional recreation therapists. All of these individuals possessed a minimum of a bachelor's degree and had been exposed to training in behavior analysis.
5. *Behavior analysts* consisted of individuals who were responsible for the design of some behavioral programs and were the direct-line supervisors of the staff implementing the behavioral programs.
6. *Interns* consisted of both graduate and undergraduate students from various colleges and universities. By and large, they were psychology and human services students.
7. *Other professionals* consisted primarily of individuals whose positions required a high level of skill in their own field, but that field did not provide formal training in behavior analysis.

A minimum level of competency was targeted for each participant based on the assumption that different jobs required different levels of skill. This was generally established jointly between the individual, the program manager, and the project staff. The level chosen reflected the skills the individual needed to successfully perform the programming duties in their current position. Additional participation beyond minimum requirements was encouraged. The testing and training processes were designed to be responsive to the need for continued training for persons already employed within the human services field. An effort was made to have the materials self-paced and as instructor-free as possible. As a result, the individual competencies were designed so that they could be worked on separately. Each participant started by pretesting on all the competencies at the first level. If the person met the criterion on each of the competencies at the first level, she or he would pretest at the next level and so on until the target level was met. Remediation was provided in the form of training packages for individuals not meeting the criterion. A training package consisted of a collection of readings pertinent to the specific competency.

Following remediation, the individual posttested on the competency. Successfully meeting the criterion resulted in continuing on with the process. On those occasions when the posttest was not passed, individual tutoring was provided to supplement the written training materials.

EVALUATION OF THE ASSESSMENT AND TRAINING PROCEDURES

The following results are based upon test scores obtained by the participants. These data constitute initial findings. They provide a perspective on the current set of materials and are the basis for additional study.

Test scores were examined to determine the relationship between job classification and performance. The means of all pretest scores for each of the groups are presented in Figure 1. In this figure, it can be seen that graduate behavior therapists ranked first, followed by the behavior analysts, human services specialists/behavior modification, special teachers/recreation therapists, paraprofessionals, interns, and other professionals, respectively. The only exception to the consistency of these rankings occurred within the intern category at Level II, and this appeared to be a function of the selection process. Only graduate-level interns participated at Level II. If the performance of graduate behavior therapists is the yardstick against which to measure the validity of the assessment devices, then these results support the tests.

An analysis of variance between subject groups was conducted for the overall scores on each of the levels as well as for the individual competencies. For the overall scores at each of the various levels, there was a significant difference between the groups ($p < .002$).

On the individual competencies, the same pattern emerged. There was a significant difference across job categories for all of the tests at

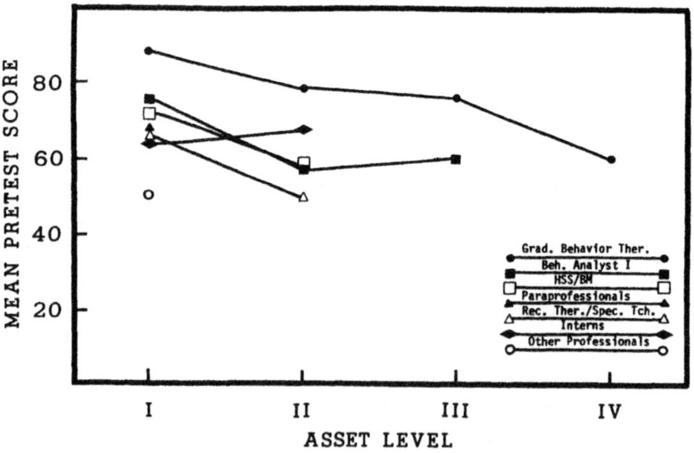

Figure 1. The mean pretest scores for the four levels of ASSET across occupational categories.

Level I ($p < .02$). The analyses conducted on Level II yielded similiar results. Of the 12 analyses conducted, 7 were significant ($p < .05$). At Level III, the only categories with sufficient numbers of participants for statistical analysis purposes were the graduate behavior therapists and the behavior analysts. Of the 10 tests that were analyzed at this level, 5 were significant at the .05 level. Ranking, using the mean scores, placed the graduate behavior therapists above the behavior analysts. There were no analyses performed on the Level IV competencies because only the graduate behavior therapists participated at this level.

The percentage of individuals within each group reaching the criteria (i.e., passing the test) on the competencies at each level is shown in Figure 2. As was the case with the mean scores obtained, the percentage of each group reaching the criteria can be used as a rough measure of relative rank of the groups. Virtually the same pattern emerged with the exception of the paraprofessionals who ranked above the interns and the special teacher/recreation therapists at Level I.

To determine whether the proportion of individuals reaching the passing criterion differed among the identified groups, a chi-square analysis of each of the competencies was conducted. This analysis compared the number of each of the previously cited groups who met the criteria on the pretest. As in the case with the analyses of variance, the number of groups declined as the level of the testing increased. The chi-square was significant ($p < .05$) for 7 of the 11 tests at Level I (64%), 5 of the 12 tests at Level II (42%), and for 3 of the 11 tests at Level III

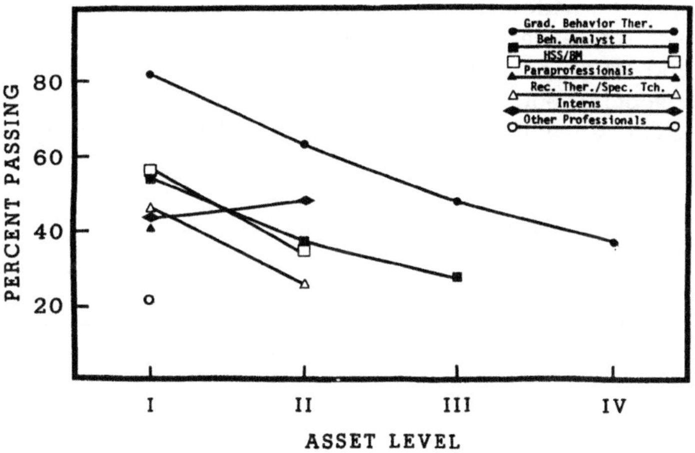

Figure 2. Percentage of individuals across occupational categories reaching criteria on the competencies at each level of ASSET.

(27%). No analysis was possible at Level IV due to inadequate numbers of participants for statistical purposes.

These data display a relationship between formal training and experience with behavioral procedures and performance on the competency assessments. However, no single individual passed all of the competencies on the pretest. Considering that a number of the graduate behavior therapists held their doctorate degrees and the majority of the master's-level individuals received the training in specifically behavioral programs, this fact becomes important. At the same time, no competency was failed by all of the individuals taking it. Combined, these results suggest that although there is a relationship between formal training and performance on the competency assessments, formal training does not ensure that the individual is able to perform all of the identified competencies. The inability of the highly trained therapists to demonstrate all of the competencies strongly suggests that using degree criteria as the basis for authorizing a therapist to use intrusive procedures may be an error.

Mean change scores were computed to determine whether test scores changed as a function of training. Change scores reflect the difference between the percentage scores obtained on the pre- and posttests. Summary data for the mean change and the range for each level are shown in Table 6. There was a consistent increase in posttest scores for all levels. The greatest change in scores was seen in Level III. This may be accounted for, in part, by the fact that more people in the lower scoring groups (i.e., BAs, special teachers, recreation therapists) took Level III tests than took tests at Level IV.

Due to the wide variety of formal education of the participants in the project, the readability of the materials was examined. Samples of testing and training materials were analyzed for level of reading difficulty. In general, both testing and training materials were in the 11th to 12th grade range of reading difficulty. The level of reading difficulty

Table 6. Pretest/Posttest Change Scores

	Mean change	Range	Percentage of posttests passed
Level I	+21.80	6.2–45.9	68
Level II	+29.13	9.9–53.3	64
Level III	+35.40	6.7–70.0	66
Level IV	+29.70	4.0–48.3	84

ranged from 7th grade (the Fry Readability Test at Level III) to "scientific, professional, technical" (the Raygor Reliability Estimate at Level III).

DISCUSSION

There is a multitude of issues that could be reviewed in any discussion of therapist competencies. The fears of members of the community of behavior analysts reflected some of those issues. The conferences of behavior analysts in the early 1970s regularly led to intense disagreements. Participants argued about the steps that could and should be taken to protect the clients being treated with behavior modification programs and the staff responsible for that treatment. Technically correct application of behavior modification procedures without recognition of the clients' constitutional rights creates an unsafe environment for both clients and therapists. Misuse and abuse of behavioral technology also establish increased risks for both clients and therapists. Consequently, it is highly desirable to ensure that therapists avoid both misuse of the technology and violation of clients' rights.

Because of the great variability in graduate training programs, it is impossible to determine for any given graduate whether the competencies have been developed that are essential for protecting client rights while providing effective treatment. Existing degree-granting programs tend to emphasize completion of a variable course load with no specification of minimum skills required to complete each course. The transcript of graduate credits provides evidence of participation in a variety of course offerings. The transcript cannot be interpreted as documentation for the presence of any targeted set of skills.

Advocates, lawyers, consumers or clients, and employers all have a legitimate interest in whether a particular therapist has developed the skills necessary to work safely and effectively with a particular client. The traditional means of ensuring therapist competency include both licensure and certification. Unfortunately, both of these systems present serious problems. Licensure of a specific profession to use behavior modification procedures could unnecessarily restrict appropriately trained people from delivering services. At the same time, certification that is usually based on the completion of some targeted course of training does not ensure that a therapist can do any particular procedure competently. The dilemma is real. The greatest potential for a positive solution may lie in the adoption of training programs that emphasize the development of particular competencies. Unfortunately, there has not been a consensus about the particular competencies that can be judged essential.

The surveys conducted to identify critical competencies relating to the use of intrusive behavior modification procedures cannot be interpreted as establishing a professional consensus regarding all essential skills. The surveys do provide an initial, data-based step toward the identification of a broad array of therapist competencies. In addition, in the area of providing therapy to control behavioral excesses, the survey-based competencies do appear to reflect an important level of professional agreement.

The ability to identify particular skills of a clinician aids both in the initial hiring of individuals and in the credentialing process. Although there remains no professional consensus regarding certification, accrediting bodies require that professionals be granted privileges to perform certain duties based upon their experience and training. The current set of tests allows for a much more objective assessment of these skills. Accreditation professionals are also suggesting that continued privileging be based on measures of the professional's ongoing performance on the job.

This type of training program has led to several overall program benefits. It has provided direction from administration that staff competence be highly valued. This in turn has set the tone of active programming throughout the facility. The involvement of staff from a wide variety of disciplines in the training has enhanced the ability of individuals to communicate with each other, even though their professional backgrounds and orientations were quite divergent. Development of a shared or common language has led to a reduction in conflicts regarding the approach to be taken with any given case. For example, discussions regarding the merits or problems with punishment procedures are put aside, and the particulars of a given procedure become the focus of planning.

From the administrator's perspective, the current system of training has increased the confidence that errors and abuses have been minimized. As Mager and Pipe (1970) have suggested, any analysis of a discrepancy in performance should include an analysis of the training that the employee has received. This system of training allows the manager to determine this with relative ease.

Current Status

Since the completion of the federally funded project, the ASSET training progran has continued. During fiscal year 1985, 227 individuals have begun or continued to work on the testing and training sequences.

Tests have been revised and updated. Training materials have been revised, and specific study objectives have been provided. The program has expanded as well, with the full set of materials available at Cambridge State Hospital. The Minnesota Department of Employee Relations has adopted portions of the materials for use in its screening process for behavior analysts.

Future Direction

A central issue related to the concept of competency-based instruction is whether the training is having an effect on actual staff performance. That is, did the training that was provided result in actual changes in on-the-job performance?

Systematic assessment of job performance is made difficult by the nature of the specific competencies as well as the setting in which they are to be measured. Virtually all residential treatment centers rely on the interdisciplinary team approach to design and provide structured treatment. In this approach, the treatment program provided is a composite of all of the skills of all individuals on the team. Within this framework, the determination of individual performance becomes most difficult. Additional problems in the verification of training effects arise with the development of programming aids, such as standard treatment formats, which delineate elements for inclusion, standard consent forms that are designed to meet legal requirements, and standard report formats for providing information regarding treatment effects. All of these steps are designed to enhance the overall treatment of the client and, as such, are necessary elements. However, because the training provided is designed to prevent the occurence of problems even though no problems were found, there would be no assurance that the individual was demonstrating training effects because the organizations system of checks and multiple reviews may have prevented the errors.

The current system of training has increased confidence that errors are being minimized. As Mager and Pipe (1970) suggested, any analysis of a discrepancy in performance should begin with a determination of whether the individual knows what to do and how to do it. Criterion-referenced assessment of staff knowledge allows a beginning analysis of discrepancies between what staff do and what they should have done. Program managers can improve program services by emphasizing training or by changing other parameters. For example, it may be found that a therapist knows how to conduct a particular treatment but does not use the therapy appropriately because organizational policies prohibit the correct actions. In other cases, of course, assessment will reveal that the therapist did not know essential facts or could not perform targeted procedures. Improving methods for examining the relationship between the training process and the on-the-job performance is one of the foremost tasks to be undertaken. Currently, practicums are being developed to accompany certain of the competencies. This area looks most promising for assessing the effectiveness of the current training.

Refinement of Training Techniques

Another source of continued interest is improving the effectiveness of the training packages. To date, the training materials have relied heavily on published work that relates to the competency area. The data on posttest performance, although indicating overall positive change, need to be examined more closely as a function of exposure to the training materials. One possible source of difficulty is the reading level required, which is considered by the authors to be too high. Study guides have been developed to structure the trainee's exposure to the material. These guides are seen as a positive advance by those particiipating in the training. However, additional development in this area is definitely needed. With the advent of microtechnology, the possibilities for providing individualized instruction are increased. Pilot work has been completed within this area, and it appears to be most promising. Such a system will allow the individual to move very quickly through the material that has been mastered and to concentrate on the areas in need of remediation. The major drawback to this type of instruction is the amount of initial development time required for each training package.

Expansion of Competency Areas

Although the competencies that have been identified have provided an enormous wealth of source material for the development of training materials, there is no illusion that they constitute the entire set of skills required by practitioners in the field of behavior analysis. Although the targeted competencies were identified by professionals, it remains to be seen whether an individual who is taught to demonstrate them will be a more effective therapist. Continued effort is being made to identify additional skills needed by practitioners at all levels.

The next steps, of course, should involve efforts to validate the competencies by conducting research that demonstrates improved client results as a function of acquisition of the target competencies.

SUMMARY

The process of competency-based instruction as an ongoing source of continuing education has begun. The impetus for the development of systematic training in the field of behavior modification has come from a variety of sources, ranging from legal challenges to the establishment of bureaucratic rules. A competency-based, criterion-referenced model was chosen because it ensures that each of the participants demonstrate each of the skills and knowledge at a predetermined criterion, thus allowing a greater degree of confidence that errors made in the delivery of treatment are not due to a lack of training. The competencies identified for this training, along with their associated criteria, were subjected to extensive peer review in an attempt to ensure some uniformity and consensus on their content. An assessment and training program was developed based on these competencies and criteria and were field-tested on a wide array of individuals. Data resulting from the assessments indicate that the tests appear to correlate with the amount of formal training that the individual has received and that the training materials bring about positive change in test performance. Test performance data also indicate that no individual, regardless of his or her formal training, was able to perform at the criterion level on all of the identified competencies without some additional training. Questions that remain to be answered relate to the effect of training on actual on-the-job performance. Continued attempts to answer these questions as well as the continued refinement of training materials constitute directions that the project will pursue.

ACKNOWLEDGMENTS

The 10 years of work summarized in this chapter represent the collective contributions of over 40 participants. The tasks included writing and analyzing competency surveys, developing assessment procedures, contracting training materials, administering tests, conducting training, and the like. Although many of the participants were listed by name in a letter of thanks published in *The Behavior Therapist* (Vol. 4, No. 3, p. 3, 1981), the number grows each year, and space limitations prevent a detailed review of each contribution.

Finally, detailed results of the competency and criteria surveys can be obtained by writing to Dr. Jeffrey Grimm, Blick Clinic, 640 West Market Street, Akron, OH 44303.

REFERENCES

Griffith, R. G. (1980). An administrative perspective on guidelines for behavior modification: The creation of legally safe environment. *The Behavior Therapist, 3,* 5–6.

Jackson, A. T., & Thomas, D. R. (1974). *Rationale for a career ladder of job classifications in Minnesota Civil Service for behavior analysts.* Brainerd, MN: Minnesota Learning Center, Minnesota Department of Human Services.

Mager, R. F., & Pipe, P. (1970). *Analyzing performance problems or you really oughta wanna'.* Belmont: Fearon Pitman Publishers.

Naumann, C., Maus, M., & Thomas, D. R. (1982). An analysis of guidlines controlling the use of locked room timeout. *Behavioral Engineering, 8,* 77–89.

Parry, J., Rapoport, D., Dooley, J., Lampson, M., Tao, L., Spruell, W., Byrd, I., & Taylor, J. (1984). *Mental disability law, a primer.* Washington, DC: American Bar Association.

Pollack, M. (1981). *Guidelines for the use of behavioral procedures: A review of state and local standards and recommended strategies.* Association for Advancement of Behavior Therapy: Toronto.

Stolz, S. B., Wienckowski, L. A., & Brown, B. (1975). Behavior modification, a perspective on critical issues. *American Psychologist, 30,* 11, 1027–1048.

Sulzer-Azaroff, B., Thaw, J., & Thomas, C. (1975). Behavioral competencies for the evaluation of behavior modifiers. In W. Scott Wood (Ed.), *Issues in evaluating behavior modification* (pp. 47–98). Champaign, IL: Research Press.

Thomas, D. R., McAllister, L., & Thompson, T. (1976). *Minnesota guidelines for aversive and deprivation programs.* Chicago: Midwestern Association for Behavior Analysis.

Welch v. Likins, 373 F. Supp. 487 (M.D. Minn. 1974).

Welch v. Noot, United States District Court, District of Minnesota, Fourth Division. No. 4–72 Civil. 451 (1980).

APPENDIX

Therapist Competencies and Assessment Criteria

1. **COMPETENCY:** Identifies target behaviors in relation to antecedent and consequent environmental events that are associated with them and identifies direction of desired behavior change.

Criterion: (simulation exercises). Given videotaped examples of a behavioral deficit, a behavior excess, and inappropriate stimulus control, the candidate identifies the appropriate targets, the associated antecedent and consequent events, and specifies the direction of desired behavior change.

2. **COMPETENCY:** Conducts reliable measurement of targeted behaviors.

Criterion: (simulation exercises). Given a videotaped presentation of target behavior, a recording procedure, response definition, data sheet, and other necessary equipment, the candidate measures with 80% or better reliability using each of the following measurement techniques: (a) frequency count; (b) time sampling; (c) interval recording; and (d) duration recording.

3. COMPETENCY: Selects a measure and develops a scoring method (data sheet design, instrument selection, procedure, instructions, etc.) for a specified target behavior, including identification of relevant collateral behaviors.

Criterion: (simulation exercise). Given a videotaped presentation of a behavior to be targeted for deceleration, the candidate operationally defines the targeted response and at least two relevant collateral behaviors, specifies and defines the type of recording procedure to be used, gives specific directions on how the procedures are to be used, designs a sample data sheet, and justifies the selections made.

4. COMPETENCY: Operationally defines and illustrates observational recording techniques.

Criterion: (written test). Given five recording techniques (frequency count, interval recording, time sampling, duration recording, and permanent product), the candidate operationally defines each and matches each technique with appropriate examples.

5. COMPETENCY: Identifies variables that may prevent appropriate evaluation of treatment effects.

Criterion: (written test). Can explain the effects of at least five of the following: maturation, noncontingent reinforcement, concurrent shifts in multiple independent variables, sensory abnormalities, improper definitions of dependent variables, and inconsistent implementation of treatment procedures. Given two reports of treatment effects, can identify variables that confound the relationship between treatment and outcome.

6. COMPETENCY: Is familiar with ethical issues, standards, and practices.

Criterion: (written test). Given bibliography of selected readings, the candidate will score at least 90% on an objective examination.

7. COMPETENCY: Incorporates ethical standards in program design, implementation, communication, and evaluation.

Criterion: (simulation exercise). Given an illustrative problem situation, an aversive and/or deprivation program designed by the applicant is rated for consistency with a checklist of ethical standards. The checklist on ethical standards will be derived from the standards recommended by the Association for the Advancement of Behavior Therapy to the APA.

8. COMPETENCY: Identifies major ethical issues: (a) Whose agent is the therapist? (b) Who decides what is best for the client? On what grounds? (c) Who has responsibility for the client? (d) How does one decide who receives treatment and who does not? (e) What are the pros and cons for changing behavior; using aversive consequences; and reporting procedures and results? (f) How much and what type information is given to the client? (g) How are the human rights of the individual and the family best safeguarded?

Criterion: (oral interview). Given an illustrative problem situation, the candidate will relate these major issues to the problem solution.

9. COMPETENCY: Identifies federal and state laws and legal precendents as they affect the conduct of education–treatment activities.

Criterion: 1. (written test). Given a bibliography of appropriate laws and legal precedents, the candidate will pass an objective examination with 90% accuracy. At a minimum, the bibliography will reference the following principles: (a) treatment with trained staff in adequate numbers; (b) the least restrictive alternative in treatment settings and procedures; (c) freedom from deprivation of normal goods and services without due process; (d) freedom from participation in programs without consent being given; (e) right to withdraw consent from treatment programs; (f) education regardless of handicap for school-aged individuals; (g) minimum wage in nontherapeutic work situations; and (h) individualized treatment plans. 2. (simulation exercise). Given an illustrative problem situation, the candidate will correctly identify violations of legal precedents and/or laws.

10. COMPETENCY: Is familiar with the Department of Human Services (DPW) Rule 40.

Criterion: (written test). Passes objective exam on the details of the Association for the Advancement of Behavior Therapy/Association for Behavior Analysis (AABT/ABA) model guidelines for the use of restrictive procedures with 90% accuracy.

11. COMPETENCY: Knowledge of current regulations and utilization of aversive stimulation devices approved by the Food and Drug Administration (FDA) including types of instrumentation, knowledge of dangers and side effects, and knowledge of dangers associated with the operation of apparatus.

Criterion: (written test and simulation exercise). The candidate will pass an objective test over this area and will correctly identify hazards shown in at least three videotaped segments with 80% accuracy.

12. COMPETENCY: Demonstrate familiarity with current literature on application of widely validated aversive and deprivation procedures.

Criterion: (written test). Given bibliography of selected readings, the candidate will pass, with at least 75% accuracy, an objective test on content. In addition, the candidate will appropriately reference this literature in proposing procedures to alter a problem behavior in the simulation exercises required to demonstrate competencies in designing programs.

13. COMPETENCY: Programming for behavior change: Lists the essential steps in designing and conducting behavior change activities directed toward altering a behavioral excess or deficit.

Criterion: (written test). Given a brief narrative description of the problem and its history, the candidate can describe in writing the steps necessary to design a behavior change program based on positive reinforcement. The description must include at least the following: (a) the target behavior stated in objective and quantifiable terms; (b) the objective or goal of the treatment program; (c) the change procedure to be employed, including the stimulus circumstances and environment under which the treatment would take place, the baseline procedures, the positive consequences to be provided, and the schedule or other procedure of delivering the consequences contingently; (d) the method of measuring the behavior and consequences throughout the treatment program; (e) control or probe techniques to determine the necessity of continuing treatment; (f) a plan for program generalization and maintenance; and (g) the conditions under which the program would be changed or terminated.

14. COMPETENCY: Writes a proposal for a behavior change (i.e., habilitative/educational) program.

Criterion: (simulation exercises). Given a brief narrative description of the problem and its history and a videotaped demonstration of the problem behavior, the candidate will write a program that incorporates the following: (a) the targeted behavior stated in objective and quantifiable terms; (b) the objective or goal of the treatment program; (c) the change procedure to be employed, including the stimulus circumstances and environment under which the treatment would take place, the baseline procedures, the positive consequences to be provided, the schedule or other procedures of delivering the consequences contingently; (d) the method of measuring the behavior and consequences throughout the treatment program; (e) control or probe techniques to determine the necessity of continuing treatment; (f) a plan for program generalization and maintenance; and (g) the conditions under which the program would be changed or terminated.

15. COMPETENCY: Provides a written report of program effects.

Criterion: (simulation exercise). Given illustrative case study material, the candidate will write a report suitable for submission to a county or state agency at the time of termination of treatment or transfer. The report will include the following elements: (a) client description, name, age, sex, diagnostic, and other psychometric information; (b) a brief history leading to the problem that was treated; (c) an objective description of the problem including quantification of the pretreatment problem intensity and the current levels of behavioral occurrences (frequency, duration, etc.); (d) a description, in minimally technical but accurate language, of the procedures employed; (e) a quantitative (preferably graphic) summary plus a narrative description of the results; and (f) recommendations for methods of increasing the probability of program generality to a new setting.

16. COMPETENCY: Identifies variables that may contraindicate specific treatment procedures.

Criterion: (written test). For each of five procedures, the candidate can identify the possible client or program characteristics that would indicate rejection of these procedures as inappropriate or unsafe. Examples include (a) using Gatorade or milk for hydration in the Foxx–Azrin toilet training program;

(b) painful shock; (c) physically enforced overcorrection; (d) food/candy reinforcement; and (e) seclusion time-out.

17. COMPETENCY: Is familiar with important therapeutic concerns regarding procedures that are frequently used in behavior therapy and educational/habilitative programming.

Criterion: (written test). The candidate can identify for each item on a selected list of procedures, the following characteristics: degree of instrusiveness (i.e., not intrusive vs. mild to very intrusive), time to become effective (very short vs. moderate to long), durability and generality of effect (very durable and easily generalized vs. limited durability and generalizability), likelihood of side effects (none or minimal vs. occasional to frequent), and risk of harm to client or staff (none to minimal vs. significant). At a minimum, the list of procedures will include the following: (a) extinction; (b) reinforcement of incompatible behaviors; (c) time-out in room; (d) graduated guidance; (e) restitution; (f) response cost; (g) required relaxation; (h) time-out (separation); (i) restraint; (j) noxious noises, smells, and the like; (k) deprivation of food or water; (l) slapping; and (m) painful skin shock.

18. COMPETENCY: Is familiar with procedures for arranging contingent relationships between targeted responses and consequences that are available in the natural environment.

Criterion: (written test). Given as examples three target behaviors that are measured respectively by their duration, intensity, and frequency, the candidate will specify consequences for each that should increase the behaviors and will also specify consequences for each that should decrease the behaviors. The consequences indentified should already exist in the environment or be available without substantial additional funds or resources. The candidate will also specify the treatment environment (preferably the candidate's work settings).

19. COMPETENCY: Must be able to devise at least two alternative treatment procedures in each of three levels of instrusiveness of intervention.

Criterion: (simulation exercise). Given a videotaped example of a behavior to be decelerated, the candidate will briefly describe two alternative treatment procedures from each of the three levels of instrusiveness, all of which can be justified as having a reasonable likelihood of reducing the problem behavior.

20. COMPETENCY: Is familiar with learning principles and the treatment procedures that have been derived from them.

Criterion: (written test). Given a sample of at least 20 written definitions and/or examples, the candidate will correctly match from a list of phenomena and procedures with at least 90% accuracy. The pool from which the examples will be taken will include at least the following definitions: operant conditioning, positive reinforcement, negative reinforcement, differential reinforcement, punishment, avoidance, time-out, respondent conditioning, respondent extinction, covert sensitization, differential reinforcement of other behavior, differential reinforcement of high-rate behavior, differential reinforcement of low rate behavior, baseline, probe, deprivation, escape, required relaxation, token economy, electroshock therapy, shock punishment, reliability, validity, steady state, restitution. Examples: stimulus control, shaping, chaining, fading, continuous reinforcement, interval schedule, multiple schedule, extinction, response cost, satiation, desensitization, aversion therapy, overcorrection, positive practice, reversal, restraint, graduated guidance, flooding, superstitious reinforcement, Premack Principle. Procedures: (simulation exercise). When shown videotape samples of the following procedures, the candidate can correctly identify the procedure with at least 70% accuracy on a multiple-choice test: positive reinforcement (social, token), stimulus control, extinction, seclusion time-out, time-out, response cost, reinforcement of incompatible bahavior, desensitization, aversion therapy, positive practice, overcorrection, differential reinforcement of other behavior, contingent observation, restraint, graduated guidance, flooding, superstitious reinforcement, and restitution.

21. COMPETENCY: Identifies a pool of procedures that may be used in human services settings to alter staff behavior in order to enable implementation of treatment programs.

Criterion: (oral interview). Describes procedures that can be used without violating work rules, union contracts, or personnel policies and procedures.

22. COMPETENCY: Is able to communicate in written and graphic form.

Criterion: (simulation exercise). 1. Written: Explicitly describes a treatment program in writing so that a naive individual who follows the program does not make errors in demonstrating the procedure. (The task specified in Competency 14 is used for evaluative purposes.) 2. Graphic: Given a videotaped simulation of data-collection situation and the raw data that result from the observation, the candidate will design a graph, plot the data, label the ordinate and abscissa, and otherwise identify the variables shown so as to graphically communicate the behavioral changes shown in the videotape presentation. (The task specified in Competency 2 is used for evaluation purposes.)

23. COMPETENCY: Conducts reliable measurement of targeted behaviors.

Criterion: Treatment programs submitted for committee review include reliability checks on data required to evaluate effects.

24. COMPETENCY: Incorporates ethical standards in program design, implementation, communication, and evaluation.

Criterion: Two aversive and/or deprivation programs designed by the applicant are rated by the review committee for consistency with a checklist of ethical standards.

25. COMPETENCY: Does not violate federal and state laws and legal precedents as they relate to the conduct of educational-treatment activities.

Criterion: The review committee evaluates programs designed by the "expert" in terms of their consistency with a checklist of legal issues.

26. COMPETENCY: Does not violate pertinent guidelines controlling the use of aversive and deprivation procedures.

Criterion: The review committee will assess compliance with pertinent guidelines for aversive and deprivation procedures by comparing the job performance with the requirements of the guidelines on a standard checklist.

27. COMPETENCY: Written proposals for behavior change (i.e., habilitative/educational) programs and provides written reports of program effects.

Criterion: The review committee certifies that treatment plans submitted to them include at least the following: (a) the targeted behavior stated in objective and quantifiable terms; (b) the objective or goal of the treatment program; (c) the change procedure to be employed, including the stimulus circumstances and environment under which the treatment would take place, the baseline procedures, the positive contingencies; (d) the method of measuring the behavior and consequences throughout the treatment program; (e) control or probe techniques to determine the necessity of continuing treatment; (f) a plan for program generalization and maintenance; (g) the conditions under which the program would be changed or terminated. In addition, the committee certifies that reports suitable for submission to a county or state agency have been prepared at the time of termination of treatment or transfer. The reports will include the following elements: (a) client description, name, age, sex, diagnostic and other psychometric information; (b) a brief history leading to the problem that was treated; (c) an objective description of the problem including quantification of the pretreatment problem intensity and the current levels of behavioral occurrences (frequency, duration, etc.); (d) a description in minimallly technical but accurate language of the procedures employed; (e) a quantitative (preferably graphic) summary plus a narrative description of the results; and (f) recommendations for methods of increasing the probability of program generality to a new setting.

28. COMPETENCY: Identifies variables that may contraindicate specific treatment procedures.

Criterion: The regular performance checklist completed by the review committee will certify that the therapist obtains appropriate interdisciplinary consultation (medical, dental, social work, psychodiagnostic, etc.) regarding possible client characteristics that would contraindicate proposed behavior change program procedures prior to implementing the treatment programs.

29. COMPETENCY: Assessment, goal formulation, and targeting.

Criterion: The review committee evaluates the candidate's specification of appropriate and realistic program goals with a checklist. The checklist includes items such as operationalized target behaviors, the employment of the normalization principle, the availability of trained staff in adequate numbers, and so forth.

30. COMPETENCY: Can apply and demonstrate the effectiveness of procedures for various types of behavioral change categories.

Criterion: The review committee certifies that the programmer applies at least one procedure for each of the following categories with a concomitant demonstration of procedural effectiveness: (a) increase in behavior; (b) decrease in behavior; (c) maintenance of behavior; (d) teaching a new behavior; and (e) stimulus control.

31. COMPETENCY: Supervision: Coordinates behavior change program.

Criterion: The review committee certifies that the candidate monitors program procedures at regular intervals; acts as supervisor for line personnel; and consults with family members as necessary.

32. COMPETENCY: Communication: Written, oral, and graphic.

Criterion: The review committee will rate the effectiveness of the behavioral programmer in two types of oral and written reports: (a) Ratings will be given on the clarity of description of program procedures and rationales; and (b) ratings will be given on the clarity of the descriptions of program results.

14

Continuing Professional Education for Clinical Psychology

A Practice-Oriented Model

CARL A. LINDSAY, MARY BETH CROWE, and DURAND F. JACOBS

Quality assurance in the delivery of services has become a fact of life for professionals. The demand for high-quality care arises from ever more critical consumers and the increasing presence of third-party payers as well as from professions themselves in protecting the services they render (Houle, 1981; Jacobs, 1974). Evidence for professional quality assurance activities in the practice of psychology that are sponsored by national professional organizations and licensing boards includes accreditation requirements for academic and internship programs (American Psychological Association [APA], 1979), ethical and practice standards (APA, 1981a,b), and provision for their monitoring. This chapter focuses on a particular aspect of professional quality assurance—the role of continuing learning. It reports on the work of the

CARL A. LINDSAY • Professional Planning Consultants, State College, PA 16801. **MARY BETH CROWE** • Office of the President, The Pennsylvania State University, University Park, PA 16802. **DURAND F. JACOBS** • Psychology Service, Jerry L. Pettis Memorial Veterans' Hospital, Loma Linda, CA 92357.

Continuing Professional Education Development Project (CPEDP) as it developed, implemented, and evaluated a unique practice-oriented model of continuing professional education for clinical psychology.

The need for continuing education for practicing psychologists has long been noted (Dubin, 1972; Jones, 1975; Webster, 1971). Dubin's notion of the half-life of professional training (i.e., the amount of time required to render one-half of professional training obsolete) dramatizes the need for professional updating. Over 10 years ago, Dubin (1972) estimated the half-life of competence for professional psychologists to be 10 to 12 years. He also noted that in many professions the half-life steadily decreased with the passage of time due to the rapid expansion of knowledge and technology.

Knowledge updating, alone, is too limited an approach for meeting today's demands for continuing professional education. Jensen (1979) differentiates between an education model that dispenses knowledge in a formal manner and a professional development model that holds that

> (a) knowledge is a framework for action that is acquired, itself, by acting, (b) given a suitable background, individuals may aquire knowledge by self-directed actions, (c) the need for knowledge emerges from the nature of the problem at hand, and (d) under certain conditions, even highly trained professionals may choose a formal course of study. (p. 386)

Jensen's model suggests that continuing learning must be closely related to the demands of professional practice and be concerned with skills as well as knowledge. This approach calls for the exercise of astute clinical judgements based on current knowledge and implemented by currently accepted methods. The model also stresses the uniqueness of the individual practitioner and the variety of methods that can be used to meet continuing learning needs. Traditionally, psychologists have pursued continuing education by reading journals, participating in case conferences and collegial discussions as well as attending formal courses (Brown & Briley, 1979; Clark, Waden, Brownell, Gordon, & Tarte, 1983; McNamara, 1977).

Documented hours of continuing professional education of the type noted previously has been accepted as evidence demonstrating continuing competence of licensed psychologists in the 29 states that have mandatory continuing education requirements for relicensure (APA, 1981c). To date, this approach has been much preferred by practitioners over alternatives such as periodic reexamination for license renewal (Vitulano & Copeland, 1980). There is, however, a growing number of persons holding that traditional forms of continuing education are but one factor contributing to quality assurance (Cooper, 1981; Gonnella & Zeleznik, 1983; Sanazarro, 1982). These critics distinguish between competence and actual performance, noting that educational programs are a necessary but not a sufficient basis for competent practice. Competence is comprised of the necessary knowledge, clinical skills, sound clinical judgment, and ethical attitudes that together contribute to the ability to perform acceptably (Sanazarro, 1982). However, actual practitioner performance is subject to the influence of a variety of contextual factors that include organizational and societal factors and characteristics of the clients themselves. Furthermore, acceptable professional performance cannot guarantee desired client outcomes because of the influence of these factors on the client as well (Gonnella & Zeleznik, 1983; LaDuca, 1980; Suter, Green, Lawrence, & Wathall, 1981).

The challenge to continuing professional educators is to maximize the potential of their efforts to influence practice directly. This requires a linkage between the realities of the practice situation and continuing learning activities. It calls upon continuing professional educators to be practice facilitators as much as knowledge providers in order to meet the vast array of individual needs among their clientele. The Continuing Professional Education Development Project specifically sought to address the first of these requirements: to develop a practice-oriented continuing education model. The project's general rationale is described in the next section. Its focused application to clinical psychology is reported in the remainder of this chapter. Although primarily concerned with continuing professional education, many elements in the project's program development process, such as role delineation and performance assessment, are relevant to training and certification issues in general.

OVERVIEW OF THE CONTINUING PROFESSIONAL EDUCATION DEVELOPMENT PROJECT

Project Goals

The CPEDP is an explicit effort to bring together higher education and five selected professions to work toward the fundamental goal of Houle's (1981) concept of professionalization—maintaining and enhancing the competence of professionals (Smutz, Davis, & Lindsay, 1982). Begun in 1980, it was a 5-year research and development effort funded by the W. K. Kellogg Foundation, The Pennsylvania State University (Penn State), and 14 participating professional associations representing the five different professional groups.[1] The project had three major goals: (a) to establish collaborative relationships between the university and each of the concerned professions in order to strengthen the development and implementation of continuing professional education programs; (b) to develop and implement practice-oriented continuing professional education for selected professional groups through application of a seven-phase needs assessment/program development process called the "practice audit model" (Smutz, Kalman, Lindsay, Pietrusko, & Seaman, 1981); and (c) to develop models of university/profession collaboration for continuing professional education (Lindsay & Smutz, 1984; Toombs, Lindsay, & Hettinger, 1985).

The Practice Audit Model

The basic framework that guided project activities is the practice audit model that emerged directly from an effort begun in 1977 to develop quality continuing professional education programs for pharmacists (Smutz *et al.*, 1981). However, its roots go back to earlier work on continuing professional education needs assessment and program development at Penn State. These included Dubin's (1972) challenge to the profession of psychology issued more than 10 years ago that it recognize and deal with the phenomenon of professional obsolescence, Dubin's multi-dimensional model of the updating process (1971), and the content-based group assessment model for defining and assessing obsolescence in physical educators (Lindsay, Morrison, & Kelly, 1974). Several key concepts from this collective research provided the initial basis for the pharmacist project, whereas others were added and integrated as it unfolded. Among the concepts are an operational definition

[1]The five professional groups and their respective organizations participating in the project were (a) clinical psychology, American Association of State Psychology Boards, American Psychological Association, Pennsylvania Psychological Association, The Pennsylvania State University/Department of Psychology; (b) public accounting, American Institute of Certified Public Accountants, Pennsylvania Institute of Certified Public Accountants, The Pennsylvania State University/Department of Accounting; (c) architecture, American Institute of Architects/Pennsylvania Society of Architects, National Council of Architecture Registration Boards, The Pennsylvania State University/Department of Architecture; (d) clinical dietetics, The American Dietetic Association, Pennsylvania Dietetic Association, The Pennsylvania State University Nutrition Program; (e) nursing, American Nurses' Association, National Council of State Boards of Nursing, Pennsylvania Nurses Association, The Pennsylvania State University/Department of Nursing.

of competency, a data-based description of professionals' practice-oriented needs, role delineation, practice standards, and performance-based educational needs assessment. These are developed in collaboration with representatives from each concerned profession and culminate in systematic continuing education program development. These issues are discussed in detail in a monograph describing the pharmacists' project (Smutz *et al.*, 1981). A more recent paper (Smutz, 1984) examined some important assessment and programming issues that grew out of the practice audit model's application to the five professions involved in the CPEDP.

Essentially, the practice audit model rests on the assumption that professional competence and continuing education needs assessment are intimately interwined. Both require an understanding of what is demanded of a professional in practice. To assess competence requires detailed knowledge of the professional's roles and practices (Kalman, 1979; LaDuca, 1980; Shimberg, 1983); to determine needs requires operational criteria against which performance may be judged. The systematic determination of professionals' responsibilities and tasks is the basic mix from which subsequent needs assessment and competency measures must evolve and upon which continuing education programs must focus. The importance of the systematic determination of the requirements of professional practice cannot be overemphasized. Despite the variability of approaches to job analysis and role delineation, a clear consensus exists on one point: The determination of professionals' roles and practices must be empirically derived rather than simply defined by "experts" who do not venture into the field to collect data (D'Costa & Schreck, 1984).

Systematically addressing the practice needs of professionals is an arduous process requiring extensive resources, a multifaceted set of perspectives, skills, knowledges, and abilities within a team of investigators and their long-term commitment. For this reason a final, critical element is close, formal, and continuing collaboration among participating groups (Lindsay & Toombs, 1980; Lindsay, Queeney, & Smutz, 1981). For too long, many of the groups concerned with providing continuing education professionals have worked independently. The barriers erected between professionals and educators have been particularly detrimental. Given the complexity of the task of maintaining professional competence, various types of expertise are needed. Continuing education professionals are experienced in the delivery of programs, university faculty members work on the frontiers of knowledge and are experienced in program development, and professional associations are in the closest touch with the concerns of practicing professionals and those they serve, often promulgating guidelines for practice. Because each has something valuable to contribute, it is assumed that working in collaboration can produce a better product than each working separately.

The fundamental goal of the practice audit model is to provide for the systematic development of continuing professional education programs that will assist professionals striving to remain competent. The foregoing descussion has identified some of the key concepts that influenced the model's development. The seven-phase process that evolved is shown in Figure 1.

Phase I required formation of a profession team consisting of representatives of higher education professional associations and licensing boards. The rationale for this team was that each of the members has a different kind of expertise that could be put to better use when they worked together rather than separately on the development of continuing professional education programs. This team made the key decisions affecting each additional phase of the model.

Phase II, which provided the foundation for the remaining steps, involved the development of a practice description. This is a heirarchical set of domains, responsibilities, and tasks that describe the scope of practice for a given profession. Each profession team developed these documents, utilizing considerable background literature from the concerned profession's archives. In addition, Pennsylvania practitioners were surveyed to determine how closely the description reflected their actual practice, thereby validating the experts' judgments.

Exercises to assess practitioners' performance were developed in Phase III. Two points are important here. The first pertains to what constitutes a representative "work sample." Given that it is impossible to assess everything in the practice description, choices had to be made. Three considerations guided those choices: data from the survey of practitioners reflecting their views on the importance and performance frequency of various responsibilities, the potential for actually assessing a given responsibility in a workshop setting, and the judgment of team members. The second issue pertains to exercise design. Because of the model's practice orientation, assessment exercises that realistically reflect situations encountered in the practice setting must be developed, incorporating devices such as written case studies, videotaped interactions and live simulations, using actors as clients.

In Phase IV, the practice audit session, practitioners were assessed in order to identify deficiencies and learning needs. For each profession, a sample of 40 to 45 Pennsylvania practitioners volunteered to participate in exercises lasting approximately 1 day. These audit sessions

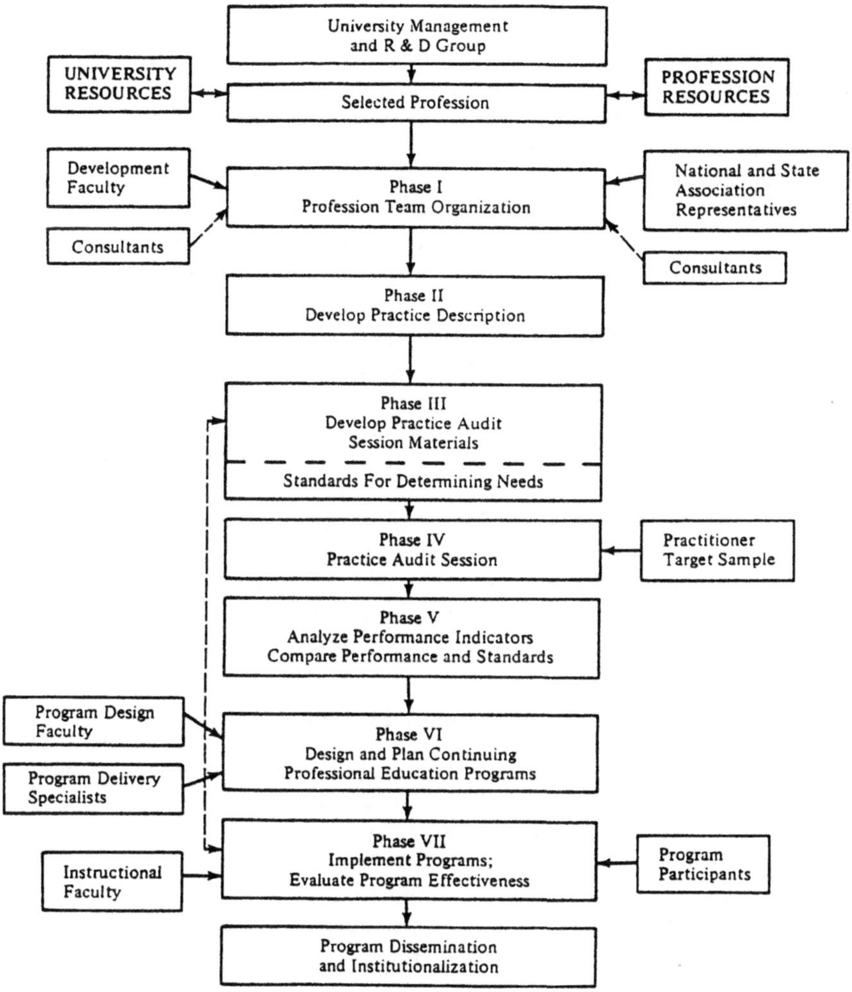

Figure 1. Practice audit model.

involved considerable effort, but they also were experiences that the participants found interesting and useful in terms of what they learned about their own practice skills.

Phase V was devoted to scoring practitioners' performance and thereby identifying strengths and weaknesses. Prior to the practice audit session, profession team members consensually agreed upon acceptable responses to the various exercises. Based on these criteria, individual scores were aggregated to provide group scores on each of the various exercise components. These, in turn, were tied to the responsibilities in the practice description. Team members then reviewed the performance results to determine a profile of strengths and weaknesses for what was assumed to be a representative sample of that profession. Generally speaking, the areas of weakest performance were targeted for continuing education program development for that profession.

Phase VI involved the design and developmenet of continuing professional education programs that addressed the identified needs for each profession. The five respective profession teams each structured their own basic programs in terms of purposes, objectives, and format. After that, staff members worked with university and nonuniversity design and marketing specialists and instructors to develop the programs in detail and to produce effective learning experiences. The general format developed by the Clinical Psychology Profession Team became the model for the other professions involved in the project.

The final phase, Phase VII, involved the delivery and evaluation of programs. To date, at least one continuing professional education program has been delivered to each of the five participating professional groups. Participant response has been uniformly positive to the learning experiences provided by the project's programs.

Participation of Clinical Psychology in the Project

Clinical psychology was chosen to be one of the project's five participating professions because it met selection criteria designed to identify professions prepared to focus on the performance aspects of service delivery (Queeney & Melander, 1984). That is, in Houle's (1981) framework, clinical psychology was identified as a profession having an established practitioner subculture, concerned with defining its basic mission, and developing a formalized system for determining the competence of its members. However, the selection process was a mutal one requiring commitment and participation by both parties; not only did the project select clinical psychology, but organized psychology, through academic and professional association representatives, selected the project.

Clinical psychology, rather than the profession of psychology at large, was selected for project participation for conceptual and practical reasons and because of time and resource constraints. It also should be noted that the project was limited to Pennsylvania practitioners for the same practical reasons. Nonetheless, members of the clinical psychology profession team were continually cognizant of the broader context of professional psychology when completing project activities and recognized that many project activities were relevant to other specialty groups within their profession.

The concept and operation of collaboration between the university and the professions was manifest in the composition of the profession team. For psychology, the six-person profession team was comprised of a representative from the American Association of State Psychology Boards, one each from the APA and the Pennsylvania Psychological Association, and three senior clinical faculty from Penn State's department of psychology. These were supported by two project staff members.[2]

THE PRACTICE DESCRIPTION FOR CLINICAL PSYCHOLOGY

The practice audit model first requires a current description of practice. This in turn provides the basis for constructing relevant performance assessment exercises that are then used to identify areas of strength and weakness in important practice roles. Areas empirically identified through this assessment as needing attention then become the target for continuing education activities. In this way, the program of continuing professional education that evolves is, by explicit design, practice oriented.

The Role Delineation Study

Standard role delineation procedures were used to develop the practice description for clinical psychology. D'Costa (1982) defines *role delineation* as the process for obtaining a rational description of the responsibilities of a specific occupational group. In contrast to job analyses conducted for specific jobs, role delineation attempts to encompass the diversity of jobs and situational variables that exist within a large occupational group such as a profession. Thus the product of a role delineation study is a generic description of the scope of practice of a profession (or in this case, of the specialty of clinical psychology). It does not refer to the practice of any individual or the application of

[2]Representatives of these associations were S. Joseph Weaver, American Association of State Psychology Boards; Durand Jacobs, American Psychological Association; Noel Plummer, Pennsylvania Psychological Association; Thomas Borkovec, Leon Gorlow, and Richard Lundy were from the department of psychology, The Pennsylvania State University; project staff members were Carl A. Lindsay (project director) and Mary Beth Crowe (research project associate) from Planning Studies in Continuing Education, The Pennsylvania State University.

services to a particular problem or within a specific setting but describes the collective practice of members of the profession. The role delineation product was labeled a *practice description* for project purposes.

Three sources of information were used in the role delineation study: a panel of experts (i.e., the profession team), a review of relevant literature, and a survey of practitioners. The profession team held two 2½-day meetings during the 1-year period in which role delineation activities took place. The group used a consensus-based decision-making process, facilitated by a group process consultant.

Developing the Practice Description. The profession team used a review of literature as initial input to the identification of dimensions underlying the practice of clinical psychology. No completed role delineations were available at the time this research was initiated. However, several sources documenting partially completed role delineations or other descriptions of psychological services were used as reference materials (American Boards of Professional Psychology, D.W. Bray, personal communication, December, 1980; Clement, 1977; Committee on Professional Standards, APA, 1981; Educational Testing Services (ETS), 1982; Richman, 1980). Working from these sources and their own experience, team members developed an array of broad practice dimensions

Table 1. Responsibilities under the Three Domains of Clinical Psychology Practice

Direct client services
Collects information for clinical inference
Integrates sources of information
Recognizes own limitations
Develops intervention plan
Implements intervention plan
Evaluates intervention plan periodically
Establishes and maintains a professional relationship with client
Maintains confidentiality
Organization and administration of services
Organizes service setting
Trains and supervises interns and staff
Establishes an information-management system
Establishes new client services
Promotes the welfare of the client
Professional activities
Maintains personal and professional standards
Participates in training of clinical psychologists
Promotes the profession of psychology
Promotes mental health through prevention
Conducts research and evaluation studies

(i.e., domains) and within each labeled customary responsibilities of clinical psychology practitioners. Specific tasks for each dimension were then generated. The preliminary draft of the practice description was revised after the profession team's initial meeting. The revised list of domains, responsibilities, and tasks formed the basis of the second phase of the role delineation process, the survey of practitioners. The final practice description contained 18 responsibilities and 95 tasks, representing 3 major domains of professional activities: (a) direct client services, (b) organization and administration of services, and (c) professional activities. These domains and responsibilities are listed in Table 1.

At their second meeting, the profession team reviewed the results of the practitioner survey described next, made minor changes in the practice description, and deleted two tasks that had received relatively low ratings of importance in the practitioner survey.

The Practitioner Survey. Providers of clinical psychological services in Pennsylvania were asked to rate each task in the practice description on two dimensions: (a) the time spent on the task and (b) the importance ascribed to the task. The survey was limited to obtaining practitioner response to which of the tasks listed were viewed as important and commonly performed and was not designed to obtain support for the exhaustiveness of the practice description.

Respondents were asked to rate each task in the practice description in terms of time spent and importance; these scales are commonly used in job analyses (McCormick, 1976). Two 5-point scales were used. On the time spent scale, tasks were rated from "I do not perform this task" to "I spend an extreme amount of time on this task." The importance scale ranged from "this task is of no importance in my practice" to "this task is of extreme importance in my practice."

In the fall of 1981, surveys were mailed to all 858 current members of the clinical division of the Pennsylvania Psychological Association. Due to project time constraints, no follow-up to the original request was made. A total of 302 usable questionnaires was returned, representing 35% of those sent. For a detailed description of the demographic characteristics of the sample, see Crowe, Grogan, Jacobs, Lindsay, and Mark (1985).

Ratings for each responsibility were obtained by averaging the ratings for the tasks comprising a given responsibility. This resulted in a set of time spent and importance ratings for each of the 18 responsibilities. These ratings were rank ordered on the two dimensions (time spent and importance) to create a profile of practice for the entire group of respondents.

Table 2. Mean Time Spent and Importance Ratings for 18 Clinical Psychology Responsiblities[a]

Responsibility	Time spent Mean	Importance Mean	Importance Rank
Establishes and maintains relationship with client	2.78	3.36	2
Implements intervention plan	2.55	3.01	7
Maintains personal and professional standards	2.23	3.28	3
Develops intervention plan	2.23	3.06	6
Integrates sources of information	2.21	2.86	10
Maintains confidentiality	2.19	3.57	1
Evaluates intervention plan periodically	2.19	2.92	8
Promotes the welfare of the client	2.14	3.15	4
Collects information for clinical inference	2.05	2.66	11
Recognizes own limitations	1.92	3.12	5
Establishes an information-management system	1.88	2.88	9
Promotes the profession	1.56	2.60	12
Organizes service setting	1.52	2.49	13
Trains and supervises interns and staff	1.48	2.39	14
Participates in training of clinical psychologists	1.44	2.31	15
Promotes mental health through prevention	1.06	2.21	16
Establishes new client services	1.03	1.98	18
Conducts research	.85	2.10	17

Note. $N = 302$.
[a]Responsibilities are ordered from high to low in terms of mean time spent.

Profile of Clinical Psychology Practice. Table 2 contains the mean responsibility ratings. Survey respondents reported spending the most time on those responsibilities involving direct client services. The importance ratings indicated that the respondents were highly concerned with ethical behavior. The five most important responsibilities involved confidentiality, client relationships, personal and professional standards, client welfare, and recognizing one's own limitations. The lowest ratings (both for time spent and importance) were given to responsibilities that involved research, administration, training and supervision, and the promotion of the profession and mental health other than through direct client services.

THE PRACTICE AUDIT FOR CLINICAL PSYCHOLOGY

A key feature of the practice audit model is the assessment of professional performance in order to identify continuing learning needs. This approach to needs assessment creates a direct linkage between continuing education program content and the performance requirements of professional practice. Thus continuing education programs developed through the practice audit model tend to emphasize skills development and making accurate clinical judgments rather than knowledge acquisition *per se*.

The project's assessment for clinical psychology focused primarily on clinical skills because the practictioner survey had indicated responsibilities involving direct client services to be most prominent. Assessment exercises included client simulations, written client vignettes, and videotaped therapy vignettes. A multiple-choice test regarding legal and ethical issues and a survey of self-perceived continuing education needs were also included. Each of these is described later. Because the client simulation comprised a major portion of the assessment and because this exercise highlights problems encountered in developing the assessment exercises in general, the simulation is described in more detail than the other exercises.

The exercises, which required approximately 8 hours to complete, were incorporated into a practice audit session. The session resembled a work evaluation center with participants moving from station to station to complete individual exercises. However, the project's focus was on the average performance of the representative group of Pennsylvania psychologists and not upon evaluating individual scores. A conscious effort was made during the practice audit session to remind participants of this broader objective and to minimize their individual anxiety by encouraging a collegial atmosphere and emphasizing the participants' contribution to the research at hand. This was accomplished chiefly by organizing participants into small groups, with a member of the profession team serving as a group leader. Participants moved with their group through the entire session, providing frequent opportunity for discussion with other group members. This not only created a supportive environment for the assessment but provided informal peer feedback to participants as well.

The membership of the clinical division of the Pennsylvania Psychological Association who were licensed psychologists was invited through a mailing to participate in the assessment. Forty participants who met designated criteria concerning licensure and extent of clinical practice were selected from among the 102 volunteers; the group included practitioners with both masters'- and doctoral-level training because Pennsylvania grants licenses to psychologists at the master's level. The practice audit session was held in June 1983, in conjunction with the annual meeting of the Pennsylvania Psychological Association.

Client Simulation

The client simulation was developed to sample skills ordinarily used in clinical assessment and treatment. These included observation, conceptualization, and interpersonal interaction. The simulation format was used to create as realistic an assessment setting as possible. The client simulation consisted of two parts; each part contained both an interactive and a written section.

In the simulation, practice audit session participants interviewed a "client" who was portrayed by an actor. The five actors used to portray the role followed a scenario developed for the case and were trained to be fairly passive in order to maintain uniformity of the stimulus condition. The first interview represented the first meeting with the client, a 27-year-old male. The second interview represented the second meeting between client and therapist. Each interview lasted approximately 25 minutes and was videotaped for later evaluation. The only information provided to the clinician prior to the first interview was the following note:

> Self-referred. Bill has been having difficulty working; his supervisor suggested counseling. He is a 27-year-old male married with a 1-year-old child.

After each simulation interview, participants responded in writing to several questions regarding their clinical impressions of the client. The questions concerned observations, identification of strengths and weaknesses, hypotheses about client problems, and treatment plans.

Ratings. Two sets of ratings were developed for the interactive portion of the client simulation. The first set consisted of 10 global dimensions of clinical behavior. The second set contained a checklist of behaviors specific to the case used in the simulation.

The global clinical behavior dimensions were developed by team members based on the practice description and other available clinical rating scales. They are defined in terms of behavioral anchors describing excellent and poor performance on each dimension. These dimensions are listed in Table 3. Ratings were made on a 5-point scale; a rating of 1 represents poor performance and a rating of 5 represents excellent performance.

The specific behaviors on which participants were rated were also derived from the practice description by the profession team and were defined with respect to details of the case used in the simulation. For example, participants were rated on whether they responded to the client's expressed concern about his parents. These ratings were also made on a 5-point scale; a rating of 1 indicated no evidence of the

Table 3. Ten Global Clinical Behavior Dimensions Used in Evaluating Therapy Simulations

SPEAKING: Psychologists who have excellent speaking ability talk clearly, distinctly, and fluently; they use words that are appropriate for those with whom they are speaking; they avoid jargon.

Psychologists who have poor speaking ability may speak too rapidly; they may use words either too technical or too simple and give unclear or incomplete messages; they may use many place holders such as "like," "uh," "you know," and the like.

INFORMATION GATHERING: Psychologists with excellent information-gathering skills use open-ended probes whenever appropriate instead of closed questions; they help clients give expansive answers and frequently check with the client to make sure he or she understands the information provided; they complete thorough questioning in one area before moving on to another; they investigate all relevant areas.

Psychologists with poor information-gathering skills ask rapid-fire, closed questions or do not ask questions at all; they fail to clarify unclear or inconsistent client responses; they settle for brief or incomplete answers and may leave important questions unasked.

PERSONAL COMFORT: Psychologists with high personal comfort display verbal and nonverbal behaviors during an interview that indicate they are at ease and confident in their abilities. They smile when appropriate, have a relaxed posture, and show no nervous mannerisms, even if clients become upset or introduce shocking material.

Psychologists with low personal comfort display verbal and nonverbal behaviors during an interview that suggest they are nervous or uncomfortable; although relaxed for part of the interview, their demeanor may change as clients create a more tense atmosphere.

STRUCTURING: Psychologists with excellent structuring skills tell clients the purpose of therapy, its ground rules, and what they can expect from the interviews.

Psychologists with poor structuring skills do not give clients any indication of what they can expect from therapy; they do not present ground rules for the client–therapist relationship.

EMPATHY: Psychologists possessing a high level of empathy convey a clear understanding of what clients are thinking and feeling.

Psychologists with a low level of empathy do not appear to understand what clients are thinking and feeling.

NONJUDGMENTAL ACCEPTANCE: Psychologists high on nonjudgmental acceptance communicate to clients that it is safe for them to explore their deepest concerns; they enable clients to talk about whatever they wish and to display whatever emotions they are feeling; they are never critical of clients and clearly convey respect for clients, regardless of what is disclosed or displayed in the interview.

Psychologists low on nonjudgmental acceptance appear opinionated or disposed to making judgments about clients' behavior; they may assign "good/bad" or "right/wrong" labels to what clients are saying; they do not convey to clients that it is safe to reveal whatever thoughts or feelings they may have.

(continued)

Table 3. (*Continued*)

CARING: Psychologists high on caring appear involved with clients; they demonstrate verbally and nonverbally that they actively want to help their clients; they show personal concern for their clients.

Psychologists low on caring appear indifferent to clients; they lack concern for clients as individuals; they are not committed to helping clients.

PAYING ATTENTION: Psychologists who are excellent at paying attention note all client communications, both verbal and nonverbal. The client is the focus of the interview rather than the psychologist's agenda. These psychologists respond immediately to significant messages and information from clients.

Psychologists who are poor at paying attention do not listen to clients; they do not pick up all client cues. It is apparent that these psychologists have an agenda from which they will not deviate and therefore miss important client messages.

CLARITY OF PURPOSE: Psychologists high on clarity of purpose demonstrate that they have a plan or agenda underlying their interaction with clients; however, their guiding purpose is not so rigid as to prevent responding to clients' cues.

Psychologists low on clarity of purpose have no discernible intent in their interactions with clients. It is difficult to determine what they are trying to achieve with their clients.

CONTROL: Psychologists who are high on control are able to accomplish their purpose without being rigid or overbearing; they are unhurried and make good use of silence; they are prepared for their clients; they are sure of what to say.

Psychologists who lack control appear at a loss as to what to say or do; they do not make good use of silence; their behavior is erratic.

behavior, and a rating of 5 indicated the behavior was clearly demonstrated. These behaviors are listed in Table 4.

Trained raters, who were clinical graduate students, coded the videotapes. Each simulation interview was rated by one of two teams consisting of two raters each. Ten of the tapes were rated by both teams as an ongoing check on interteam agreement. Each member of a rating team rated a tape independently and then compared ratings with the other rater. When ratings differed by more than two points, raters discussed a score until consensus was achieved. Before consensus, rater reliability was moderate to excellent; coefficients of rater reliability for each of the two simulation interviews ranged from .21 to .88, and most of the coefficients were .51 or higher. The team average for a scale, or the consensus rating when one existed, was used in evaluating the results of the simulation exercises.

The written responses to the simulation were rated with respect to the following dimensions: observations, information gathering,

Table 4. Clinical Behavior Checklist Used in Evaluating Therapy Simulations

1. Talk specifically about confidentiality and other ground rules for the therapeautic relationship.
2. Speak at the client's level of comprehension and vocabulary.
3. Gather information on the client's strengths and weaknesses.
4. Respond to the nonverbal cues given by the client.
5. Display facilitative nonverbal behaviors such as good eye contact, appropriate body positioning, calm demeanor, head nods, and the like.
6. Provide continuity by discussing plans for subsequent sessions or referral.
7. Close the interview with a summarization of what had transpired and what would happen next.
8. Respond specifically to client's concerns about his parents.
9. Respond specifically to client's concerns about the cost of therapy.
10. Respond specifically to client's request that the therapist call his boss.
11. Respond specifically to client's feelings of helplessness.

hypotheses or diagnoses, treatment plans, and overall competence. The same teams of raters were used as for the videotapes. Ratings were made on 5-point scales, with each rating point defined by example responses. Moderate-to-good rater agreement was achieved on all dimensions. The coefficients of rater reliability were the following: observations, .83; information gathering, .82; hypotheses, .44; treatment plan, .68; and overall competence, .65.

Other Exercises

Although the client simulation was a major focus of the practice audit for clinical psychology, other exercises were included to examine a broader sampling of clinical psychology practice. These are briefly described next.

Written Client Vignettes. These were brief written case scenarios describing a variety of clients. The purpose of the client vignettes was to provide a sample of therapist judgment across a range of situations. Five different vignettes were used to assess case conceptualization and alternative approaches to assessment and/or treatment planning. They were intended to evoke the practitioners' reaction to different situations rather than provide an in-depth response to any particular situation. Participants' responses were rated on two dimensions, issues identified and recommended actions, using 5-point scales.

Videotaped Therapy Vignettes. Three videotapes were used to provide a sampling of participants' evaluations of difficult situations they might encounter with clients. The tapes were selected from a set of 11 developed by the American Board of Professional Psychology on an experimental basis for possible use in the diplomate exam. These brief vignettes also provided an indication of the participant's ability to evaluate another therapist's interactions with a client and thus also addressed supervisory skills. After each viewing, participants were given 10 minutes to respond in writing to four open-ended questions regarding their evaluation of the situation and their recommended actions. These questions concerned (a) identification of the client's problem; (b) description of the therapist's behavior; (c) evaluation of the therapist's behavior; and (d) recommended actions. A selection of "good" answers, compiled by the professional team, was provided for each of the vignettes as a referent for rating response.

Legal Issues Test. A 24-item multiple-choice legal issues test was constructed by an advanced clinical graduate student who was also an attorney. The test covered Pennsylvania law and regulations regarding the practice of psychology.

Continuing Education Needs and Demands Surveys. Participants were surveyed regarding their self-perceived continuing education needs and demands. Needs were defined in terms of the potential of continuing educaiton to increase skills; demands were defined as areas in which participants would like to obtain continuing education. Participants indicated their self-perceived continuing education needs and demands for the tasks listed in the original practice description, described previously.

Practice Audit Criteria

Time and resources were not expended to perfect the assessment exercises from a psychometric perspective. This was because the focus of the clinical psychology practice audit was on group, and not individual, performance and because the purpose of the assessment was to provide input for continuing education program development, the project's ultimate goal. Nevertheless, the exercises do have potential for use in other contexts, recognizing that further development may be required in most instances. The principal concerns of the CPEDP were that measures used be reasonably reliable and that they be valid in the sense that they addressed actual performance and were relevant to a broad population of clinical psychology practitioners.

Developing content for the practice audit exercises posed two challenges: (a) that the content reflect commonly encountered situations requiring clinical intervention; and (b) that the content be generic and not biased with respect to theoretical orientation or type of client. The clinical psychology practice description provided the content domains denoting behaviors to be included in the assessment. Content in this sense was matched to assessment method in several ways. The methods used to assess clinical behavior represented a continuum with respect to the extent to which actual performance was approximated. The client simulation was considered very real by participants, who reported that they quickly forgot the artificial aspects of the situation and dealt with the actor as they would with a real client. The videotaped and written vignettes were also evaluated by participants as realistically portraying client/therapist interactions and requiring skills typically used in the clinical setting. (For certain purposes these preprepared exercises appear to offer a valid alternative to the much more expensive and time-consuming interactive client simulation.)

Keeping the exercises generic was addressed in two ways. A variety of clients and problems were employed across the various assessment exercises so that they represented a case mix that would be familiar to the group that was involved in the assessment. In the client simulation, for instance, a self-referral was built on what the profession team considered to be a set of common complaints, thereby permitting the participants to work with the client from their own theoretical perspective and exercise their own clinical approach.

RESULTS OF THE PRACTICE AUDIT SESSION

Results from the practice audit session for clinical psychology produced a total of 411 scorable variables for the 40 participants. Following the logic of the practice audit model, and for organizational and interpretive purposes, these variables were categorized under the practice description responsibilities from which the exercises were drawn. That is, the interest was in identifying group-learning needs associated with a clinician's responsibilities rather than in examining the results for a given exercise.

Space limitations allow only a cursory summary of the data, but a sample of the results and how they were organized is given in Table 5. It shows summary statistics and the percentage of the group achieving a criterion score for 16 variables associated with Direct Client Services Responsibility 1: "Collects information necessary in making clinical inferences." These variables can be placed in two categories: ratings of clinical performance (based on client simulation and client vignettes scores) and responses to survey items (i.e., needs survey and demands

Table 5. Psychology Practice Audit Session Data Summary for Responsiblity 1: "Collects Information Necessary for Making Clinical Inferences"

Exercise/variable	Median	Mean	*SD*	Percentage below criterion
Client simulation				%≤ 2.49
Information gathering (1)	4.27	4.10	.97	10.3
Information gathering (2)	3.85	3.77	.71	5.1
Clarity of purpose (1)	4.05	4.05	.69	0.0
Clarity of purpose (2)	3.88	3.82	.51	0.0
Written observations	3.53	3.45	.79	12.8
Written information gathering	3.46	3.49	1.00	17.9
Client vignettes				
#2 Identification of issues	2.13	2.18	.68	71.8
#2 Recommended actions	2.25	2.41	.99	61.5
Needs survey				%≥4.0
1. Assess intervention	2.60	2.92	1.06	38.4
2. Observe client behavior	2.32	2.67	1.13	30.7
3. Administer tests	2.41	2.77	1.31	35.9
4. Data from other sources	2.03	2.10	.97	7.7
Demand survey				
1. Assess intervention	3.55	3.21	1.44	51.3
2. Observe client behavior	2.58	2.87	1.28	35.9
3. Administer tests	3.25	3.05	1.40	46.2
4. Data from other sources	1.97	2.18	1.14	15.4

Note: $N = 40$.

survey). The former are assessments of various dimensions of observed clinical behavior, and the latter are self-reports of perceived needs and wants. By applying cutoff points to these scores, inferences about group learning needs were made.

Clinical psychology profession team members established a cutoff score of 2.49 or lower (representing a rating of less than adequate) for ratings of measured clinical behavior that indicated *performance-based* learning needs. For *self-perceived* needs, they set a score of 4.0 or higher where 4 and 5 indicated a high need. As shown in Table 5, the practice audit session participants performed very well on the six items from the client simulation exercise but less well on the two items from the client vignettes. Through the self-report data, they indicated a satisfactory appraisal of their information-collecting skills. The overall performance on this responsibility was considered satisfactory. Therefore, the basic clinical responsibility of "collects information necessary for making clinical inferences" was not identified as a high-priority learning need for this particular group.

Similar tables were constructed and inferences drawn for the remaining 17 responsibilities assessed during the practice audit session. Given time and resource constraints, not all of the 18 practice description responsibilities have been assessed fully. However, there were at least 3 variables for each responsibility, and the modal number of variables per responsibility was 20. Some highlights of the results based on clinical performance indicators and the overall conclusion regarding learning needs reached by the profession team follow.

Of the remaining seven responsibilities from the practice description's direct client services domain, four responsibilities had one performance indicator reaching the cutoff score, and three of the responsibilities had none. Under Responsibility 2, "integrates sources of information leading to clinical inferences," one of the performance indicators from the videotaped vignettes dealing with the identification of the clinical problem had a mean score of 2.51 with 51.3% of the group achieving less than a 2.49 rating. For Responsibility 3, "recognizes own limitations in providing direct client services," one item from the client vignettes exercise dealing with identification of issues had a mean score of 2.26 with 66.7% of the group achieving less than a 2.49 rating. Under Responsibility 8, "maintains confidentiality of information obtained from clients," one performance indicator from the client simulation dealing with discussing confidentiality with the client achieved a mean score of 2.67 with 51.3% of the group falling below a 2.49 rating. The other three responsibilities in the direct client services domain, "develops intervention plan," "implements intervention plan," and "establishes and maintains an effective professional relationship with client," did not have any performance indicators falling below the criterion score. This last responsibility had the most performance indicators with a total of 35 and is arguably the most important therapy responsibility. To the credit of this group of clinical psychologists, no problems emerged from either ratings of specific behaviors or from ratings of the major therapy dimensions for the client simulation on this responsibility.

Thus the impression that emerged from an examination of performance on eight major responsibilities of clinical psychology behavior was that of a relatively competent group of therapists. In reaching this conclusion, the profession team deferred pursuing purely knowledge deficiencies emerging from the practice audit session data, even though the group performed below some established criteria (e.g., concerning their understanding of legal and ethical issues in the practice of clinical psychology). The profession team considered these knowledge limitations as correctable through didactic forms of continuing education. Consequently, it was decided that the key area for continuing professional education program development was that of direct client services. This decision was strongly influenced by the practice audit session participants' reactions to the assessment exercises. At a debriefing after the session, participants reported that the small-group format not only facilitated the scheduling of exercises, but it offered them an opportunity to interact with their professional colleagues to exchange clinical experiences and to compare their views regarding case management with others. They further suggested that the practice audit session exercises themselves were learning experiences and recommended using similar assessment exercises, especially live simulations, in future continuing professional education programs. One participant expressed it this way:

> While I am quite aware that the project was designed to gather data on the practices of the group, my own experiences helped clarify areas of [my own] strengths and weaknesses. I couldn't help but think that the audit session itself became a very viable working model of education.

Thus the profession team adopted the view that *all* clinical psychologists can improve their clinical skills and proceed to design a workshop to meet this objective.

THE CLINICAL SKILLS WORKSHOP

The clinical skills workshop was based on the premise that, although all clinical psychology practitioners can achieve professional growth through insights regarding their clinical skills, they rarely have time or find appropriate occasions to examine their behavior objectively and systematically. The express purpose of the workshop was to provide a unique opportunity for exercise and guided reflection upon individual clinical skills in the collegial and supportive environment of a small group of peers. The overall goal of the workshop was to measurably enhance participants' clinical skills. More specific objectives were to (a) increase sensitivity in making clinical observations; (b) increase the repertoire of available clinical behaviors; and (c) to modify individually identified verbal and nonverbal behaviors.

The program entitled "Enhancing Your Clinical Skills: An Experiential Workshop" was held in conjunction with the annual meeting of the Pennsylvania Psychological Association in June 1984. The 2-day workshop contained 15 clock hours of exercises and interaction. Thirteen participants were divided into two small groups for all exercises, and each group had two facilitators. Following the experience of the practice audit session, there were three types of exercises: live client simulations, written client vignettes, and videotaped client–therapist vignettes. Each of these exercises provided stimulus material for group discussion that provided informal feedback regarding each individual's responses. In addition, peer ratings were used in the live simulations.

Live Client Simulations. There were two live simulations, one involving the initial consultation with a "depressed female," the other an initial consultation with a "compulsive male." All participants met with actor/clients who played these roles. Each of these simulations consisted of a 30 minute interaction with the actor/client that was videotaped and then followed by 4 hours of collective viewing and small-group discussion per case. During the posttaping discussion period, each participant became the "identified student" for approximately ½ hour during which a 5-minute segment of his or her tape was viewed by the group, group members rated the segment on 10 clinical skills dimensions,[3] and a form of "round robin" verbal feedback was given by group members and by the group facilitator regarding the therapist's performance with the "client." Each participant received a written summary of the group's ratings after the discussion period ended. The second simulation was designed to (a) provide an opportunity for each participant to apply feedback received during the prior discussion; and (b) for the group and the participant to evaluate the effects of the participant's altered behavior on the subsequent therapeutic encounter. In this manner, the continuing education exposure became an active and measureable learning experience.

Written Client Vignettes. Five brief scenarios depicted a variety of clinical situations. Participants indicated in writing the clinical issues involved in each vignette and what they would do in this situation. (This was done in the time allocated for taping the client simulation because a 90-minute period was required to tape all members of each small group.) One hour was scheduled for group discussion of their responses to the vignettes. At the conclusion of the discussion, participants were given copies of the profession team's response to each vignette for comparison purposes.

Videotaped Therapy Vignettes. The same three videotaped therapy vignettes used during the practice audit session were included in the Workshop. During the 90-minutes scheduled for this exercise, participants responded in writing to four questions concerning the client/

[3]The 10 clinical skills dimensions are described in Table 3.

therapist interaction and later discussed their responses with their small group. Profession team member responses were also provided for comparison.

Workshop Evaluation

Three kinds of evaluation information were collected on the clincal skills workshop. The first was the typical survey of participants' reactions to the workshop obtained at its conclusion. In general, all participants were enthusiastic about the workshop experience. Most indicated that they had expected to obtain specific feedback regarding their professional skills and that the workshop generally met their expectations. All participants indicated that the workshop was worth the time and money ($300) invested. All but two of the participants said that they implemented suggestions made by their group during the second simulation. The opportunity to talk to the actresses and actors about their reactions as "clients" in the clinical interviews was held to be one of the best learning opportunities in the workshop, according to many participants. The written vignettes and videotaped vignettes were received somewhat less favorably than the live simulations. Average ratings of the major features of the workshop (made on a 5-point scale with 5 being excellent) ranged from a low of 3.3 for the written vignettes to 4.5 for the videotaped vignettes to a 4.9 for both simulations. Also rated very highly were the small-group format (4.0), peer feedback (4.8), and group leaders (4.5).

A second type of evaluation information was obtained through a follow-up questionnaire sent to the workshop participants 6 weeks after the workshop. The questionnaire was intended to get feedback regarding the usefulness of the workshop in the participants' actual practice. Of the 10 respondents who returned the survey, 9 indicated that their practices of clinical psychology had been positively influenced by their workshop participation. Those who indicated their practice had been affected by the workshop also were asked to describe specific examples citing the situation, the type of client, what the therapist did, and how their participation in the workshop influenced what they did in the given situation. An example will provide the flavor of the types of responses received. One of the respondents indicated that his practice of clinical psychology was influenced during a subsequent intake interview with an angry, confused young man, suffering from a panic disorder with paranoid ideation. The therapist said, "I was able to keep the interview under good structure, making my client focus on his main problems. This had been difficult for me to do in the past." The therapist went on to say that his participation in the workshop influenced his behavior in the situation because "my fellow group members made me aware of my [former] tendancy to keep the interview too unstructured or too loose."

The third type of evaluation information involved a statistical analysis of the ratings on the 10 clinical dimensions that had been developed for the practice audit. This involved examining reliabilities of the ratings and changes in mean scores from Simulation 1 to Simulation 2. Two clinical psychology graduate students were trained in using the workshop's 10 dimensions of clinical behavior for the purpose of rating the 13 workshop participants' videotapes from the two live simulations. This provided two groups of raters: (a) the trained graduate students, and (b) the workshop participants themselves, who had rated their fellow participants' videotapes following each simulation. These are referred to later as "trained raters" and "peer raters," respectively. Coefficients of interrater agreement for each rater type and simulation are given in Table 6. The coefficients are intraclass correlations derived from rater × item analyses of variance for each of the two simulations (Guilford, 1954) and have not been adjusted by the Spearman–Brown formula. In general, the trained raters show somewhat higher agreement than the peer raters. The coefficients for peer raters increased from Simulation 1 to Simulation 2, suggesting that practice improved their rating skills; coefficients for trained raters did not change appreciably.

A summary of mean ratings for the two types of raters is given in Table 7. Looking first at the overall mean rating for the trained and peer raters, it is seen that the peer raters tend to be more lenient than the trained raters on both simulations. However, this is incidential to the main point of the table that is that there was an increase in the participants' clinical skills from Simulation 1 to Simulation 2 for all dimensions except caring. The increase for peer ratings was significant (t-test for correlated means, $p < .05$) for information gathering, control, and

Table 6. Overall Agreement[a] by Rater Type and by Simulation for Clinical Skills Workshop Participants

Type	Simulation 1	Simulation 2	Overall
Peer raters (N = 13)	.34	.61	.57
Trained raters (N = 2)	.75	.64	.69
Combined raters (N = 15)	.29	.49	.50

[a]Coefficients are intraclass correlations derived from rater × item analyses of variance. Because peer ratings were nested within group, overall coefficients for rater type are the average of the intraclass correlations obtained separately for Group 1 and Group 2 ratings.

Table 7. Comparison of Clinical Skills Ratings for Clinical Skills Workshop Participants by Simulation Experience with Actor/Clients and Rater Type

	Mean ratings[a]			
	Peer raters		Trained raters	
Clinical dimension	Simulation 1	Simulation 2	Simulation 1	Simulation 2
Means of speaking	4.00	4.15	3.82	4.08
Information gathering	3.27	3.89*	3.35	3.83*
Personal comfort	3.82	3.87	3.74	3.91
Structuring	3.68	3.87	2.96	3.43*
Empathy	3.71	3.75	3.26	3.39
Nonjudgmental	3.90	4.08	3.39	3.39
Caring	3.94	3.90	3.43	3.30
Paying attention	3.99	4.17	3.48	3.70
Clarity of purpose	3.64	3.70	3.09	3.61*
Control	3.79	4.03*	3.65	3.83
Overall mean	3.78	3.94*	3.42	3.65*

[a]Peer ratings are averaged across 13 raters and 13 participants. Trained ratings are averaged across 2 raters and 13 participants. Means for Simulations 1 and 2 were compared using t-tests for correlated means.
*$p \leq .05$.

the overall rating. The increase in trained ratings was significant for information gathering, structuring, clarity of purpose, and the overall rating.

The pattern of these ratings and the general agreement between the two types of raters suggest that the simulation techniques used during the workshop were successful in increasing the clinical skills of the participants from Simulation 1 to Simulation 2. This finding, coupled with the anecdotal information about program impact provided by the respondents, indicates that the workshop did have an immediate impact on clinical skills that may have carried over after they returned to their practice. One can confidently conclude from these findings that the clinical skills training model has considerable promise for future applications.

PRACTICE-ORIENTED CONTINUING PROFESSIONAL EDUCATION

Within the 5-year life span of the Continuing Professional Education Development Project, there has been an increasing interest in the issue of quality in all aspects of continuing education for the professions (e.g., Council on the Continuing Education Unit, 1984; Green, Grosswald, Suter, & Walthall, 1984). Under the general rubric of *educational quality assurance*, the entire continuing education system has been callled upon to identify, define, and use formal criteria of quality to assess the impact of its continuing education programs. The project's work with clinical psychology and the other four professional groups has been conducted in this environment, and it has not been insensitive to the issues associated with quality continuing professional education. Indeed, the project's two main concepts, practice-oriented continuing professional education and collaboration between the professions and higher education, directly address these issues. On the other hand, scant attention has been paid to implications regarding costs to either provider organizations or participants for efforts aimed at enhancing quality assurance. This concluding section will draw upon project experiences to critically review the practice-oriented continuing professional education model, the costs associated with its development, design, and implementation, and speculate about its future prospects.

Comparison of Knowledge-Based versus Practice-Oriented Approaches

The CPEDP's approach to the educational needs assessment and program development process relates directly to what is seen as an emerging issue regarding the definition and format of continuing education for professional groups and indirectly to its quality. This issue can be initially characterized as large-group oriented versus individually targeted programming for professionals. The former type characterizes most traditional continuing education, whereas the latter is a newer approach advocated by the CPEDP. The newer trend closely follows Houle's (1981) performance mode of learning. It is in sharp contrast to traditional continuing education that has been primarily knowledge-oriented. Traditional group- or knowledge-oriented continuing professional education has these characteristics:

1. Content is academic-oriented
2. Large groups
3. Lecture format
4. Stresses knowledge acquisition
5. Little or no interaction
6. Little or no feedback on performance
7. All participants treated as same
8. Formal instructor/student atmosphere

9. Learner is primarily passive
10. Cost efficient (for the most part)

Parenthetically, its cost efficiency may be the overriding attribute, insofar as the popularity and survival of this type of continuing professional education program is concerned.

Performance-oriented continuing professional education in marked contrast to the traditional form has the following characteristics:

1. Content is practice oriented
2. Small groups
3. Interaction with peers and group leaders
4. Stresses experiential learning and skill refinement
5. Individually oriented
6. Conducted in collegial atmosphere
7. Learner assessment and feedback on performance
8. Learner active
9. Cost intensive (for the most part)

Although both approaches espouse similar goals, that is, enhancing the performance and competency of practitioners, the two approaches have marked differences in development and implementation costs and, consequently, different implications for how they are priced, marketed, understood, and accepted by practitioners.

Cost Consideration

All of the identifying characteristics of practice-oriented continuing professional education were present in the clinical skills workshop. This is not surprising, given that an explicit goal of the project was to develop programs with these characteristics. What is surprising, however, and what may not be known generally, is the high cost of developing and implementing this kind of continuing professional education. Without going into precise dollar amounts, the following briefly discusses some of the cost differences between knowledge-oriented and performance-oriented continuing professional education. For purposes of this discussion, assume that the provider organization is a university, required to at least break even financially on the programs offered in a given year. Also assume that promotion, overhead/indirect costs, location, program coordination, and other typical program costs are the same for both types of offerings.

Knowledge-oriented continuing professional education is largely instructor-centered, and thus its content comes with the instructor or lecturer. Consequently, there are practically no direct program development costs that must be factored into the registration fee. Implementation costs also are low, consisting principally of the fee paid to the principal lecturer and other program leaders. Knowledge-oriented continuing professional education has yet another desirable characteristic: When the income from program registrations reaches the program cost, each additional registration represents a "profit" to the provider unit. Thus large enrollments are possible for this kind of programming. Together, these characteristics encourage the use of nationally known speakers who are a "draw" in programming for professionals. For example, at a recent annual meeting, a state psychological association featured a "name" psychologist who charged the association a flat $20 per head for his services with no minimum guarantee. The association charged $35 for his lecture. Over 200 psychologists attended, the lecturer went away happy, and the coffers of the association were enriched by several thousand dollars.

By contrast, performance-oriented continuing professional education is individual-centered and is much more expensive to develop and implement. Under direct development costs, the program material finally incorporated in the clinical skills workshop was gleaned from the previous practice audit results and conclusions. These involved case studies, media, simulations, and rating instruments, all subsidized by the project's sponsoring agencies. This required much expensive preparation. In particular, actors and actresses had to be trained for the simulations, and skilled clinicians were needed to serve as group leaders and facilitators. Under program implementation costs, these same individuals must be paid for conducting each workshop program. In addition, television recording and playback equipment plus at least one technician are required for the simulations. Added to program implementation costs for a 2-day workshop were room and board costs for a large program staff. Finally, this kind of program is not geared to volume. Because of exercise scheduling constraints, including available rooms, equipment, and actors/actresses, the workshop must be planned for a fixed number of groups and individuals per group (we have found groups of five to be a workable arrangement). Given these parameters, it is seen that a total of 20 to 30 registrants must be charged a rather high fee to even begin to cover direct program development and implementation costs. For the project's clinical skills workshop, a fee of $300 (which practitioners considered expensive) was charged for the 2½ day program. Workshop income did not meet direct workshop expenses. The bottom line is that without a substantial subsidy from the participating organizations, it could not have been held. For these reasons, the future of this clinical skills workshop program and similar offerings appears to be rather dim.

Prospects for Practice-Oriented Continuing Professional Education

In contrasting these two types of continuing professional education under the rubric of quality assurance and its costs, some interesting opportunities and challenges emerge. It is likely that performance-oriented continuing professional education is more successful in producing a direct and lasting impact on practitioners than is knowledge-oriented programming. However, both types serve useful purposes, and their respective trade-offs must be carefully considered when formulating a given continuing education offering (Cervero & Rottet, 1984). There are very few programs for professionals that can be characterized as performance oriented. Nonetheless, the project's ability to effect measurable changes in participants' clinical behaviors clearly recommends that university, professional associations, and other groups concerned with professional competence, such as regulating agencies, carefully consider this approach as a viable option for improving clinical performance. The challenge, of course, is how to make this approach cost-effective for the sponsoring organization and affordable from the practitioner's point of view.

A possible solution to this quality/cost dilemma may rest on changing the values and attitudes of professionals toward continuing professional education. The features of the clinical skills workshop were not unlike many features of graduate training for clinical psychologists. Typically, these include the use of simulations, a mentoring relationship, feedback from peers, videotaping of clinical performance, and a nonthreatening collegial atmosphere. How can positive attitudes about these performance-oriented learning experiences and their associated costs be carried into and through the professional's career? Houle poses this question succinctly:

> If continuing education is crucial to the profession and therefore to the people who are preparing to enter it, some attention should presumably be given in the admission process to the selection of individuals who have already given evidence that they have a thirst for knowledge and that they are likely to retain that thirst throughout their careers. (1981, p. 82)

In a study of the 1956 freshman class of the University of Chicago School of Medicine, Gunzberger (1983) demonstrated relatively strong relationships between the professional's level of involvement in continuing learning activities in 1978 and factors such as high school rank, parent's level of involvement in continuing learning, and a tendency toward change. Gunzberger's conclusion that it is possible to identify characteristics that may predict a proclivity toward becoming a continuing professional learner suggests that it may be feasible for admissions committees to take Houle's (1981) challenge seriously. We would stop short of recommending that a similar study be undertaken for clinical psychology because the importance of an individual's earlier learning experiences and later felt needs for continuing learning appears self-evident. At a minimum, the concept of continuing learning and updating of professional skills should be imbedded in all clinical training curricula. If effected, this could not help but have a positive impact on the continued competence of clinical psychology practitioners and the quality of services they deliver.

REFERENCES

American Psychological Association. (1979). *Criteria for accreditation of doctoral training programs and internships in professional psychology*, Washington, DC: Author.

American Psychological Association. (1981a). *Ethical principles of psychologists* (Rev. ed.). Washington, DC: Author.

American Psychological Association. (1981b). *Specialty guidelines for the delivery of services*. Washington, DC: Author.

American Psychological Association. (1981c). *A summary of laws regulating the practice of psychology through (L) licensure of (C) certification*. Washington, DC: Author.

Brown, R. A., & Briley, P. L. (1979). Continuing education activities for Maryland psychologists: A survey. *Professional Psychology, 10*, 285–292.

Cervero, R. M., & Rottet, S. (1984). Analyzing the effectiveness of continuing professional education: An exploratory study. *Adult Education Quarterly, 34*, 35–146.

Clark, H. B., Waden, T. A., Brownell, K. D., Gordon, S. G., & Tarte, R. D. (1983). Sources of continuing education for behavior therapists: The utility of journals, conferences, and other informational sources. *The Behavior Therapist, 6*, 23–26.

Clement, P. W. (1977). *Report from the ad hoc committee on performance criteria in psychology*. Pasadena, CA: The Psychological Center, Fuller Graduate School of Psychology.

Committee on Professional Standards, American Psychological Association. (1981). Specialty guidelines for the delivery of services. *American Psychologist, 36*, 639–651.

Cooper, S. S. (1981). Myths about continuing education. *Mobius, 1*, 69–75.

Council on the Continuing Education Unit. (1984). *Principles of good practice in continuing education*. Silver Spring, MD: Author.

Crowe, M. B., Grogan, J. M., Jacobs, R. R., Lindsay, C. A., & Mark, M. M. (1985). Delineation of the roles of clinical psychology: A survey of practice in Pennsylvania. *Professional Psychology, 16*, 124–137.

D'Costa, A. (1982, March). *Enhancing rationality and empiricism in role delineation*. Paper presented at the annual meeting of the American Educational Research Association, New York City.

D'Costa, A. G., & Schreck, A. (1984, April). *A conceptual design in role delineation methodology.* Paper presented at annual meeting of the American Educational Research Association, Chicago.

Dubin, S. S. (Ed.). (1971). Professional obsolescence. Lexington, MA: D. C. Heath.

Dubin, S. S. (1972). Obsolescence or lifelong education: A choice for the professional. *American Psychologist, 27,* 486–498.

Educational Testing Service, The Center for Occupational and Professional Assessment. (1982, June). *Inventory of responsibilities of licensed psychologists.* Princeton, NJ: Author.

Gonnella, J. S., & Zeleznik, C. (1983). Strengthening the relationship between professional education and performance. *New directions for continuing education: Strengthening connections between education and performance, 18,* 59–72. San Francisco: Josssey-Bass.

Green, J. S., Grosswald, S. J., Suter, E., & Walthall, D. B. (1984). *Continuing education for the health professions.* San Francisco: Jossey-Bass.

Guilford, J. P. (1954). *Psychometric methods.* New York: McGraw-Hill.

Gunzberger, L. K. (1983). Can lifelong learners be identified during the selection process for professional schools? *Mobius, 3*(3), 45–52.

Houle, C. O. (1981). *Continuing learning in the professions.* San Francisco: Jossey-Bass.

Jacobs, D. F. (1974). The agony and ecstasy of professional role change. In A. I. Rabin (Ed.), *Clinical psychology: Issues of the seventies (pp. 74–85).* Lansing, MI: Michigan State University Press.

Jensen, R. E. (1979). Competent professional service in psychology: The real issue behind continuing education. *Professional Psychology, 10,* 381–389.

Jones, N. F. (1975). Continuing education: A new challenge for psychology. *American Psychologist, 30,* 842–847.

Kalman, S. A. (1979, August). *Continuing professional competence.* Paper presented at National Council of Engineering Examiners, Norfolk, VA.

LaDuca, A. (1980). The structure of competence in health professions. *Evaluation and the Health Professions, 3,* 253–288.

Lindsay, C. A., & Smutz, W. D. (1984). Professionals and professors: A change strategy for institutionalizing collaborative continuing professional education program development. In D. S. Queeney (Ed.), *Mainstreaming continuing professional education: A conceptual approach and an empirical study* (pp. 1–33). University Park, PA: The Pennsylvania State University, Continuing Professional Education Development Project.

Lindsay, C. A., & Toombs, W. E. (1980, March). *Continuing professional education and the university: The practice audit model for needs assessment and program development.* Paper presented at the annual meeting of the Association for the Study of Higher Education, Washington, DC.

Lindsay, C. A., Morrison, J. A., & Kelley, E. J. (1974). Professional obsolescence: Implications for continuing professional education. *Adult Education,* 25(1), 3–22.

Lindsay, C. A., Queeney, D. S., & Smutz, W. D. (1981). *A model and process for university/professional association collaboration.* University Park, PA: The Pennsylvania State University, Continuing Professional Education Development Project.

McCormick, E. J. (1976). Job and task analysis. In M. D. Dunnette (Ed.), *Handbook of industrial and organizational psychology.* Chicago: Rand McNally.

McNamara, J. R. (1977). Patterns of continuing education for Ohio psychologists: A survey of interests and activities (1972–1974). *Professional Psychology, 8,* 368–376.

Queeney, D. S., & Melander, J. J. (1984). *Establishing foundations for university professional association collaboration: The profession selection process.* University Park,

PA: The Pennsylvania State University, Continuing Professional Education Development Project.

Richman, S. (1980). Research on the examination for professional practice in psychology. An interim report. *Professional Practice of Psychology, 1*(1), 45–50.

Rosenfeld, M., Shimberg, B., & Thornton, R. F. (1983). *Job analysis of licensed psychologists in the United States and Canada.* Princeton, NJ: Center for Occupational and Professional Assessment.

Sanazarro, P. (1982). Continuing education, performance assessment, and quality of patient care. *Mobius, 2,* 34–37.

Shimberg, B. (1983). What is competence? How can it be assessed? In M. R. Stern (Ed.), *Power and conflict in continuing professional education (pp. 15–37).* Belmont, CA: Wadsworth.

Smutz, W. D. (1984). Developing and marketing practice oriented continuing professional education: Prospects and implications. In *Proceedings of the National Conference on Continuing Competence Assurance in the Health Professions* (pp. 94–100). Bal Harbour, FL: National Commission for Health Certifying Agencies.

Smutz, W. D., Kalman, S. H., Lindsay, C. A., Pietrusko, R. G., & Seaman, J. J. (1981). *The practice audit model: A process for continuing professional education needs assessment and program development.* University Park, PA: The Pennsylvania State University, Continuing Professional Education Development Project.

Smutz, W. D., Davis, D. M., & Lindsay, C.A. (1982). Enhancing professionalization through collaboration for continuing professional education: A role for the university. In G. C. Whaples & W. M. Rivera (Eds.), Proceedings of the Lifelong Learning Research Conference (pp. 215–219). College Park, MD: University of Maryland.

Suter, E., Green, J. S., Lawrence, K., & Wathall, D. B. (1981). Continuing education of health professionals: Proposal for a definition of quality. *Journal of Medical Education, 56* (Suppl.), 687–707.

Toombs, W. E., Lindsay, C. A., & Hettinger, G. A. (1985). Modifying faculty roles to institutionalize continuing professional education. *Research in Higher Education, 22*(1), 93–109.

Vitulano, L. A., & Copeland, B. A. (1980). Trends in continuing education and competency demonstration. *Professional Psychology, 11,* 891–897.

Webster, T. G. (1971). National priorities for the continuing education of psychologists. *American Psychologist, 26,* 1016–1019.

Index

GPSR Compliance

The European Union's (EU) General Product Safety Regulation (GPSR) is a set of rules that requires consumer products to be safe and our obligations to ensure this.

If you have any concerns about our products, you can contact us on ProductSafety@springernature.com

In case Publisher is established outside the EU, the EU authorized representative is:

Springer Nature Customer Service Center GmbH
Europaplatz 3
69115 Heidelberg, Germany

Batch number: 10844655

Printed by Printforce, the Netherlands